Patron Saints of Early Medieval Italy AD c.350–800

This book provides the first translation into English of the Latin biographies of nine holy men and one archangel who became the patron saints of the areas where they evangelized, documenting the conversion of pagan Roman Italy to Christianity at the dawn of the Middle Ages. These *Lives* or *Passions* recorded for early medieval audiences the difficulties their local patron saints encountered in promoting the new religion, and their sufferings at the hands of resistant pagans and Roman authorities – ordeals that qualified these saints as special protectors or guardians over their cities or regions. Full of tales of courage, torture, assistant angels, mischievous devils, dragons, and monsters, these earliest *Lives* also served as literary and devotional touchstones for later elaborations, medieval and modern, on the saints' lives, careers, and cults.

With a comprehensive introduction and historical commentary to each biography, *Patron Saints of Early Medieval Italy* provides new evidence for understanding the transition from the ancient Roman world to the Middle Ages. In assessing the technical problems relating to the origin and date of composition of each text, *Patron Saints* also contributes to redeeming these valuable but neglected sources for the history of medieval Italy. It also discusses the historical and literary significance of these biographies within the contexts of hagiography as a literary genre and early medieval religious life.

I0895899

Durham University

Institute of Medieval and Early Modern Studies

DURHAM MEDIEVAL AND RENAISSANCE
TEXTS AND TRANSLATIONS 5

Patron Saints of Early Medieval Italy AD c.350–800

History and Hagiography in Ten Biographies

Translated with an introduction and commentary by

NICHOLAS EVERETT

Institute of Medieval and Early Modern Studies
Durham University

Pontifical Institute of Mediaeval Studies
Toronto

Library and Archives Canada Cataloguing in Publication

Patron saints of early medieval Italy AD c.350–800 : history and hagiography in ten biographies / translated with an introduction and commentary by Nicholas Everett.

(Durham medieval and Renaissance texts and translations ; 5)
Includes bibliographical references and index.
Text in English; translated from the Latin.
ISBN 978-0-88844-565-0 (paperback)

1. Christian patron saints – Italy – Biography – Sources – Early works to 1800. 2. Christian saints – Cult – Italy – Sources – Early works to 1800. 3. Christian hagiography – History – To 1500 – Sources – Early works to 1800. 4. Christian literature, Latin (Medieval and modern) – Italy – Sources – Early works to 1800. 5. Catholic Church – Italy – History – Middle Ages, 600–1500 – Sources – Early works to 1800. 6. Italy – Religious life and customs – Sources – Early works to 1800. 7. Italy – Church history – Sources – Early works to 1800. 8. Italy – History – 476–1268 – Sources – Early works to 1800. I. Everett, Nicholas, writer of added commentary, translator II. Pontifical Institute of Mediaeval Studies, issuing body III. Series: Durham medieval and Renaissance texts and translations ; 5

BX4659.I8P38 2016 270.092'245 C2016-906608-8

Pontifical Institute of Mediaeval Studies
59 Queen's Park Crescent East
Toronto, Ontario, Canada M5S 2C4
www.pims.ca

MANUFACTURED IN CANADA

Patri meo

PHILLIP C. EVERETT
1936–2016

Contents

Abbreviations

AA. SS.	*Acta Sanctorum*, ed. J. Bollandus et al., 68 vols. (Antwerp, etc.: 1643–1940).
BHL	*Biblioteca hagiographica Latina antiquae et mediae aetatis*, 2 vols. Subsidia Hagiographica 70. Brussels: Socii Bollandiani,1898–1901; repr. 1914; *Novum supplementum*, ed. Henricus Fros, Subsidia Hagiographica 70 (Brussels: Boulevard Saint-Michel, 1986).
Bib. Sanct.	*Biblioteca Sanctorum*, ed. I. Vizzini et al., 12 vols. (Rome: Istituto Giovanni XXIII nella Pontificia Università lateranense, 1961–1970; Suppl. 1987).
CCL	Corpus Christianorum, Series Latina (Turnhout: Brepols, 1952–).
CLA	*Codices Latini antiquiores*, ed. E.A. Lowe, 12 vols. (Oxford: Clarendon Press, 1935–1966).
Gregory, *Dial.*	*S. Gregorii Magni Registrum epistolarum*, ed. Dag Norberg (Turnhout: Brepols, 1982).
HL	Paul the Deacon, *Historia Langobardorum*, in *Pauli Diaconi Historia Langobardorum*, ed. G. Waitz and L. Bethmann (MGH SS rer. Lang. 48 : 12–187).
LP	*Liber pontificalis: Texte, introduction et commentaire*, ed. Louis Duchesne (Paris: Thorin, 1981).

MGH Auct. ant.	Monumenta Germaniae Historica: Auctores antiquissimi (Berolini: Weidman, 1877–).
MGH Capit.	Monumenta Germaniae Historica: Capitularia regum Francorum (Hannover: Hahn, 1996–).
MGH Epp.	Monumenta Germaniae Historica: Epistolae (Berolini: Weidman, 1883–).
MGH Poetae	Monumenta Germaniae Historica: Poetae aevi Carolini (Berolini: Weidman, 1978–).
MGH SS	Monumenta Germaniae Historica: Scriptores (Hanover: Hahn, 1826).
MGH SS rer. Lang.	Monumenta Germaniae Historica: Scriptores rerum Langobardicum et Italicarum, saec. VI–XI (Hannover: Impensis Bibliopolii Hahniani, 1878).
MGH SS rer. Merov.	Monumenta Germaniae Historica: Scriptores rerum Merovingicarum (Hannover: Hahn, 1937–).
PL	Patrologiae cursus completus: Series Latina, ed. J.-P. Migne, 222 vols. (Paris: Migne, 1844–1864).

Italy, c.700. Main cities, castra, monasteries, and locations mentioned.

Introduction

This book presents ten biographies of patron saints written in early medieval Italy in the period AD 500–850, translated from Latin into English, which provide insight into the religious and cultural life of Italy after the collapse of the Roman Empire and ascendancy of Christianity. In promoting their saint's cult, church, or holy site, these biographies reconfigured the past in ways that helped early medieval Italians understand how pagan Roman civilization was replaced by the Christian, post-Roman world they witnessed in the churches and shrines of their cities and neighbouring countryside. The ten hagiographic texts presented here were selected for two main reasons: firstly, they serve as examples of accomplished works of Latin literature from a sparsely documented period usually considered Italy's Dark Ages; secondly, the introductions to each *Life/Passion* attempt to establish these biographies as historical sources for the period by considering their configuration of history, their more earthly claims for jurisdiction or authority, and philological clues in the texts that help date their composition and the contemporary concerns of their audiences. The twofold intention of this book, therefore, is to present new evidence for early medieval Italy and offer examples of analysis that might be used to redeem the historical value of many more hagiographic works that survive from this period.[1]

Although they document important patron saints in early medieval Italy, these biographies have been ignored by historians with good reason: they are nearly all of anonymous authorship and uncertain date of composition, and are full of fantastical claims and historical inaccuracies that jar modern historical sensibilities. The fantastical elements may gain our sympathy as literature, for we can comfortably ascribe them to traditions of genre and symbolism and

1 Surveys of early medieval Italian hagiography are Lanéry 2010 and Gioanni 2010; Godding 1994, 1996, 1998; Everett 2000. Anti 1998, 3–36, provides a handy list for northern Italy from the fourth to the twelfth century. For southern and central Italy, see D'Angelo 2006; Paoli 2002; Vuolo 1996; Susi 1995; Granier 1996, 2006.

enjoy the dramatic scenes painted by these texts: *Senzius* of Blera and his friends fight dragons; *Michael* the archangel visits Mount Gargano (Puglia) and founds a cave-church; *Apollinaris* of Ravenna, *Eusebius* of Vercelli, and *Cetheus* of Pescara miraculously withstand cruel tortures; *Vigilius* of Trent bravely ventures into the pagan countryside to imitate the neighbouring martyrdom he wrote about. All of these holy people perform miracles of healing illnesses or defeating demons, sometimes after they are dead and buried. Blatant historical inaccuracies and extravagant ahistorical claims further undermine the notion that these texts offer anything of historical value. The claim that *Sirus*, first bishop of Pavia, and *Apollinaris* of Ravenna were disciples of St Peter in Rome is particularly bold; coupling the reign of the Emperor Constantius II (337–361) and the Vandal invasions of Africa (429–442) to explain *Senzius*'s arrival in Italy is wild anti-Arian distortion (see *Eusebius*, introduction); and other claims, such as *Zeno* of Verona (c.362–380) curing the daughter of the Roman Emperor Gallienus (252–268), seem historically clueless.

But these hagiographic texts may be used as historical sources in another way: as guides to the concerns and aspirations of Italian churches and their cults at the time in which these texts were written. For in reconfiguring local history in celebration of their patron saints, churches and their hagiographers often betray earthly concerns that offer clues to the composition of the text: claims for prestige, authority, jurisdiction over neighbouring churches, and possession of miracle-performing saintly relics. This last is often stated: several of the *Lives/Passions* studied here openly promote the possession of miracle-performing relics, graves, or sites (see below). But claims for jurisdiction over neighbouring churches (*Eusebius, Vigilius, Barbatus, Gaudentius*), independence from other churches (*Sirus* and *Michael*), appropriation of monastic cults (*Senzius*), and the promotion of doctrinal and political harmony (*Apollinaris*) are only revealed when they are held up against the evidence we do have. Philological clues such as place names, details of churches later obliterated, and titles of secular or ecclesiastical office or rank further help us to match the text against the historical record and measure its claims.

These texts also contain historical value in the conventional sense that they preserve knowledge that would otherwise be lost to us, such as the hagiographer's account of the council of 355 and inclusion of otherwise lost documents in the *Passion of Eusebius*, and the accounts of early Christian cults in some cities (Novara, Vercelli, Trent) and of pre-existing churches or monasteries in others (Pescara, Pavia, Verona). Securing the date of composition allows us to assess that information and configure it among other sources of evidence.

The biographies collected here mainly represent northern and central Italy, with the exception of *Barbatus* of Benevento, *Cetheus* of Pescara, and *Michael* at Gargano: most southern hagiographic texts, such as those from Napoli and Sicily, date from the ninth century or later and have received scholarly attention concerning their immediate audience, political orientation, and date of composition.[2] The introduction to each text translated in this book provides the historical setting for the saint's cult and the composition of the work, along with details of the text's transmission, Latinity, and issues of translation. The following draws on those specific studies to offer some general reflections on the character of early medieval Italian hagiography, its purpose and audience, and its recurring theme of relics, most of which are still venerated in Italian churches, often the town's cathedral church (as with Sirus, Eusebius, Gaudentius, Cetheus, Vigilius, and Barbatus).

Early Medieval Italy, Its Churches, and Their Hagiography

Most of the Italian *Lives* and *Passions* that can be posited as having been written from the sixth to the tenth century are concerned with the distant past, as early as the apostolic era (as here with *Sirus* and *Apollinaris*), frequently during the persecutions under the Emperor Diocletian (303–311) and just as often in the fourth century, when the earliest Christian churches with diocesan clergy were established (*Vigilius, Eusebius, Gaudentius*). This concern with Christian origins some three to four centuries later was due to a number of factors. One is the prestige and influence of Rome, with Christ's own disciple Peter, the prince of apostles, as its patron saint, who provided the model for associating a saint not merely with a particular church or monastery but as the holy patron of an entire city. Bishops of Rome such as Liberius (352–366) and Damasus (366–384) also promoted Roman martyr cults, and Roman martyr narratives played a role in shaping Latin hagiography, especially in Italy, by providing models of sanctity in the form of the first Christian presence in an area.[3]

2 See D'Angelo 2006; Paoli 2002; Vuolo 1996; Susi 1995. On Naples, see Granier 1996, 2001, 2006; for Sicily, see Sardella and Zito (eds) 2006, and Nef and Prigent 2006. The corpus of texts concerning Spoleto and towns on the Via Flaminia present problems of late transmission and textual interdependence hard to untangle: Everett 2002a, 117–124; Susi 1995, 2005.

3 See the Martyr narratives in Musurillo 1972. On Italian hagiography c.300–550, see Lanéry 2010 and Gioanni 2010. For the martyr as model of sanctity, see Leonardi,

As with pagan Roman religious culture, Christian sanctity in Italy was found in the hallowed antiquity of great predecessors. Pope Gregory I noted this tradition in justifying the composition of his *Dialogues*: in the prologue, Gregory's deacon Peter complains, "I do not doubt that holy men existed in this land, but I reckon that either their deeds and miracles never happened, or now they are so buried by silence that we have no idea what they did."[4] To write about recent and present-day holy men in Italy, Gregory employed the desert-fathers model of hagiography and focused on ascetic heroes like Benedict of Nursia, who shared Gregory's monastic sensibilities (see *Senzius*, introduction). While the *Dialogues* were immensely influential in Italy (for example, its use in *Senzius* and *Zeno*) and elsewhere in early medieval Europe, the dominant trend in Italian hagiographic writings remained the commemoration of a city's earliest Christian presence, and predominately the figure of its bishop. Exceptions here are *Senzius* and *Michael*, but their stories were written because their cults were appropriated by the cathedral clergy, a development that explains other (seemingly) non-episcopal saints' lives, though certainly not all.[5]

Another reason for the historical focus of these texts is the caesura in Italian life that took place over the course of the sixth century due to the Gothic wars, the Justinianic plague, and the Lombard invasions. Pope Gregory lamented the Italy of his day:

> Now the cities have been depopulated, fortresses razed, churches burned down, monasteries and nunneries destroyed, the fields abandoned by mankind, and destitute of any cultivator the land lies empty and solitary.

Degl'Innocenti, and Santi (eds) 2011, 73–86, 101–142, 161–184.On Liberius and martyr cults, see the introduction to *Eusebius*, and for comparisons with the development of cults elsewhere in Europe, Thacker and Sharpe (eds) 2002, as well as Thacker 2002a. In contrast, Merovingian hagiography was focussed on contemporary figures: Van Uytfanghe 1987; Fouracre 1990; Fouracre and Gerberding 1996.

4 Gregory, *Dial.* I.1.

5 For the episcopal appropriation at Verona (concerning the *Passio Firmi et Rustici*, BHL 3020), see Everett 2002a, 87–90, and below, *Life of Zeno*, introduction; *Vita Cerbonii*, BHL 179, and *Vita Reguli*, BHL 7102, of Populonia, appropriated by Lucca, see *Senzius*, introduction; in Pavia (concerning the *Passio Dalmatii*, BHL 2082), see Everett 2000, 75–79. Exceptions are monastic texts such as the *Vita Walfredi*, ed. Schmidt 1991; Jonas's *Vita Columbani abbatis discipulorumque eius*, BHL 1898, ed. Krusch (MGH SS rer. Merov. 1902: 61–152); and possibly the *Vita Iohannis Penariensis*, BHL 4420, Everett 2002a, 104, though arguably these all reflect episcopal politics.

> No landholder lives on it: wild beasts occupy places once held by a multitude of men.[6]

Gregory's picture is apocalyptic, but other contemporary sources and archaeology testify to a peninsula economically impoverished and politically divided.[7] As battered communities re-emerged from the debris of a war-torn and factional government, caught between imperial and Lombard authorities (as seen in *Senzius* and *Cetheus*) and divided on questions of doctrinal orthodoxy in the Three Chapters dispute (evident in *Sirus*, *Apollinaris*, *Vigilius*), local churches sought to play a leading role in the re-establishment of a strong communal identity that could withstand the vicissitudes of shifting external powers. The figure of the bishop often provided the ultimate focal point (as in eight of our ten selected texts), for he connected the community's past with its present. The bishop was essentially an urban figure, and post-Roman Italy was a highly urbanized world, control of the peninsula being dependent on control of networks of towns, despite the seismic economic and demographic shifts throughout the fifth and sixth centuries that made cities smaller, poorer, and less populated.[8] By the end of the fourth century, most of Italy's towns had established diocesan clergy under a system of three metropolitan authorities (Rome, Milan, and Aquileia; for Ravenna, see *Apollinaris*, introduction), though the boundaries of jurisdiction were far from certain, and some were disputed for centuries (see Figure 1).[9] Despite urban and economic decline, Italy's churches became wealthy landowners in this period, benefitting from aristocratic patronage and assuming responsibilities of city administration as the remnants of Roman town councils (*curiae*) were swept away along with the presence of empire. The bishop effectively became a town mayor, and an important political figure, who could negotiate with emperors, generals, and barbarians in defence of his flock.[10] Hagiography that recounted the trials and tribulations of a past bishop strug-

6 Gregory, *Dial.* III.38.

7 Christie 2006; Wickham 2005, 591–594, 644–656; Zanini 1998, 120–208; Brogiolo and Gelichi 1998, 45–154; Balzaretti 1996, 2013.

8 On bishops as town patrons, see Orselli 1976; Picard 1988; Golinelli 1996.

9 For northern Italy, see Picard 1988; Golinelli 1996, 2004; Bertolini 1960; elsewhere in Italy, see Pellegrini 2009, and Lanzoni 1927. On episcopal palaces, see Miller 2000. Comparisons with localities of cults elsewhere in Europe are found in Thacker and Sharpe (eds) 2002. On Carolingian bishops, see Patzold 2008

10 For example, Ennodius of Pavia's *Life of Epiphanius of Pavia,* trans. Cook 1942, and *Sirus*, introduction. On bishops as political figures elsewhere in late antiquity, see Rapp 2005, Elm 2003, Sterk 2004.

gling to create a sense of unity in a hostile world served to provide a sense of continuity among the real discontinuity experienced over three or four generations of political instability coupled with demographic and economic decline. The community had experienced destruction and dissension before, but the bishop, the representative of Christ, kept the spirit of unity alive through his work and his suffering.

Episcopal authority, therefore, is a central theme in early medieval Italian hagiography, because of Italy's long history of urban infrastructure, the establishment of diocesan clergy in the fourth and fifth centuries, and the influence of Rome, whose bishop was the self-proclaimed head of Christendom. Underlining the dominance of the episcopal model is the almost complete absence of female saints in early medieval Italian hagiography, reflecting the very few cults dedicated to women on the peninsula in this period.[11] This is particularly lamentable for the historical record in that hagiography was a genre that gave women a literary voice for the first time in Greco-Roman culture – a genre in which they could be both authors and subjects of biography.[12] Women do play important roles or are given voice in some texts (in this collection, Thecla in *Apollinaris*, Duchess Theodora in *Barbatus*, Bona in *Cetheus*, the emperor's daughter in *Zeno* – though she is really the devil) and make minor appearances as people cured by the holy men (*Senzius, Sirus*). But this seems a poor harvest when we consider the documentary evidence for the important role women played in founding monasteries and endowing churches in this period, reflecting their central role in religious life, despite their exclusion from church hierarchy and their absence in hagiography. Despite this omission, the hagiography of this period has much to offer students of history and helps to fill out our picture of cultural life in early medieval Italy, containing the types of tales and legends that were told about the founders of their churches and the protectors of their towns.

Hagiography as Genre

Hagiography is notorious for being a genre where "facts" and the particular historical circumstances of the actors and places in the text in chronologically

11 See La Rocca 2009. On female saints in Carolingian Europe, see Smith 1995, who notes a similar lack south of the Loire. On later female cults in Italy, see Leonardi, Degl'Innocenti, and Santi (eds) 2011, 455–737. On women in early medieval Italy, see Skinner 2001. Cf. Merovingian hagiography, which produced a new model of "the great monastic lady": McNamara 1992, 8.

12 See Everett 2009; Ashbrook Harvey 2004; Salisbury 1997; Coon 1997; Dronke 1984.

configured time and space are of the least concern to the author. This authorial stance, or choice, derives from a complex mixture of theological perspectives and ancient literary conventions.[13] First and foremost is that Christ himself claimed that his followers will be able to work miracles in his name and in doing so illustrate the truth of their preaching (Matt. 18:19). Christ's own career and miracles as recorded in the Gospels provided a model for signs that a person enjoyed God's favour and was preaching the correct doctrine. These "Christomimetic" miracles – healing the sick, raising the dead, curing the blind, deaf, and dumb, exorcising demons, feeding many from little (Cannae), resisting Satan's temptations, and so on – abound in hagiographic texts. But the association between miracles and divine favour was fundamental to Jewish belief scriptures also, so that Old Testament miracles and monsters often served as models or are alluded to in hagiographic works, as did other New Testament books such as Acts and Revelation.[14]

It is also important to remember hagiography's worldly origin in legal texts, the *acta* or Roman court proceedings that recorded saint's interrogations before Roman authorities and the form of their torture and eventual martyrdom for the faith. Christian communities collected copies of these *acta* and added biographical details of the martyr and further accounts of torture, and sometimes posthumous miracles, in the form of a "passion" (*passio*), a narrative of their "suffering."[15] These legal origins, combined with ancient classical traditions of biography, created a vibrant genre of popular hagiographical literature from the fifth century onwards. But hagiography's legal origins should remind us that these texts purport to document the truth and make claims about the past to justify a present course of action or concern. The *Life of Eusebius* in this volume is an early example of incorporating documents into a hagiographic work, a trend that really takes off in the ninth century as a means of recording and defending property claims, and the use of hagiographic accounts to support existing documents.[16] Hagiography in early medieval Italy was certainly employed to justify claims of authority or jurisdiction over neighbour-

13 Leonardi, Degl'Innocenti, and Santi (eds) 2011, 161–196; Wilson 1983, 1–57; Brown 1981; Head (ed) 2001, xiii–xxvi.

14 Grégoire 1987; Wilson 1983; Leonardi, Degl'Innocenti, and Santi (eds) 2011, 31–72.

15 Examples in Musurillo 1972. See Leonardi, Degl'Innocenti, and Santi (eds) 2011, 101–143; Grégoire 1987, 12–23.

16 On these developments in Italy, see Sennis 2013. In the Frankish world, see Innes 2013, Hummer 2013 and Geary 1994. The bishops of Le Mans on several occasions used their *gesta episcoporum* to protect territorial rights: Sot 1978, 442–445.

ing churches: most of the texts in this volume serve as examples (*Apollinaris, Barbatus, Eusebius, Sirus, Cetheus, Michael, Senzius*).[17]

The *acta-passio* tradition must also play some role in a curious feature of early medieval Italian hagiography, that hagiographers rarely identify themselves (an exception is *Zeno*) and almost never provide details that would help us date the text (an exception is *Gaudentius*), despite speaking in the first person in prologues and epilogues, professing their lack of ability in artful, recherché phraseology, and declaring their research on the saints (*Eusebius, Gaudentius, Vigilius, Zeno, Barbatus, Senzius*). Italy's lack of authors from Pope Gregory I to Paulinus of Aquileia and Paul the Deacon (c.780–800) supports the period's epithet of the "Dark Ages," and that the Lombard kingdom (568–774) deserves some blame. But there are signs of theological and literary activity in Italy before Italians like Paul, Paulinus, and Peter of Pisa gained the patronage of Charlemagne, and other factors like the use of papyrus (until the end of the seventh century), preservation, and institutional instability may explain the silence.[18] Nonetheless, these hagiographic texts demonstrate that literary composition was alive and well in Italy, even if anonymous and ahistorical.

Audience and Purpose

Most of our hagiographic texts were probably written as sermons to commemorate the saint's feast day, a practice attested as standard by Gregory of Tours (590s).[19] Some *Lives* explicitly say this (*Gaudentius, Eusebius*); for some it can be inferred from references in the text (e.g., *Senzius*, ch.9). But other, lengthier texts like the ambitious *Passion of Eusebius* and the *Life of Gaudentius* would have required several readings. It is possible that many of these texts were the fruit of rhetorical exercises in Latin composition practised in cathedral schools, demonstrating a continuity of Roman educational techniques and practices put to Christian service.[20] Scriptural quotations were woven into

17 Further examples in Everett 2000. On hagiography as a political tool, see Paoli 1997. On its use in Merovingian Francia, see Fouracre 1990; Fouracre and Gerberding 1996; in Ireland, see Picard 1982; Ó Cróinín 1995, 208–211.

18 Everett 2003a.

19 *Glory of the Martyrs*, 85, ed. and trans. Van Dam 1988b. On Gregory's audience see De Prisco 2000; Van Uytfanghe 1987. On later Italian audiences, see Golinelli (ed) 2000. On feast days, see Grégoire 1987; Leonardi, Degl'Innocenti, and Santi (eds) 2011, 31–72.

20 As suggested by Viscardi 1939 for the wordy *Vita Gaudentii* (see *Gaudentius*, introduction). This theme for Italian hagiography deserves further study.

hagiographic texts like classical allusions in *suasoriae*, the pretend speeches used for prose composition in late antique schooling. The little evidence for schooling in this period, in churches or elsewhere, certainly suggests that reading hagiographic literature alongside study of the scriptures and holy fathers was encouraged.[21] Saints' lives were considered edificatory reading, but they also conferred authority on the saint, guaranteeing his reputation for sanctity and the holiness of the church where he worked or where his body resided. In 791 Pope Hadrian I advised Charlemagne that "the Lives of the fathers which are not written by proved authors (*probabiles auctores*) shall by no means be read in the church. But those written by accredited orthodox authors shall be accepted and read." Three years later, the Council of Frankfurt declared "that no new saints are to be venerated or invoked, and no shrines for them to be put up along the roads; but those alone are to be venerated in the church who have been deservedly chosen on the basis of their passions or lives."[22] We have no such declarations from Italy, but Italian bishops attended the Council of Frankfurt, and legendaries and passionaries that begin to survive from the ninth century onward in Italy show a common stock of hagiographic texts obviously considered authoritative and packaged together as a collection of "greats," the form in which nearly all of our texts survive.[23]

In terms of how well these texts were understood when read out, early medieval Italy presents us with a broad spectrum of evidence for the survival and teaching of Latin with classical norms for spelling and grammar, and for a significant linguistic shift towards proto-Romance (and proto-Italian by the tenth century), especially in the documentary evidence from Ostrogothic and Lombard Italy. Unfortunately, the manuscript tradition for Italian hagiographic texts mostly begins from the ninth century onward, after the Carolingian reforms and the return to classical standards and pronunciation, which divorced written Latin from its everyday, spoken forms. Texts from central and southern Italy (see *Barbatus, Michael, Senzius*) offer a similar problem in that we cannot be certain that the southern traits go back further than the scribes of our tenth- and eleventh-century manuscripts for most texts.[24] An exception included here is the *Life of Apollinaris*, for which we have an eighth-century

21 Riché 1976, 1979; Everett 2003a. Heene 1989.

22 Hadrian *Ep.* 36, ed. Hampe (MGH Capit. 1899:. 1.28); ed. Boretius 1883: "qui ex auctoritate passionum aut vitae merito erecti sint." On regulation of saints in Carolingian France, see Fouracre 1999; Bosworth 2010.

23 Dolbeau 2008; Philippart 1977, 1994; Degl'Innocenti 1999, 2012. A case study on one Italian ninth- or tenth-century passionary can be found in Everett 2002a.

24 See D'Angelo 2006; Paoli 2002; Vuolo 1996; Susi 1995.

manuscript (*Codex Petropolitanus*) that was probably written in Ravenna (see *Apollinaris*, introduction). Undoubtedly, clergy in seventh- and eighth-century Italy spoke a Latin that was far from classical and closer to proto-Romance. They were happy to write documents that way, but when they quoted the holy scriptures they wrote a more orthographically and grammatically classicized Latin.[25] For early medieval Italians, classical Latin norms were simply the formal version of their speech, and there was no great gap between written and spoken forms. Moreover, classicized Latin was undoubtedly read out with local dialects and pronunciations that were far removed from classical letter sounds and the one-letter-per-sound norm, just as developed in French and as is especially common in modern English, wherein the same combination of letters is pronounced many different ways.[26] Although hagiography provides little help for assessing the development of Latin in this period beyond suggesting the continued comprehensibility of classicized norms, it does offer the occasional linguistic gem (e.g., *marmoriolus* in *Cetheus*, *civitate papia* in *Sirus*, *metabolarius* in *Senzius*).

Relics

Many hagiographic texts explicitly promote the healing power of their saints' relics, and most of the *Lives/Passions* collected here do likewise, some promoting relics interred in churches built by the holy patrons themselves (i.e., *Senzius, Gaudentius, Eusebius, Sirus, Vigilius,* and *Zeno*; the Archangel *Michael* created a cave-church and left a healing spring instead). The relics of some saints are still housed inside their town cathedrals today (i.e., *Eusebius, Gaudentius, Sirus, Zeno, Vigilius, Cetheus*; *Apollinaris*'s are housed in nearby Classe). Human remains were incorporated into hagiographic traditions early, and relic cults with reputations for divine interventions into human affairs drew pilgrims, who brought prestige, patronage, and material compensation for the guardians of the holy relics.[27]

25 Everett 2003a, 221–234

26 Wright 1982, (ed) 1991; Herman 1988; Zamboni 2000. Note Gregory's comment in *Dial.* I.1 about his rustic oral sources: "If I wished to relate carefully the very words used by every single person, the things said in rustic speech are not well rendered by writing" (*quia si de personis omnibus ipsa specialiter verba tenere voluissem, haec rusticano usu prolata stylus scribentis non apte susciperet*).

27 The earliest account of relics is found in the *Martyrdom of Polycarp*, dated to AD 156: trans. E.C.E. Owen in Stouck (ed) 1999, 2–9. See Freeman 2011, 219–227; Head 1999, 296–299.

Rome actively promoted its martyr cults, and services and hospices catered for the many pilgrims drawn to the capital of Christendom to visit the sites where apostles and martyrs worked and suffered for the faith. In northern Italy, Ambrose famously "discovered" the remains of Protasius and Gervasius outside Milan and had them interred inside the city as a means of bolstering his see's prestige; the *Life of Sirus* (and its continuator, the *Life of Iuventius*) sought to insert a major role for Pavia's clergy in these events.[28] Vigilius of Trent's concern with the relics of the martyrs of the Val di Non (397), a *cause célèbre* at the time that caught the attention of emperors and major church figures like Augustine of Hippo (see *Vigilius*, introduction), demonstrates how popular and powerful relics had become in Italy, an expression of piety that was also turned on the bones of bishops themselves. Relics were hotly contested among rival Italian cities,[29] and relics from Italy, especially Rome, were bought or stolen for export over the Alps during Carolingian and Ottonian rule.[30]

Collecting, preserving, and displaying decomposing bodies for worship are macabre practices, and some of our texts provide curious information. Gaudentius of Novara's body, thankfully "redolent of fragrant perfume," was left on a wooden plank in the sacristy of his half-completed church for over six months (22 January to 3 August) until his successor completed the church: during that time Gaudentius's hair and nails continued to grow every day, a sign of his sanctity (*Gaudentius*, ch.18). Similarly, the body of Gaudentius's mentor and neighbour Eusebius of Vercelli was so fragrant when he was buried "that it was as if a rivulet of balsam was coursing into that church," and the odour of the blood from his head "like every kind of balsam and incense mixed together" was so specific it could still be smelled by the faithful at Eusebius's tomb in the hagiographer's day (*Eusebius*, ch.41). But a closer look at the development of Eusebius's cult elsewhere reveals that the hagiographer's comments about the saint's fragrant blood is targetted, for he also tells us that Eusebius made his disciples swear to bury his clothes and vestments with him and that no clippings of his hair or beard be made: "it is because of this that relics of him are seldom encountered" (ch.42). With a few strokes of the quill, the hagiographer both answered a critique of a lack of relics and challenged competing cult sites that claimed the legacy of Eusebius. The *Passion of Cetheus* records that

28 See McLynn 1994; Tomea 1998; Lizzi 1990; and the introduction to *Sirus*.

29 Golinelli 1996; Paoli 1997. In the south, Granier 2001, 2007a, 2012a. See also *Senzius*, introduction.

30 See Geary 1979; Head 1999; Smith 2000; Freeman 2011.

after the bishop was thrown into the Pescara River with a five-hundred-pound weight around his neck, his body miraculously floated across the Adriatic and landed on the shores of Zadar (in modern Croatia), where he was worshipped as "the martyr Peregrinus" (meaning "foreigner" or "traveller"). It is an odd epilogue to an otherwise very local history, but it reveals the close connections between coastal Italy and Dalmatia in maintaining Byzantine control over the Adriatic and the imperial presence in Italy. Hence, the promotion of relics also promoted connections of the cult site with other locations, as also seen in *Senzius* (episcopal links with monastic communities), *Sirus* (connections with Milanese martyr cults), and *Apollinaris* (doctrinal solidarity with Rome).

Sanctus, Holy and Most Holy

The Latin *sanctus* simply means "holy," and there was no established sense of "sainthood" or approved pantheon of saints in the period in which these texts were written,[31] despite the Carolingian legislation and consensus in the content of surviving legendaries mentioned above. For that reason I have translated *sanctus* as "holy" rather than "saint" when the hagiographer applies it to his subject. For church dedications, such as *ecclesia sancti Thomae* (in *Cetheus*), I have followed convention in keeping "S[aint]" ("church of S. Thomas"). Latin epithets are generally rendered as found, including repetitive superlatives such as "the most blessed" (*beatissimus*) or "the most holy" (*sanctissimus*), or soubriquets such as "man of God" (*vir Dei*). These are often used for rhetorical effect, but the manuscripts frequently vary on this score (see *Apollinaris*, Text and Translation), and the fact that they are almost always written in abbreviated form (such as *scs̄* for *sanctus*) allowed for much freedom on the part of copyists and readers whether they followed what they found or adapted. Epithets initially did correspond to status: *beatissimus* was often reserved for bishops, particularly archbishops, including the pope. But by the date of our surviving manuscripts hagiographers and copyists were fairly carefree with the epithets they borrowed.

31 Leonardi, Degl'Innocenti, and Santi (eds) 2011, 73–86, 101–142; Wilson 1983; Brown 1981; Delooz 1969.

Latin Texts and Editions

The editorial introduction to each text here contains a section discussing the edition of the text used, its manuscript tradition, and any instabilities or uncertain readings. Some of these Latin texts have enjoyed the fortune of more recent editions (*Gaudentius*: Colombo 1983, Gavinelli 2013; *Sirus*: Everett 2002a; *Cetheus*: Everett 2015) or alternative readings from different manuscripts (*Apollinaris*: Orioli 2001). For many texts we still stand on the shoulders of antiquarian scholars whose standards for editing still inspire when we consider the advance of historical knowledge and tools of inquiry between then and now. Three of the texts used here (*Zeno, Senzius, Vigilius*) were translated from the great Bollandist collection of hagiographic texts, the *Acta Sanctorum*, originally published in the seventeenth and eighteenth centuries. Two of the texts (*Michael* and *Barbatus*) were edited in the volume of Italian sources (ed. Bethmann and Waitz 1878) in the *Monumenta Germaniae Historica* series. Another (*Eusebius*) was taken from Ferdinand Ughelli's *Italia sacra; sive de episcopis Italiae et insularum adjacentium*, 2nd ed. 10 vols. (Venice 1717–22). While newer editions of these texts are needed, attention is paid to any issues that have arisen from subsequent scholarship on the texts or their traditions.

Order of Lives

The *Lives/Passions* in this book have been placed in the order of *per curriculum anni*, that is, arranged according to their saints' feast days throughout the year, which became the standard method for arranging saints' lives in legendaries and passionaries from the tenth century onward.[32] We pay homage to this later medieval tradition of collecting different saints' lives together in a single book because that was how the texts presented here, as with most hagiographic texts, enjoyed their widest readership in the Middle Ages and beyond.

32 See Philippart 1977 (on *per curriculum anni*, 68–72), 1994; Degl'Innocenti 1999, 2012; Dolbeau 2008; Everett 2002a, 904–913.

22 JANUARY

The Life of Gaudentius of Novara

The *Life of Gaudentius of Novara*[1] is one of the wordier hagiographic texts from early medieval Italy. It is the source of nearly all of our information on Novara's first bishop and patron saint, whose body lies in the cathedral of Novara today. In its concern to locate its subject in real historical time, the *Life of Gaudentius* compares well with the *Life of Eusebius* (also in this volume), for Gaudentius is claimed to have been a disciple of Eusebius and is associated with other big names of the fourth-century church: Gaudentius was a student of Martin of Tours, met Ambrose of Milan, who predicted his bishopric, and was consecrated by Simplicianus, Ambrose's successor and a key figure in the conversion of Augustine of Hippo. These associations may be legendary, even literary. Given the paucity of information on Gaudentius, we assess these claims below in some detail, along with issues of sources and textual influences, in the attempt to gauge the historical worth of the *Life of Gaudentius* and achieve a stronger foothold on its date of composition. It is demonstrated here that the *Life of Gaudentius* makes a serious contribution as an historical source for early medieval Italy and can be dated with some certainty to the period of c.685–725. Its high Latin style is a reminder that we should not readily characterize this period as the Dark Ages, despite its lack of surviving evidence.

Novara's Patron and His Cult

The *Life of Gaudentius* itself is the source for most, if not all, of our information about this saint, so its veracity is difficult to measure. The earliest mention of the cult in historical sources (outside of the *Life*) is found in a charter of 729, drawn up in Novara, in which a layman provides an altar for a local shrine, along with land to support its maintenance with candles, addressed to Bishop

1 BHL 3278; V. Gilla-Gremigni, *Bib. Sanct.* 6: 56–58; Colombo, Temporelli, and Perotti (eds) 1983; Picard 1988, 459–456; Gavinelli 2001, (ed) 2013.

Gratziosus, "who holds the see of the blessed Gaudentius."[2] Otherwise, liturgical manuscripts that mention the saint or his feast day date from the tenth century onward, testifying to a firmly established cult of a patron saint for the town.[3] The earliest attestation of the church dedicated to the saint at Novara is found in a donation of 841 (recorded in a twelfth-century copy) from Viscount Maginard of Pombia to "the church of the most blessed apostles in honour of Holy Gaudentius, which was founded outside the walls of the city of Novara."[4] The *Life* itself explains why Gaudentius enjoys two different feast dates, with different traditions choosing one or both: the *dies natalis* is 22 January, but since the church of San Gaudentius was not yet built, as the *Life* precisely notes (ch.19), six months and twelve days were required before Gaudentius's body could be transferred to the new location (3 August).[5]

By positioning Gaudentius among some of the biggest names in fourth-century Italian church history, the *Vita* makes some bold claims about its hero that might be easily dismissed as the sort of historical aggrandizement common to these texts: that Gaudentius studied with Martin of Tours in Milan; that he followed Eusebius of Vercelli into exile and was then sent to Vercelli by Eusebius to administer his see for three years; that he met Ambrose of Milan, who miraculously predicted his episcopacy, and was ordained by Ambrose's successor, Simplicianus, whom Augustine famously described in his *Confessions* (8.2–5) as a key influence on his own conversion.

As to the first claim, that he studied with Martin at Milan and even became his notary (*notarius*: *Life*, ch.6,), this is plausible, but the chronology is strained. The *Life* claims that Gaudentius went to study with Martin in Milan after the death of Laurence in Novara, but the next chapter (ch.7) states that this was at the time of Constantius (337–361), and more precisely, when Eusebius of Vercelli was exiled (355), so that Gaudentius went with him. Now, in his *Life of Martin* (ch.5), Sulpicius Severus records that Martin was warned in a dream to return to his native land and try to convert his parents in Pavia, an endeavour encouraged by his mentor Hilary of Poitiers, who had ordained Martin as an

2 CDL 44 (1:148–149): "Domno sancto et meritis beatessimo apostolorumque meretis quohequando patri nostro Gratzioso episcopo, sedem tenens beati Gaudenti." The layman, Radoald, stipulates that the charter was to be preserved in the archive (*scrineum*) of the church. The surviving single-sheet charter is the original.

3 Picard 1988: 636–637; Berschin 1986, 2:141;Visonà 1999; Beccaria 2011.

4 Salsotto 1937, 5, doc. 1. On the location of churches in Novara and its Roman *forum*, see Maggi 1995; Uglietti 2010; and Capra 2010.

5 On the feast date in liturgical sources, see Colombo 1974; Colombo, Temporelli, and Perotti (eds) 1983.

exorcist. The chronology and topography that follow are far from clear: crossing the Alps, Martin was taken captive by a robber, whom he converted (ch.5), then (ch.6) Martin seems to have "travelled beyond Milan" ("cum Mediolanum praeterisset") and presumably to Pavia, for after dismissing a demon, he managed to convert his mother but not his father. After this, we are told,

> when the Arian heresy had spread through the whole world and was especially powerful in Illyria, [Martin] was fighting most strenuously against the treachery of the priests and had been subjected to many punishments – for he was publicly scourged and at last was compelled to leave the city – he again returned to Italy, since he found the Church in the two divisions of Gaul in a distracted condition through the departure also of the holy Hilary, whom the violence of the heretics had driven into exile, and he established a monastery for himself at Milan. There, too, Auxentius, the originator and leader of the Arians, bitterly persecuted him and, after he had assailed him with many injuries, violently expelled him from the city.[6]

Leaving aside the confusion generated by the comments about Illyria, fighting alone the treachery of priests, and being compelled to "leave the city" before returning to Italy, it would appear that Martin visited Italy on separate occasions, but his residence in Milan, at least as known to Sulpicius, took place after Hilary's condemnation, enacted in Béziers in 356. How long Martin was in Milan before Auxentius (355–374) had him thrown out is difficult to say, but Hilary seems to have returned from exile in 360, when Martin unsuccessfully tried to meet him in Rome, and shortly thereafter the two were back in Poitiers. Hence, Sulpicius places Martin in Milan c.355–360,[7] precisely when the *Life of Gaudentius* would have Gaudentius following Eusebius into exile, only to be sent back by Eusebius to govern the see of Vercelli until Eusebius's return three years later. Our hagiographer, therefore, seems to have the dates wrong, but Sulpicius is also notorious for the chronological inconsistencies and uncomfortable gaps in his narrative, which seem to suggest that Martin was in Italy, and probably in Milan, on several different occasions. Moreover, Hilary's later return to Milan and defeat by Auxentius in a debate resulted in his expulsion from the city. Sulpicius fails to mention this, but it may have afflicted his

6 *Life of Martin,* ch.6, ed. Fontaine 1967–1969; BHL 5610.

7 Stancliffe 1983, 112–113, locates Martin in Italy 357–360. But other problems of chronology (ibid., 112–124 et passim) demonstrate that precision was not a major concern for Sulpicius.

memory and therefore affected his narrative of Martin. If the two holy men did meet in Milan, it must have been before 355.

But there are two further problems that render this connection suspect. Firstly, it is difficult to imagine that Gaudentius would have become Martin's *notarius*, an office of diocesan church hierarchy, while Martin was supposedly residing in a monastery and himself had only been ordained as an exorcist. But it certainly suits the hagiographer's theme of progression, from Laurence (entry into minor orders, *adiutor* and *lector*) to Martin (made notary) to Eusebius (made companion and trusted deputy), "so many and such skillful teachers" (ch.7), so that the acknowledgement and recognition of Ambrose and subsequent consecration as bishop by Simplicianus seem a natural if delayed development. Secondly, the *Life of Martin* was a bestseller, and there are some signs that the author of the *Life of Gaudentius* consulted Sulpicius's work: particularly, one almost verbatim phrase that seems to have been taken from this very section of the *Life of Martin* (ch.5) where his desire to convert his parents is mentioned, and Eusebius's desire is expressed in the same terms.[8] Moreover, Martin's cult was well known in Italy, as is evident in early–sixth century writers like Ennodius of Pavia and Venantius Fortunatus, and Martin's association with Milan is well attested in Gregory of Tours, who recorded how Ambrose claimed to have assisted at the funeral of Martin, miraculously, while he was asleep at the lectern in Milan.[9]

It may well also be this type of renown, captured and promoted in the literary heritage of early medieval clerics, that lay behind the appearance of Ambrose and Simplicianus in the *Life of Gaudentius*. But in these cases the dates are perfectly plausible; the only question is why Gaudentius had to wait, long after Eusebius's return (c.365) and death (371), to be consecrated as Novara's

8 *Life of Martin*, ed. Fontaine 1967–1969, 5.3: "... parentesque, quos adhuc gentilitas detinebat, religiosa sollicitudine ad fidei gratiam visitaret"; *VG* 3: "... seu etiam et parentes, quos adhuc gentilitas detinebat, religiosa sollicitudine ad fidei gratiam provocabat." This commonality was spotted by Lizier 1910, who points out two other parallels in theme but not language: both extinguish a fire (*Gaudentius* ch.10; *Martin* ch.14) and both perform a posthumous miracle (*Gaudentius* ch.20, *Martin* ch.17). The further parallels in language adduced by Colombo, Temporelli, and Perotti (eds) 1983, 4, are not convincing, nor is the detection of further sources by Gavinelli 2001, who posits direct use of Paulinus of Nola (*Ep.* 5), Augustine (*In Ioahnnis evang.*; *Enarrationes in Psalmos*), Pope Leo (*Tractatus* 97), Pope Gregory I (*Dialogues*), and Rufinus (*Historia ecclesiastica*); only the latter seems evident, but the borrowing is not verbatim as it is for the *Vita* of Sulpicius Pius (see below).

9 *Mirac. S. Martin*, 1.5, ed. Krusch 1885 (MGH SS rer. Merov. 1: 591).

first bishop by Simplicianus (397–400). Perhaps that is the true motif of Ambrose's prophecy, "You will be bishop," and Gaudentius's tart and somewhat macabre response, "Certainly. But I shall be consecrated by another" (ch.11–12). The story is also found, nearly verbatim, in a hagiographic work called *On the Life and Merits of Ambrose* written in late–ninth century Milan.[10] As noted below, this has caused some confusion for dating the *Life of Gaudentius*, but it is clear that the later Milanese author borrowed it from the Gaudentius text. Ambrose is signalled at the start of the *Life of Gaudentius* as somehow uniting Gaudentius and Laurence in a brotherhood of faith (ch.1); hence, although a distant figure in Gaudentius's career, Ambrose's historical importance granted him a central place in the narrative of Gaudentius's *Life*.

The figure of Simplicianus also touches upon another hagiographical work presented in this volume, for Vigilius of Trent sent to Simplicianus a letter describing the fate of the three martyrs of the Val di Non, along with their relics, which Simplicianus then interred in the "basilica uirginum" built by Ambrose, later known as the "basilica Simpliciani" after Simplicianus was buried there. Simplicianus himself is an important figure in Italian ecclesiastical history.[11] Already considered an old man when he officiated Ambrose's baptism (374), he played a key role in Augustine's period of conversion while in Milan (c.384–387) by recounting to Augustine the story of Marius Victorinus, a philosopher of Neoplatonism who converted to Christianity, encouraged by Simplicianus, who himself was well versed in philosophy but had been a Christian from his boyhood. It was Simplicianus who explained to the high-minded Victorinus that being a Christian meant not only studying scripture but attending church also ("It's the walls that make Christians, then?" Victorinus cheekily replied – a joke clearly appreciated by Augustine). When on his death bed, Ambrose dimly heard his clergy discussing his potential successors, and upon hearing the name of Simplicianus, Ambrose cried out three times "Old, but good" (*Senex sed bonus*). Aside from the letter of Vigilius, letters to Simplicianus from Ambrose and Augustine survive, containing responses to Simplicianus's

10 *De vita et meritis Ambrosii*, 70–72, ed. Paredi 1964. The two versions are conveniently printed side by side in Colombo, Temporelli, and Perotti (eds) 1983, 4–5, also in Courcelle 1973, 49–121 (at 100–101 and 138).

11 His feast day is 15 August. On Simplicianus, see A. Rimoldi, *Bib. Sanct.* 11, 1194–1197; Picard 1988, 46–48, 67–68, 616–623; Augustine, *Confessions*, 8.1–5. For Ambrose's deathbed, see Paulinus, *Life of Ambrose*, ch.46–48. The *Vita Simpliciani* (BHL 7786; AA. SS. Aug. III: 282–284) is usually dated to the eleventh century, but Picard 1988, 622 n145, suggests it might be earlier.

theological questions, and in 396 Augustine even worked one of these letters into a two-book treatise entitled *To Simplicianus, On various questions*,[12] which gave preliminary accounts of his conversion and his doctrine of grace, themes to which he would return in the *Confessions* written immediately after.

While the literary heritage concerning Simplicianus was considerable (he was noted by Gennadius, Ennodius, and Prosper of Aquitaine), it is perfectly reasonable to presume that he did consecrate Gaudentius during his brief episcopacy, as is claimed in the *Life of Gaudentius*. Simplicianus was actively involved in exercising his metropolitan authority during those three years: he received letters from the Synod of Carthage in 397, from that in Toledo in 400, and possibly attended the Council of Turin in 398. He was also well aware of Ambrose's final duties before he died: he intervened in a disputed election of a bishop at Vercelli (alluded to in the *Life of Gaudentius*, ch.11) ordained his friend Gaudentius as bishop of Brescia, and then ordained the bishop of Pavia in February 397, before retiring to his sick bed. Simplicianus may have simply continued the policy of solidifying Milan's metropolitan authority in northern Italy by ordaining Gaudentius, whose barb at Ambrose in the *Life* may reflect a contemporary concern that it was high time Novara had its own bishop. The *Life* (ch.7) seems to make this very point when Gaudentius chooses to support Eusebius of Vercelli and join him in exile; in doing so, "he sought martyrdom rather than attain the pontifical rank." Gaudentius's subsequent appointment as Eusebius's deputy in Vercelli certainly gave him credentials, and at this point the hagiographer is at pains to stress the connection between Vercelli and Novara, personified in the partnership of Eusebius and Gaudentius, so that the two churches enjoyed a shared direction, "and now even up until today they seem by the will of God to endure as undivided" (ch.8). We can only wonder if this contemporary reference is a clue to a contemporary audience and purpose for the *Life*, say, some dispute between Vercelli and Novara c.685–725 (see below for the dating).[13] There is no evidence that the author knew the *Life of Eusebius* presented elsewhere in this book, with its portrait of Vercelli's ecclesiastical primacy in fourth-century Western Europe and the fiery Eusebius who challenged a Roman emperor. Indeed, the *Life of Gaudentius* makes no further mention of Eusebius, nor is Eusebius's martyrdom mentioned at all: he is referred

12 Ed. Mutzenbecher (CCL 44) 1970; Trans. J.H.S. Burleigh 1953.

13 Cassani 1954 suggested that the *Life* was written in conjunction with the dedication to Gaudentius of a pre-existing Novarese church previously dedicated to the apostles (that mentioned in ch.18), but evidence is lacking.

to as "the greatest confessor." On the other hand, the whole chapter (ch.7) evokes the theme of Gaudentius's willingness to undergo "martyrdom" by following Eusebius into exile, only to suffer the bad luck of not being killed: "his desire for martyrdom would have been granted if only there were a murderer." This type of language, which describes exile as "martyrdom," is certainly found in the *Life of Eusebius*, because Eusebius and his contemporaries described themselves that way (see *Eusebius*, introduction, and further, Everett 2006). It seems that Gaudentius's hagiographer knew some of those sources and knew that Eusebius and Vercelli were important in the fourth century, but he did not know the *Life of Eusebius* itself. This then suggests a *terminus post quem* for the *Life of Eusebius* of 685–725.

Finally, the *Life of Gaudentius* introduces the mysterious figure of Laurence (ch.5–6), a priest who (apparently) had been actively evangelizing around Novara, constructing baptismal fonts outside the city and preaching, until he was martyred by pagans ("cultists of the mausoleum"), along with a large number of children whom he had baptized. We have no other information about this Laurence and no evidence of his cult in Novara until the eleventh century, when we hear of a church (outside the walls of the northern gate) and a monastery dedicated to the saint. The end of that century witnessed the redaction of a *Vita Laurentii* (BHL 475m), written before the *Vita Agabii* (BHL 377), and both texts relied heavily on the *Vita Gaudentii* as a source.[14] Thanks to the *Life of Gaudentius*, an important early Christian presence in Novara is documented.

Date of Composition

The date of the *Life of Gaudentius*'s composition has been the subject of debate, but we can confidently assign it to the late seventh or early eighth century. A *terminus post quem* is provided by the use of Pope Gregory I's *Homilies on the Gospels* (on Matt. 25:14–30, see below, *Life*, ch.15 n61), but the most important clue is given by the hagiographer, who in the epilogue refers to enjoying the support (*fultus*) of a *papa Leo*, "the latest to possess the see of the blessed Gaudentius in the city of Novara" (*Life*, ch.22). The earliest episcopal list of Novara, which was inscribed sometime in the eleventh century onto a consular diptych made of ivory (itself originally dating from c.525), records only one bishop of

14 Picard 1988, 461–462.

that name, who appears as the twenty-fifth bishop. Unfortunately, the list only begins to provide dates and/or lengths of episcopacy from the thirty-first bishop (Atto, AD c.829) onward, but we do have historical dates for the twenty-second bishop (Gratianus, c.680) and the twenty-seventh (Gratziosus, in a document of 729, noted above).[15] Given two successions on either side of those dates, Leo's episcopate falls in the range of c.685–725. The use of *papa* for bishop is unusual if not impossible in this period; it was the term for bishops up to the fourth century but became increasingly restricted to the bishop of Rome in the Latin West in the fifth and sixth centuries.[16] But *papa* was still used occasionally for bishops into the ninth century and beyond, and it is not inconceivable that the author of a text describing famous fourth-century bishops might affectionately apply that term to his patron, the bishop of Novara, who then occupied Gaudentius's see. The final sentences of the *Life* ("And now, having narrated these deeds ...") appear verbatim in a *Life* of Sulpicius Pius, bishop of Bourges (d.c.646), which appears to be an elongated version of an earlier and shorter text and has been dated to the ninth century,[17] thereby providing a possible *terminus ante quem* for the *Life of Gaudentius*.

The literary Latin of the *Vita* does not fit with the usual characterization of this period as one of barbarism and with little concern for literary culture. This has led some scholars to argue for a much later date, most recently and forcefully Colombo (1974, 1983), who suggests it was written in the late eleventh century in the climate of religious reform against the Patarine movement (hence, *papa Leo* supposedly refers to Pope Leo IX, 1049–1054). These arguments have been comprehensively refuted[18] and are also invalidated by the

15 There are in fact two lists, one on each plate of the diptych, preserved in different churches: the earliest, that relevant here, was preserved in San Gaudenzio and goes up to 1070; the other, preserved in the cathedral of S. Maria, goes up to 1355. There are differences of opinion on their date of redaction: see Picard 1988, 459–461, also Mor 1967 and Hlawitschka 1972. The early part of the diptych is reproduced by Lanzoni 1927, 2: 1033; a concordance of the two lists is given by Picard 1988, 743, tab. 11. The addition of "anni XX" next to Gaudentius's name seems to be taken from the *Vita*. On the basis of the "papa Leo" reference, Gavinelli 2001, (ed) 2013 dates the *Life* to the period of King Liutprand (712–744), finding cultural concordance with the religiosity of his legislation and reign; she does not consider the hagiographer's possible use of the *Life of Eusebius* as dated here and Everett 2006.

16 Moorhead 1985. We also find *papa* (even *papa et episcopus*) in sixth-century papyri documents from Ravenna: Tjäder 1955–1982, P.34, P.49.

17 BHL 7930, AA. SS. Ian. II: 168–174. For shorter versions, see BHL 7927–7928 and parallel text ed. Krusch 1902 (MGH SS rer. Merov. 4: 364–368).

18 Tomea 1998, 190–202; Everett 2000, 92–99; Gavinelli 2001, 2007.

manuscript tradition, which begins from the late ninth century. Two other aspects of the *Life*, however, have prevented scholars (such as Picard 1988: 636–640) from identifying *papa Leo* with bishop number twenty five in the episcopal lists: the lack of mention of Gaudentius in any of the ninth- century Frankish martyrologies and the use of an almost identical passage – that in which Ambrose predicts Gaudentius's future consecration (ch.11–12) – in the *On the Life and Merits of Ambrose*, written in late ninth-century Milan (see above). But in the first case, there is no reason to marvel that a local Italian patron saint was not noted in martyrologies prepared by Franks, whose interest in Italy was centred on Roman martyrs. In the second case, the author of the *Life and Merits of Ambrose* simply borrowed from the *Vita Gaudentii* (not the other way around). Nothing argues against that except prejudice against the Lombard period and bias towards the Carolingian. We now know enough about literary traditions in the Lombard period, including the composition of hagiography, to put those prejudices aside. The *Life of Gaudentius* can be comfortably dated to the period AD c.685–725, until new evidence can be offered to the contrary.

Text and Translation

The literary ambitions, even pretensions, of the *Life of Gaudentius* are evident right from the prologue. One eminent Italian scholar of Latin literature even suggested it demonstrated continuity of Latin rhetorical traditions from antiquity.[19] Occasionally, the piling up of adjectives or lofty abstract nouns obscures the meaning, though that too may be owed to corruptions in the manuscript tradition. Our earliest manuscripts date from the late ninth century, and a recent edition by Gavinelli (2013) uses two ninth-century Carolingian manuscripts: one is a collection of hagiographic and patristic material preserved at Milan's Biblioteca Ambrosiana, S 55 Sup. 122v–131v, and probably written at Bobbio; the other manuscript is a passionary preserved at Intra, Archivio capitolare, 12 (10), previously dated by Colombo and others to the eleventh century, but its script and contents suggest it is contemporary with Ambrosiana S 55 Sup.[20] Colombo's edition of 1983 utilized around eighteen manuscripts, includ-

19 Viscardi 1939, 373–375.

20 Full descriptions in Gavinelli, 2001, 2007, (ed) 2013; Gavinelli's edition includes an Italian translation by G. Benedetto. Another of Colombo's earliest manuscripts was Naples, Biblioteca nazionale, XV AA 12, fols. 229–232, copied c.976–1025, in the region of Florence (Poncelet 1910, 145–147), which also ruled out his dating of the *Life* to the eleventh century.

ing many from Novara itself, most of which date from the eleventh century onward (except for Intra, Archivo capitolare, 12, as above, which Colombo also used). Colombo's edition supersedes that of the Bollandists, AA. SS. Ian. III, first ed., seventeenth-century; rev. ed., 1865, 30–34, which itself was based on Mombritius (AD c.1480; rev. ed., 1910), I.564–569. Colombo's edition was used for the translation below but is rare and difficult to obtain. The Bollandist version is still serviceable. Significant differences between the two versions are commented upon in the notes. Likewise for the edition of Gavinelli 2013, which came to the author's attention after submission of the present book to the publisher. Attempts have been made to incorporate any variant readings that alter the meaning of the text or affect the commentary offered here.

The Life of Gaudentius of Novara

[Chapter I][21]

1. When I was zealously reflecting upon the life and works of the saints who have gone before us, suddenly, by divine will, my memory recalled the most celebrated acts of the blessed Gaudentius. Although the Lord ordained that Gaudentius should shine through so many and such great signs [*signa*], I, being simply a humble servant and correspondingly rude in speech, cannot narrate them all well enough, because I am unequal to, and unworthy of, so great a burden. Nevertheless, there is reward in this work, so that supported by divine authority, which says, "open your mouth, and I shall fill it,"[22] and also enwrapped in the merits of the aforesaid pontiff and patron, I should attempt to narrate at least a few of the many things about him, shunning inaction. But this also requires some notice on the blessed Laurence the martyr,[23] in order that the equal triumph of those whom Ambrose,[24] radiant in his own right, united in brotherhood in a bond of faith may resound. Indeed, the already mentioned sacred Gaudentius, skillfully keeping to the paths of this man [Laurence],[25] has trampled over the obstacles of the world, shunning its wealth. For that reason, he, the victor, seated on a chair in heaven, triumphs with the angels.

2. Blessed Gaudentius of Ivrea, a city in *Esperia* [northern Italy] known to be in the vicinity of the Alps, right beside the border of Europe, was born from a noble family, among the most important citizens of the town. But later he shone as the distinguished pastor of the city of Novara, in *Ausonia* [Italy], where he occupied the bishop's chair for twenty years, and was made our patron by his glorious death. Indeed, radiant with the heavenly brilliance of divine grace, in addition to the splendour of his mind, he walked amongst the stars as if he were the glittering morning star. This blessed man burned from the very cra-

21 These chapter divisions appear in the editions of Mombritius 1910 and AA. SS. and are repeated here; the numbered paragraphing follows Colombo, Temporelli, and Perotti (eds) 1983.

22 Ps. 81:10.

23 On this mysterious figure, known only from the *Life*, see the introduction above and Picard 1988, 461–462.

24 Ambrose (374–398). See also below, ch. 11–12.

25 Although grammar (*huius*) suggests Ambrose, the sense suggests Laurence.

dle for the highest religious way of life, and was nursed with such great wisdom in the stages of early infancy that even upon becoming a young man he followed the ecclesiastical rule by divine inspiration, loving it with all his might. He restrained himself strictly by his own discipline, offering a preview of what sort of priest he would later become in the temple of God. For although he appeared to be very young and even immature for his years, he nevertheless openly proclaimed and perfectly maintained a vow of chastity, thereby establishing abstinence in his heart as a basic foundation, upon which he built his other virtues. To repress his youthful passions and ensure his progression to wisdom, he controlled himself with the restraints of prayer and abstinence, and educated the many who came to him in the teachings of the perfect life.

3. Not only did he begin to sow evangelical seeds [by his eloquence][26] among the crude locals but also with spiritual guidance he brought his parents, still held by paganism, to the grace of faith. He was a blessed person of the greatest merit and virtue, to whom it was granted to be a teacher first, before becoming a priest, for what he taught with words he fulfilled in manifest examples. During this time he began to become famous for his acts [*signa*] and the power of his miracles. For he both cured the sick with his prayers and put demons to flight with his words. This most humble of men exerted himself so that, although he enjoyed the riches of favour in this world, he avoided tainting his ears with the pollution of arrogance.

4. While this most blessed man was doing these things, that virulent seducer and enemy of all goodness [of the human race][27] discerned that people were being brought daily to join with Christ the Lord by the painstaking exertions of Gaudentius. So [attempting to assail the minds of many with seditious counsel and call them back from their good conduct][28] the enemy devised a clever trick against the servant of God, and caused the people to attack him as proud and contemptible. In him, therefore, was fulfilled that which is written: "A prophet is only without honour in his homeland."[29] They subsequently stopped believing in him, and he no longer seemed to have worked his many miracles there. For just as the splendour of the light had illuminated some pious believers, a

26 Gavinelli (ed) 2013.
27 Gavinelli (ed) 2013.
28 Gavinelli (ed) 2013.
29 Cf. Matt. 13:57; Mark 6:4.

foul fog had suffused other impious dissenters. His supporters sped towards glory, and the faithless were dragged towards their punishment. When the most blessed man eventually learned about their defiance, he was afflicted with great sadness, after the example of the blessed Apostle Paul, who wished to be made anathema from Christ for the sake of his brothers and kindred in flesh.[30] Nevertheless, pondering carefully that this was done by a subtle and mysterious judgement of God, he understood that holy preaching may be held back from certain ears for the reason that they do not deserve to be awakened through grace: just as it is written, "Let the ungodly man be taken away, that he should not see the glory of God."[31] Putting aside ties of blood relations, he abhorred them as enemies of the Catholic religion. Detesting association with each and every one of them, he sought support in the example of David: "Let me not sit in the company of the malign; I shall share in their crimes no longer, but shall stay with the innocent and go about your altar, O Lord, lest I be tempted into sin by sharing a table with the ungodly."[32] He soon began to meditate on the acts of the ancient fathers, how they obeyed the divine commandments and deserved to obtain the kingdom of heaven and become companions of its angelic citizens. And when he contemplated how Abraham, the friend of God, departed from his land and people at God's command,[33] and how many other elect of God left behind earthly things yet received heavenly rewards a hundred times over, he hastened to fulfil the divine commandments with all speed. Renouncing everything, he became an attentive listener to the Gospel. He denied himself, took up his cross, and followed Christ.[34] So it happened that the farther he withdrew from his ancestral land for the name of Christ, the more he deserved every day to be closer to heaven.

[Chapter II]

5. And so he left Ivrea, and after a few days reached the city of Novara. There he learned that the blessed Laurence, a priest worthy of God, had arrived from the western lands a little while earlier for the name of Christ, and that Laurence had been waging battle against the faithlessness of the pagans, like a warrior raging among the enemy, a standard-bearer clothed in the fervour of faith,

30 Cf. Rom. 9:2–4.
31 Isa. 26:10.
32 Cf. Ps. 26(25):4–6.
33 Cf. Gen. 12:1.
34 Cf. Matt. 16:24 and Luke 9:23.

ramming through the midst of their battle lines. Protected by faith, he built sacred fonts with his very own holy hands just outside the city, where he continually performed baptisms in the name of the Holy Trinity. Nor did he cease to introduce God, perfect in the Trinity [which he knew],[35] to the pagans. By setting his judgement and mercy before all, he strove little by little to unite with God their souls, which the devil had stolen. And so, amazingly, it happened that an armed mob did not have the power to stand against one defenceless man. For the Lord deigned to perform such great wonders [*virtutes*] through Laurence that he won over the hearts of the rebels as much by his preaching as by miracle. Then one day, when as usual Laurence had consecrated to the Lord an innumerable multitude of children to be born again through the grace of baptism, he then proceeded fearlessly amongst the ranks of the cultists of the mausoleum. And it was then that he was crowned with martyrdom, together with the little ones he had just baptized, by the aforesaid evil ones. His life in the present world ended, having secured eternal life in heaven with the angels, he revels still as the victor. His venerable corpse still astonishes even unto the present day, with many signs and miracles of healing in the aforesaid city of Novara. Thanks be to you, Lord Jesus, for you prevented the arrows of an attacking enemy from wounding your faithful, offering proof that you grant great rewards for their toils, and prevent the enemy from rejoicing in their cowardice.

6. But since the focus of the work I have undertaken is intended to be the specific deeds of our patron, I cannot describe in detail the many things done by the most blessed Laurence the martyr. It is enough that I have not been unmindful of him, for in these matters it is best that the faithful simply believe, rather than consider what human narration can describe. Therefore, when the blessed Gaudentius came to Laurence, that most blessed athlete of God, he was received by him with the greatest pleasure. Gradually, by keeping close by Laurence's side and following his spiritual guidance, Gaudentius became a lawful sacrificer[36] and was fully instructed in the doctrine of the Holy Trinity. For some time they fed the royal flock in equal brotherhood. But after the glorious death of Laurence, it should be known that Gaudentius, because of his faith and

35 Gavinelli (ed) 2013.

36 *iuredicus immolator*, qualified in the following chapter as ordination into minor orders (*adiutor*, *lector*). Gavinelli (ed) 2013 reads *veridicus immolator* and notes (as does Colombo, Temporelli, and Perotti [eds] 1983) *iuridicus simulator* for MS Intra, Archivio capitolare 12. The phrase is possibly a corruption of *veridicus aemulator*, "true imitator," though no manuscript supports it.

religious learning, became the companion and notary of the most blessed Martin,[37] the eminent confessor, in the metropolitan city of Milan.

7. This was at the time of Emperor Constantius,[38] when the Arian heresy had sprouted forth like a poisonous flower from a toxic root. The aforesaid emperor was persuaded by certain enemies of the Catholic faith, Valens and Ursacinus, to condemn into exile Eusebius,[39] bishop of Vercelli, along with other pontiffs pleasing to God. And so it happened. Now, at this same time, the blessed Gaudentius, steadfast in hope[40] and clothed in the fervour of his faith, was not at all afraid of his own death in following his love of Christ. Instead, showing that he held within him that special and sublime love with which Christ taught to lay down one's life for one's friends, he openly and without delay supported Eusebius, the most blessed man and holy confessor, and sought with keen spirit to join him in exile, following him voluntarily as his attendant and companion, fully prepared to die [and was made exile from his companions by heavenly favour].[41] For as it is written, "love is as strong as death."[42] O truly this was a most perfect man [whose imitators desired to be priests themselves, and][43] who from his very earliest instruction burned with such great love in his heart that from the beginning he attached himself to Laurence, the most blessed martyr, and became his assistant [*adiutor*], performing with complete expertise the duties of his rank like the lowliest *lector*. After that he became a follower of the most blessed Martin, the eminent confessor, and was found to be the most skillful of all notaries, proving worthy of ascending the ranks of the second order.[44] But now bound to Eusebius, the greatest confessor, during this most serious crisis, he sought martyrdom rather than attain the pontifical rank. O truly

37 St Martin of Tours, who went to Milan and established a monastery there (c.355–360) but was eventually driven out by the Arian Bishop Auxentius (on whom see *Eusebius*). Gaudentius's association with Martin may be legendary but is plausible: see introduction above.

38 Emperor Constantius II (337–361).

39 See introduction above.

40 *spe stabilitis*. Gavinelli (ed) 2013 reads *timore motus* ("moved by fear").

41 Gavinelli (ed) 2013.

42 Song of Sol. 8:6.

43 Gavinelli (ed) 2103.

44 Following Gavinelli (ed) 2013, "quasi secundi ordinis gradus ascendendo scandebat"; likewise, Colombo, Temporelli, and Perotti (eds) 1983, "quasi secundi ordinis gradus ascendendo monstrabat." Cf. AA. SS./Mombritius, "quasi seculi ordinis gradus ascendendo scandebat."

blessed man in all ways, who wished, just like the blessed apostle, "to depart and be with Christ,"[45] and to whom "to live is Christ and to die is gain!"[46] From this it may be understood with how much love he cherished Christ, while fearing nothing of the supreme power of Constantius. Indeed for the love of Christ he threw himself into certain ruin, and his desire for martyrdom would have been granted if only there were a murderer. And so it is clear how this most blessed man, who had so many and such skillful teachers, had himself become an instructor. But now let me return to the order of our sermon.

8. Soon the ancient enemy observed that the people of Vercelli were destitute in the absence of their pastor, and strove with certain malicious intrigues to foment civil war and so assail the aforementioned church of God and all its people. But then quickly, with God's help, divine mercy appeared in the arrival of the blessed Gaudentius, for he had been sent to Vercelli by that pious pastor the blessed Eusebius to guard his flock. Keeping close watch on all things,[47] Gaudentius's vigilance ensured that the flock of God was not mangled in the jaws of the wolf.[48] Indeed, he took every care – just as the Prophet says, going up to the breaks in the wall and repairing them for the House of Israel so that it might stand firm in the battle on the day of the Lord[49] – to represent the eminent pastor of that church, keeping watch over his flock long through the night with all his resourcefulness, right up until he could present the inviolate sheepfold of the Lord to its returning pastor. Three years had passed when Eusebius finally returned,[50] and he venerated the blessed Gaudentius as a colleague and a friend. Thanks to this turn of events, the two men became joint guardians of both of their peoples, looking out for both of their churches of God with a shared direction, as if two flocks had been made one sheepfold. For both flocks were joined by an indivisible love, and now even up until today they seem by the will of God to endure as undivided. God is surely amongst them, to be magnified wondrously in his saint, to continue the work of virtue begun by Gaudentius and Eusebius unto more propitious outcomes, and like a light

45 Phil. 1:23.
46 Phil. 1:21.
47 Literally, "on the far side and the near side."
48 For the imagery of this chapter, cf. John 10:1–21.
49 Cf. Ezek. 13:5.
50 The phrase "reduce vero sancto Eusebio tribus evolutis annis" may also mean that Eusebius had returned for three years before the subsequent events mentioned (e.g., joint pastorship) occurred. The period of Eusebius's exile was around seven years (c.355–362): see *Eusebius*.

beaming down from heaven, to illuminate the entire world with the brightness of heavenly light.

[Chapter III]

9. Around this same time, the most blessed Gaudentius sought out within the walls of the city a certain small domicile or cloister enclosed by gates in which to dwell, not far away from where the holy mother of churches is situated. When he first approached it, armed with faith and fearless with courage, he surrendered himself wholly to a great many abstinences, fasts, and vigils, to the point that if ever physical need demanded some sleep, he never once enjoyed the softness of a bed, but instead laid himself down on only a mat of rushes and a hair-blanket.

10. And there, while passing a night in vigil, there suddenly erupted a fire along the city walls in the middle of night, due to some accident. The blaze grew huge and surrounded them on all sides. It swiftly reached nearly all the way to Gaudentius's cell, where he was drifting in a light sleep. Learning what was happening from a disciple who had rushed to him, Gaudentius quickly ran about to circle the centre of the flames with spiritual chanting, trying to oppose the towering flames with the sign of the cross. But when the flames reached the neighbouring and adjoining houses on each side, they could no longer burn and were turned back upon themselves. Gaudentius went back to his cell exulting and singing the praises appropriate to the hours of matins.

11. Shortly after this event, Gaudentius performed a prophetic miracle, thanks to divine intervention. One time the most blessed man and the glory of the churches, Ambrose, the bishop of the holy church of Milan, hastened to the aforesaid city of Vercelli on account of a certain dissension amongst its people. While there he illuminated the entire city with his rays, equal to the sun, and left behind a perpetual peaceful concord. He had intended to return quickly to his own see, so as he passed by the city of Novara and the day was already growing dark, he hurried on towards his destination, postponing a visit to the blessed Gaudentius, saying to his companions, "We ought to see the most reverent man Gaudentius, but the day is already fading to night." Saying this, he continued on the route he had chosen. But before he had gone much farther, suddenly the horse of the blessed Ambrose stood still, and he could not budge it to move forward. He began to strike the horse with his whip and bloody it with his

spurs, but it remained immobile, as though it feared the chosen journey as a mortal danger. When the great man became weary from whipping the horse at length, he suddenly changed his mind, and radiant with the divine spirit as usual he said to himself, "We are not allowed to complete our journey unless we have seen the blessed Gaudentius." Upon saying this, he immediately retraced his steps and went back willingly to the city where he had been unwilling to go.

12. Now when the blessed Gaudentius learned, through an apparition of the Spirit, that the great man was coming to him, he immediately endeavoured to run out to meet him. Ambrose first stared at him, then warmly embraced and kissed him, and then announced a prophecy [*mysterium*], almost shouting it, saying to Gaudentius, "You will be a bishop, as I see it." Now Gaudentius, foreseeing the future by the same grace, with his face calm as usual, chided in response, but not in a cheeky way, "Certainly. But I shall be consecrated by another."[51] And so it happened that, speaking with one spirit about the same miracle, both prophesied the future, one discerning the event, the other discerning its appropriate time. After they bade each other farewell, Saint Ambrose returned to his city, but after a short time, just as the prophecy of the blessed Gaudentius foretold, he departed for the Lord in a glorious death, but nominated beforehand the most blessed Simplicianus[52] as his worthy successor.

13. But now the desired time wished for in everyone's prayers drew nigh, when the people of Novara, hoping for so long that the most blessed Gaudentius would be their bishop, pleaded with the earthly sovereign about him who they knew was wholly acceptable to the heavenly sovereign.[53] Wherefore they sent him a petition, weighty of purpose but using few words to make clear the desired outcome, beseeching him to become a merciful hearer of their prayers, so that Gaudentius,

51 This episode is also recorded in the *On the Life and Merits of the Blessed Ambrose* (ed. Paredi 1964, 70–72), composed in late–ninth century Milan: see introduction above. The text is almost verbatim and was likely taken from the *Vita Gaudentii*.

52 Simplicianus (397–400), who played a key role in St Augustine's conversion (*Confessions*, 8.1–5): see introduction above.

53 The phrase is obscure: "terreno principi illum [scil . Gaudentium] orando expeteret, quem noverat omnino caelesti principi conplacuisse." Secular (imperial) confirmation was only required for archbishops; the hagiographer is probably using the model of Ambrose, a special case because he was previously governor: McLynn 1994, 4–10. The sovereign (*princeps*) in this period would have been the Emperor Honorius (395–423), in the West; Arcadius (395–408), in the East.

worthy of God, might at last undertake the office of their guidance and be exalted to the sacred summit. As a gift from heaven, the prince unexpectedly ordered without delay to fulfil that which had been predestined by divine providence, for he had enjoyed the acuteness of their counsel, and all his greed had been restrained. And so, by the Lord's arrangement, he was the first to earn the episcopal office of the see of Novara. Once he received the pontifical honour from the most blessed Archbishop Simplicianus, he became all things to all men.[54]

14. He was seeking not his own good but the good of many, so that they might be saved.[55] The Lord quickly deigned to illuminate his priest like some sort of lantern, augmenting daily his power to preach the word and to sow the salutary seeds of the kingdom of heaven. He soon freed infected people of the ancient poison, so that even the worshippers of the impious mausoleum, who had earlier killed the blessed martyr Laurence, seemed to gaze upon the new light of truth, so that none of them remained without the grace of baptism in the city given to him by heaven. For he who deserved to become a confessor did not hesitate as a preacher to enlighten savage peoples. He beseeched the Lord continually for their conversion, and taught them that through baptism they would have remission for their sins, and that they could not be saved otherwise. Then they were astounded, as if rays of the true sun had shone brightly in their hearts. Contemplating with unveiled faces the glory of God,[56] they repented their ancient error, and came with faithful confession to be baptized by that very pontiff. And so, through divine grace, the eminent warrior Gaudentius carried off the plunder from the Enemy and restored it to the Author.

15. A little while after this, the grace of miracles had accumulated in him so much that signs occurred through him no less than they did through the apostles long ago. For, as I said a little above, during his youth he could already put to flight demons with his words and cure the sick with his prayers. The Lord was further magnified daily by performing miracles through his saint, so that over time he restored sight to the blind, hearing to the deaf, speech to the mute, and mobility to the lame. He has done very many other things that would be tedious to narrate one by one. Because in the past, when the Lord and Saviour was present on earth, he said to his disciples, "If you believe in me, works that

54 Cf. 1 Cor. 9:22. Carolingian MS (Gavinelli [ed] 2013) adds "more burden than honour."

55 Cf. 1 Cor. 10:33.

56 Cf. 2 Cor. 3:18.

I do you will do also, and you will do greater things than these."[57] He therefore ignited the blessed Gaudentius with spiritual fire that burned with a love of the faith so great that if anyone secretly pilfered water dripping from his hands while he washed himself, and used it to touch the body of a sick person, the sick person was immediately free from most infirmities. Only those who can vouch for these signs could believe how many or what kind of signs the Lord ultimately delivered through him. Yet still the most blessed Gaudentius strove without pause to reinvigorate the hearts of his sheep with divine feasts, lest they should overlook the divine commandments, completely replicating that edict of the Saviour: "Do not possess gold or silver."[58] Indeed, just like the apostle, he taught them to be content with food and clothing.[59] Meanwhile he exerted himself with all his strength, punishing his body and reducing it to servitude, lest perhaps he himself, preaching to others, should be proven reprobate.[60] As long as he was preaching and toiling, he yielded double the profit to the Lord from his activity.[61] And there is no doubt to anyone that, according to the voice of the Saviour, he who taught things that he himself had done first in all respects would be great in the kingdom of heaven.[62] He was a priest of God, bearing the pontifical *petalon*,[63] and by crucifying himself and attacking his sins, won a new martyrdom by the mortification of his flesh.

[Chapter IV]

16. But when he had constructed enough churches, monasteries, and sanctuaries throughout his parishes, and had become the father of innumerable clerics,

57 Cf. John 14:12.
58 Cf. Matt. 10:9.
59 Cf. 1 Tim. 6:8.
60 Cf. 1 Cor. 9:27.
61 Cf. Matt. 25:14–30 (the parable of the talents). However, the exact phrase in the text of the *Life* ("eatenus ut predicando et operando, duplicatum de negotio lucrum ad dominum reportaret") seems to have been taken from Pope Gregory I's homily on this Biblical passage: *Homiliae in Evangelia*, 9(18).1: "cumque et intelligendo et operando aliis praedicant, quasi duplicatum de negotio lucrum reportant."
62 Cf. Matt. 5:19.
63 Isidore of Seville (d. 636) defined a *petalon* as "a golden plate worn against the high priest's forehead; it would have the *Tetragrammaton*, the name of God, written on it in Hebrew characters," *Etym.* 19.21.7, ed. Lindsay 1911. Curiously, the phrase used in the *Life* ("fuit sacerdos Dei pontificale petalum gestans") is a verbatim (Latin) translation of a description of John the apostle found in a letter of Bishop Polycarp of Smyrna (d. 155) quoted in Eusebius of Caesarea, *Ecclesiastical History*, 3.31 and 5.24.

exulting in the thorough dedication of his sons, he hastily took up from the Eternal Father the final reward that was in store for him. Truly the Lord is always there to comfort and reward a faithful servant.[64] Therefore, when he had already completed twenty years in the pontifical rank, and recognized that his own death would take place soon, he thought it would be more beneficial, while he remained present in his body, to announce who was to be his successor, lest afterwards any dispute should arise concerning the future shepherd of the flock entrusted to him by heaven. Once all the clergy and people had been brought together, he advised them first to remember the words of God that they had heard with their own ears, although divinely revealed through him, and to dread the danger of eternal damnation, while preparing themselves every day for the heavenly kingdom. Then he admonished them about many other matters, and added that everyone should know that his successor in office, and their future shepherd, a prudent man by the name of Agabius,[65] had been foreordained by God, and that all of them should steadfastly remain in harmonious agreement about his selection, lest ignorant people rebel against divine prescience.

17. After he gave this advice, with whatever strength he had left, the most blessed man never ceased to teach his people before his glorious time of ending arrived. [And so, a few days later, perfecting his allotted time by sparkling in the splendour of his miracles.][66]While he was entrusting his earthly limbs unto the earth, his spirit, which had long desired to join the heavenly choirs of angels, ascended high above. Immediately a crowd of innumerable people quickly flocked together from every direction at his passing; the town walls, the houses, and all the streets were packed with people. All were in deep mourning, all suffered intolerable grief. Amidst the sobbing and groaning of the distressed only the following cries would be wrenched into the form of words: "Alas, desolate flock, what will you do? Behold, will you disperse at the loss of your shepherd? And who will be able to free you from the swift jaws of the wolves?" At that time the basilica, which the priest of God had begun to construct with great effort, and where he now lies interred in wondrous beauty awaiting the time of resurrection, remained unfinished. The blessed man Agabius later brought this basilica to completion with all honour. But at the

64 Cf. Matt. 25:21 and 25:23.

65 Agabius's feast day is 10 September; the dates of his episcopate are unknown. The *Vita Agabii* (BHL 0117m) dates from the eleventh century: see Picard 1988, 461–463.

66 Gavinelli (ed) 2013.

time the people were afflicted by a double sadness, for the death of their shepherd, and for his unfinished basilica. Unable to endure such anguish, they prostrated themselves on the pavement and bellowed with every ounce of strength, to the point that even the ministers of the church were not allowed to perform the divine offices.

18. In time the most holy man Gaudentius hastened to visit spiritually his people whom he had left behind in body, but not in affection. He suddenly imbued the hearts of everyone with divine inspiration, indicating that they should lay his venerable corpse in the holy mother church of God[67] and not inter it in a tomb, but instead merely place it on the ground, until the church that he had begun to build should be brought to completion by his successor, the most reverent man Agabius. Then an entire multitude of people, radiant with divine illumination, and also strengthened by his past miracles, cast aside all their uncertainty about the corruption of his sacred body, and placed his holy and venerable body on a wooden plank in the sacristy. There they celebrated his holy obsequies with all reverence, and decided that divine offices should be performed continually there. Let no one doubt[68] that his sacred corpse, gleaming with roseate radiance and redolent of fragrant perfume, had remained unburied from the eleventh day before the Kalends of February[69] all the way until the third day before the Nones of August.[70] Indeed, his corpse was seen daily by his sons to demonstrate a considerable miracle in and of itself. For the hair on his head and cheeks, and also the nails of his hands and feet, remained as they had been before on his most blessed body, so that they continually grew while many people looked on. The most blessed man deigned to display such great signs in his body so that he might make it understood to all who saw him that the man whom they were previously mourning inconsolably as being in the land of the dead was instead living in heaven with the angels. After these signs, he revealed himself to be present by healing those suffering from various infirmities.

Like a light shone down from heaven, or some ray of the sun bursting forth, he illuminated the entire world with the brightness of celestial light. From very many towns and cities an immense multitude of people gathered together at his holy and venerable corpse for different miracles of healing.

67 On possible locations, see Cassani 1954.

68 *nullus ambigat*. Gavinelli (ed) 2013 reads *quis ambigat* ("who could doubt ... ?").

69 22 January.

70 3 August.

19. His illustrious reputation spread quickly to reach not only neighbouring cities but also ones far away.[71] Meanwhile the blessed Agabius, together with the entire people, raised the aforesaid basilica at great expense and with exceptional care. Once it was completed, they diligently consecrated it with all due ceremony. Then, six months after his death, and twelve days in addition, they delivered his holy body, as uncorrupted as a day-old corpse, into his tomb with all honour. And every day there, through the power of Jesus Christ the Lord, his miraculous powers are revealed to the crowds, who learn how much they should honour the servant of God, when blindness recovers sight and lameness mobility, and the blocked ears of the deaf are opened to sound.

20. [The miracle][72] when the right hand of Christ extended unto one girl, whom a bunch of demons had invaded, in order to reveal his servant. When this girl was born of noble stock in the city of Rome, she possessed limitless wealth and countless riches. On a certain day, while she was roaming through the remote parts of the woods on her property, she fell unawares[73] to the darts of demons, and her breast, suddenly corrupted, became a temple of their legions.[74] Eventually her companions[75] found her too aggressive:[76] being few, they were not strong enough to hold her when she was raging. She raved furiously at everyone and gnashed her teeth, and her venomous mouth made her companions hostile towards her. They surrounded her from all sides, imprisoned her in chains, and led her to the church of the blessed prince Peter, conducting her by force to the site of his sacred tomb. Then, the phalanx of demons throughout her possessed body imitated all sorts of voices in the manner of an organ: now, with her mouth quivering, she emitted the hissing of a serpent; now the lowing of cattle or the bleating of sheep; now the cawing of birds, and finally she roared like a wild beast. At last, the most blessed Peter, prince of the apostles, deigned to manifest his mystical power through a certain most holy man. He advised her companions to undertake a long journey,

71 Gavinelli (ed) 2013 reads "but also took wing to every kingdom on earth."

72 The opening use of *quod* with the sentence that follows suggests a rubric or chapter heading (hence incomplete editing).

73 Reading "improvida" instead of "in provida," see Colombo, Temporelli, and Perotti (eds) 1983, 20.

74 *legionum*: the alternative reading of *religionum* (Colombo, Temporelli, and Perotti [eds], F5) is equally plausible: "a temple of their rites."

75 *sodales*, though a little below they are called *parentes* (parents, guardians, elders) who take her to Novara, and her kinsmen or family (*cognati*) were left in Rome.

76 *petulcus*: literally, "prone to head-butting."

to traverse all of Italy along its western axis and make for the city of Novara at a rapid pace to heal the wretched girl whom the chains of demons had fettered. If they reach the threshold of the blessed confessor Gaudentius to receive the aid of his miracles, the captive girl might recover her former health through the prophet [*uates*]. At the command of the heavenly gate-keeper, her guardians [*parentes*] immediately took to the road, heading for the city of Novara, roughly five hundred miles from the city of Rome. As soon as the girl set foot in the temple of the blessed man, the faith immediately put the dreadful demons to flight. Indeed, the girl, stripped of her abominable pestilence, and released from her iron chains by her companions, hurried to the walls of his tomb and at last reached the shrine of his blessed body. There, groaning heavily, she bathed her cheeks with flowing tears. Then, suddenly healed, she lifted her face unto the holy mysteries and rendered thanks unto God for his gift of health. Next, to the amazement of her companions and the people, she repaid Jesus Christ the Lord with mighty and unceasing praise, and rejoiced that she would return healthy and see her kinsmen whom she left when stricken. And so she took the journey home and arrived safely back in the city.[77]

21. Meanwhile the reverent people were marvelling at the achievement of his grace. His glittering fame was relayed through every mouth, so that the entire people cried out together with the Prophet, "You have visited the land, O Lord, and watered it."[78] O how great is your glory, O Christ, through the ages, you who, to show that your servant is equal to the blessed Peter, were willing to glorify him with such a great miracle through the answers of the same heavenly gate-keeper. And this miracle, besprinkled with a sheen of glory, shimmers amidst his other miracles so far and wide that the entire populace of the city of Novara sang in praise to the Lord, and said, "You have turned, O Lord, the desert into pools of water, and the parched earth into flowing springs."[79] And even now the church cries out, "The right hand of the Lord has done a mighty thing, the right hand of the Lord has exalted me."[80] Truly, O Lord, your gifts

77 Gavinelli (ed) 2013 reads "... to the amazement of her companions and the people, she rose strong, and gave praise to Lord Christ while she rejoiced, and hastened to see her kinsmen safely ... back in the city. Favourably impressed by these events, all rejoiced together and received their salvation."

78 Ps. 65:9.

79 Cf. Ps. 107:35.

80 Cf. Ps. 118:15–16.

are free.[81] You pour fresh water from the font of mercy onto the ignorant, and fill their empty hearts.

22. But neither my barren mind nor this worthless paper is sufficient for me to retrace the miracles and deeds of such grand virtue. I have dared to run through these things briskly, and have imprinted them in unlearned words to be re-read by the faithful, supported by the merits of the blessed *papa* Leo,[82] who, by God's design, is the most recent occupant of the seat of the blessed Gaudentius in the city of Novara, whose entire citizenry rejoices in him as their patron. And now, having narrated these deeds of the blessed man, even if with words unworthy of their subject, I determine that the time is right to make an end. I place my hand over my mouth,[83] and hasten to return inwards to my conscience. And indeed, while we, unworthy servants, cannot imitate him, we may ask through prayer that he become our patron, so that we may be aided by the merits of him whose nativity we celebrate, and with the support of him who, together with the Father and the holy spirit, lives and reigns forever and ever. Amen.

81 Cf. Rom. 3:23–24.
82 Probably Bishop Leo of Novara (c.685–725): see the introduction above.
83 Cf. Prov. 30:32, "If you have played the fool and exalted yourself, or if you have planned evil, clap your hand over your mouth!"

The Life of Barbatus of Benevento

The *Life of Barbatus of Benevento* (BHL 973) is one of the few Italian hagiographic texts in which the Lombards are central characters of the story (cf. the *Passion of Cetheus*), and its focus is on the holy man's activities in converting the Lombards from paganism to Christianity. As a result the *Life of Barbatus* has been cited as evidence for the alien character of the Lombards on Italian soil, because of their continued adherence to ancestral pagan practices – here recorded as eating food hung on a sacred tree that is used for spear practice, and worshipping a gold statue of a viper – until the 660s, the period in which the *Life of Barbatus* is set: the narrative of the text centres on the invasion of southern Italy by the Emperor Constans II (641–668) in 663. This event is the conversion motif for the *Life*: on the verge of defeat, Barbatus convinces Duke Romuald of Benevento (662–667) and the Beneventans to abandon their pagan customs and fully convert to Christianity. The salvation of the town results in Barbatus's election as bishop.

The anonymously written *Life of Barbatus* is an inventive and undeniably literary text that offers little historical testimony for understanding seventh-century Italy, and certainly should not be used as evidence for Lombard religious practices in the duchy of Benevento or elsewhere (discussed below). Instead, the *Life of Barbatus* reflects the aspirations of the Beneventan cathedral church in the early ninth century, and its links with secular power in the now independent principality of Benevento after the fall of the Lombard kingdom (774–1053). A good number of hagiographic works were written in Benevento during this period, the majority of them *translatio* texts that describe the importation of relics and their internment at Benevento, such as the *Translation of Saint Mercurius* (BHL 5936–5937), the *Translation of the Twelve Brothers* (BHL 2302), and the *Translation of Saint Helianus* (BHL 3799). The *Life of Barbatus*, however, constitutes the only biography among early Beneventan hagiography and was tremendously influential among literary productions from the principality.[1] It is argued below that the key to determining the *Life*'s immediate audience and date of composition is its mention that Duke Romuald granted Barbatus jurisdiction over the shrine of St Michael of Gargano, which had been neglected by the church of Siponto (ch.7). The *Life of Barbatus,* therefore, was another shot fired in the dispute over control of the shrine concerning the *Book Concerning the Apparition of St Michael on Mount Gargano*, which reflects the Sipontine claims for jurisdiction.

Barbatus, the Invasion of 663, and the Ducal Court of Benevento

The episcopal record for early medieval Benevento is "full of holes and broken," and contains nothing about Barbatus, apart from what derives from the *Life of Barbatus.*[2] Our anonymous hagiographer, who "put aside shame" at his meagre literary ability (prologue) to promote the cult of Barbatus, whose relics, he claimed, still cured many people of "demons" in his day (ch.3), concluded by noting that Barbatus was seventy-nine years old when he died and occupied his see "for eighteen years and eleven months" (ch.11), and we are told earlier (ch.7) that he was "elected" bishop after Constans II's withdrawal in 663. Hence Barbatus was born AD c.602 and took up his episcopacy (663–681) at sixty-two years old. Despite the *Life*'s concluding chronicle-like notice, Barbatus is unattested elsewhere in the historical record except for his attendance at the Roman council of 680, when he subscribed, alongside another 125 or so bishops, the dogmatic statement against Monothelitism drawn up by Pope Agatho to be

1 For example, the *Translatio Heliani* opens with the same line as the *Vita Barbati,* exchanging Grimoald for Arichis. On the dating of these texts and their context, see Vuolo 1996, who dates the above-mentioned *translatio* texts to the early ninth century and cites earlier literature; this whole volume of conference papers (Andenna and Piscasso [eds] 1996) offers much for re-evaluating Beneventan history in this period. See also Paoli 2002. The above-mentioned texts are all set in the time of Arichis II. The tenth-century *Chronicle of Monte Cassino* (1.9) claimed that Arichis imported the relics of thirty-one saints: Belting 1962.

2 Lanzoni 1927, 254–263: "lacunoso e guasto," 255. Only a few bishops of Benevento pre-600 are securely attested elsewhere: Aemelius c.394–409, Dorus c.448, Epiphanius c.494–499. Whether the martyr Januarius of Naples (d.c.303) was bishop in Benevento or simply from there depends on which text is consulted: BHL 4132 claims he was bishop of Benevento and martyred along with his deacon Festus and *lector* Desiderius (Vuolo 1996, 223–224).

presented at the Council of Constantinople that year.[3] There is some doubt about whether this list of subscriptions is authentic. An eleventh-century manuscript of the *Life* states that Barbatus was the twentieth (*vicesimus*) bishop of Benevento, and later antiquarian catalogues, such as that of Mario De Vipera (published 1636), place him as the twenty-third.[4] Later hagiographic works or ecclesiastical literature that used the *Life* presented here added more details about Barbatus's biography: that Barbatus was born in Vandano (Cerreto), that he studied at Benevento, that he belonged to the church of Morcone for a while, and that he succeeded a Bishop Hildebrand to the Beneventan see.

None of these legends has any foundation, and highlight just how little the author of the *Life* tells us about Barbatus himself. Barbatus is introduced (ch.1) as simply a "priest renowned for his deeds and miracles in Benevento"; he somehow was "staying with" (*morabatur cum*) Duke Romuald and his retinue on the walls of Benevento when Constans II attacked the city (ch.4); the *Life* claims that Barbatus was unanimously "elected" (ch.7) bishop by men and women of all ages, but Duke Romuald offered him the bishopric before that (ch.6). The closing melt-the-viper story (ch.8–10) suggests Barbatus enjoyed close relations with Duke Romuald and his wife, Theuderata, and the *Life* merely concludes that he conducted himself "justly and wisely" for his nearly nineteen-year episcopacy (ch.11), mentioning no other events or miracles, or anything about his burial or the interment of his relics; we can only surmise that they were in the cathedral church dedicated to Mary to which the *Life* refers frequently. Falco of Benevento recorded that he witnessed the rediscovery of Barbatus's relics under the altar by Archbishop Rodfred in 1124, who then moved them elsewhere in the cathedral church; Falco records several miracles at the new location.[5] Today Barbatus's relics are housed in the sanctuary of Montevergine (Avellino), with the exception of a piece of his arm bone, which is kept in the church of San Nicola in Castelvenere (Cerreto), where he is also considered a patron saint.[6]

3 Mansi 1775–1190, XI: 299–300. Barbatus is the eleventh bishop to sign after Pope Agatho as one of eleven Campanian bishops whose subscriptions appear before other prelates. The subscription is formulaic: "Barbatus gratia Dei episcopus sanctae Benventanae ecclesiae provinciae Campaniae hanc suggestionem quam pro apostolica nostra fide unanimiter construximus similiter subscripsi."

4 Naples, Biblioteca nazionale VIII B 6 (olim Troianus); Waitz 1878, 563. On the later catalogues and notices, see Lanzoni 1927, 254–255; Martin 1974, 137–141.

5 See Oldfield 2014, 25, 73, 103, and BHL 975.

6 Pratesi 1964.

Date of Composition

The *Life of Barbatus* has been variously dated from the mid-ninth to the tenth century[7]: the *terminus post quem* is established from its verbatim use of Paul the Deacon's *HL* to describe the invasion of Constans II in 663, and the *terminus ante quem* from the date of its earliest manuscripts, which begin from the tenth and eleventh centuries (on which, see below). With good reason the anti-Byzantine stance of the text has been interpreted as a reflection of the threatening Byzantine presence in the late ninth century: in 883, Nicephoras Phocas reclaimed nearly all of Calabria from the Arabs and continued with his army up the Adriatic coast in a manner reminiscent of Constans II's invasion of 663; in 887 a Byzantine general (*strategos*) claimed several towns in the Beneventan principality while dealing with Arabs at Garigliano; and after the death of Prince Aio (884–891), Benevento was captured by the Byzantines and became their new administrative capital for three years, in place of Bari.[8]

But there are compelling reasons why the *Life of Barbatus* should be dated to the first half of the ninth century, the most important of which is the mention, in a court case of 839, of the decree (*praeceptum*) of Romuald granting Barbatus control of the grotto of S. Michael at Gargano, which is also mentioned in the *Life* (ch.7). As we have seen, the *Book Concerning the Apparition of St Michael on Mount Gargano* defends the church of Siponto's claim over control of the shrine, originally granted to the bishop of Siponto by the archangel himself. The *Life of Barbatus* documents Benevento's appropriation of the grotto, which likely happened in the aftermath of the invasion of Constans II, allowing Grimoald and Romuald to tighten Benevento's hold on its surrounding territory, including the peninsula of Gargano.[9] Inscriptions carved into the sanctuary wall at Gargano record that Duke Romuald enriched the shrine, which may have included the installation of a staircase, and another inscription may refer

7 Different dates are given as follows: mid-ninth century: Vuolo 1996, 217–220, Montesano (ed and trans) 1994, and Cicco 2006, 358–359; tenth century: Paoli 2002, 304–312. Martin 1974 sees two different stages of redaction in the early and then late ninth century, but the language and literary plot of the text suggest a single author, as argued by Montesano 1991 and (ed and trans) 1994.

8 Kreutz 1996, 62–63, 65. The presence of the Carolingian Emperor Louis II, resident in Benevento with his wife, Angilberga, from 866 to 871, also prompted Beneventan patriotism against foreign rule: they were remembered for insulting Beneventan military ability, e.g., *Chronicon Salernitanum* ch.109, ed. Westerbergh 1956. See Granier 2007b.

9 Paul, *HL* VI.1; Palmieri 1996.

to Grimoald also.[10] We discuss elsewhere (*Michael*, introduction) the theories of Bognetti and other historians that King Grimoald promoted the cult of Michael as patron saint of the Lombards as a means to unite southern Lombard Italy with the northern kingdom he had usurped. Nonetheless, the inscription at Gargano testifies to Duke Romuald's patronage of the grotto: the court case before Prince Sicard of Benevento in 839 refers to a decree (*praeceptum*) made by Duke Romuald to Barbatus that transferred control of the diocese of Siponto to Benevento. The *praeceptum* was cited by the monks of S. Maria in Locosano, defending their ownership of a baptismal church against the current bishop of Benevento, who claimed that by canonical law all churches belonged to the diocese. But the monks knew their local history too well, and in court they retorted,

> If he (the bishop) wishes to judge matters by canon law, then how did Bishop Barbatus obtain from Duke Romuald, as is well recorded, permission to usurp the holy see of Siponto, and because of his supplication that see was usurped (*usurpata*) and designated [his] (*denominata*), and was handed over (*contradita*) to the holy see of the Beneventan church, so that ever since then and even now a bishop has not been consecrated there? If what happened to this church, which is against the canons although common in this province, has no validity, then why do you wish to observe the canons? If so, then let a bishop be ordained for the city of Siponto, and moreover you should destroy many monasteries that earlier dukes had donated by decree (*praeceptum*), just as happened concerning Siponto and its diocese, which was granted through the decree of Duke Romuald (I), which seems to us to have happened quite against the dictates of canon law![11]

The monks won their case: Prince Sicard would have opened a judicial can of worms if he had decided in the bishop's favour. The caustic tone and language (*usurpata*, *denominata*, *contradita*) reflects the lasting bitterness behind this dispute between Benevento and Siponto, as does Barbatus's comment in the *Life* that under the bishop of Siponto "everything is depraved" (*omnia depravantur*) at the shrine of Michael (ch.7). The language that follows in the *Life* describing the

10 Carletti 1980, no.82: see *Book Concerning the Apparition of St Michael on Mount Gargano* (introduction). On the shrine and inscriptions, see Everett 2003a, 265–274.

11 CDL 5.47, ed. Zielinski 1986, from *Chron. Vult.* doc. 67, ed. Federici 1925. The Latin is difficult in places, but the sense is clear. Cf. Wickham 1981, 146–147; Everett 2002b.

terms of Romuald's *praeceptum* seems to have drawn from a copy of the decree itself, for its *sanctio* formula (warning against future infringement) matches formulae found in Beneventan charter traditions.[12] Barbatus's specifications for the fourfold division of the shrine's income, in which a quarter went directly to the bishop himself, was likewise probably lifted from the *praeceptum*. In the *Life of Barbatus,* only control over the shrine of Michael is mentioned, but the court case of 839 reveals that the grant to Barbatus involved the complete suppression of the Sipontine see as part of the process. The matter is complicated by the preservation at Benevento of a false papal decree purporting to date from 668, in which Pope Vitalian (657–672) confirms, at the request of Barbatus, the Beneventan bishop's jurisdiction in neighbouring territories, including the diocese of Siponto and the sanctuary of Michael at Gargano.[13] It has been argued that this privilege was a product of the tenth century, and that the *Life of Barbatus* was drawn up at the same time.[14] However, the language of the *sanctio* found in the *Life* and the false papal privilege matches that found in a Beneventan episcopal charter of 879, so both documents can be comfortably dated to the ninth century, and it may well be that both were produced by the Beneventan church in the same period.[15]

Romuald's grant to Barbatus was well known to Beneventan monks in 839, suggesting that the *Life of Barbatus*, which quotes the terms of the grant concerning Gargano, was written earlier. This narrows the composition date to roughly the first three decades of the ninth century (from c.800 [Paul's *HL*] to the 830s). We have suggested that the *Book Concerning the Apparition of St Michael on Mount Gargano* was written in response to Benevento's annexation of the shrine and Siponto in 663. The *Life of Barbatus* may have been a literary response to the immense popularity of the *Book* and its pro-Sipontine origin legend, combined with the growing popularity and prestige of the cult as a pilgrimage site in the eighth and early ninth century. As Paul the Deacon wrote in the epitaph for the Lombard Queen Ansa (d. post 780), whose daughter Adelperga was duchess of Benevento and Paul's patron, the Queen's endowments have

12 The phrase "et us resonat in futuro, anathematizaverunt qui contra haec agens irritam hanc facere voluerit concessionem" (*Life,* ch.7) resonates with other ducal charters: see Zielinski 1996a and 1996b.

13 Ciaralli, De Donato, and Matera (eds) 2002, 1–7, doc. 1.

14 Paoli 2002, 304–309.

15 Ciaralli, De Donato, and Matera (eds) 2002, 7–11, doc. 4. Cicco 2006, 359, argues further that the *castellum* built outside the grotto at Gargano (completed in 871) was instigated by Bishop Ursus and plays a role in the renewed documentary attention to Barbatus in the *Life* and the false privilege of Vitalian.

ensured that "All you pilgrims who come from the West, take to the road in safety when you come to venerate the shrines of St Peter's land or when you seek the venerable cave of Garganian rock."[16] It seems that soon after Paul, the *Life of Barbatus* also promoted Lombard patronage of Gargano by emphasizing Benevento's legal rights over the site, and the authority of the city's bishop.

That Barbatus's relics were in the cathedral church of S. Maria, rather than the church of Santa Sofia founded by Duke Arechis II (c.760), also supports an early ninth-century date of composition for the *Life*. In the early decades of the ninth century the Beneventan clergy began to associate themselves with the cathedral church of S. Maria, which seems to have been founded under Arechis II also, but was refurbished and enlarged under Prince Sico (817–833). Sico also organized a number of saints to be venerated there, most famously the body of the martyr Januarius, the patron saint of his neighbouring enemies, the Neapolitans, as recorded by the *Translatio S. Januari*, which was supposedly written immediately after the body's internment, sometime around 831. We have already mentioned above that several other *translatio* texts written in this period ascribe the importation of relics to Arechis II, but other similar texts also appear: the *Translatio S. Bartholomaei* records how in 838 Prince Sicard (833–839) stole the body of Bartholemaeus from the island of Lipari (north of Sicily); the *Translatio S. Felicitatis cum septem filiis* and the *Translatio Marciani episcopi Frigentini* record similar holy imports organized by Bishop Ursus (c.830–850), who we know also organized a cathedral school in this period.[17] This shift of energy away from S. Sophia towards the cathedral of S. Maria, also represented in the *Life of Barbatus*, signals a transition away from the Lombard court's dominance over the religious landscape of the city, and the growth of episcopal ties with Rome, as witnessed also in changes to the liturgy at this time.[18] A series of frescos depicting Barbatus in the crypt of the cathedral can be dated to the ninth century, affirming that his cult was established.[19] Unfortunately, the *Life of Barbatus* offers no further clues to its date. The hagiographer's note that Barbatus's curse on the family of the fellow who would chop his wife's head off if she acted like the Duchess Theodora (ch.10) came true, for "even up until now anyone who descended from this man is

16 *Carm.* 9, ed. Neff 1908.

17 Cicco 2006. See also Fioretti 2010.

18 Vuolo 1996, 223–226; On liturgy, see Kelly 1989, 29. Churches dedicated to Mary are found in Benevento from the seventh and eighth centuries: Palmieri 1996, 70–72. On Mary's role as protector in Constantinople, see Baynes 1949 and Barnay 1992, 45–60.

19 Bove 2000.

always seen to be disturbed by an evil spirit," which seems to reflect the aristocratic factionalism of Beneventan politics.[20] But without names, the allusion, and a possible clue to a date, is now lost to us.

Sources: The Invasion of 663 and Lombard Paganism

The hagiographer's extremely wordy prologue belies his humility about his literary talents, and his claim to have used "reports of the faithful" concerning Barbatus should be measured against his use of extant sources. Paul's account (*HL* V.6–7) of Constans II's invasion of 663 is cited verbatim by the hagiographer, but is also truncated and embellished to distort the event and make Duke Romauld and his brave Beneventans the sole heroes. The hagiographer leaves out altogether Paul's information that Romuald gave his sister, Gisa, as hostage to Constans II to sue for peace while he summoned his father, King Grimoald, to bring the Lombard army from Pavia, at whose very presence the emperor abandoned the siege and headed for Naples.[21] The complete excision of King Grimoald from the story is surprising given the mention of Grimoald and Romuald in the opening sentence of the *Life*, and the author cites nothing from the tale recorded by Paul a few pages later in which Romuald refuses his father's help in fighting a general called Saburrus, whom the emperor had sent to try again to capture Benevento. Yet Paul's tale surely inspired our author: Romuald refused Grimoald's help by telling him, "You don't need to give me part of your army; I will fight him with God's favour," and Romuald returned home victorious, bringing joy to his father and security to the Beneventans, for he "eliminated the fear of their enemies."[22] The *Life*'s particular version of the invasion of 663, with Grimoald excised to enhance Romuald's stature, was used by many sources dating from the tenth century, including the *Chronicle of Benedict of S. Andrea* of Mount Soratte, the

20 Wickham 1981, 146–157.

21 *HL* V.6–7. The interpolations from Paul are clearly marked by different fonts in the edition of Waitz 1878, 558. On Gisa, see *HL* V.8; she died in captivity on arrival in Sicily (V.14). Also ignored is the motif, central to Paul's narrative, of the soothsayer consulted by Constans II about whether he could beat the Lombards (V.6): the response, that the Lombards were invincible until Queen Theudelinda's church of St John in Monza fell into neglect, is a key structural device in Paul's text: Goffart 1988, 400–412.

22 *HL* V.10: "*Ego Deo favente cum eo pugnabo*"; *sublato hostium timore*.

Vita Sancti Pardi written by Radoin, deacon of the church of Larino, and the late tenth-century *Chronicon Salernitanum*.[23]

Scholars looking for the alien character of the Lombards, as Germanic warriors ruling native Romans, have often cited the *Life of Barbatus* as proof of their residual paganism long after their initial settlement in Italy in 568. As such the *Life* is often discussed alongside Gregory the Great's portrait of Lombard paganism in the *Dialogues*, which records that the Lombards worshipped a goat's head while dancing around it singing songs and eating sacrificial food, which they then forced Christians to do.[24] Gregory's portrait, which seems known to the hagiographer judging by the quotation from Romans 1:25, which both authors cite, owes more to biblical exegesis than reality (cf. Leviticus 16–20, 17–7): Gregory said the Franks also sacrificed to animal heads.[25] Our earliest sources suggest the Lombards were orthodox Christians, though clearly many professed Arianism: Gregory attests to both persuasions among Lombards. No doubt some Lombards were pagan, as were many of Italy's other inhabitants in this period, including many "Romans" living on papal estates.[26] But the proposition that Beneventan Lombards, and Duke Romuald himself, were worshipping sacred trees and statues of vipers in the 660s is difficult to reconcile with other, less literary evidence. Romuald's patronage of the grotto at Gargano was mentioned above. Paul records that Theuderata founded a church dedicated to St Peter outside the walls of Benevento and instituted a congregation of nuns there. While it is true we know nothing of Grimoald's religious sensibilities, he claimed his laws were "favourable to God" (*Deo propitio*) and was buried in a church dedicated to St Ambrose in Pavia, which he himself built; this hardly signals paganism.[27]

The literary precursors which served as models for the tropes of paganism in the *Life of Barbatus* are numerous, for "the genre of hagiography abounds

23 *Benedicti Sancti Andreae monachi chronicon*, ed. G.H. Pertz (MGH SS 3: 695–719). *Vita Sancti Pardi* (BHL 6465), AA. SS. Mai. VI, 368–370. Oldoni, *Anonimo Salernitano del sec. X* (1972), 76–84. On use of Paul's notice of 663, see Corsi 1975.

24 Gregory, *Dial.* III.27–28; Manselli 1972; Gasparri 1983, 32–45. Cf. Everett 2003a, 56–65.

25 Gregory, *Reg.* VIII.4.

26 See Fanning 1981; Everett 2003a, 56–65; Brown 2009.

27 Theuderata, *HL* VI.1; Grimoald, 5.33. His church of St Ambrose was destroyed in the later Middle Ages: see Bullough 1966; Arecchi 2006, 24–27. On the laws, see Grim. *prol.* ed. Bluhme 1868, 91. A charter purporting to date from Charles the Fat's reign (881–888) records that Grimoald granted a church to the bishop of Bergamo: Bosco et. al. 1988, 197–199.

with saints who demolish trees sacred to pagans and battle against serpents."[28] Our hagiographer, however, did not slavishly copy previous models, but attempted to craft his own images of missionary courage in the face of alien, evil customs. The opening scene (ch.1) of the custom of Lombards on horseback shooting at hides hung on a tree probably reflects a real tradition of military practice at equestrian skills. The comment by one Lombard that they remember their glorious ancestors by name may likewise reflect the martial, aristocratic culture of Benevento in this period, but was surely common among military elites whether barbarian or Roman. The place name "Votum," supposedly retained from the profane vows (*vota*) Lombards took at their sacred tree there and still retained in the hagiographer's day, has inspired a few learned guesses on the topography of Benevento,[29] but Carolingian sources recording Saxons taking a *votum* before sacred trees[30] may caution against searching further. The golden viper-cum-chalice and the *dénouement* of Romuald unwittingly drinking from it on Easter Sunday display considerable literary skill, drawing on traditions of hagiography (pagan statues) and patristic lore (imagery of serpents), and as with Pope Gregory's goats' heads, biblical exegesis (in this case of Numbers 21:4–9 and John 3:14). But it also may reflect common folklore about serpents in central south Italy, well attested for neighbouring Marsica (Abruzzi). The concentration of quotations from 1 and 2 Corinthians in the viper section demonstrates the hagiographer's art, for Paul was the apostle of the gentiles, and his immunity to snake-bites (Acts 28:1–6) made him a popular antiophidic figure. The implicit association of the two missionary saints assures the reader that Barbatus, just like his biblical archetype Paul, was a "teacher of the pagans" (ch.8).

Text and Translation

The following translation is based on the text edited by Waitz in MGH SS rer. Lang., 555–563, which likewise served as the basis for the Italian translation by

28 Montesano (ed and trans)1994, 16, also includes possible Latin sources as appendices, 62–85. See also Martin 1974.

29 See Montesano (ed and trans) 1994. It is now identified with the village of Piano Cappelle, c.5 km southeast of Benevento.

30 On the Penitential of Egbert 8.1 and Charlemagne's capitulary concerning the Saxons, see Martin 1974, 148–149. On sacred trees in early medieval hagiography, see Cusack 2011.

R. Valli (in Montesano 1991, 57–94) and Montesano 1994, 34–55, the only other translations of the *Life* into a modern language. Waitz noted that the manuscripts varied considerably, so that determining the author's original text was very difficult, and based his edition upon the collation of eleven manuscripts, dating from the eleventh and twelfth centuries. The Bollandist website lists these and a few more: renewed attention to the manuscript tradition is warranted, and closer attention should probably be paid to Naples, Biblioteca nazionale, VIII B 6 (olim Trajanus), one of the earliest manuscripts that contains more vulgar Latin readings that may get us closer to the scribe's original. The text which appears in AA. SS. Feb. III, 142–146 (BHL 973a), is a shorter version based on eleventh-century Beneventan manuscripts; likewise, the edition of Ughelli, *Italia sacra*, VIII: 25–32, was edited from a single manuscript that once belonged to S. Sophia. Another short version (BHL 794), from an eleventh-century Vatican manuscript (Biblioteca Apostolica Vaticana, Vat. lat. 7810), begins "Considerandum est, dilecti fratres, quomodo mater ecclesiae ... ."

The *Life of Barbatus* contains many spellings and Graecisms (e.g., *celeps* for *celeber, colonibus* for *colonis*) that are common to other Beneventan texts of this period, including the *Book Concerning the Apparition of St Michael on Mount Gargano*. The author has a predilection for gerundives that is evident right from the prologue ("qui non philosophandi sed simplicibus verbis suos discipulos evangelizandi"), but appearing throughout (ch.5: "et capiendos se fore universi predonibusque dirimendos ..."), and can be tedious to reproduce in translation. The text also contains some curious scriptural paraphrases and expressions, such as *subversor protoplaustus* (ch.3), *annuente mentium scrutator* (ch.6; cf. Proverbs 25:27, *scrutator maiestatis*, and Wisdom 6, *cordis eius scrutator*), the combination of Luke 15:7, Ezekiel 33:12–13, and Psalms 15:3, 51:1–4 (ch.6), *hac instabile luce* (ch.8), and the use of *non per speculum in enigmate* (ch.12: 1 Corinthians 13:12, also in Augustine, *De cat. rud.*).

The Life of Barbatus, Bishop of Benevento

Prologue

Just as we have learned most vividly from reports of the faithful about the celebrated character [*mos*] and merits of the holiest father Barbatus, and although I am unworthy to compose praises for so extraordinary a bishop, and am inferior to all students of philosophy, I hasten to describe faithfully and make known the glory that heaven shone down upon the most blessed Barbatus, even if in uncouth speech. However, I do so with the consent of the scrutinizer of souls,[31] who ordained his disciples not to philosophize but to evangelize the sacred mysteries with simple words. If anyone well learned in the liberal arts might attentively read these deeds of so great a man set out in letters,[32] let him not judge the inadequacy of the narrator but instead consider the distinction of merits of him about whom I speak recklessly but with the utmost effort of the mind, putting aside my shame.

1. During the time when Grimoald held the reins of the Lombard kingdom and his son Romuald was ruling over the Samnites,[33] a distinguished priest by the name of Barbatus, as I mentioned, famous for his deeds and resplendent with miracles, became renowned in Benevento through the will of the Redeemer. Although in those days the Lombards had been cleansed with the waters of holy baptism, they still clung to their former pagan rites (*ritus*). Since they remained with bestial minds, they bent their necks to the statue of a beast, commonly called "the viper," when they should have rightly bent to their Creator.[34] Moreover, not far from the walls of Benevento, on some sort of

31 *annuente mentium scrutatore*. Cf. Wisd. of Sol. 6, Prov. 25:27.

32 Difficult passage: *accuratius … . apicibus prenotata*; *praenotata* in late antique authors often means "prefigured" as used in biblical exegesis: see Mastrangelo 2010, 63–64.

33 Grimoald I, duke of Benvento 647–662, king of the Lombards 662–671. Grimoald appointed his son Romuald as duke of Benevento (662–671) when he became king: Paul, *HL* IV.51. *Samnites* is a literary conceit: cf. *HL* IV.44, 46; VI.2, 29; *Passion of Cetheus*, ch.1.

34 *quae debite suo debebant flectere Creatori*. Cf. Rom. 1:25. A similar phrase was used by Gregory, *Dial.* III.28 ("et cervicem quam semper Creatori flexerant creaturae inclinare contempserunt"), for his notorious description of Lombard paganism, which he claimed involved sacrificing a goat's head to the devil and running around it singing pagan songs, and forcing Christian captives to do the same. Gregory's depiction of goats' heads may owe more to Biblical exegesis than reality: cf. Lev. 16:20, 17:7.

ceremonial feast day, they worshipped a sacred tree and hung an animal hide on it. Everyone who gathered turned their backs to the tree and quickly took flight, bloodying their horses with their spurs in trying to overtake each other. Then they turned around,[35] still following the same course, and threw javelins at the hide, and if they hit the hide they then received a small piece from it to eat in a superstitious manner. Because they rendered foolish offerings (*vota*) at this place, they named it "Votum" after this practice, as it is still called today.

2. Seeing these things, the man of God, Barbatus, preached incessantly that those who served two lords could not be saved, and those who subjected themselves to the authority of the apostate angel were not entitled to be counted among the number of God's children. Running about here and there, the most blessed Barbatus preached these and other things relentlessly, anxious to present those purged from error to their Creator. But they, blinded by bestial madness, thought of nothing but the skills of war, and professed that the best form of worship was to respect the law of their ancestors, who they asserted were the greatest warriors and whom they could name one by one,[36] and therefore completely rejected the warnings from the man of God. But God the almighty and ineffable, who assumed the form of a servant and poured forth his blood for the sins of humanity, and wishes that no one perish, did not cease to draw even the ungrateful to him in appropriate ways so that they could be saved. This most dutiful physician urgently attends to the sick man and compels him to seek his own salvation.

3. When God considered the charity of Barbatus and the illness of those men, he granted that the words of Barbatus's preaching should be strengthened with miraculous signs, since the most holy man was trying to cleanse them with

35 Reading *restroversi manibus* [*corium iaculabant*], which at least one manuscript supports, rather than *retroversis manibus* (ed. Waitz), although some sort of skill with javelin in hand may have been intended, otherwise *manibus* is superfluous. Likewise, see Martin 1974, 147, and Montesano (ed and trans) 1994, 36 n2.

36 *quos nominatim bellicosissimos asserebant*. Gasparri 1983, 82–83, draws attention to a law in the Lombard King Rothari's *Edict* (ch.153), which requires those claiming the inheritance of family property to name their ancestors ("… nominatim unicuique nomina parentum, antecessorum suorum dicat"). But the naming of glorious ancestors is hardly a "Lombard" or "Germanic" phenomenon (cf. Romans), and the author of the *Life*, writing more than three centuries after the Lombards settled in Italy, and more than a century after the demise of the Lombard kingdom (774), may have simply employed here a Christian *topos* of pagan warriors before conversion.

divine medicine from the fevers of sin and the squalid puss that oozed from their hearts (*intimis*) and lead them from the servitude of the subversive first man[37] towards the liberty of God's children. In this way, if not by his words then by observed miracles they might be directed to their salvation. For Barbatus cast out demons from possessed bodies, sometimes with entreaties to the Lord, sometimes with threats alone. Even now, with God assisting, we witness many people saved from demons as they approach the relics of his body. Moreover, the water that flowed through the hands of the holy man when he washed them after completing the solemnities of the mass immediately restored the faithful from whatever illness plagued them to their former health when they drank it. Since limbs weakened from chronic disease cannot be cured with bandages and simple ointments, but require harsh medications which draw the infection hardened with age from deep in the wound to the surface of the skin and allow the putrefaction to be removed quickly, so too merciful God, when he saw that neither the preaching of his servant nor an abundant display of miracles had any effect in securing their salvation, grieved for their damnation, but did not forget his compassion. He brought the mighty kingdoms of the world against them, so that those who disregarded warnings about their salvation in a time of peace, and refused to follow their Creator properly, were finally compelled by the necessity of facing these forces they could not resist to convert to their Redeemer and be rescued by divine aid.

4. During this time, Constantius, also called Constans, was ruling the Constantinopolitan empire.[38] He wished to snatch Italy from the hands of the Lombards and subject it to his authority, just as it had once been under the rule of his predecessors, and gathered an immense multitude of his men, crossed the sea, and entered Taranto. From there he continued on to plunder nearly all the cities of Apulia. Along the way he captured the rich city of Lucera, after the heaviest of battles, and levelled it to the ground once it had been completely pillaged by his bands of looters. The destruction of this city thrilled the emperor and incited him to move his armies swiftly and camp them near the walls of Benevento. Without delay, he mustered the army and ordered his magnates to storm the city with various war machines. Inside the town was Romuald, whom I mentioned above, with only a few but the most powerful Lombards.

37 *subversor protoplaustus* – that is, Adam.

38 Emperor Constans II (641–668). The account of the invasion is partly taken verbatim from Paul, *HL* V.6–7, 8, but the hagiographer excised from the story altogether King Grimoald, whose army rescued besieged Benevento: see above and n21.

Also staying there with them was the most holy father Barbatus. Once the city had been surrounded, they fought for the longest time in a terrible and unprecedented way to seize it with renewed attacks. But against them stood the magnanimous and fearless Romuald, who fiercely resisted: now defending from the walls, now with surprise attacks, he wore down a large contingent of his enemies. For he was afraid to meet them in open battle because of the small size of his army. Nevertheless, by quick and relentless sorties here and there with lightly armed soldiers he defeated the troops of his enemies. Yet the more successful Romuald appeared to be in resisting, the more fervently the abovesaid emperor arranged new attacks against them.

5. When the aforementioned prince (*princeps*) and his fellow citizens realized they were surrounded on all sides and could no longer go outside the walls, and were repeatedly attacked by the most frenzied assaults, completely destroying their hope of salvation (*salus*), they all wept with loud groans that they would be captured and divided up among the plunderers. They therefore decided to open the city gates and send out both men and women to fight to the death. Immediately, the most holy father Barbatus stood before them and said, "Convert to your Creator, children, so you can be saved. For he eliminates war, condemns to hell, saves, humbles, and exalts.[39] Therefore abandon this falsehood that you have followed until now at the devil's connivance that causes you to hurry as fast as you can to the destruction of your body and soul. Instead sing praises in a harmonious voice only to God the Father, the Son, and the holy spirit, three persons but only one in God coeternal and consubstantial. Pour forth prayers to the one who judges your affections and hearts,[40] promise that you will most faithfully serve him alone, and he will free you from those who seek your souls."

6. Upon hearing this, Romuald said, "If it is as you say, and we will not be captured by our enemies, then I shall renounce everything I had worshipped according to the rite [*ritus*] of my people and promise to serve God alone. And I shall endow you with estates and serfs throughout every city of my province, and allow you to become bishop of this city, so that you consent to caring for me like the best father." Then everyone said they agreed with this declaration, and those who had once despised the warnings of blessed Barbatus now

39 Cf. 1 Kings 2:6–7.

40 *renes et corda*; lit. "kidneys and hearts." The kidneys were sometimes considered to be the source of emotions. Cf. Ps. 138:12, Apoc. 2:23.

crowded together, compelled by necessity, to listen earnestly to his instructions for their salvation. Immediately the pious father Barbatus, caring for neither honours nor riches, but worried for the salvation of these people, entered the church of the mother of God and prostrated himself on the ground. Sobbing and in tears he prayed to her that the Redeemer of all mankind might deign to bestow his glorious favour and rescue the Lombards from the hands of foreign enemies, and that when freed from the servitude of evil spirits through [this] temporal deliverance, they might deserve to partake in eternal glory. Almighty God did not spurn the prayers of his servant, and complied just as [Barbatus] had requested. For God himself professed with his own mouth that there is greater joy in heaven over one man's repentance than over ninety-nine just men who have no need for repentance,[41] and testified elsewhere that the moment a sinner converts from iniquity, his past transgressions will be forgotten, and he will live in his righteousness, and carry it out.[42] When divine mercy was shown, the blessed Barbatus realized that he had been heard, whereupon he returned to Romuald and said, "Consider carefully that you and your people, who promised to serve only Jesus Christ the Lord God when rescued from your attackers, do not invalidate a pact of agreement, and cause worse things to befall you, because no one can rescue you once abandoned by God. Know for certain that Christ, to whom you converted, will free you. Indeed, the march of Caesar and his people will not cross the entrance to Benevento, but instead will retreat quickly and return to their lands. And so that you may know what I preach is true, let us mount the wall together, where I will show you the most pious Mary, mother of God, who poured out salutary prayers to God on your behalf, and now, having been heard, comes to your aid."[43] Hearing this, Romuald cried tears of joy and approached the wall together with Barbatus. When he saw the mother of God, the prince fell flat on his face, overcome with panic and nearly unconscious, and lay on the ground in a state of bewilderment. The man of God, Barbatus, comforted him and lifted him from the ground. Coming to his senses, [the prince] gave thanks to God, who consented to lead him to knowledge of his mystery.

41 Luke 15:7 .

42 Ezek. 33:12–13. Cf. Ps.15:3, 51:1–4.

43 The cult of Mary as protector was well established in Constantinople and the Byzantine East (Baynes 1949; Barnay 1992, 45–60), and churches dedicated to Mary in Benevento date from the seventh and eighth centuries: see Palmieri 1996, 70–72. The cathedral church of Mary at Benevento (mentioned in ch.7) dates from the time of Arichis II (Belting 1962) but was enlarged and refurbished in the early ninth century, when the *Life of Barbatus* was probably composed: see the introduction above.

7. On the following day, he who tried to destroy the city entirely and massacre its inhabitants, and who could not be bent towards mercy by immense weights of silver and gold, nor by an enormous number of precious stones and pearls, took only Romuald's sister, deserted Benevento, and went to Naples. Immediately, the most blessed Barbatus grabbed an axe and headed towards Votum. With his own hands he cut down the abominable tree that the Lombards had long used to perform their pernicious sacrilege, uprooted it entirely, and covered the hole with soil so that no one could find any trace of it. With the enemy now in retreat, men and women of all ages gathered to elect unanimously the most blessed Barbatus to the bishopric, rejoicing that they were worthy of having such a father who could repel the enemy with his prayers. Once [Barbatus] was elected to the episcopal office, Romuald wished to endow him with estates and serfs from every city in his province, just as he had promised. But Barbatus, a man of God, refused to accept. [Romuald] then insisted, saying, "If you refuse this reward that I wish to give for my salvation, then I do not believe that I can be counted among the number of your sons." Compelled by these entreaties, the most blessed Barbatus said, "If you wish to offer me a gift for your salvation, then grant me one favour (*beneficium*). Place under the jurisdiction of the see of the most blessed mother of God, where I now preside unworthily, the shrine of the blessed Archangel Michael, which is situated in Gargano, and all which is under the authority of the bishopric of Siponto. For since everything becomes depraved in the absence of worshippers, proper services for God cannot be performed there, so it is better that everything that pertains to your salvation be administered by us." The prince immediately agreed to the requests of the man of God, in the manner that we said, so by his order, just as is customary, everything was conceded to the see of the mother of God. And so that it might resound for the future, they anathematized anyone who might wish to challenge the validity of this grant.[44] Obtaining everything he requested, the holy man did not forget the mandates of God. He decreed that the entire revenue of the church be always carefully distributed in four parts: the first to the destitute, the second to those who give assiduous praises to God in church, the third he ordered to be distributed for the restoration of churches, and the fourth part the bishop received to take care of his own needs. And right up until now everything still seems to be divided just as he arranged it.

44 This decree was also cited in a Beneventan court case of 839. The *sanctio* (warning) clause here matches Beneventan charter traditions, suggesting it was taken from the decree itself; likewise, the fourfold division of property. See above and Everett 2002b.

8. Thereafter, Romuald and his companions were blinded by their former error, for although the Almighty had miraculously rescued them from the snares of their enemies through the prayers of his servant, and they openly confessed that they worshipped one God according to the preaching of the most blessed Barbatus, in secret they adored the image of a viper unto their ruin. This, however, did not escape the notice of the man of God. Because the charity of God was within him, upon discovering the deadly pestilence he worried about how their crime would lead to their future destruction. He then wept profusely before God, since there is nothing that cannot be achieved with his power, in the manner that pleases him, and so asked that he deign to rescue them from the insanity inside their minds, and not condemn them to the eternal fires of hell because of an error owed to the deceiver of the human race. He prayed in this way because he was filled with that spirit that filled Paul, the illustrious preacher and teacher of the pagans, when he said, "Who is weak, and I am not weakened? Who is offended, and I burn not?"[45] Meanwhile the wife of the abovementioned Romuald, Theuderata by name, had abandoned all error and was worshipping the true Lord Jesus Christ according to canonical rule, completely renouncing the error of her husband. When Romuald went out hunting, the man of God Barbatus took the opportunity to visit Theuderata. He began to converse with her about the weakness of her husband, but she sighed heavily and responded by saying, "If only you had poured out prayers to the Almighty on my husband's behalf! I know for certain that with your interventions the Lord might have pardoned him so that he would walk along the path of truth." The man of God Barbatus responded, "If, as I believe, you truly have faith in God, then fear not. Take my advice: give me the statue of the viper, and your husband will be saved." She responded, "If I do that, father, I know for certain that I will be killed." The blessed Barbatus then said, "Remember the rewards of eternal life, daughter, because there is no death, only a great reward when you are removed from this uncertain light[46] because of your faith in Christ, and you will reach the place where Christ himself dwells in glory with all of his angels and saints. In this glory no one suffers from cold or heat, deterioration from disease does not occur, poverty tears no one apart, sadness never comes to pass, nor do weary limbs require rest. Neither the hateful, nor the envious, nor the discontented are found in that place, and any notion of death

45 2 Cor. 11:29.

46 *ab hac instabuli luce*; the phrase appears only elsewhere in Desiderius of Cassino (later, Pope Victor III, 1086–1087), *Dialogi de miraculis Sancti Benedicti* 3.3 (PL 149: 1008).

or deprivation of glory has been erased. Why do I try to discuss these one by one, when it is said that 'no eye has seen, no ear has heard, no human heart has received what God has prepared for those who love him'.[47] And when you believe without any doubts in all these things we have said, go forth joyfully, if it profits, because when you have left behind this wretched life, you will be led to that life in which you will live in glory without want and without end. Nevertheless, have faith in my promises that nothing adverse will happen to you from this matter. Only bring the statue of the beast to me, so that it can be achieved through you what was once written, 'The unfaithful husband will be saved by his faithful wife.'"[48] Placing her complete trust in the promises of the man of God, she quickly brought the statue before him. Upon receiving it he immediately melted it in the fire, and summoned several goldsmiths, ordering that before the prince returns they mold the gold into a plate and chalice of extraordinary size and beauty from which the body and blood of Christ could be offered, for it would also serve as a reminder for future times in the blessed church of the mother of God, through which they were saved from both an internal and external enemy.

9. After everything had been carried out according to the orders of Barbatus, man of God, it so happened that Romuald was due to arrive in Benevento from his hunting expedition on the holy day of Easter. The most holy Barbatus orchestrated the prince's return route so that he would arrive at the church of the mother of God and celebrate mass before going on to the royal palace. Romuald complied with the arrangements of the man of God and along with his entire retinue he entered the church to celebrate the Lord's mass. At the appropriate moment, the vessels fashioned from the statue of the beast and now bearing the body and blood of the Lord were brought forward and offered to the Lord almighty by the hands of the man of God Barbatus. When the solemnities of the mass were completed and all divine sacraments had been performed, the man of God approached the prince and said reproachfully, "Behold, O prince, we stand here in the presence of God and his mother. Be mindful because you yourself have seen how God rescued you from your enemies through the intercession of his mother. You had vowed to serve the catholic God alone and abandon all idols, yet now in the inner sanctuary[49] of

47 1 Cor. 2:9. Cf. Isa. 64:4.
48 1 Cor. 7:14.
49 *penetralibus* following the suggestion of Waitz ed., instead of *penetrabilibus*.

your house you worship the statue of a beast. Do you think that if you hide something from men, you can hide it from God? Does it not seem measly to you to tempt God so many times to punish you for your sins even after you have converted? Will the statue of the viper protect you in his presence? Or say to God 'do not strike him down'? Will it snatch you from his hands? Be careful, lest the day of retribution comes and there is no one to rescue you, nor hear the sound of your screams."

10. Hearing this Romuald was humbled and confessed that he had made a grave mistake. He begged Barbatus to ask forgiveness from the Lord on his behalf and promised to abandon the statue of his ruin immediately and hand it over to Barbatus to be destroyed as he wished. The man of God said, "There is no need for you to give me the statue, because with God's favour, the vessels from which we received the Lord's body and blood were fashioned from that statue. What was once furnished by the devil and existed for your destruction is now used for the salvation of all." To this Romuald said, "I ask you, most beloved father, to explain to me how the statue was brought to you." "I admit," said blessed Barbatus, "that after speaking to your wife with great sorrow about your damnation, I demanded it from her and took it." Suddenly, one of the bystanders said, "If my wife had done such thing, I would have cut off her head without a second thought." The most blessed Barbatus turned to him and said, "Because you endeavour to help the devil, you are enslaved to him." At once the man was seized by a demon and began to be violently tormented. Barbatus then added, "Since you conspired with the devil, let this be a warning to future generations of the Lombard people: for every generation that follows you, there will never be a time when someone from your family is not tormented by the devil." Indeed, it is not remembered how many generations he established, but even up until now anyone who descended from this man is always seen to be disturbed by an evil spirit. The rest of the people there were truly terrified with fear, and after rejecting all that they had worshipped superstitiously, converted to God with all their effort. Thereafter they were fully instructed in the Catholic faith through the teachings of the man of God, which they still preserve even until now, God willing.

11. And so that most pious father, trusting in the solace of the Almighty, occupied the office of bishop justly and wisely for eighteen years and eleven months. Called by divine mercy to receive the reward for his works, and freed from this unstable light, he was conveyed to the heavenly kingdom on the eleventh day

of the Kalends of March in the eightieth year from his birth, where he dwells in eternal glory with the holy angels. Now joyful among them, he embraces through love (*caritas*) and not through the reflection of a mirror but face to face[50] those things that he embraced daily when he lived in mortal flesh and were reflected in his faith and hope. With our Lord Jesus Christ willing, who lives and reigns with the Father in unity with the holy spirit through the ages of time.

50 Cf. 1.Cor. 13:12. The phrase was used by Augustine, *De catechizandis rudibus*, 2.4.

12 APRIL

The Life of Zeno of Verona

The *Sermon of the Notary Coronatus on the Life of Zeno, Bishop and Confessor*[1] is one of the few hagiographic texts from early medieval Italy in which the author identifies himself. Unfortunately, that provides no clear date for the text, which describes the career of Zeno of Verona (c.362–380), though it was written centuries later, for it borrows a story from Pope Gregory's *Dialogues* about Zeno's church miraculously resisting a flood in 590. Zeno's reputation and cult seem to have gained popularity quickly after his death, but it was not without rivals in early medieval Verona, and his status as patron of the city may have been in part secured by composition of the *Life*, which dates from the middle of the eighth century (as argued below), when ecclesiastical reorganization and the promotion of other cults threatened Zeno's status and the location of his relics. Coronatus's *Life* was used as a source for the liturgy in Verona for centuries afterwards, and for the scenes of Zeno's career and miracles in bas-relief on the bronze panels of the door of San Zeno Maggiore, dating from the twelfth century.[2]

City and Cult

Verona was situated on the convergence of three main Roman roads (Via Postumia, Via Claudia Augusta, and Via Gallica), and the magnificent Roman buildings which still adorn the city testify to its wealth and prestige in the imperial period.[3] Verona's importance as a strategic military centre, to defend north-

1 BHL 9001. Text in Marchi 1972, 18–23; PL 11: 199–204; AA. SS. Apr. II, 70–71: details below. For date and cult, see A. Amore, *Bib. Sanct.* 12:1477–1479; Lanzoni 1927, 932–934; Picard 1988, 673–678.

2 Fishing in Adige: ch.3–4; Ox and cart: ch.3; exorcism of Gallienus's daughter: ch.5; Gallienus offers crown to Zeno: ch.6. See Mellini 1992.

3 Tosi 1995.

ern Italy from barbarian incursions, increased as the empire disintegrated in the fifth century. King Theoderic the Ostrogoth kept his treasure there, and the Lombard King Alboin established his court at Verona, where he was murdered by his wife and buried under the stairs of his palace.[4] The rich epigraphic and archaeological evidence of Verona attests to many established pagan cults, of the traditional Greco-Roman pantheon, including the imperial triad of Jupiter, Juno, and Minerva, but also of eastern religions such as Isis and Mithra cults. Zeno's efforts to establish Christianity in the region can be compared to those of Vigilius of Trent, and although Zeno was not martyred, his reputation and cult seem to have gained popularity immediately.[5] Perhaps it was because he was not a martyr that other cults sprang up in early medieval Verona.

We know little about the historical Zeno, and the dates of his episcopate are uncertain. The *Life* translated here dates his career to the time of the Emperor Gallienus (252–268), which is most unlikely: the notice may reflect the memory of Gallienus's construction of Verona's second defensive wall to the north in 265.[6] Ambrose of Milan (c.340–397) refers to him as a "holy bishop of memory ... some years ago" in a letter to Syagrius, bishop of Verona (c.385–395).[7] Retracing the episcopal record in Verona relies on difficult sources, one of which is an eighth-century chasuble preserved in Classe, near Ravenna, hence known as the Velo di Classe, which depicts thirty-five bishops of Verona, and which includes Zeno.[8] Another source is an anonymous poem, discovered by Mabillon in the monastery of Lobbes (Belgium), which names Zeno as the eighth bishop of Verona. Scholarly consensus posits years of 362–380 for his activity in Verona, which is also documented in a group of (105) sermons discovered by two Dominicans in the sixteenth century in Verona's Biblioteca Capitolare, and which they attributed to Zeno. In the eighteenth century the Ballerini brothers published their own version of these and deduced, among other things, that Zeno was originally from Africa, and was a tireless supporter

4 Paul, *HL* II.28. Paul notes that in his day Duke Giselpert of Verona opened the grave to steel Alboin's sword and boasted that he "had seen Alboin." Alboin's successor, Authari, married Queen Theudalinda on the outskirts of Verona (campus Sardis): III.30. For archaeology in early medieval Verona, see La Rocca Hudson 1986.

5 The best overview of the development of Christianity in the Veneto is Golinelli 1989. For the Veronese church to 1000, see Cervato 2004. On the cult of Zeno from the eighth to the twelfth century, see Sala 1989, 1990, 1991.

6 Gallienus's wall was extended in the Ostrogothic period: Cervato 2004, 69; Christie 2006, 322–323, 362–363.

7 Ambrose, *Ep.* 5.1, ed. Banterle 1988: "..sanctus episcopus memoriae ... post tot annos."

8 On the Velo di Classe, see Frattaroli 2004; Picard 1988, 515–518 and fig. 55.

of orthodoxy against the Arian heresy. Scholars since then have impugned many of the Ballerinis' conclusions and have reduced the number of sermons attributed to Zeno.[9] One sermon entitled "On the Construction of a House of God as the Work of Solomon" seems to refer to converting an existing house into a church. Archaeological investigations confirm that in the region between today's cathedral and the Adige River there was a small structure, probably a private house, with adjoining structures, including a baptistery, which dates from the fourth century, and which was renovated in the fifth century. The church was later dedicated to Mary in the seventh century, but continued to function as the cathedral until the eighth century, when Santa Maria Matricolare was constructed on the same site, under the inspiration of Bishop Anno (c.750–780s), on whom more below.[10]

Zeno's cult seems to have been well established soon after his death. Sometime around the middle of the fifth century a certain Petronius, who may have been the bishop of Bologna (c.431–449), or bishop at Verona (c.425–450), composed a sermon celebrating "The feast day of Holy Zeno" (*In Natale sancti Zenonis*) and mentions that many miracles take place at his tomb, in language very reminiscent of the *Life*, suggesting it served as a source.[11] Despite this local fame, and Ambrose's awareness of him, Zeno failed to get a mention in the *De viris illustribus* of Jerome and continued by Gennadius of Marseille (c.496). We learn that there existed a Gothic church dedicated to Zeno in a suburb of Ravenna, Caesaria, for it was one of the Gothic churches "reconciled" by Archbishop Agnellus (557–570) after Justinian's decree confiscating Gothic property and transferring it to the Ravennate church.[12] It is possible of course that the dedication refers to another Zeno, as could Pope Gregory I's reference to a "monastery of Laurence and Zeno" at Cesena.[13] But Gregory was certainly

9 Edited by Löfsted 1971, reprinted in 2008 with Italian translation and updates by Banterle, Fedalto, and Ravazzolo.

10 On excavations, see Lusuardi Siena 1987, 26–36. On the fortunes of Zeno's church, see Fiorio Tedone 1987. On the church of Verona in the tenth and eleventh centuries, see Miller 1993 (*Zeno*, 87–88).

11 On the sermon, see Lodi 1967. For Petronius as a bishop of Verona, see S. Tonolli, *Bib. Sanct.* 10: 532–534; likewise, Cervato 2004. Discussion of the cult of Zeno in liturgical sources found in Segala 1982 and Orlandi 2003.

12 Agnellus, *LP* 86. That this church was Arian seems to have received little notice by scholars, but Verona had Arian churchmen too, judging from the Arian sermons written c.500 and conserved in Verona, Biblioteca Capitolare LI (49) (CLA 4.504). See Gryson 1982.

13 Gregory, *Reg.* XIV.6. See Orlandi 1990.

aware of Zeno's stature in Verona, for a story in his *Dialogues* was used by the hagiographer as a "postscript" in the *Life* (ch.9), the tale of the "church of the blessed martyr and bishop Zeno," as Gregory calls it, miraculously holding back flood waters as high as the building. No other source claims Zeno was a martyr: Paul the Deacon's repetition of the story followed Gregory in calling the church the "*basilica* (*ecclesia* in Gregory) of the martyr Zeno," but our hagiographer discretely changed "martyr" to "confessor" in his otherwise direct borrowing from Gregory.[14] The floods were connected to those of 589 in Rome, which also devastated other parts of Italy, and two months later much of Verona was burnt in a fire.[15]

But Verona rebounded and enjoyed prosperity and patronage during the Lombard period, with dukes Lupo (c.720) and Giselpert (744–745) establishing the churches of Santa Maria in Organo and Santa Maria in Solaro, respectively, while another five or six churches in and around the city can be attributed to the eighth century, and several parish churches further into the countryside.[16] A monastery dedicated Zeno is first attested in a charter of the Lombard King Desiderius (756–774), and in a charter of his officer (*gasindus*), Taido, both of whom donated land to the abbey, which was destroyed by fire sometime before 806, when Bishop Rathold rebuilt it.[17] How early this monastery was established is unknown, but this ecclesiastical prosperity in eighth-century Verona, the emergence of competing cults, and later legends about Zeno's relics being transferred to this monastery under Rathold point to a context for dating the *Life of Zeno*.

Date of Composition

The text of the *Life* is as difficult to date as Zeno's career. A *terminus post quem* is provided by the use (ch.9) of Gregory's *Dialogues*, written c.593–594, for the

14 Gregory, *Dial.* III.19, ed. De Vogüé 1978. Gregory claims he heard the story from a tribune who was there with the Lombard King Authari at the time.

15 Paul, *HL* III.23–24; Christie 2006, 200–205.

16 See Cervato 2004. On other, later dedications to Zeno in Italy, see Orlandi 1990; outside Italy, see Orlandi 1991. On Zeno in liturgical sources, see Segala 1982 and Orlandi 2003.

17 On the monastery, see Fainelli 1958; Brugnoli and Maroso 1986; and Brugnoli (ed) 1986. Taido, CDL 293: Desiderius's charter is cited in a *notitia iudicati* of 806 (*CDV* 52, 1: 71, 88–89) and a charter of Louis the Pious from 815 (*CDV* 117). These charters must be used with caution: see La Rocca 1995.

story of Zeno's miraculous flood-resistant church in Verona. The *terminus ante quem* of the ninth century is established in the *Life*'s earliest manuscripts (see below), matched by its first attestation elsewhere in the martyrology of Usuard (post 865), yet the slightly earlier martyrologies of Adan and Hrabanus Maurus mention only the miracle recorded by Pope Gregory, and do not seem to know of the *Life*,[18] despite the possibility that Hincmar of Reims may have owned a copy of the *Life* as a preface to Zeno's sermons (see Text and Translation, below). Can we do better than c.600–850?

The *Life* claims that, prior to his missionary work in Verona, "smashing idols and building churches," Zeno lived in a monastery "in a hidden part of town." The image of a monastic Zeno who reluctantly became bishop may reflect close relations, or an attempt to build better relations, between the cathedral church and the monastery dedicated to the saint, which was enjoying Lombard royal and noble patronage in the mid-eighth century. A later, eleventh- or twelfth-century *translatio* text, known as the *Legenda translationis S. Zenonis*, written by a monk of St Zeno who used Coronatus's *Sermon/Life*, claims that Bishop Rathold arranged for the transfer (*translatio*) of Zeno's body from his original church to the monastery of St Zeno, "when Pippin, the son of Charles the Great, was king, whom Pope Adrian himself baptized."[19] The legendary and derivative nature of this text does not inspire any certainty, but references in liturgical texts confirm that a translation of Zeno's relics took place around this time.

However, there are grounds for attributing both the translation of relics and the composition of the *Life* to activities of Bishop Anno (c.750–780s) and his reform of Verona's religious landscape. Anno established his new cathedral on the site of the pre-existing church dedicated to Zeno, and he seems to have reorganized other cults: he consecrated the *martyrium* of Saint Theuteria (751), and around 759 he arranged for the relics of the martyrs Firmus and Rusticus to be interred in a church dedicated to them, now San Fermo Maggiore, where their relics repose today. We know little about Firmus and Rusticus: their *Passion*, which was probably written around the time their relics were interred, claimed they were imprisoned and tortured to death at Verona during the reign

18 Hrabanus, *Martyrologium*, ed. McCulloh 1979, 45 (12 April); Usuard, *Martyrology*, ed. Dubois 1965, 211.

19 BHL 9011. Text in PL 207–212. Possibly the same author wrote another *Vita Zenonis* (BHL 9010; Picard 1988, 675).

of Emperor Maximian (286–310).[20] The *Passion* also claims that their bodies ended up in Istria (after a sojourn in Carthage), from where Anno arranged to import the bodies (by then in Trieste), "along with those of Primus, Mark, Apollinaris, and Lazarus," to be buried "in a church that was earlier constructed in their honour" outside the walls of the town. Anno's importation of the relics is confirmed in the civic praise poem known as the *Versus de Verona*, composed during the reign of King Pippin in Italy (781–810), and modelled to some degree on the Milanese praise poem of the 740s (see *Life of Sirus,* introduction).[21] The *Versus* claims that *praesul* Anno brought back the lost relics of Firmus and Rusticus "at the time of kings Desiderius and Adelichis" (759–774), and that Anno adorned the martyrs' tombs with gold cloth interwoven with white, black, and purple designs.

The *Versus de Verona* exhibits the sense of civic pride and competition found in the Milan praise poem and, as this book tries to demonstrate, in the hagiography of this period. The *Versus* boasts that due to the many bodies of saints in Verona, "the only city in Italy with one hundred of them," Verona receives praise from Rome, Pavia, Aquileia, Ravenna, Mantua, and Brescia, and is the "gateway to all Liguria." But the *Versus* begins celebrating Verona's first eight bishops, and its references to Zeno's miracles suggest knowledge of Coronatus's *Sermon/Life*, while nothing suggests the poet knew the *Passion of Firmus and Rusticus*, also probably written during Anno's episcopate. This suggests that Coronatus's *Life of Zeno* was written before the *Versus de Verona* (781–810), and was also written during Anno's episcopate, perhaps in response to the *Passion of Firmus and Rusticus*, which portrayed the Bishop Proclus of Verona (c.342) as inept and ineffective, hiding in a monastery for fear of pagans. Alternatively, the *Life* may also have been an attempt to prevent the transferral of Zeno's relics to the monastery, for it clearly states that Zeno was buried in a *basilica* built by a member of Gallieni family (emphasizing its antiquity), near the river "where his

20 BHL 3020. On the cult of Firmus and Rusticus, see Golinelli and Brenzoni (eds), 2004. *Passio* text in Mombritius 1910, 1: 455–447, and ed. Ruinart 1859, 636–640. These editions are superseded by Golinelli 2004, who provides a new text of the *Passio* and *Translatio* (BHL 3021) texts from Verona, Biblioteca Capitolare LXXVII (s.XI–XII) and lists twenty other manuscripts. Golinelli 2004, 21–22, believes the *Passio* and *Translatio* were written at the same time during Anno's episcopate; likewise, Everett 2000, 87–92 (for the *Passio*). Picard 1988, 515–517, 676–677, dates both texts to the tenth century. On the liturgical evidence for their cult, see Segala 2004.

21 *Versus de Verona*, ed. Duemmler (MGH Poetae 1881: 1, 120–121). See Avesani 2004 and Granier 2009.

holy body now rests, a venerable place resplendent with miracles" (ch.8), and the citation from Gregory's *Dialogues* about the supernatural powers of the church (removing Gregory's "martyr" references) serves as a reminder of its fame: even people from "remote regions" (*de longinquis regionibus*) came to be cured at Zeno's tomb there (ch.9). Moreover, Coronatus qualifies himself as *notarius*, which would identify him with the cathedral clergy.[22] It is also possible the *Life of Zeno* reflects efforts by Anno and his clergy to annul any religious separatism of cults in Verona and to channel religious devotion within the city on the figure of the bishop. In either case, Anno's reforms and activities provide a fitting context for Coronatus's sermon on the *Life of Zeno*.

Text and Translation

The *Life of Zeno* (BHL 9001) translated here was edited by Marchi 1972, 18–23, reprinted by Sala 1990, 29–32, and is identical to that given by the Ballerini brothers (reprinted in PL 11, 199–204), who copied it from the now lost "Codex remensis ... exaratus ante saeculum IX." This was probably our oldest manuscript of the *Life*, and was used by the Ballerini brothers for the edition of Zeno's sermons (published 1758), where the *Vita* served as a preface. The manuscript once belonged to Hincmar of Reims (845–882), who gave it to the church of St Remigius. But this manuscript was burned in the fire of 1774, and we only have the Ballerinis' handmade facsimile example of its script to judge its date, which must remain speculative: Lazzarini 1904, 5. The earliest surviving manuscript is Paris, Bibliothèque nationale de France, lat. 5593 (fols. 182–184v), which dates from the ninth century, and was used by the Bollandists for their edition AA. SS. Apr. II, 70–71 (confirmed by Poncelet 1889–1893, 2: 497), as was Vatican City, Biblioteca Apostolica Vaticana, Barb. lat. 586, fols. 16–17, s. XI/XII (Poncelet 1910, 459), reprinted in Mombritius 1910, II, 651–652.

The Latin of Coronatus's *Sermon/Life* is fairly simple and straightforward, generally eschewing high-blown rhetorical expression common to late antique texts, except for its wordy prologue expressing humility. The *Life*'s simplicity perhaps explains why it became popular and sparked new compositions on Zeno. We have mentioned the eleventh-century *Translatio* (BHL 9011) and another *Life of Zeno* (BHL 9010), both modelled heavily on Coronatus's work, but as early as the ninth century the *Life* was converted into a poem in rhyth-

22 On the meaning of *notarius*, see Everett 2003a, 197–210.

mic metre (BHL 9009), which became a favourite among the many liturgical commemorations of Zeno developed throughout the Middle Ages, during which Coronatus's *Life* echoed for centuries.[23]

23 On the *Vita rythmica*, see Pighi 1960, 1974. On liturgy, see Segala 1982, Orlandi 2003; also, Sala 1990, 1991. The *Life of Geminianus of Modena* (BHL 3296) used Coronatus's *Life* extensively: Anti 1996.

The Sermon of the Venerable Coronatus on the Life of the Holy Bishop and Confessor Zeno

1. We have investigated the miracles of such a great man from those days, in the province of Italy, in the city of Verona, where the acts of the blessed Zeno were famous. For the human mind desires to know the lives of the saints, like a thirsty man parched by the heat of the sun desires a flowing stream, or like someone waiting anxiously to hear some important news, or like someone raised on sumptuous delicacies, and then placed on a long journey, who then longs to reach a place where he can satisfy himself to his heart's content. And so I, although incapable of setting down everything that such a great man did by word or through miracles, nevertheless do not shirk from narrating as much as I have been able to ascertain, lest any reader disparage it, or anyone listening accuse the reader of possessing a lazy mind, as it is written, "Those who repay my good with evil slander me," and because of that which the Lord himself said to those who perform good works: "I knew you before I formed you in the womb, and I sanctified you before you were even born."[24] For he himself was sanctified in the womb and was blessed in his crib, and having deserved this distinction he then earned his place as pastor among the people by virtue of his holy life, and that is why in every land his words have resounded and his sanctity has sparkled. And now let all people listen who are eager to know of his miracles[25].

2. He resided in a monastery in a remote corner of the town of Verona, beseeching the Lord with continual fasting and incessant prayers, asking that the way be opened for him to preach to the people. For all day every day he was committed to converting the minds of men to the love of Christ. Truly the holy spirit was his teacher, just as the very truth spoke through him, saying, "For it

24 Ps. 37:21; Jer. 1:5.

25 The edition of Ughelli 1643–1662, V: 680, gives an alternative prologue found in later manuscripts: "Although we are found to be incapable of setting out for you a suitable narrative covering all the miracles for which the blessed Zeño, bishop of Verona, was famous, it seemed more right that, even if by a stumbling effort at a sermon, we might [learn] something about him, rather than have him obscured by the darkness of ignorance because his wonders, through which he truly scintillated back then, are left to silence. For indeed we know that he rightly belongs with the assembly of the saints, but he must be all the more honoured by human ceremony, since his deeds have been written down for the people's understanding, and should [be] read out."

is not you who speaks, but the spirit of the Father who speaks through you," and likewise, "I am your good shepherd, and I give my life for my sheep."[26] Thus he was friendly in his speech, mild in manner and character, so that all who came to visit him praised God, and soon enough they happily abandoned their idols and believed in Jesus Christ the Lord.

3. In that time he once left his monastery and took a short trip to the Adige River not far from the city of Verona. While he was fishing there he looked up and saw before him a man sitting on a cart with the oxen submerged in the river. The man was being swept by at such a speed that it was clear to everyone that this was the work of the devil. The holy man lifted his eyes to the heavens, for he recognized immediately that the devil had done this. He raised his hand and made a sign of the cross a number of times, saying, "Get back Satan, do not destroy a man whom God has created." As soon as the devil saw the sign, he vanished like smoke, shouting in a horrid yell as though falling from a high cliff, saying, "Since you do not allow me to acquire the souls of men, I am prepared to go into the unknown lands around these parts to obstruct you." Then Zeno the holy man of God said, "The Lord will not allow you to act against his servant."

4. After this exchange, with a wail and a shout the demon took off, but immediately hurried to the palace of Gallienus[27], seized his daughter, the only child he had at that time, and began to torture her cruelly. Soon her father and the entire imperial household were in a state of misery because the girl was suffering so cruelly from her torment. While she was possessed by this cruel afflic-

26 Matt.10:20; John10:11, 14.

27 Gallienus (253–268) shared the imperial title with his father, Valerian (253–260), ruling the western and eastern parts of the empire respectively until the latter's capture by the Persians in 259. Eusebius (*Historia Ecclesiastica* 7.14) reports that Gallienus reversed his father's policy of persecuting Christians, and cites imperial edicts in which he declared freedom of worship and restored some lost property to Christians (see Keresztes 1975). But Gallienus certainly never converted to Christianity: he travelled to Athens to receive initiation into the Eleusinian cult of Demeter and issued coins honouring at least nine deities (Apollo, Diana, Hercules, Jupiter, Juno, Liber Pater, Mercury, Neptune, and Sol) as "protectors of the emperor." Gallienus also cultivated a friendship with the Neoplatonic philosopher Plotinus, who nearly convinced Gallienus to found a city in Campania governed by philosophers and called "Platonopolis" (De Blois 1976). On coins, see Weigel 1990. Gallienus repaired and extended Verona's defensive walls in 265 (see introduction above); corrupted records may explain his appearance in the *Life*.

tion, the demon began to cry out through the mouth of the emperor's infant daughter, saying, "I will not leave this body unless Zeno the bishop comes, and only leave at his command." As soon as the Emperor Gallienus heard this, he immediately began to investigate and sent out special agents to find the holy man. And so by order of the emperor the soldiers came upon the man of God. He himself was sitting on a rock near his monastery, fishing in the river. When the soldiers approached, because they did not know him, they immediately began to interrogate the holy priest of God, saying, "Who are you, a man of God? Tell us if you have seen the Bishop Zeno, whom we seek by order of the emperor." He responded, saying, "Since there are many in our monastery of that name that you ask about, say also why you have been sent. For although I am insignificant, I am also a servant of God, and my name is Zeno." The soldiers then deliberated among themselves, saying to one another, "Why do we keep talking? Let's explain why we've been sent to find this man!" They turned and said to him "The emperor asks for you, and wishes to see you." Zeno responded, "Why does the emperor, who continues to be the enemy of all Christians, wish to see humble little me?" They then said, "The emperor asks you to restore to health his only daughter, who is possessed by a demon." He said to them, "The Lord Jesus Christ is omnipotent. Go, then, and I shall follow you, because the miracles of God should be revealed to everyone." When he said this, the soldiers left.

5. Zeno got up from the rock, said a prayer, then set out for the palace, where the emperor was in anguish and despair for his daughter. The holy bishop of God reached the palace before the soldiers who had come to find him. Upon entering the palace the priest of Christ made a sign of the cross when immediately the demon began to shout through the mouth of the little girl, "So it is you, Zeno! You have come to expel me, and because of your holiness I cannot stay." As this was said the priest grabbed the hand of the girl and said, "In the name of the Lord Jesus Christ, I command you, demon, to leave this girl." The demon began to shout in an obscene voice, saying, "Since you have you expelled me from here, I shall go to Verona, and there you will find me in those whom I shall possess waiting for you in the main square." And that is how the priest of Christ restored the daughter of the emperor to health.

6. When the Emperor Gallienus saw this he was struck with admiration, and offered the imperial crown that he wore on his head to the holy priest, saying, "To such a physician, who restored my only daughter to health, I could not

offer in reward anything less than my own crown." While this was happening, a large crowd of people who had come to the palace saw all this and were turned from their pagan error and believed in our Lord Jesus Christ. They beseeched the priest of Christ to show them the way of salvation, and to receive baptism for the forgiveness of their sins. And when the priest accepted the crown of the emperor, he immediately gave it to the poor, saying, "If God works miracles, then the glory must go to him."

7. After this, the most blessed Zeno asked that he be given permission to destroy all idols and build churches in the name of Christ. Listening to his entreaties, the emperor granted him everything he asked. The priest then returned to the city of Verona and bravely preached the word in the name of Christ, whereby idols of the devil were destroyed and churches were built in the name of Christ. Because of this, a good number of pagan people seethed with anger, and ceaselessly plotted to obstruct the servant of God. But Christ, vigilant for his servants, defeated the deceit because Zeno kept a pure faith in his heart.

8. With this out of the way he continued to work and intercede for the salvation of the people, which he was accustomed to do from a young age for the love of Christ. Yet while he worked at this so diligently, not long after by the will of God he was received in peace. And because through his miracles he was famous to all peoples, a member of the Gallieni family built in honour of God and his holy priest a basilica dedicated to the saint not far from the river, where his holy body now rests, a venerable place resplendent with miracles in the name of Christ.

9. Sometime later in this same city of Verona, when the people devotedly gathered together with the clergy and priests to celebrate the solemnities in a mass on the day of this saint's nativity, the Adige River suddenly swelled up in a great flood over the bank where his body was known to be buried, and the water whooshed up from the river until it reached the windows and climbed toward the roof.[28] *But although the doors of the church were open, the water did not*

28 This miracle story is taken verbatim (as indicated by italics) from Gregory, *Dial.* III.19, who says it took place "in our days" when the Tiber also overflowed and flooded Rome upon his election to the papacy, 590. The Lombard King Authari (584–590) apparently witnessed the miracle. Note that Gregory used the term "martyr," not "confessor" as here (see above).

enter through them, and then shut the door of the church: although an element of liquid, it was transformed into the solidity of a wall. At the sight of this the people were struck with wonder, and those who came there for the honour of God and the holy priest were shouting that they were going to perish from hunger and thirst. *And when many had gone inside and the whole church was surrounded by a huge amount of water, they realised they could not get out. Terrified of dying from hunger and thirst, they went to the door of the church to drink and drew from the water that, as I said before, despite reaching right up to the windows, never leaked into the church anywhere. The water could be drunk, but it could not flow inside. It just stood before the doors to demonstrate the worthiness of the* confessor, *for it was water that assisted, not water for flooding the place.* This was a veritable flood of water, which rose up and surrounded the church like a wall, yet still no water entered inside. We know that this was owed to the power of his prayers to influence God, when water rises up like a type of wall, but does not dare to enter a holy place. And so veneration for and fear of the priest of Christ increased, for if they came with faith, the sick were healed, and those possessed by demons were freed. And if anyone invokes his holy name in true faith, without doubt he will grant their request. And many who suffer bodily infirmities arrive from the neighbouring regions at his tomb to lay next to it for his intercession, then return home in health and happiness.

Behold, whatever I, Coronatus, worthless notary, could find out about his many miracles, I have set out here in brief, lest I annoy readers and listeners. With the help of our Lord Jesus Christ, to whom go honour and glory forever. Amen.

8 MAY

The Book Concerning the Apparition of St Michael on Mount Gargano

The *Liber de apparitione Sancti Michaelis in Monte Gargano* is a short, enigmatic text that describes how the Archangel Michael founded a cave-church with miraculous healing waters among the rocks high up on Mount Gargano in Puglia – a church that became one of the most important pilgrimage points in Western Europe from the seventh to the ninth century, and was made a World Heritage Site in 2011.[1] Although of uncertain date and anonymous authorship, and set in a timeless early Christian past, the *Book Concerning the Apparition of St Michael on Mount Gargano* is quite unlike other hagiographic works of Italy, in that its subject is the archangel, whose divine power physically alters the landscape of Italy to create a church on a site that was known for its healing powers in the ancient world. The *Book* therefore chronicles the Christianization of a pagan shrine, but also contains hints of an ecclesiastical squabble over control of the site, echoed also in the *Life of Barbatus,* between the churches of Siponto and Benevento, which helps to date the *Book*'s composition to the late seventh or early eighth century. The *Book* was undoubtedly read by many pilgrims who came to the shrine to scratch their names into the cave wall, was immensely popular in the Middle Ages (over 150 different copies survive), and inspired later imitations for shrines in Europe devoted to Michael with their own apparition texts.[2] The

1 BHL 5948. Text edited by Waitz (MGH SS rer. Lang. 1878: 541–543). On the shrine, see Carletti and Otranto (eds) 1980, (eds) 1994; Everett 2003a, 265–274. On Puglia in the Middle Ages, see Martin 1993; Lanzoni 1927, 278–284. On UNESCO's listing, see the coverage in *Il Gargano*, June 2011 (anno 37, no. 6).

2 The *Apparitio in Monte Tumbae* (BHL 5951; text in AA. SS., Sept. VIII 1865: 76–78), dating from c.850–900, celebrates the foundation of the monastery of Saint Michel in Normandy. See Bettocchi 1994. Another *apparitio* text (BHL 5947b–c) from the tenth or eleventh century concerns Monte Tancia in Lazio (c.10 km from Rieti), where Michael defeated a dragon: text in Poncelet 1906 and Aulisa 1994. Another *apparitio* text was found in a tenth-century manuscript (Paris, Bibliothèque nationale de France, lat. 2873A), but the location of the church foundation it celebrates is not stated: Sivo 1995. On the inscriptions at Gargano, see Carletti 1980 and Everett 2003a, 265–274.

Book was translated into Greek from as early as the tenth century, and probably earlier.[3]

The Cult of Michael and the Shrine at Gargano

Michael, which means "Who is like God?" in Hebrew, appears in different books of the Old Testament (Daniel, Jude, Joshua), but was probably best known to Christians for his role in the Book of Revelation as the leader of God's armies against the forces of Satan.[4] The first attestation of a cult of Michael is in Phrygia, and it has close parallels with our Gargano cult. According to a text known as the *Miracle of the Archangel at Chonae* (of uncertain date; the version we have dates from the eighth century), Michael appeared to man in a dream and instructed him to take his mute daughter to a natural spring that the archangel had created among the rocks. After his daughter drank the water and was cured, in gratitude the man built a church over the spring from which Christians were healed, and also pagans, causing them to convert.[5] Both the *Miracle of the Archangel at Chonae* and *Book Concerning the Apparition* constitute a subgenre of hagiography that has been termed hagiotopography, for Michael's appearance on earth is accompanied by dramatic physical changes in the landscape – the divine power of his interventions move earth and rock to leave very real and tangible traces of his presence, and of his benevolence. The creation of the grotto at Mount Gargano by Michael in *Book Concerning the Apparition* may also represent the Christianization of a known healing site of the ancient world, associated with pagan supernatural powers. In this sense the *Book* forges a new, Christian identity for the wild landscape of the Gargano peninsula.[6]

Exactly when Gargano received a church, from Michael or otherwise, is unknown: an interpolation in the *Liber Pontificalis* claims that Michael's *apparitio* took place during the papacy of Gelasius I (492–496), but the earliest secure testimonies to the shrine at Gargano in written sources are brief notices in late eighth-century manuscripts of Jerome's *Martyrology* and Paul the Deacon's

3 Leanza 1985 (from Vatican City, Biblioteca Apostolica Vaticana, Vat. gr. 821, s.XI, and Vat. gr. 866, s.XI–XII); 1994.

4 On Michael in scripture and pagan traditions, see Arnold 2013; Muehlberger 2013.

5 Halkin (ed) 1957, 1282. Greek edition and Latin translation in Bonnet 1889. See the insightful analysis of Peers 1996. On early Michael cults, see Arnold 2013.

6 On this theme and classical references to the site, see Arnold 2000; Otranto 1983; Petrucci 1963; Paul, *HL* IV.46, and see *Life of Barbatus*.

History.[7] Paul claims that the Greeks came to attack the shrine, which was valiantly defended by Duke Grimoald of Benevento (c.647–661). Inscriptions inside the grotto testify to its patronage by Grimoald's son Duke Romuald as early as the 670s, and archaeological evidence suggests late fifth- or early sixth-century foundations, which lends support to the Gelasian date.[8] The 159 graffiti inscriptions inside the grotto date from the seventh century to 875, and record the names of 182 pilgrims, including Franks and Anglo-Saxons, which they scratched onto the walls of the cave, sometimes with a little message ("May you live with God forever," *biba [vivas] in deo semper*; "Pray for me," *ora pro me*).[9] As noted in the introduction to the *Life of Barbatus*, by Paul the Deacon's day Gargano enjoyed royal Lombard patronage and had become part of the pilgrimage route to Rome, and even beyond to the Holy Land.[10]

Michael held a special place among Lombard elites from the later seventh century. The historian Gian Piero Bognetti proposed that that Duke Grimoald of Benevento brought the cult of Michael with him when he seized the Lombard royal throne in Pavia to become king (662–671), and promoted it as a way of uniting Catholic and Arian Lombards.[11] But there is no evidence for Grimoald's involvement with the cult (or for Bognetti's vision of a religiously divided kingdom), and it seems there was already a church dedicated to Michael in seventh-century Pavia, as well as several such in Milan.[12] Nonetheless, Paul the Deacon records a tale of how Michael appeared among the spears of King Cunincpert (688–700) as he headed out to battle against the rebel Alahis, and from Cunincpert's reign onwards the Lombards minted coins with images of

7 Manuscripts and literary references are documented in Otranto 1981 and Everett 2002b. See also Paul, *HL* IV.46 and the *Life of Barbatus*.

8 Inscription in Carletti 1980, no. 82: "+d[e] donis d(e)i et [(san)]c(t)i a[rcha]n/ +geli fiere iusse et don[avit/ +Romoald dux age[r]c pietate/ +Giademari fecit." Another inscription may record Grimoald's involvement (Carletti 1980, no. 44: "h[i]c patri eius [r]egni [c]umsor[t]ior/ e[re]ctor sic terre[n]a su[m]tsit/ [c]elestia n[u]m[q]ua[m] relinqui[t]"). *Pater* and *consortior regni* may refer to Grimoald and Romuald, respectively. Romuald may have sponsored the extended staircase (*longa porticus*): see Trotta and Renzulli 1998 and Arnold 2013, 87.

9 Inscriptions collected in Carletti 1980. For discussion, see Everett 2003a, 265–274.

10 On Gargano as pilgrimage site, see Piemontese 2000; Sensi 2014; and Bouet, Otranto, and Vauchez (eds) 2003.

11 Most prosaically in his essay "I 'loca sanctorum' e la storia della chiesa nel regno dei longobardi," Bognetti 1966–1970, 3: 303–346 (orig. pub. 1952), though the theory appears throughout Bognetti's corpus of writings.

12 Bullough 1966, 124–125; Cagiano de Azevedo 1979. On Arian-Catholic factions, see Wickham 1981, 34–36; Everett 2003a, 59–64.

Michael.[13] The significance of this has been over-interpreted by scholars looking for the "Teutonic" nature of the Lombards, and who see a belligerent Germanic people replacing Wotan with the archangel, yet another martial deity.[14] We can leave aside such theories, but Cunincpert's coins document the popularity of Michael at the turn of the century, and this may in part be owed to the fame of the Gargano shrine. It seems worth noting that the Beneventans, despite their proximity to the Gargano shrine and direct patronage of it, did not mint coins with Michael on them until 806.

Purpose and Date

Fixing a date for composition of the *Book* is difficult, and suggestions have ranged from the sixth century to the ninth century: a secure *terminus ante quem* is provided by Hrabanus Maurus's verbatim citation of the *Book* in his homiliary *Sermons for Major Feast Days,* written around 816. The run of surviving manuscripts begins in the ninth century also.[15]

The *Book* goes out of its way to avoid historical or chronological points of reference – perhaps one reason for its later popularity and adaptability – but the information afforded by the *Life of Barbatus*, and the Beneventan court case of 839, allows us to see through the text's ahistorical disguise and expose it as a claim for Siponto's original control over the shrine. The annexation of the Gargano peninsula by Grimoald and Romuald in the aftermath of Constans II's invasion (663) facilitated the appropriation of the grotto by the cathedral church of Benevento, now closely allied with the ducal court. As we have seen, the *Life of Barbatus* records that process and seems to quote from a copy of the decree (*praeceptum*) of Duke Romuald granting control of the shrine, which was still cited in 839 as a deviation from the law in Beneventan courts. The *Book*, therefore, is a complaint against dispossession. Siponto was the main ecclesiastical authority in the region in the 590s,[16] and Michael's appearance to

13 *HL* V.41. For the coins, see Grierson and Blackburn 1986, 64–65; on Cunincpert's reign and the cult of Michael among Lombards, see Antonopoulos 2010 (coins at 120).

14 Fischetti 1973; Gasparri 1983; Troiano 1989.

15 Otranto 1981; Everett 2002b. On manuscripts, see Sivo 1994 and Everett 2002b, 365 n8, for another (possibly the earliest) manuscript.

16 Clear from Gregory, *Reg*. 1.15, 3.41–42, 4.17, 8.8, 9.113, 9.170, 9.175. On the Sipontine church, see Lanzoni 1927, 277–284; Martin 1993, 113–160; Mazzei (ed) 1999; Fabbri 1999; Giuliani 1999.

the Sipontine bishop, and the nod to papal authority in the text, serves to remind readers that the Sipontine church was the original caretaker of the grotto, as mandated by Michael himself. The complaint resurfaces in a later hagiographic work (ninth or tenth century), the *Life of Laurence of Siponto*, which picks up where the *Book* left off: perceiving through his prophetic powers that Italy would be destroyed by barbarians, Laurence, bishop at the time of Pope Gelasius I, painted the walls of the churches in Siponto with images of the Sipontine cathedral next to the Gargano shrine, and declared, "though this picture that you see, I perceive the future fate of this episcopate." Although saddened by the forthcoming disasters, Sipontines rejoiced that "God had revealed to their bishop that their church will be restored."[17]

Scholars who focus less on the earthly realities of hagiographic production and its immediate audience are often charmed by the *Book*'s enigmatic qualities and postulate earlier dates for redaction, often in agreement with medieval traditions ascribing Michael's appearance to the papacy of Gelasius: the pagan Neapolitan attack that unites Sipontines and Beneventans has been interpreted as a reference to the Gothic wars.[18] Another argument for an early date is to envisage different stages of redaction, for the *Book* itself tells us that the details of Michael's apparition can be read in a "little book" (*libellus*) placed inside the church (ch.1), interpreted as the "core text" of the one that has come down to us, and it has been suggested that parts of the *Liber* exhibit the features of rhythmic prose, *clausulae* and *cursus*, that reflect a sixth-century usage, but the analyses do not hold.[19]

Text and Translation

The Latin text translated is that edited by Waitz 1878 (MGH SS rer. Lang., 541–543), which he cobbled together from the two previous editions of Ughelli

17 BHL 4790–4791. Text in AA. SS. Feb II, 57–60 (*Vita major*), 60–62 (*Vita minor*). Lanzoni 1927, 281, dated the *Vita minor* to 870–900, and the *Vita major* to the mid-eleventh century, when the see of Siponto was briefly granted independence from Benevento; Campione 1992 and Catallo 1991 date both *vitae* to the mid-eleventh century, but not convincingly (cf. Everett 2002b, 371 n22). Scholars have doubted Laurence's historicity: Martin 1993 115–116. On the restored church, see AA. SS. Feb. II, 61 (*Vita minor*): "post angustias consolationem etiam suam restaurandam ecclesiam pontifici Deus revelaverat."

18 Otranto 1983, 1988; Arnold, 2013, 67–70.

19 Petrucci 1963. On rhythmic prose, see Quacquarelli 1980. On scepticism, see Everett 2002b, 366 n10.

1643–1662, VII: 1107–1109, who used a manuscript "ex Vaticano," and of the Bollandists, AA. SS. Sept. VIII, 65–67, who used five or six "ancient manuscripts," one of which was at Trier. Re-examinations of the manuscript tradition have identified some of these witnesses but also earlier manuscripts and recognition that a new critical edition of this popular text is needed: see Sivo 1994; Otranto 1981, 1988. Another English translation is found in Johnson 2005, 110–115, with commentary on its reception in later medieval England.

The Latin of the *Book* demonstrates some of the same southern Italian traits of orthography found in the *Life of Barbatus* and the many hagiographic texts from Benevento; as always, it is difficult to tell how far back these morphological, orthographic, and grammatical features can be dated, and how much they reflect the scribal culture of the tenth and eleventh centuries. Arnold 2000 identifies several "Virgilian tags" from the *Aeneid* in the text; others see Latin of different periods in the text, as noted above.

The Book Concerning the Apparition of St Michael on Mount Gargano

Here begin a few words concerning the apparition of St Michael and the dedication of his church.

1. The church founded by the labour of the blessed Archangel Michael himself and consecrated in his name commemorates his memory for his veneration throughout the entire world. It was not endowed with the gleam of metals but with the privilege of signs, fashioned of simple design, but provided with celestial power, for the archangel, mindful of human frailty, came down from heaven and deigned to build it by his own hand so that there mortals may earn entry into the fellowship of those above. Accordingly, situated on the summit of a lofty mountain, the church can be seen in the form of a cave hollowed out from the mass of this same rock. Its location is within the boundaries of Campania, where the city of Siponto sits between the gulf of the Adriatic and Mount Gargano, and rises up on the highest peak twelve miles from the walls of the city, where it bears the church of the blessed archangel that I mentioned above. A little book placed in this very church reveals how it was made known to mortals in the following way.

2. In this same city there was a certain rich man by the name of Garganus, who gave the mountain its name because of his adventure. While his cattle, of which he owned a countless multitude, were grazing on the sides of the sloping mountain, it happened that a bull, spurning the company of the of the gathered herd, wandered off alone as usual, but quite far away, and did not come back home with the returning herd. Its owner gathered a number of servants and searched high and low for it until he finally found the bull standing on the summit of the mountain outside the entrance of a certain cave. Seething with anger because the bull wandered off alone, he grabbed his bow and fired a poisoned arrow at it. But the arrow turned back as though blown by a gust of wind to reverse its course and struck him who had fired it. The townsfolk [*cives*] were alarmed and amazed by this event, and sought advice from their bishop on what they should do, for they did not dare to go near the place. He advised that the answer must be sought from God, and announced a three day fast. When this was completed, the Lord's holy archangel addressed the bishop in a vision, saying,

> You did well now to seek from God that which is hidden from men. May you know that the mystery that struck a man with his own weapon was something done by my will. For I am the Archangel Michael, who forever stands within sight of the Lord. Resolving to protect this place and the inhabitants of this land, I wanted to demonstrate by this sign that I am the guardian and custodian of this very place and everything that happens here.

After this revelation was disclosed the townsfolk made it their custom to beseech the Lord and the holy Michael here. They discovered two doors there; the one on the southern side, which is the largest, could be reached by several downward-sloping steps, but they did not dare to enter further into the grotto, and instead devoted themselves to prayer in front of the doors.

3. Around the same time the Neapolitans, still wandering astray in pagan rites, declared war on the Sipontines and Beneventans, who live around 250 miles from Siponto. The latter,[20] as instructed by their bishop, requested a three-day truce so they could institute a three-day fast to implore the protection of the holy Michael, just as if he were their faithful patron. At the same time, the pagans called upon the assistance of their false gods with theatrical shows. Behold, however, on the night before the day of war, the holy Michael appeared to the bishop in a vision, and said that the prayers had been heard, and promised that he would be present and would meet the enemy in battle at the fourth hour of the day.[21] In the morning, therefore, happy and certain of an angelic victory, the Christians went out to meet the pagan Neapolitans, who were debilitated by a demonic spirit. At the first preparations for battle Mount Gargano was shaken by an immense tremor, lightning bolts flew thick and fast, and a dark fog shrouded the entire mountain top, fulfilling the prophecy that praises the Lord, saying, "He makes his angels winds, his servants flames of fire."[22] The pagans took to flight, some repulsed by the swords of their enemy, some by the arrows of fire, and were chased by their adversaries, who pursued them all the way back to Naples before withdrawing to their respective lands,[23] until finally the pagans, nearly dying, snuck back behind the walls of their

20 The Latin relative pronoun *qui* here implies that both Sipontines and Beneventans "sought the advice of their bishop," but the overall context suggests only the Sipontines were intended as the subject.

21 That is, 10:00 a.m., counting forward from prime, 6:00 a.m.

22 Heb. 1:7; Ps. 104:4.

23 "... atque extrema quaeque cedentibus adversariis."

town. Those who escaped the danger realized that an angel of God had come to the aid of the Christians, for they had seen nearly six hundred[24] of their own killed by lightning. Immediately, they bowed their heads to Christ, the King of kings, and took up of the arms of faith. When the victors returned home they gave vows of thanks to the Lord at the temple of the archangel. In the morning they saw footprints like those of a man imprinted close together in the marble before the northern door I mentioned above and which is like a small back gate,[25] and they recognised that blessed Michael wished to make his presence known with this sign.[26] Later they put a roof over this spot and placed an altar there, and this church was called "Apodonia"[27] because of the sign of the footprints.

4. Meanwhile the Sipontines were very uncertain about what they should do with this place, where the entrance to this church should be, and how it should be consecrated. They called a meeting together and decided to found a church to the east of that place and dedicated it in the name of the blessed Prince of the Apostles, Peter, and inside they set up altars of the forever-blessed Virgin Mary and the holy John the Baptist. Eventually the bishop, when he learned of these salutary plans, consulted the bishop of Rome through messengers about whether these plans should be carried out. By chance, he was then sojourning on a mountain nearly fifty miles distant from the city of Rome, which the locals there call by the name of San Silvester, for Silvester himself at one time had been exiled there and because of the persecution of the faith had taken refuge on Mount Soratte. The bishop of Rome sent back the following instructions:

> If it is the duty of man to dedicate that basilica, it should certainly be done on the day that the victory was granted. But if, however, another time

24 Cf. Judg. 3:31.

25 "... iuxta ianuam septemtrionalem, quam praedixi, instar posteruli pusilla." That is, the other of the two doors mentioned at the end of previous chapter (2): *instar posteruli pusilla* should read *instar posterulae pusillae,* following Waitz's suggestion (MGH SS rer. Lang. 1885: 542).

26 The footprint motif is common in ancient sources: see Dunbabin 1990.

27 Possibly from the Greek ἀπό + πούς, as in ἄποδος and ἄπους, "footless." Waitz (MGH SS rer. Lang. 1885: 542 n2) unenthusiastically suggests it derived from the verb ἀποδίδωμι (ἀπόδοσις), meaning "to give back" or "to return" (Latin *reddo*). For the scriptural resonance (esp. Matt. 27:58 and Rom. 2:6), see Arndt and Wilbur Gingrich 1979, 89, and Lampe (ed) 1976, 191. Cf. the Greek text edited by Leanza 1985, 306: "προςποδάριον."

> might please the provider,[28] his will on this matter should be sought on that very same day. And since this time is almost at hand, let us both conduct three-day fasts with our citizens, and beseech the Holy Trinity that the gifts that it has deigned to bestow through the greatest minister of its see might arrive at a final resolution.

And so it was done just as the bishop had suggested. On the last night of the designated fast, Michael the Lord's angel appeared to the bishop of Siponto in a vision, saying,

> It is not your task to dedicate this basilica that I myself have built. I founded it, and I have dedicated it. You are only to enter the place and offer your prayers while I stand by as your patron. And tomorrow, when you celebrate the mass there, let the people take communion as usual. But it shall be my task to show how I have consecrated that place through my very self.

5. When they came the next morning with offerings and many earnest prayers, they entered through the southern hall, and here a long colonnade extends to the north until it reaches that door we mentioned that has the footprints impressed in the marble outside. But before you come to this point, to the east there appears a large basilica that is reached by a set of stairs.[29] This church and its colonnade together seemed to hold nearly five-hundred people, and displayed its altar for veneration covered with red cloth near the middle of the southern wall. For that house[30] was full of corners, not because of walls erected the way humans fashion them, but like a cave was rough with stone jutting out at steep angles and its rocky roof was of uneven height, which here could be touched by one's head but elsewhere could hardly be reached with one's hand. I believe that the Lord's archangel teaches us here not to seek and cherish the ornamentation of stone, but purity of heart instead. Outside, the summit of the mountain is partly covered with cornel wood forest, and partly widens out into verdant plain.

6. Once the celebration of the mass was finished they returned to their homes inspired with great joy. After the bishop had appointed the offices of the min-

28 *provisor*, that is, Michael. Cf. 2 Macc. 4:2.
29 On the architecture and structures in the grotto, see Trotta and Renzulli 1998.
30 *domus*. Cf. Vergil, *Aeneid* 6.81; 10.101.

isters, priests, and cantors and lodgings were built for them, he prescribed an entire course of psalms and masses to be celebrated there in the proper order every day. No one, however, dared to enter the place at night, but at the break of dawn they sung matins hymns there. From the very rock that crowns this sacred temple near the northern altar, sweet, crystal-clear water trickles out by drops, which the locals here call "the drop." A glass vase made for collecting the water hangs there on a silver chain, and it is a custom that the people go after mass to climb the stairs one by one to this little vase and taste the gift of the celestial liquid. For it is both sweet to taste and good for one's health. In fact, some people who have long suffered from the flames of fever immediately experience the swift cooling of restored health upon drinking this "drop." Crowds of the sick are healed there in innumerable other ways as well, and many miracles that could only have happened due to angelic power have been attested there. The greatest miracles, however, take place on his feast day,[31] when a larger crowd than usual gathers from the neighbouring provinces to return there, and a greater concentration of angelic power is believed to be somehow present, and what the apostle said spiritually also seems to have happened corporally, "For angels are ministering spirits, and have been sent to minister to those who make themselves the heirs of salvation."[32] In Jesus Christ our Lord, Amen.

31 Never stated here in the *Book*; Frankish martyrologies such as that of Hrabanus Maurus (above) give 29 (sometimes 30) September, but Erchempert of Benevento (writing c.890) notes that it was locally celebrated on 8 May, which Beneventan liturgical manuscripts confirm. See Everett 2002b, 378–379, and Otranto 1981.

32 Heb. 1:13–14.

The Life of Senzius of Blera

The *Life of Senzius* is a rollicking tale that is really the story of two holy men, the monkish priests Mamilianus and Senzius, who escape from persecutions in Vandal Africa (c.439–450) and sail to various islands in the Tuscan archipelago, where Mamilianus defeats a dragon and dies. Senzius ventures to the Italian mainland to live as a hermit sandal-maker just outside Blera, where he too defeats a dragon, performs miracles, and baptises pagans.[1] Today Blera claims its patron saint to be Viventius, supposedly the town's first bishop, for whom we rely on later traditions: an annual procession along the Via Clodia towards the church dedicated to him in Norchia celebrates Viventius's patronage.[2] There exist few reminders of Senzius today in Blera itself: the name of a small street near the train station, and a cave and fountain of San Sensia further along the Via Clodia, reputed to be the ascetic refuge mentioned in the *Life*.

The *Life of Senzius*, however, reflects knowledge of the early medieval Tuscan archipelago, and was undoubtedly written in early medieval Blera. Our earliest manuscripts date from the eleventh century, but it is argued here that the text dates from the seventh or eighth century, and that it reflects the appropriation of local monastic cults by the cathedral church at Blera, barely attested

1 *BHL* 7581; AA. SS. Mai. V, 70–72 (*BHL* 1741, 536–539); Amore 1968; *Bib. Sanct.* 9: 496–498; Grégoire 1983, 348–349; Lanzoni 1927, 523–526; Burattini 1990; Saxer 1984. There is considerable variation for the name in medieval sources: Sensia, Sensio, Singizio, Sensigio, Sentius, Sentiate, etc. I follow here the AA. SS. text (Senzius). Cf. *LP* AD c.850: church of "Synzgius," below. Everett 2000, 100–107, anglicized [wrongly] to Sentius. Modern Italian uses both Sensia and Sensio. In his *Storia di Bieda*, published in 1822, Fedele Alberti claimed that in his day Sensia was a common name for newborns.

2 Viventius's relics rest in the (now-deconsecrated) church of San Nicola, Blera, which was built in the fourteenth century: Draghi 1998. San Nicola possessed an altar dedicated to Senzius, which was appropriated by the Italian government in 1914 and destroyed sometime after: see Santella 1981. Later medieval legends claimed that Senzius's relics were interred there also and were stolen by Spoletans and interred in a church in Spoleto: Susi 2010.

in the historical record and only revealed by archaeological excavations at the end of the twentieth century. Blera's position in the early Middle Ages as a frontier town on the border of Roman-controlled Lazio and Lombard-controlled Tuscany increased its strategic importance to both sides, but the conflict caused its eventual obsolescence as a town and bishopric, and the obliteration of Senzius's cult in the city today. Re-examination of the historical evidence at our disposal helps us to understand the connection between Blera's contested status in this period and the claims of the *Life of Senzius*, which adds to our fragmentary documentary record for early medieval Tuscany.

Blera: A Frontier Town

Before tackling the issue of dating our text it is worth considering Blera's position and its subsequent difficulties in the early Middle Ages. Blera contains many sites of Etruscan tombs dating from the sixth to the third century BC, and like other Etruscan towns on the coast, it came under Roman influence with the construction of the Via Clodia in the third century BC, and became a Roman *municipium* in the first century BC, when its agricultural organization was improved enough for the appearance of luxurious houses, baths, and mausoleums.[3] Although poorly attested in the sources of the imperial period, Blera maintained its status as a Roman *civitas* into the early Middle Ages. Throughout the Gothic war (535–553), the city became a strategic stronghold of the Byzantines, but the Lombard invasion of Italy, which had extended to Tuscany by the time of Gregory the Great, exposed Blera's vulnerability, located near the boundaries of the two conflicting powers, though Blera was nominally loyal to the empire. Pope Gregory's successor, Pope Sabinian I (604–606), was from Blera, and it was later the birthplace of Pope Pasquale II (1099–1118). We have no information on Blera for the seventh century (besides the *Life of Senzius*, as suggested here), but we learn of its troubles as a war-torn frontier town in the eight century from the *Liber Pontificalis*. Demonstrating the weakness of Byzantine authority in the area, in 730 the citizens of Blera, along with those of Luna and Monterano, swore fealty to a usurper named Petasius, also called Tiberius, whose failed bid resulted in bloodshed and his head being sent to Constantinople. In 739 King Liutprand invaded Blera as part of his march on

3 On the topography of Blera, see Quilici Gigli 1976; Santella 1981. Later medieval Blera (or "Bieda," as it was called then), discussed in Marcelli and Santoni 1996.

Rome that year; this and similar incidents prompted Pope Gregory III in 740 to write to the bishops of Lombard Tuscany and remind them of their ordination oaths to St Peter and their need to stay loyal.[4] We hear nothing of Blera's fate in the ensuing conflict that resulted in the Franco-papal alliance, but in 773 it suffered tremendously in the attempts of the final Lombard king to retain control of Italy, when

> King Desiderius sent the whole army of the districts of Tuscany to Blera, and when the people of that city, thinking they were at peace, came out as a whole with their wives and sons and dependants to harvest their crops, the Lombards suddenly fell on them and killed the chief men that held power in that city, and stole many men and much property as booty, laying waste to everything around with fire and sword.[5]

This comes after nearly two centuries of hostilities between the two major powers being played out in Blera. With Charlemagne's conquest of Italy the following year, the town came under papal rule, as part of the "republic of St Peter."[6]

Our only information on Blera in this period is the record in the *Liber Pontificalis* that Pope Leo IV (847–855) provided: "... in St Synzgius' church in the city of Blera ... 1 golden interwoven cloth with gold studded panels in the middle with an effigy of the Savior, with 3 prase jewels on his head, and of St Synzgius and of the blessed prelate; and 4 gold-interwoven veils."[7] This is our earliest and only mention of the church dedicated to Senzius in Blera besides the *Life of Senzius*, and it suggest that Senzius's cult and the church were well established by the mid-ninth century, while the *Life* seems to be promoting a newly established church and cult (ch.9), for Senzius's body was "placed in a sepulchre by the fearful men who built the basilica, where even until today many miracles and blessings take place." The *Life* reflects a degree of tension between Senzius's monastic sensibilities, lifestyle, and original companions and his role as patron saint of a cathedral church, a role that emphasizes that saint's pastoral duties. Senzius's work baptizing pagans and building a baptistery is

4 *Ep*.16 (MGH Epp., 3: 708). The text of the oaths is found in the *Liber diurnus*, nos. 75–76, ed. Foerster 1958, 136–138. On oaths in Italy, see Everett 2011.

5 *LP* 97.18, trans. Davis 1992, 131; Petasius, *LP* 91.23; Liutprand, *LP* 93.2. On these events, see Noble 1984, 61–132.

6 Noble 1984, 128–133; Toubert 1973, 367–368.

7 *LP* 105, trans. Davis 1995, 144. *Synzgius* is a Hellenized form of *Senzius*.

noted at the end and justified with the comment that Senzius then "revealed that he was engaged in the priestly order" (*patefecit Sanctus Senzius quia presbyteri fungebatur ordine*). Other comments stress Senzius's relationship to Blera, though his career in "Olim" suggests a monastic vocation.[8] It is suggested here that this tension is the key to understanding the text's original purpose in justifying the appropriation of Senzius's cult, and with it at least two monasteries, by the cathedral clergy of Blera. Further support for this is found in the letters of Pope Gregory concerning the two monasteries, and the example of the see of Lucca's appropriation of monastic cults in Populonia and Lucca and the production of texts (*Life of Regulus*, *Life of Cerbonius*) similar in style and content to the *Life of Senzius*.

Ecclesiastical History and Monastic Settlement: Pope Gregory I and Archaeology

Exactly when Blera became a bishopric is uncertain. Christian inscriptions once thought to date from the fourth or fifth century record the name of Viventius, whom local tradition has claimed as the first bishop (c.457–487), though we have no information that might confirm this, and subsequent scholarship has cast doubt on the inscriptions. Different recensions of the *Martyrology of Jerome* record for 25 May that "in the *Tuscan island* [or *town*] of Blera, Senzius, Vincentius, and Sancta" were martyred, but the notice is confused and gives no idea when it happened.[9] Our earliest historical reference is to a Bishop Romanus of Blera, who attended the twenty-third synod of bishops at Rome in 591 and was a signatory on the encyclical letter of Pope Gregory.[10] The decrees from this synod give some idea of church life at the time: the clergy

8 On angelic guidance to Blera, see ch.6; the marked lamb was the first miracle "in Blera," but it took place at Olim (ch.7); on healing the sick of Blera as a precursor to expulsion of the dragon, see ch.8. Senzius and Mamilianus are qualified as *viri religiossimi Domini servi presbiteri* (ch.1), and their three companions are *monachi* ("monks of Mamilianus" in ch.5), but all perform *opera Dei* of praising God with hymns and psalms "night and day" at every stage of the journey.

9 On inscriptions, see *Corpus Inscriptionum Latinarum*, ed. T. Mommsen et al. (Berlin, 1853–), I: 3357, 3359; De Rossi 1887; Lanzoni 1927, 522–523. Later traditions record sixteen bishops between Viventius and 1093.

10 Gregory, *Reg.* V.57A (not included in Norberg's edition: see Martyn [trans] 2004, 2: 388). The Bishop Maximus referred to in a letter of Gelasius I (J-L 713) was erroneously located in Blera, rightly dismissed by Lanzoni 1927, 524.

should no longer sing at mass, for those with beautiful singing voices forget their duties in delighting the congregation; lay secular boys should no longer help bishops to dress; church administrators were appropriating lands and writing false documents; placing "dalmatics" (woollen cloth) on the tomb of a bishop of Rome was banned; and charging fees for ordinations, consecrations, or papal bulls was prohibited. Gregory's last decree is worth noting: too many of those "freed from human servitude" in the church, that is, slaves who belonged to the church, were hurrying to join monasteries; Gregory believed they should prove their good standing as freedmen first. As it happens, Gregory also wrote to a monastery in Blera, and to another monastery on the island of Montecristo, which is specifically mentioned in *Life of Senzius* – both of which have implications for dating the *Life*, and are discussed below.

Also important for considering the origins and context of the *Life of Senzius* are the recent excavations (1998–2000) in the north-east section (Petrolone) of present-day Blera, which have revealed three church structures that date from the early Middle Ages: one is a church, thirty metres long, in the form of a Latin cross, with a western apse and the entrance facing east onto the Via Clodia. Among the ceramic finds there was a type of African red slip ware that dates from the sixth and seventh centuries, and matches the type and number found in other parts of Byzantine Italy, in decreasing numbers through the seventh century.[11] To the north of the transept is a quadrangular structure (7x6x4 metres) of uncertain function. Next to the thirty-metre church is a small structure in the form of a Greek cross, which demonstrates some similarities, in terms of dimension and building techniques, with the church of the Holy Cross in Ravenna known as the mausoleum of Gallia Placidia and other structures around the late antique Mediterranean. Excavation of this structure also revealed a number of graves dating from the eighth and ninth centuries, according to their stratigraphy, including a closed tomb made of stone slabs (*cista litica*).[12] The structure therefore may have served both funerary and baptismal functions: it is tempting to link this small cruciform structure with the church built for Senzius's burial in the *Life* (ch.9: see below), or the baptistery where he baptized pagans, since the chronology matches, but nothing confirms the link. Nonetheless, the combination of these buildings, in consideration of the defensive system of Blera as a *castrum* that controls traffic on the Via Clodia, suggests an episcopal complex of some sophistication and importance, and

11 Zanini 1998, 677–688; Christie 2006.

12 The tombs are of the "family" type that are common from late antiquity to the early modern period: see Possenti 2002.

probably reflects Blera's status as a key strategic foothold for maintaining *Tuscia Romana* against *Tuscia Langobarda* and the increasing Lombard incursions into the area, especially during the reigns of King Liutprand (712–744) and King Desiderius (756–774).[13]

By the eleventh and twelfth centuries the larger church was drastically reduced in size (to four metres long), while the rectangular and the Greek-cross structures were largely abandoned, and despoiled over following centuries.[14] The archaeological remains match what can be determined from the scant written sources: the diocese of Blera was amalgamated with that of Civitavecchia to create the diocese of Tuscana at sometime around 1051–1093, but was assigned to the diocese of Viterbo a century later. The small castello built there was owned by different noble Roman families.[15]

Although not attested in the archaeological record (yet), Pope Gregory I attests to a monastery in Blera that was experiencing economic difficulty. In 590 Gregory instructed his notary in Tuscany to grant the "monks of Blera" a thirty-year lease of lands and a ten-acre field from a papal estate near Viterbo, because the monks were "enduring a very severe shortage over their lands." Gregory ordered the transaction be done quickly, that the monks could "continue to praise God with a freer mind," and noted that the ten acres had already been granted to them some time ago.[16] It is difficult to identify this monastery with Senzius's hospice on the nearby mountain of "Olim" (*Life of Senzius*, ch.7: the name, literally "once upon a time" in Latin, may be a literary conceit), since Gregory refers to this particular monastery as "situated inside the city of Blera." But Gregory's letter testifies to a monastery in economic difficulties, relying for its survival on landed interests twenty kilometres north in Viterbo, another contested border city that we know was certainly in Lombard territory by the

13 A charter of Charlemagne (774), preserved in a confirmation charter by Lious the Pious (817), records that *Tuscia Romana* consisted of Porto, Civitavecchia, Blera, *Manturanum*, *Ceri*, Sutri, Nepi, Gallese, Orte, Bomarzo, Amelia, Todi, and Perugia: *Tuscia Langobarda* included Città di Castello, Orvieto, Bagnoreggio, Viterbo, Castro, *Orclae*, Marta, Tuscania, Sovana, Populonia, and Roselle. See Raspi Serra 1987, 159–163.

14 See Ferracci and Agneni 1998, 2000; Ferracci 2001a, 2001b; Aureli, Brolli, and Del Lungo (eds) 2006.

15 Marcelli and Santoni 1996; Santella 1981; Petrucci 1984. Ancient monastic settlements are thought to be behind the place names of Monte Monastero and Massa Gratiliana in Blera: Quilici Gigli 1976. Santella 1981, 25, claims the crypt of St Maria, the eighteenth-century parochial church of Blera, has tombs dating from the eighth century.

16 Gregory, *Reg.* IX.97 (599). Interestingly, Senzius enjoys a feast-day celebration (13 June) in Viterbo in modern times.

time of Pope Zacharias (741–752).[17] It is therefore likely that the monastery at Blera, and whatever property it still possessed, came under the control of its bishop, still located inside Roman territory and loyal to the empire, despite Lombard attacks.

The *Life of Senzius* claims that the monks on the Isola del Giglio have a right to house the body of Mamilianus, even though he died in Montecristo (ch.4). We know there was a monastery on Montecristo by Pope Gregory's time, for in 591 Gregory wrote to censure the monks for their laxity, complaining that they observed "none of the precepts of monastic rule." Gregory sent his own agent, Abbot Orosius, to temporarily oversee the monastery's management: other letters from this year demonstrate that Orosius was also used to reform a monastery on the island of Gorgona (thirty kilometres south-east of Livorno) and to establish a monastery on Corsica. In these letters Gregory also repeated the concern he expressed in his cyclical letter that year (591, cited above) about the intake of unsuitable people for monastic life on the islands of Eumorfiana (today Scoglio della Botte, near Ponza), Palmaria, and elsewhere, because of the Lombard invasions of the area. Gregory warned that "on the islands cohabitation of monks is rough," and he banned women and boys under eighteen years old from joining. Nonetheless his letters give the impression of a boom in monastic settlements that needed to be controlled.[18]

Gregory's very curt letter to the monks of Montecristo made no mention of the cult of Mamilianus at the monastery, but his cult is attested there in the tenth century, at the same site where the existing thirteenth-century Camoldese monastery was built, above Cala Maestra, four hundred metres above sea level.[19] Not far from the monastery is a cave-shrine now known as the Grotta di San Mamilano (and also Grotta del draco). Mamilianus's cult spread far and wide: later legends claim that he was bishop of Palermo, and that Elba and Genoa stole pieces of Mamilianus on his burial day, explaining his cult in those locations and elsewhere throughout Italy.[20] The *Life of Senzius*'s claim that the Isola de Giglio rightly possesses Mamilianus's body, suggesting that Mamilianus's cult existed there in the writer's day, has no corroborative evidence from

17 *LP* 93.11 and note Davis 1992, 40 n39. See also *LP* 97.25 and Noble 1984, 131.

18 On Montecristo, see Gregory, *Reg.* I.49; on Gorgona and Corsica, 1.50; on Eumorfiana and Palmaria, 1.48. Note also 1.46 on a monastery in Sardinia and 1.52 concerning the establishment of the cult of St Agata at a monastery in Capri.

19 Camici 2010.

20 Peria and Ferruzzi 2010. On images of Mamiliano (and other saints) in Tuscan churches, see Casini 2013.

the Middle Ages, but Mamiliano today is the patron saint of the Castello on the Isola del Giglio, which claims to preserve Mamiliano's arm.

The *Life of Senzius*'s concern with monasticism, in legitimating the Isola del Giglio's right to the body of Mamilianus, and in promoting a monkish priest as the patron saint of Blera, where an impoverished monastery existed, suggests that the church of Blera was defending its authority over these monasteries in some way. Further support for this can be seen in two similar texts from this era and period, the *Life of Cerbonius* (BHL 1728–1729) and the *Life of Regulus* (BHL 7102), both of which recount how these two saints fled Vandal Africa to arrive at Populonia on the Italian coast. Like the *Life of Senzius*, these two texts borrow heavily from Gregory's *Dialogues*: Cerbonius actually appears in Book 3, as a bishop of Populonia who fled to the island of Elba because of the Lombards (*Dial.* III.11). Recent research has revealed how the cult of Regulus at Populonia was appropriated by the church at Lucca, via complicated relations with the monastery of St Regulus at Gualdo, just outside Lucca, which is first attested in a charter of 744/745, and subjected to the bishopric by 750. In 780/781, Bishop John of Lucca transferred Regulus's relics to the church of St Martin in Lucca, completing the episcopal appropriation of the cult. The two *Lives* of Cerbonius and Regulus reflect Lucchese claims over Populonia, which was outside of the diocese of Lucca but had come under Lucchese control at some point during this period, along with the monastery at Gualdo.[21] Lucca's singularly rich archive of surviving documentation from this period allows us to trace these developments: the relationship between bishopric and monastery in Blera is lost to us other than what the *Life of Senzius* can tell us.

Date of Composition

The *terminus post quem* is the *Life*'s use of Gregory's *Dialogues*, which is cited almost verbatim at the conclusion of the text in describing whether Senzius should be considered a confessor or a martyr, because he tortured himself (ch.9), but is behind many other episodes and phrases in the text (see below). This chronology narrows the composition date for the *Life of Senzius* down to between c.620 (the general reception date of Gregory's *Dialogues* and subsequent literary modelling) and c.850 (when the church was dedicated to

21 Brand 2008, 2014; Collavini 2007. On Lucca and Populoni, see Rossetti 1973, 241–247; Susi 2005, 23–65.

Cetheus). Eugenio Susi has suggested that the text originates from a late tenth-century dispute between the abbey of Farfa and a Roman monastery over possession of the monastery Santa Maria del Mignone, which owned a boat landing at the mouth of the Mignone: Susi would identify the "little port called Columns" where Senzius disembarks onto the Italian mainland (ch.6) with Santa Maria's landing. But the identification is insecure: nothing in the *Life* or its tradition supports association with Santa Maria del Mignone, and no evidence correlates the *Life* with later disputes.[22] The *Life*'s reference to Senzius's landing "on the Roman shore" after the stay at Montecristo (ch.6) reflects an Italy divided between two powers, as it was in Blera's region until 774. The remains of the cathedral church recently excavated suggest a seventh- or eighth-century date. Considering the troubles of the monasteries of Montecristo and Blera during Gregory's pontificate, and the *Life of Senzius*'s direct concern with monastic cults at these sites, the hagiographer's efforts appear to be documenting the episcopal appropriation of local sites by the clergy of Blera, perhaps beginning in the seventh century: the bishop of Lucca's appropriation of the cult of Regulus of Populonia in the period 750–780, and the resulting production of hagiographic texts (*Life of Regulus, Life of Cerbonius*), offers a comparator for Blera and the *Life of Senzius* that suggests the eighth century. It has been argued that the dragons in the *Life of Senzius* represent the Arian heresy, cited in its opening chapter, and therefore the text can be read as an anti-Arian tract against the Lombards and dated to the seventh century.[23] Arguably, the dragon that harasses the city in the *Life of Senzius* represents the dangers of secular power, which thrive on the pomp and vanity of this world: these are the most dangerous dragons in the thought-world of Gregory, particularly in the *Dialogues*.[24]

Text and Translation

The *Life of Senzius* cites the *Dialogues* directly (ch.9), but there are hints of the *Dialogues* behind other episodes also, particularly Gregory's second book ded-

22 Susi 2000. Cf. Everett 2015c. On Santa Maria del Mignone, see Del Lungo 1994.

23 Susi 1995; Arguments against this interpretation found in Everett 2000, 100–107. On sauroctone saints in the West, see Orselli 1989, 783–784.

24 E.g., *Dial.* II.25, IV.38; see also *Homiliae in Evangelia* 19 ("draco [est] antiquus serpens"); cf. *Moralia* 5.9 and *Homiliae in Ezechielem* 20.1–2. On dragons in patristic thought, see Quacquarelli 1975.

icated to the life of Benedict. The dragon slayed by Mamilianus on the island of Montecristo (ch.4), with its eyes and mouth shooting flames, is described in similar terms to Gregory's descriptions of the devil who visits Benedict (*Dial.* II.8), and its size, "like that of a giant tree" (*quasi trabem magnam*), is reminiscent of the dragon Gregory supposedly saw floating down the Tiber in Rome, according to his contemporary Gregory of Tours.[25] The weightlessness of the dragon for the holy men on Montecristo (ch.4) reflects a similar miracle in the *Dialogues* (II.9), and both Mamilianus and Senzius cause springs of cold water to erupt in a manner reminiscent of Gregory's portrait of Benedict, who did likewise for his monks at a hill-top monastic site (*Dial.* II.5). Gregory also remarks that the water continues to flow in his day, as do the springs in the *Life*.[26] Finally, when describing Senzius's initial life of hermitic solitude outside of Blera (ch.9), the *Life of Senzius* cites Matthew 5:14–16 to explain how God sent Senzius to be Blera's patron, just as Gregory cited this passage to explain how God sent Benedict to be an example to the world (*Dial.* II.1). Other books of the *Dialogues* were consulted: the opening scene of African clergy fleeing the Vandals may have been inspired by Gregory's description of such at the opening of Book 3 (III.1), as it seems to have done for the *Life of Cerbonius* and the *Life of Regulus*; the miracle of the rain not falling on the boat transporting Mamilianus's body to the Isola del Giglio (ch.4) recalls Gregory's account of Cerbonius (*Dial.* III.11). There are undoubtedly echoes of other texts though none seem later than the *Dialogues*: the use of *metabolarian* (ch.2) seems late antique/early medieval.[27]

The earliest known manuscripts of the *Life of Senzius* date from the last quarter of the eleventh century, including Rome, Archivio del Capitolo di S. Giovanni in Laterano 79 (ff.228–230), a legendary written in Lucca that was used by the Bollandists for their edition of 1741 (AA. SS. Mai. V, 70–72) and is that which is translated here: the small number of variants they record

25 *Life*, ch.4: "exibat flamma ex ore ejus, et sibilationes horrendæ, ignis etiam ex ejus oculis procedebat." Cf Gregory, *Dial.* II.8: "ore oculisque flammantibus sæuire videbatur." Gregory of Tours, *Hist.* 10.1: "magno dragone in modo trabis validae," picked up by all early biographies of Pope Gregory, including Paul the Deacon's.

26 Gregory, *Dial.* II.5: "[aqua] tam sufficienter emanavit ut nunc usque ubertim defluat." Cf. *Life of Senzius*, ch.4 and 6: "aqua emanavit/exit frigidissima usque in hodiernum diem."

27 The description of Senzius hitting the dragon (*percussit eum de baculo* [ch.8]) is similar to Venantius Fortunatus's *Vita Marcelli* (*caput eius baculo ter percutiens*). Cf. *Life of Aidan of Lindisfarne* (*BHL* 185): "baculo percussit caput bestiæ et os eius ignitum clausit." The *Life of Senzius*'s following phrase, *et excussit de crypta*, is certainly based on Rev. 20:1–3.

from two other manuscripts, from Florence and Spoleto, have been noted also.[28] The version of the *Life* preserved in the S. Giovanni in Laterano legendary is also found in another Lucchese manuscript, Lucca, Biblioteca Capitolare, C, 174v–176v, recently dated to the late eleventh century also.[29] A later version of the text (BHL 7582, 7582b), which appears in the twelfth-century legendary from Spoleto (Archivio del Duomo, cod. I, ff. 216r–218v), noted by the Bollandists, substitutes "Spoleto" for "Blera" and thereby claims that Senzius went to Spoleto and died there, where the Spoletans built a church over his body, supposedly today's church of San Salvatore, just outside the town. The legends that Spoletans stole the relics of Senzius from Blera seem to have followed soon after.[30]

28 On the legendary, see Garrison 1953–1962, 1: 177–191; Supino Martini 1987, 49 n20. A new edition of the *Vita Senzii* is needed: Susi 2000, 17 n43.

29 Pomaro 2015, 307–308; previous scholars (e.g., Garrison 1953–1962, 1: 115–125) dated it to the early twelfth century.

30 The textual transmission and some later manuscripts are discussed by Curti 1981 and Susi 2004. On Spoletan legends, see Susi 1995, 2005. The miracle of the petrified bread thief on Senzius's feast day, printed by the Bollandists at the end of the *Life* (AA. SS. Mai. V. 73 n.O), concerns Spoleto and is not translated below.

The Life of Senzius of Blera

1. At the time of the Emperor Constantius,[31] most wicked son of the Emperor Constantine,[32] this Constantius was manifestly perverted by the priest Arius to abandon the Catholic faith for heretical depravity, and from this man the heresy polluted the entire world. Also at that time the great majority of bishops and priests sank into that wicked doctrine, because they did not hold the correct belief about God, nor were they firm in their faith about the Holy Trinity. And so the Lord looked down at their evil depravity, and saw that the priests who had been put there to heal the wounds of an enfeebled people were themselves unstable in their faith, and were in danger of being seduced and captured in the snare of perdition. For these ought to have been unquestionably the salt of the earth, but this had been made mockery of in their hearts, for they did not preserve the teaching of the Gospels, and so instead swelled those hearts of theirs with all the depravities of that error. The Lord was therefore angered by them, and roused the king of the Vandals, whose name was Genseric,[33] who captured Carthage with his troops[34] and cut down its inhabitants with a massive slaughter, and wounded many more, whom he bound in chains and tortured. The hunger and destitution of the Christians increased, for there was no compassion shown to them, and many righteous people suffered because of the impiety of sinners. A great number the African people fled from persecution by the tribes and were forced to flee to Italy and landed upon Roman shores. Many also crossed over from Tuscany and Campania to the region of Africa,[35] among whom were the most religious men and servants of the Lord, the priests Senzius and Mamilianus, together with three monks, Covaldus, Istochius, and Infans,[36] who were all deported to Africa, along with their belongings.

2. Nevertheless, these men never ceased in performing the Lord's work, singing hymns by night and praises to the Lord by day, and asking the Omnipotent

31 Constantius II (337–361).

32 Constantine I (306–337).

33 Gaiseric (428–477).

34 19 October 439.

35 That the holy men first went from Italy to Africa (*transmeaverunt in Africanam regionem*) seems owed to Gregory, *Dial.* III.1, who describes similar reverse traffic due to Vandal captures: "multique essent de hac terra in Africanam regionem transducti ... ."

36 The Bolladist editors suggested this was a triple corruption of the names Eustochius, Quodvultdeus, and Epiphanius.

Father to liberate them from the hand of their evil enemy. They were badly shaken from what they had suffered, and were not strong enough to endure their misery. But the will of God, who does not slight those who hope in him, nor withhold his compassion from those who love him, prepared for them a small boat in which they all gathered together, and a metabolarian[37] wind blew to calm the seas. They arrived swiftly at the port of Sardinia which is called Cagliari, and also at Piombino. When the inhabitants of that place saw them, they threw themselves at their feet to receive their benediction. Some brought gold, some brought silver, and others brought clothing to show their approval of them,[38] but they contemptuously spurned all these gifts, taking from them only a little nourishment to survive a few days at a time. They preached to these people about fasting and almsgiving, and about having perfect charity within themselves. They also healed the sick, and the inhabitants of that place so marvelled at their religion that they tried to keep them there by force. Realizing their intentions, they asked some mariners who were also there to take them to Mount Jove. They fled that night, and after two days of sailing they came to Turarium.[39] Here the mariners, instead of continuing on to the place where the servants of God desired, went their own way. Upon being left in Turarium, these men changed neither their hearts nor their countenance, but instead, having full faith in the Lord, simply prayed for the mariners. And although they were marooned on the island of Turarium for many days, they never ceased day or night to pray to God, and ate nothing other than the creatures of the sea that they caught themselves, or the birds that fell down before them at the command of God. Nor should it be amazing that they were sustained without bread on that mountain, when God could feed five thousand men from five loaves in the desert.[40] O the ineffable power of God! The servants of the Lord, Senzius, Mamilianus, Istochius, Covuldus, and Infans, were spurned by men, but not by their Creator, who gave manna in the desert[41] and delicious

37 *metabolarius,* a rare word (from Greek μεταβολή, "change/changeable"), only attested elsewhere in Hydatius's *Chronicle* (written c.468) recording an aborted Byzantine expedition (c.466) against the Vandals: "metabolarum commutatione et navigationis inopportunitate revocatur" (ed. Mommsen [MGH Auct. ant., 11: 34]). Cf. Cassiodorus, *In Ps.* 68.17, "metabole id est iteratio."

38 "volebant eos probare"; alternatively, "for they wished to test them."

39 The name suggests Isola Tavolara (Toraira, Toraio, Turarius) off the north-east coast of Sardinia. Other possible locations include Ruraria, near Cagliari and Cunicularia; Firaria, near the promontory of Calgiari; and Capraia, toward the Pisan coast.

40 Mark 6:34–44.

41 Exod. 16:13–15, 17:5–6.

meats to the Israelites, and who commanded water to flow from a rock to sustain his servants, as it pleased the power of God.

3. They soon spied a small boat of sailors that came to them from the region of Barbaria, which was subject to the control of Sardinia,[42] and they beseeched the Lord strenuously that they might land where the servants of God were marooned. By God's design, the sailors came for cold water to the foot of the mountain which is called Turarium, and there they found the servants of our Lord Jesus Christ praying and rejoicing in the Lord. The sailors greeted them and asked them for a blessing, and they all exchanged kisses. The servants of God said, "We beseech you to take us to Mount Jove." The sailors began to mock them and refused the request of the Lord's servants, for they recognized that they did not have any money for the fare that they might receive in reward for their efforts, and so went on their way, abandoning them. When their small boat had gained some distance from Turarium, a strong wind erupted over the water and began to whip it into waves, until they thought that the Charybdis would swallow them whole. They began to weep, for they saw their death from peril before them, and reckoned that nothing could save them from this danger. Then one of them remembered the offence they had committed against the servants of God, when they had refused to help God's friends. They then said among themselves, "Let's go and help the servants of God, and escort them to wherever they want to go, otherwise we'll perish!" Suddenly the sea was calm, and they hurried back to Mount Turarium, where they threw themselves down at the feet of the holy Senzius, begged for mercy for the wrong they had done, and asked the friends of God if they would like to board their little ship. Then the dearest confessors of Christ, Senzius, Mamilianus, and the three monks, offered up a prayer and boarded their small vessel. They crossed a tranquil sea and disembarked at Mount Jove. The sailors received a prayer from the servants of God, and took to the journey they had attempted before, now praising the glory of God, because they had recognized his miraculous power. The holy Senzius and the holy Mamilianus, once they had been deposited where they had been predestined to go under the Lord's command, celebrated and

42 Barbagia, a region of central Sardinia. The name derives from a tribe called the *Barbaricini* who fled Africa during the Vandal invasions and settled in the mountains near Cagliari; Pope Gregory I wrote to their duke, Hospiton, to encourage their conversion to Christianity (Gregory, *Reg.* IV.27), and purchased slaves from them (9.124). The region is also identified with a Carthaginian tribe who settled there in the third century BC: Brigaglia and Tola (eds) 2006.

blessed the Lord who had not spurned their prayers. And they began to devote themselves solely to God, praising him day and night. Then the servants of the Lord, Senzius, Mamilianus and the monks we have mentioned, practised great abstinence, and innumerable miracles happened on that very mountain "of Jove," which today is called Mount Christ.[43] They disciplined themselves with three- and four-days fasts, and wore no other clothing at all except hair-shirts while they incessantly praised God, and by divine counsel they were pleased to live there.

4. After they had been there for many days, their weakness from fasting prevented them from climbing to the top of the mountain. But one of them, whose name was Mamilianus, collected his strength, and having said a prayer, ascended the mountain to find there a most wicked dragon the size of a giant tree,[44] horrendously hissing flames from its mouth and with fire darting from its eyes. Trembling, Mamilianus threw himself on the ground, trusting in the compassion of God, then raised his eyes and held out his palms towards heaven, imploring its infinite power: "All powerful Lord God, who snapped shut the mouths of the lions lest they devoured Daniel in the den where he was sent to perish,[45] shut the mouth of this dragon, that he may not harm me or others any longer." Then fearlessly Mamilianus approached it and struck the evil reptile[46] with the staff he was holding, and the dragon died. Mamilianus quickly descended the mountain and told his brothers what had happened to him. Each one of them marshalled their strength and climbed to the top of the mountain. The servants of the Lord then lifted the dragon, which while alive four pairs of oxen would have been unable to move, and threw it down into the sea. From that moment the coldest water began to flow from the cave where the dragon had emerged, and still flows until this day. Upon hearing this the inhabitants of the island nearby hastily made their way there, and recognizing that such great miracles were wrought through the servants of God, they sought their

43 Isola del Montecristo. A monastery dedicated to Mamilianus is attested in documents of the tenth century: after centuries of decline, it was restored in 1323 but was largely abandoned after the incursions of the pirate Dragut in 1553. See Camici 2010 and Peria and Ferruzzi 2010.

44 *trabs* (lit. "beam") can mean *tree* but also *battering ram*, *ship*, *house*, and so on, connotations that further suggest the dragon's size. The description is similar to Gregory's description of the devil in *Dial.* II.18.12 (see above).

45 Dan. 6:16–23.

46 *serpens*, often interchangeable with *draco* in patristic thought and hagiography: Quacquarelli 1975.

prayers, begging them to intercede on their behalf before the majesty of God. Others brought their weak to the servants of God, and no matter what illness they suffered they were cured of it through their prayers. And so all glorified God and returned in health to their homes.

5. They had not stayed there long when Mamilianus's day of rest with the Lord drew nigh. He gave them a sign so that all would know when God would reclaim him from this life, telling them, "When you see a cloud rising up like smoke from the top of the mountain, know then that I have departed from this world." So those who lived nearby on that island waited expectantly to find out who among them was worthy to see this sign, and so have the honour of placing the body of the Lord's servant in a sepulchre. Then, by the surpassing mercy of God, the inhabitants of the island of Egilium,[47] more excited than all the others, were the first to see the sign, and quickly gathered together on Monte Christo before everyone else, and with all haste carried the body of holy Mamilianus onto a small boat while thanking the Lord Jesus Christ. The holy Senzius and the monks sang mellifluous chants before the body of the most holy confessor Mamilianus as they carted it across the seas. But then as the boat went along it began to rock and take in water, then suddenly it rained down hard from above, so that the other ships, which had hastened towards the sign that Saint Mamilianus had predicted, could no longer keep track of its location because of the density of the downpour. And so it pleased almighty God that the ship that bore the body of Saint Mamilianus was untouched by the rain. By the power of the Lord Jesus Christ they arrived at the mountain of Egilius [Giglio] praying and singing psalms, and the inhabitants of that place came out to meet them and received with great pride the body of Saint Mamilianus, more precious to them than gold or jewels, and buried it where right up to this day it still performs many miracles and mysteries. Then Saint Mamilianus's three monks, Istochius, Covaldus, and Infans, stayed by his body day and night praising the Lord, and performed many miracles themselves in the name of God. Through their prayers many infirm were cured of the afflictions that held them. Not long after Saint Mamilianus crossed over to Christ, the three monks were buried there also, laid to rest next to the tomb of the blessed Mamilianus.

6. But the holy Senzius, by divine inspiration, found a boat and sought the Roman coast. And when he disembarked from the boat in a small port that is

47 Isola del Giglio.

called "Columnae,"[48] within the boundaries of Centumcellae,[49] he thanked the Lord as well as the sailors. Not far from the shore was a village, and when Senzius arrived there he saw that its inhabitants were suffering terribly from a shortage of water. He therefore took up a hoe by himself and dug, and the coldest water flowed out, as it still does today. And when the blessed Senzius, Confessor of Christ, sought out a place that pleased him enough to inhabit, like some doctor sent by the will of God to cure those weak in faith who were suffering from their ailments, he began the journey unaware that an angel of God was leading him to where he was headed. And so he arrived at the city of Blera, which was held captive by the evil of a dragon. The Confessor of Christ made a small refuge not far away on the mountain next to the city of Blera that is called Olim,[50] and there began to earn a living by making sandals. He never kept for another day whatever he earned from his handiwork, but instead gave it away to everyone who needed it. O truly you are the Confessor of Christ, who shunned earthly wealth, but never lost eternal wealth! You gave up earthly cities, and gained heavenly Jerusalem! O sublime priest, who surrendered your very self in sacrifice to the Lord! The unknowing Blerani were still blind despite holding among them the very light through which they were destined to be illuminated; the light wished to lie low, but could not, like a jewel hidden in a dunghill, but it remained unsullied by the dung.[51] He thought to conceal himself, who had come to win over the Blerani.

7. While the blessed Senzius demonstrated the many gifts of God in that little refuge, he devoted himself unceasingly to the Lord with hymns, singing psalms and readings day and night (and with the support of God protecting the Blerani, for God did not wish them to be denied such a patron, but instead turned up the lamp and placed it upon its stand, so that it might shine for all who were in that dark house[52]). And so it happened that a certain shepherd

48 Cf. MS *Florentium,* "portus columnae," "port of the pillar." That is, a port in which a column had been erected to aid navigation. Susi 2000, 22, identifies this port with a landing at the mouth of the Mignone river, which belonged to the monastery of Santa Maria del Mignone, a dependant of the abbey of Farfa (see introduction above).

49 Civitavecchia.

50 Lit. "formerly," "of old," or "once upon a time." It may represent a lacuna in the text ("... once called ... ."). The Bollandists note that MS *Spoletanus* (see introduction above) reads *Civanus.*

51 The motif is common to literature, e.g., Phaedrus, *Fables* 3.12, but also draws from scripture: Ezek. 7:19; Luke 14:35; Phil. 3:8.

52 Matt. 5:14–16, Luke 8:16, 11:33.

with his flock of sheep took the path in front of the humble hospice of the servant of God. Saint Senzius saw a beautiful lamb amidst the flock, and asked the shepherd to give it to him. The shepherd responded, "The lamb you ask for yourself I am reserving to be the ram of the flock." Three days later when the shepherd lead his sheep out to pasture, the aforesaid lamb, which Saint Senzius had requested, was taken by a wolf while the shepherd looked on. By God's assistance, the wolf then brought the lamb to Saint Senzius and deposited it at his feet. Seeing this very same lamb, the blessed Senzius thanked the Lord for performing such great miracles on behalf of his servant, and he nourished the lamb for the entire year. When the year was up, the same shepherd who had refused to give the lamb to Saint Senzius took the path that ran by the hospice and saw Saint Senzius, whom he reproached about his portent, saying to him, "Your request was not a good one, but was rather evil: that lamb you asked me for was taken by a wolf right before my own eyes." Saint Senzius then said to the shepherd, "Shepherd, would you recognise the brandings on that lamb, which you say was taken by a wolf a year ago, if you saw it again, or not?" The shepherd responded, "Yes, I think I would recognise it." The blessed Senzius then showed him the lamb, now grown into a ram. Seeing it the shepherd recognized from his branding that it was the lamb in question, and prostrated himself at the feet of the holy Senzius, Confessor of Christ, begging him to grant him pardon, and to intercede for the sins he had committed, for he realized that this was a man of God.

8. Now this was the first miracle Saint Senzius performed in the city of Blera. Hearing of it, the inhabitants of the city professed Christ with their whole hearts, and seeing the holy man's miracles, they brought to him their own who were restrained by illness to lay them before the feet of Saint Senzius. The holy Senzius invoked the Lord Jesus Christ on behalf of the sick, and they returned to the city in health, together praising the Lord. And since they then recognized the great powers in the Confessor of Christ, they all unanimously beseeched him to expel the dragon that was beneath the wall of city, from whose poisonous breath a great many sinners were in danger of infection. The holy Senzius instructed them to perform three-day and four-day fasts, then he fearlessly went to the place where the dragon was, knelt on the ground, raised his eyes and extended his palms upward towards heaven, and began to pray, saying, "God of Abraham, God of Isaac and God of Jacob, you who have named your triple invocation after these three patri-

archs,[53] who sent your word down from heaven to renew the world that had fallen, who made the whirlpool swallow up Pharaoh together with his haughty ministers,[54] who gave food to the Israelites in the desert solitude,[55] who caused water to flow from rock,[56] who bestowed your servant Moses on Mount Sinai with the stone tablets of law inscribed without stylus,[57] who ordered the sun to stand still over Gibeon while Joshua was at war,[58] you I invoke against this dragon, whose breath plagues the inhabitants of the city of Blera every day. Heed me, your servant, and restrain it from its evils. Designate me to banish this serpent of iniquity from this place, so that it may no longer harm the inhabitants of the city of Blera." After saying this prayer, he fearlessly went up to the dragon, bound its mouth, and beating it with his staff, drove it from the cavern in which that most evil thing dwelled as though it were a little donkey. Seeing from a distance such great miracles of God, all of the Blerani followed after him at a rapid pace. He continued to drive the dragon with his staff until he crossed the river called the Minione,[59] which empties into the great sea, and pursued it to there, where he tied it up and condemned it to the depths of the abyss in the name of the Lord Jesus Christ, and in that same place he was condemned for all time.

9. And because there were still many at that time who were strangers to the faith, the holy Senzius revealed that he was engaged in the priestly order. Then he constructed a baptismal font, and recalled to the religion of the Christians those whom he found to be pagans. O most blessed priest, not only a confessor but also a martyr! For there are two types of martyrdom, one that takes place in secret, the other in public[60]; in one you are cut down by the sword, in the other you torture yourself. Back then you destroyed dragons, now you triumph with the Blerani. Rejoice, O city of Blera, in so great a patron, you who once wept from the menace of the dragon. Hasten now all

53 Exod. 3:15.
54 Exod. 14:26–28.
55 Exod.16:13–15.
56 Exod. 17:5–6.
57 Exod. 31:18, 32:15–16.
58 Josh. 10:12–14.
59 Mignone river. Its closest point to Blera is about 8.5 km SSW.
60 The phrase is verbatim from Gregory, *Dial.* III.26; what follows differs considerably.

of you to the triumph of the holy confessor, that you may receive the grace of the Saviour. Throughout the rest of his life Saint Senzius performed many miracles, but we have not found any written down for want of a writer. And so, reader, I have set down whatever my abilities have allowed. At the order of our Lord Jesus Christ, he achieved the reward of life in peace, on the eighth day from the Kalends of June, and was placed in a sepulchre by the fearful men who built the basilica, where even until today many miracles and blessings take place, in the presence of our Lord Jesus Christ, who lives and reigns forever. Amen.

13 JUNE

The Life of Cetheus of Pescara

The *Passion of Cetheus of Pescara*, or Aternum, as the city was called before the eleventh century, is one of the few works of hagiography that mention the Lombards, who invaded Italy in 568. The Lombards play a key role in this saint's story, as villains who kill Bishop Cetheus, but also as pious town folk concerned for their property and their lives during the height of the Lombard invasions. The *Passion of Cetheus* has been mostly ignored as evidence for the period, in part because Cetheus has frequently been cited as the bishop of Amiternum (today San Vittorino d'Aquila), as portrayed in the only printed version of the *Passion*, that edited and published by the Bollandists in 1698.[1] But new evidence, including the rediscovery of an earlier manuscript of the text (Venice, Biblioteca Nazionale Marciana, lat. Z 356), which contains different readings, and recent archaeological findings in Pescara and the surrounding region, confirms that the correct location of Cetheus's career and martyrdom is Aternum, as local legend in Pescara has always maintained for its patron saint. Moreover, many elements of the *Passion of Cetheus* suggest a contemporary source behind its composition: it contains verifiable information on the late antique topography of Aternum/Pescara, which became of key strategic importance for the control of central Italy in this period.[2] A near-contemporary date for the *Passion* is also suggested by the claim in its final chapters that Cetheus's body floated across the Adriatic to Zadar, where he was worshipped and interred as the holy martyr "Peregrinus" (meaning "traveller" or "foreigner"). Previously dismissed as hagiographic fantasy, the "Zadar epilogue" reflects Byzantine and papal interests in control over Dalmatia in the early seventh century, when Zadar emerged as the new capital of the province in the wake of Slav and Avar invasions. The *Passion* demonstrates Dalmatia's close connections with Byzan-

1 BHL 1730–1731; AA. SS. Iun. II, 689–693. Exceptions to dismissing the *Passion* were Thomas Hodgkin 1892–1896, 6: 100–104, and Lanzoni 1927, 363. On Amiternum, see Clementi 2003.

2 Detailed in Everett 2015a.

tine Italy and the key role of maritime cities such as Pescara and Zadar in maintaining imperial control of the Adriatic Sea.

City and Cult

Aternum/Pescara (and its river) was on the border of what became the two Lombard duchies, remote from Lombard centres of power, and had served for centuries as a key link in the chain of maritime cities along the Adriatic used by Ravenna to maintain communication, supplies, and ferry personnel to and from Constantinople. The fate of the city is mostly unknown during this entire period: recent archaeological excavations (conducted 1990–1992 and 2002–2003) in Pescara suggest the city remained in Byzantine hands until the mid-seventh century.[3] The *Passion of Cetheus* therefore documents Pescara's brief period of barbarian captivity in the events it records, and also the city's restoration to the empire by the text's very composition and pro-Roman stance. When Pescara was retaken by the Byzantines can only be inferred: the *Passion* records that the town was under the authority of Umblo after he sentenced Cetheus to death, but Umblo "and all of his followers died" (as predicted by Cetheus), and "all of his wealth came to nothing" (ch.16), which may be more than a simple trope, given the preoccupation with property in the *Passion* (ch.4). The strategic importance of Pescara, as the next link from Ortona in the Byzantine chain of maritime towns, and what we know about Ortona from Gregory's letters and recent archaeological investigation[4] suggest that the city would have been taken back into imperial control soon after Umblo's death, perhaps by Vitalianus, the count of Ortona himself (see below).

The *Passion of Cetheus* is our only medieval notice of the saint or his cult. Our earliest testimony to the cult otherwise is the mention (in 1593) of his relics resting in the church of San Gerusalemme in Pescara, which was built in the eleventh century. By the eighteenth century, San Gerusalemme had a chapel dedicated to Cetheus and was associated with the saint.[5] Cetheus was declared patron saint of the modern town when it was formally re-established and

3 Staffa 1991, 2006b, 2010. In contrast, Amiternum (San Vittorino) was largely abandoned after the fourth century: Staffa 1991.

4 On Gregory's letters concerning Ortona (*Reg.* I.32, IV.39, IX.195), see Everett 2015a. Archaeology: Staffa 2004; Zanini 1998, 258. On these and other defensive walls in Italy in this period, see Christie 2006, 281–400.

5 Staffa and Pellegrini (eds) 1993.

deemed capital of the province of Pescara in 1927. A new cathedral was commissioned at the same time, largely thanks to the writer Gabriele d'Annunzio, demolishing the previous church, Santissimo Sacramento, apparently also dedicated to Cetheus. The new building, called the Tempio della Concilazione to reflect the pact between Mussolini's Fascist government and the Vatican in 1929, became the cathedral of the diocese of Penne and Pescara in 1949, but was not consecrated as such until 1977, when relics of Cetheus were transferred from Chieti to the cathedral at Pescara, where they remain today.[6] How and when Cetheus's relics ended up at Chieti remains unknown[7] and is at odds with the *Passion*'s claims for his body being interred at Zadar.

The Passion of Cetheus and the Lombard Invasions

The *Passion of Cetheus* opens by setting the events it records among irreconcilable dates: "In the time of the most blessed Pope Gregory [590–604], when Phocas ruled the Roman Empire from Constantinople [602–610], and Faroald governed the duchy of Spoleto [584?–590/591: see below]." Phocas's reign seems the odd one out, for it is difficult to square with the *Passion*'s portrait of the arrival in Aternum of the two Lombard warlords, Umblo and Alahis, as part of the initial Lombard invasion, when Lombards arrived from Pannonia and "scattered themselves here and there, invading the territories of the Romans, Samnites, and Spoletans." The *Passion* makes no mention of King Alboin and the initial Lombard invasion of northern Italy (568/569), and seems to be unaware of Paul the Deacon's *History of the Lombards*, our only narrative source for these events and written over two centuries later. According to Paul, the two southern duchies were created during the interregnum period (574–584), a period he describes as one of rampant, uncontrolled expansion for Lombard dukes.[8] According to Paul, Faroald was the first duke of Spoleto "around the same time" as Pope Gregory I wrote his *Moralia* while in Constantinople (c.579–585); he also informs us that Faroald invaded Classe "with an army of

6 Staffa 1991; Bianchetti 1997.

7 Lanzoni 1927, 375–376. The church of Chieti exercised considerable control over Pescara by the eleventh century: Meaolo 1996.

8 Paul, *HL* II.32. Paul may have been using the lost chronicle of Secundus of Trent (Gardiner 1983). Paul's description has received copious commentary: Goffart 1980, 1988; Pohl 1997; Everett 2003a, 72–80; Moro 2004. On historiography of the Lombards, see Mores 2011.

Lombards and stripped the wealthy city of all of its riches, leaving it naked," an event confirmed in other sources but of uncertain date and significance for the beginning of the independent duchy.[9] Faroald's successor, Ariulf, who we know from Gregory's letters was duke of Spoleto by 591, appears to have fought for the Byzantines on the Tigris river against the Persians in 582: how and why Ariulf replaced Faroald as duke of Spoleto is unclear,[10] and the situation for the establishment of Benevento is no clearer.[11] The historian Gian Piero Bognetti argued that the creation of the two large duchies of Spoleto and Benevento was initially sponsored by the Byzantine administration to create regions that would serve as buffers to more incursions from Lombard and other warlords.[12] This is plausible given what we know of other Lombard warlords and dukes in this period, many of whom switched sides for Byzantine gold, some several times, and many became loyal servants of the empire and trustees of Pope Gregory.[13]

The political intrigue recorded in the *Passion*, of a Lombard invader (and also Cetheus, according to Biblioteca Nazionale Marciana, lat. Z. 356) forming secret alliances with the Byzantine commander in the next port town, Ortona, to eliminate a Lombard rival, certainly accords with the situation in Italy in 574–604. The *Passion*'s own dating to the pontificate of Gregory and dukedom of Faroald together allows for a date of 590–591, and we have further confirmation in the career of Vitalianus, the "count" of Ortona,[14] if he was the same Vitalianus, a military commander, mentioned in Pope Gregory's letters. In 592 Gregory wrote to Vitalianus and his commander colleague, Maurice, urging

9 Also noted in the epitaph of Drotculf (also recorded by Paul), another barbarian who switched sides: *HL* III.13. On Drotculf, see *HL* III.18–19; for Faroald's sons, *HL* IV.16: only the victor's name, Teudelapius, was recorded. On the duchy of Spoleto, see Conti 1982.

10 Upon Ariulf's death, Faroald's two eldest sons fought over control of the duchy, a struggle curiously reminiscent of Alahis and Umblo's fight in the *Passion of Cetheus*.

11 On Zotto and Arichis, see *HL* IV.18. On Lombards in the south, see the studies in Roma (ed) 2010.

12 Bognetti 1966–1970, 3: 439–476. Bognetti argued that Lombard defections were in conjunction with the failed attempt of Baduarius to recapture Italy in 575. Cf. Gasparri 1978, 86–87.

13 Everett 2003a, 69–72; Brown 1984, 70–75.

14 The term *comes* was used during the period of Cetheus's lifetime (c.530–590) to designate different offices, including the commander of a garrison: Diehl, 1888, 148–149; Brown 1984. The Marciana codex calls Umblo and Alahis counts (ch.6). The title "count" may have been a logical addition for the hagiographer, who doubtless knew the term from earlier hagiographic sources.

them to attack the Lombard Duke Ariulf from the rear should the duke march on Rome. From Gregory's second, rather panicked letter that year to Vitalianus and Maurice, we learn that Ariulf had sent a letter to the pope, intimating that the town of Sovana (in Tuscany) had gone over to the Lombard side. Gregory asked the commanders to investigate, and to take hostages from Sovana and bind them with oaths, "once again ... soothing them with your words," to ensure that the "citizens of Sovana have persisted in the loyalty that they promised to the republic."[15] The scene of political intrigue at Sovana portrayed in Gregory's letters is similar to that which we find in the *Passion of Cetheus,* with the citizens first forced to choose between two warlords, one of whom, Alahis, sided with the Byzantines, but ultimately they chose to follow the victor, Umblo, even to the point of condemning a bishop who challenged his authority. Vitalianus's use of intrigue, subterfuge, and bribery, as found in both the *Passion* and Gregory's letters, matches what we know of other Byzantine commanders during the interregnum period, as they tried to prevent the Lombards from expanding into central Italy. As the Emperor Maurice (582–602) advised at the time in his war manual *Strategikon*, when dealing with light-haired peoples such as the Franks or the Lombards, use subterfuge and "pretend to come to agreements with them."[16] It seems that Gregory and Vitalianus both understood this policy well, and poor Bishop Cetheus did not.

Peregrinus at Zadar: Traces of a Lost Cult in Croatia

The curious tale of Cetheus's body floating across the Adriatic and arriving in Iadera, modern Zadar in Croatia, also offers evidence for a seventh-century date for the *Passion of Cetheus*. For Zadar was the second most important city in the Byzantine province of Dalmatia, and became the capital city (*archonty*) after Salona was destroyed by Avar and Slav raids in the 640s.[17] Moreover, the churches of Dalmatia were subject to papal jurisdiction, and popes such as Gregory and Pope John IV (640–642) strove to maintain Rome's influence in the area against local influences and direct interference from the exarch at

15 Gregory, *Reg.* II.28. See also 2.4, 2.27; Martindale 1992, *PLRE* 3B: 1379–1380, Vitalianus 3. On the letter of Ariulf, see Everett 2003a, 69–71.

16 *Strategikon*, 9.4, trans. Dennis 2001,120.

17 Brunelli 1913; Nikolič 2003, 2004. Dzino 2010, 92–154, plays down the Slav and Avar invasions and argues for a degree of continuity in Salona.

Ravenna. Gregory's surviving correspondence with the bishop of Zadar concerns a dispute with the bishop in neighbouring Salona, still Dalmatia's capital in this period, which placed Gregory in direct conflict with the exarch. From these letters we gain a glimpse of how Zadar was a key location in the Adriatic network of communications and personnel that connected Rome to Ravenna, and connected both to Constantinople. That Gregory summoned the bishop of Zadar to Rome[18] is yet another example of his strategy to invite troubling or troubled clergy to Rome to have their cases heard before the Roman curate,[19] and offers further support for the scenario given in the *Passion* of Gregory receiving the fleeing Cetheus and then welcoming an audience with the citizens of Aternum.

Preoccupation with of Dalmatia and Illyricum permeates Gregory's surviving correspondence, whether cajoling or warning Three Chapters schismatics, applying pressure on the exarch to recognise papal interests and authority, countering unwanted imperial influence in church affairs and the selection of bishops (as with Salona or Zadar), or monitoring the containment of Avar and Slav incursion into the area, for which Gregory is one of our earliest sources. "I am very much afflicted and disturbed over the race of Slavs that threaten you so greatly," he wrote to the repented and reformed Bishop Maximus of Salona in the year 600, a year after he granted Maximus the *pallium*, a symbol of Maximus's archiepiscopal authority restored.[20] Gregory might well have been disturbed, for Salona was destroyed as a viable political or ecclesiastical centre within a generation or two: the conventional date of Salona's collapse is 614/615, though archaeological evidence suggests continued, if reduced, habitation of the city and even some churches.[21] We have no reliable information on these tumultuous events, but Zadar emerges from this period as the *archonty* of the province by the 640s, a time when it also may have served as a metropolitan church with jurisdiction over Dal-

18 Gregory, *Reg.* IX.197 (July 599), receiving at the same time Honoratus, Gregory's defeated candidate for Salona. Gregory's letters concerning Zadar and the additions of the Marciana manuscript to the Zadar epilogue are discussed fully in Everett 2015b.

19 Markus 1997, 68–76; Martyn (trans) 2004, 74–81.

20 On the Slavs, see Gregory, *Reg.* X.15. See also 2.20 and 9.155. On *pallium*, see Gregory, *Reg.* IX.234. See also Paul, *HL* IV.24.

21 The conventional date of 614/615 for the fall of Salona (e.g., Fine 1991, 35, 49–59, 258; Kaegi 2003, 86) is derived from sequencing events in Constantine Porhyrogenitus's *De administrando imperii* (see below), which more recent scholarship rejects: Fine 2000; Curta 2001, 64–65. On archaeology, see Marović 1984 and Marin 1989.

matian churches.[22] The few sources we have for this period again show that the papacy was heavily invested in the province of Dalmatia. Pope John IV (640–642), who was born in Dalmatia and the son of a *scholasticus,* an imperial legal adviser of high rank, sent much money to Dalmatia and Istria "to redeem captives who had been despoiled by the barbarians." John also imported the relics of "the martyrs saints Venantius, Anastasius, Maurus, and many other martyrs whose relics he had ordered to be brought from Dalmatia and Istria" for internment at Rome.[23] Constantine Porphyrogenitus (writing in 948/949) states that Pope John IV sent missionaries to the Croats at the request of the Emperor Heraclius, and that after they were baptized, "the Croats made a covenant, confirmed in their own hands and by oaths sure and binding in the name of St Peter the apostle, that never would they go upon a foreign country and make war on it." In exchange the Croats received a benediction from Pope John IV to the effect that God himself would fight against invaders of their lands and that St Peter himself would intervene and grant them victories.[24] Constantine's *De administrando imperii* is replete with curious ethnographic tales of people's origins and habits, and this papal peace pact is clearly legendary, as is much of Constantine's description of the Croats.[25] Nevertheless, it appears that John IV was deeply involved in the political and religious life of his native Dalmatia – redeeming captives, sending in missionaries, and meddling with local cults – at the time when Zadar emerged as the capital of the province.

The period of c.600–642, between Pope Gregory's worry for Salona and Pope John IV's involvement with his homeland, offers a very likely political and ecclesiastical context for the composition of the *Passion of Cetheus*. Although Cetheus may have been killed in 590–591, the *Passion*, as it survives, may not have been written until well after Aternum/Pescara was safely back in the Byzantine fold, its church re-established, and the Lombards were settled under their monarchy in the north – sometime after c.600. The *Passion of Cetheus*, with its opening scenes of Pope Gregory bestowing benedictions on Cetheus, his

22 Fine 1991 argues that in seventh-century Dalmatia "there existed a collection of more or less equal and separate bishoprics without a suzerain bishop," but his argument is directed against tenth-century claims by the church of Split to have naturally succeeded Salona as metropolitan. On the church of Salona, see Duval 1999.

23 *LP* 74, trans. Davis 2000, 68. On *scholasticus*, see Brown 1984, 80, 132, 141. The *LP* is largely overlooked as evidence: Kaegi 2003; Curta 2001, 110.

24 *De administrando imperii,* ch.31, ed. Moravcsik, trans. Jenkins 1967, 149.

25 See Fine 1991, 49–59, Fine 2000. Likewise, Curta 2001, 64–66, but it is "the first record of a 'native' version of the past."

see, and the people of Pescara, promotes a close relationship between Rome and Pescara. Moreover, the *Passion*'s theme of a bishop battling against barbarian invaders (and losing) would certainly have had relevance for an audience of Dalmatian Christians at this time.

Text and Translation

The text translated below is primarily that edited by Papebroch for AA. SS. (Iun. II, 689–693) but incorporates the different readings contained in a twelfth-century manuscript, Venice, Biblioteca Nazionale Marciana, lat. Z 356, fol. 309r–313 (see Plate 1), which can be consulted in the diplomatic edition of Everett 2015a. The Marciana manuscript (*Marc.*), or another containing the same textual tradition, seems to have been known to some Italian antiquarians before Papebroch worked.[26] The Marciana manuscript provides a firmer foundation for assessing the *Passion*, rather than the text that appears in AA. SS., which was a composite text created from the consultation of two now unidentifiable or lost manuscripts ("Ex Ms. Bodecensi, collato cum Ms. Camaldulensi": see Everett 2015a). The Marciana codex corrects many of the misreadings that have dogged the history of Cetheus, especially his association with Amiternum rather than Aternum/Pescara (likewise Orte instead of Ortona). The different readings of the Marciana codex add or change certain events in the *Passio*, and contain additional dialogue – between Pope Gregory and Cetheus, between Pope Gregory and the citizens of Aternum, between Cetheus and his accuser, and, in the epilogue, concerning the bishop of Zadar: the most important additions are in chapters 1, 2, 5, 6, and 14–16. The Latin of the extra speeches and dialogue is more vulgar and colloquial than the rest of the text, which may reflect its pre-Carolingian composition.[27]

26 See Clementi 2003, Varrasso 2012, and Everett 2015a for these antiquarian notices.

27 Discussed further in Everett 2015a. On pre-Carolingian Latin in Italy, see Everett 2003a, 130–162; Herman 1988; Wright 1982, (ed) 1991; Zamboni 2000.

The Passion of Cetheus

1. In the time of the most blessed Pope Gregory, when Phocas ruled the Roman Empire from Constantinople, and Faroald governed the duchy of Spoleto, the tribe of the Lombards, not long after they left Pannonia, arrived at the borders of Italy, then scattered themselves here and there, invading the territories of the Romans, Samnites, and Spoletans. The two most evil and dishonourable men of this people, certainly the sons of concubines, one by the name of Alahis, the other Umblo, came to the city of Aternum[28] with their weapons of war and set up camp there, conducting raids and inflicting barbaric destruction. The venerable bishop of this city, whose name was Cetheus, could not bear their terrible cruelty, and so took flight, and made his way to the see of the most blessed Pope Gregory. When there standing before the pope, he dropped to his knees and kissed the feet of the blessed pontiff, saying, in tears, "Lord, venerable father and most holy pontiff, the city of Aternum has perished, and so I lapsed and fled to this holy see and have come to your threshold." The pontiff was stunned and trembled with fear, but then began to ask what adversity had struck the city. *When Bishop Cetheus, a man of God, described how the town had been destroyed by the tribe (*gens*) of the Lombards, the blessed pope entreated him, "Take comfort in the Lord, my son, take comfort, for the future holds that soon the tribe of the Lombards, who have forced you to flee, will be stung in their hearts and thereafter be loyal to this apostolic see, from which they will seek blessings."

[The Marciana codex contains a different ending: *Then the blessed Bishop Cetheus informed [*indicauit*] him all about how the city itself had been destroyed by the Lombard people [*gens*]. The blessed Gregory then asked him whether that people was Christian. He [Cetheus] responded, "They are Christians, and much more worship God,[29] and they venerate the miracles of the saints." Gregory said, "If they are truly Christians, we will not be sad without end: for the future holds that after a little time they will seek a blessing from this holy and apostolic see."]

28 The port of modern Pescara. On confusion over whether Cetheus was bishop of Aternus or Amiternum (mod. San Vittorino d'Aquila), see introduction above.

29 *multo magis Deum colunt*: a reference to Arianism? See Everett 2003a, 59–64, Fanning 1981. Papebroch, AA. SS. Iun. II 691 c, noted that codex C also contained this dialogue with Gregory, which reads *multo magis colunt sanctorum uirtutes*.

Plate 1: *Passio Cethei*. Venice, Biblioteca Nazionale Marciana, lat. Z 356, fol. 309r. By permission of Ministero dei Beni e delle Attività Culturali e del Turismo, Biblioteca Nazionale Marciana. Reproduction is prohibited.

2. Upon hearing this the venerable Bishop Cetheus fell silent, and immediately began to pray to the Lord all day and night, saying, "Take care of the town of Aternum with your divine powers, and breath your holy spirit into the hearts of the Lombards, until they repent the things they have done against my people and against me, and until they return me to my see where I unworthily held episcopal office, and may they all know that you alone are God, and that there is no other God except you." When he had sweated in holy prayer every night for a long time, the Lord heeded his entreaties, which he had poured out in tears, and fear of the Lord came upon that people, and they began to say to one another, "We do badly[30] not to go to the venerable city of Rome to bring back our holy Bishop Cetheus, whose blessing had always well protected us and all of our families [and everything that we possess. (*Marc.*)]. ★If we have harmed him or offended him in any way, let us humble ourselves before his presence, and he will pray for us, and we will be saved. Otherwise, unless we bring him back among us, we will all suffer a righteous vengeance from the Lord before long!" This sort of talk resounded daily throughout the entire town of Aternum until finally they all come together as one to go and retrieve the holy Bishop Cetheus from the city of Rome.

[The Marciana and Camaldolese codices have a different ending: ★and so in mourning and sorrow we shall come to our end unless he is quickly brought back and protects us with his blessing. For indeed as it is written, "whoever refuses a blessing from him will be distanced from him." We, therefore, are placed in misery, because we want to receive that blessing." This sort of talk continually rebounded about the whole city every day, until finally all met together and as one unanimously proclaimed, "Go to the city of Rome, and bring back our holy bishop." Agreed on this course of action, they then said, "We cannot travel to Rome without the command [*iussione*] of our lord.[31] But let us go to the city of Spoleto, and if the will of our lord manifests so, then with his counsel and permission [*consilio uel ordinatione*] we can travel more freely. Therefore arriving at Spoleto, they told their lord, saying, "If it is your command [*iussio*], we wish to go to the holy and apostolic see, in order that we can bring back our bishop." At this he was delighted, and said, "Let be what is

30 *male facimus*. *Marc.* reads *magnum scelus facimus*, "We commit a great crime ... ."

31 *d[omi]ni n[ost]ri*: *nomina sacra* are employed for all of these instances of *dominus*, probably a corruption of the text. The *dominus* of Spoleto here may have originally been a reference to a secular authority (Duke Faroald?): see above.

good, so that with the help of the Lord [*dominus*], his angel will be assigned to you, who can arrange your journey." To him all responded, "Amen."][32]

3. Therefore they left and arrived at the city of Rome, where they entered the church of the most blessed Apostle Peter, beating their heads, saying, "O blessed Peter, make your servant the pontiff Gregory agreeable, so that with your blessing we can return safe and unharmed to our city together with our bishop." In the meantime the most blessed Gregory was informed that [by means of the order [*per iussionem*] of their lord (*Marc.*)] the Lombards had come to receive a blessing from him, and he ordered them to come before his presence straight away. They then all prostrated themselves at his feet, crying and saying, "Holy father, we beg that you deign to restore our bishop to us." But he, rejoicing with his whole heart, responded, *"If you truly repent of your error, for which you have harassed the citizens of Aternum and forced a holy man to leave, especially since you profess to share the name of Christians along with them, then I shall bless you along with your homes and all that you possess." To this they responded by saying, "Truly we repent of whatever we have done against that town and its inhabitants. This is why we have come here with pure and simple hearts, most holy father, to receive your blessing and likewise to obtain your pardon."

[The Marciana codex ends this chapter differently: * "Listen, my sons, have you come to receive a blessing with your whole heart?" To him they responded, "With all of it." The highest pontiff was happy that they had come with their whole heart. Again he said to them, "Surely as you ask, my sons, I will hand over a blessing to you today."][33]

4. The blessed pontiff said, "The blessing of the Lord be upon you," to which they responded, "Amen." The blessed pope then added, "Let me go ahead and ask of your bishop whether it is his will to return to you, as you want."[34] Tak-

32 The same passage appears in codex C, recorded by Papebroch ("Ite ... . Amen"), AA. SS. Iun. II 691 d.

33 "Audite filii, ex toto corde uenistis benedictionem suscipere. At illi responderunt ex toto. Gauisus autem pontifex summus quod ex toto corde uenissent. Iterum dixit eis: Certe dicitis filii, ut homines benedictum hodie uobis tradam." *Homines* here is superfluous, probably a corruption.

34 *Marc.* adds here "... And I will give him to you with my own hands. And they said, 'Do what seems right to you, most holy father.' Then Gregory questioned the Bishop Cetheus, saying ... ."

ing some of them with him, he went to where the blessed Cetheus was and questioned him, saying, "My son, do you wish to return to your homeland, where you held episcopal office?" Cetheus [threw himself at his feet and in tears (*Marc.*)] said to him, "If it pleases your holiness, then I shall do as you say." The holy pontiff then said, "May it please the omnipotent Lord, for it greatly pleases me." Then Bishop Cetheus responded, "If it pleases God and yourself that I return there, I will fulfil your command without hesitation, especially for the sake of church property not being dispersed or sold off." At this the men who were present who had been sent there said, "Far be it from us to presume to disperse or sell off church property. On the contrary, for the remaining days of our lives we will increase its property, as will our descendants." The blessed Gregory said, "If it seems right to you, confirm this with an oath that church property will not be dissipated." They responded, "Whatever pleases you, holy father, we shall do." Immediately, they went out with the blessed Gregory and Bishop Cetheus to the body of the blessed Apostle Peter, and there swore an oath, saying, "We swear on this venerable body, holy father, and we steadfastly promise to your authority, that we will not sell off the property of the church, but will instead increase and preserve it, and that we will restore our father the Bishop Cetheus to his see with honour, and we shall undertake with a humble heart everything that your paternity has ordered us to perform, and preserve it with the greatest care."

5. Hearing their devotion, the blessed Gregory took satisfaction in the Lord, and after he blessed them, said, "Peace be with you, children." In response the blessed Cetheus said to the apostolic one, "and with your spirit." The holy Gregory said a prayer over them, granted them pardon and a blessing, and concluded by saying, "Go, children, and receive your bishop, and conduct him with dignity back to his see, and obey him in everything." They then retrieved their bishop and with great joy and festivity guided him back to his see, singing, in praise to him, "Glory to God in the highest," and so on. As they approached the city of Aternum, the priests and the entire clergy came out to meet them, and received the holy Bishop Cetheus with great joy and festivity, with hymns and canticles, and with every honour, as was befitting. He entered through the eastern gate, and was conducted to the church, and there he stayed for some time.

[The Marciana codex contains a different version of this chapter:
5a. Then the blessed Gregory said, "Peace be with you my sons." Bishop Cetheus said, "and with your spirit." At that same hour they received their

bishop from the hand of the pontiff with psalms and hymns and spiritual chants, exulting and saying, "Glory on high to the Lord" and "peace and goodwill be among men." Others said "Amen." Then[35] they all threw themselves at the blessed Gregory's feet and said, "Protect our journey, Lord, with your blessing." The pontiff said, "Blessing and glory and salvation be among you at all times until the end of time." To this all responded, "Amen." Then in all confidence they escorted back the blessed Bishop Cetheus, exulting and singing psalms. When they arrived at the river which is called the Piscaria, they stayed there almost half an hour.[36] And all the priests came and received their holy bishop with great joy and happiness, and they led him into the city of Aternum, saying, "Enter, blessed Lord. Your see is prepared for you." He entered through the eastern gate, and was led to the church where he remained for some time.]

6. Meanwhile, the aforementioned nobles, Alahis and Umblo, who had seized the command of the city for themselves[37] with Alahis occupying the eastern gate, Umblo the western, began to fight with each other after rivalry flared up between them, and sought to kill one another. And there was great sadness for all Christians in that city. Alahis, however, took counsel with his followers and decided to destroy the city [by using enemies [*per inimicos*] (*add. Marc.*)]. He sent an embassy to Vitalianus, count of the city of Ortona,[38] requesting that he come in the middle of the night to invade the town of Aternum, and destroy it completely. The blessed Cetheus was in his cell and was unaware of Alahis's

35 Papebroch, AA. SS. Iun. II, 691 g, recorded that codex C contained this blessing ("Then .... Amen"); it is unclear whether the whole chapter as found in the Marciana codex was there, but see the next note.

36 *dimidia hora*. This reference to Cetheus stopping at the Piscaria river, preceding that in chapter 12 below, was found also in codex C: Papebroch, AA. SS. Iun. II, 691 h.

37 *qui ducatum civitatis usurpaverant*. The Marciana codex opens this chapter differently: "In these days there were two counts there, one by the name of Alahis, the other Umblo, and Cetheus kept company (*conversatur*) with them in the city ... ," a detail that perhaps helps to explain the townsfolk's suspicion towards Cetheus (see above). Papebroch, AA. SS. Iun. II, 692 a, notes that C also read *comites duo*.

38 Following the Marciana codex, whereas the AA. SS. text has "Verilianus, count of Orte" (*Hortanensis civitas*) rather than Ortona (*Hortensis civitas*). Geopolitical logic demands Ortona as the place intended, and Ortona's key role in military affairs in this period is confirmed by recent archaeological investigation of the city: see Staffa 2004 and above. Pope Gregory (*Reg*. II.28; see also II.4 and II.27) wrote to a Byzantine military commander called Vitalianus stationed on the *Via Flamminia* in 591–592, who was commissioned to attack and destabilize Duke Ariulf of Spoleto's army in a manner reminiscent of the political intrigue described here.

scheme and how he sought to betray the city to enemies. But in this same city was a most Christian man called Fredo, and his wife, called Bona, a pious and God-fearing woman.[39] That evening they had entered the church and prayed, and after they finished praying they received a blessing from the bishop and returned home. When it was time for bed, they both lay on the bed as they usually did, but Fredo refused to take off his clothes, and tucked himself in with them on. His wife said to him, "Why did you lie down with your clothes on?" He answered her, "I am struck by severe trembling and am extremely frightened, because tonight this city will be destroyed." His wife said to him, "God will not allow[40] this city to be destroyed." But he said to her, "Bring me my weapons of war, place them near my head, and then we will rest secure."

7. In the middle of the night a shout went out in the midst of the city, "Get up, get up, a hostile people is invading this city." The most Christian Fredo therefore rose from his wife's side, seized his weapons of war, and hurried out, shouting, "Rise up, most holy father Cetheus, and pray for us, because this city is in peril, we are losing everything we have, and today we ourselves shall be killed by the sword." Cetheus quickly rose and jumped out of bed, then headed out into the main square and prayed to God, saying, "Lord Jesus Christ, Son of the living God, who liberated David from the hand of Goliath, the three boys from the burning fire, Daniel from the lion's den, and who also liberated Susannah from false accusations and Thecla from beasts, have pity on us, and liberate this city and its people from the enemy."[41] As he said this he banged his forehead on the ground in tears, and after he had prayed a while suddenly all of the enemy who were approaching were completely terrified by divine miracle, and so were humbled,[42] and many of them were killed that night.

39 The domesticity of Fredo and Bona is reminiscent of some tales of Lombard noble couples found in Paul the Deacon's *HL* (e.g., II.28–30, III.30, IV.37). *Marc.* contains a few extra phrases of dialogue between the couple, in a lower register of Latin: Everett 2015a.

40 *non faciet Deus*; cf. *Marc.*: *non satiat Deus*.

41 This sequence of prayers, known as the "*Libera* petitions," is a funeral liturgy from the early church: it was quoted by Augustine and appears in martyr narratives from the fifth century onwards. See Brown Tkacz 2002, 10–37, and Sicard 1978.

42 *Marc.* adds "and rising he made a sign of the cross over himself and immediately his enemies were humbled." See also codex C: Papebroch, AA. SS. Iun. II, 692 c.

8. On the morning of the following day, the inhabitants of the city gathered together to see how the enemy had managed to enter the town.[43] They found a ladder set up at the back of the church of the blessed Thomas,[44] by which the enemy had come and left. They learned from some reports that everything that had happened was planned by Alahis. They chained Alahis and brought him in the midst of the people, and everyone shouted together in one voice, "Let's kill this most evil man, who wanted to kill by sword so many Christian souls, and hand over everything we have to the enemy to be destroyed."[45] And again they shouted, "Let him be killed as quickly as possible, because he deserves to die from many torments." While they debated about which tortures to use to kill him, the blessed Bishop Cetheus said to him, "Child, why did you commit such a crime against this city, only to be compelled to suffer a grievous death now?" Then he turned to the people standing around them and said, "Listen to me, children, and do not lay a hand on this man, lest God consider it a sin on your part. If it pleases you, hear my plan: put him in prison, and let him stay there for some time[46]; then let there be a meeting of everyone in this town, from the youngest to the oldest, and taking him from his prison, force him to perform penance for many days until his spirit might be saved in the Lord God."

9. When the blessed Cetheus said this, the most wicked Umblo came up to him and said, very violently, "And you also, Cetheus, were part of this plan, whereby the city was to be betrayed to enemies, for that ladder that we found at the back of the church of the blessed Thomas was placed there through your magical tricks, and therefore you are no longer worthy of holding the office of bishop." The blessed Bishop Cetheus responded, saying, "May God never allow me to be contaminated by such an evil affair, my child; nevertheless, since the

43 *Marc.* adds the (correct) detail that the church and ladder were at the *porta orientalis* and that "because of these stairs behind the church the most wicked Umblo applied many tortures to the holy Bishop Cetheus." Likewise, codex C, Papebroch, AA. SS. Iun. II, 692 d.

44 The presence of this church in Pescara is corroborated in documents dating to 991 and 1078, which describe it as next to the gated wall by the sea; it was no longer extant by the sixteenth century. The topography described here in the *Passio* matches these later documentary sources and recent archeological excavation of late antique Pescara: see Staffa 1991, 2006b, and above.

45 *Marc.* adds "For indeed he is truly a traitor and an Arian minister of the devil" (*Nam certe uerus temptator est et arrianias minister diaboli*). Other references to Arianism, ch.11 (*Marc.*) and 12. *Marc.* also contains another, similar passage wherein the townsfolk call for and justify putting Alahis to death: Everett 2015a.

46 *Marc.* reads "for some time or days of suffering" (*uel dies malos*).

people are gathered here, I swear on the crucifix of the Son of God, on the inseparable Trinity, the holy Gospels of Christ, and even upon that holy episcopal blessing, which I undertook although unworthy, that I am ignorant of and uninvolved in this plan, nor did I ever wish to sell off or betray this city to enemies, nor take part in such a plan, nor allow it. Instead I have prayed humbly day and night that God would deign to grant us peace and harmony." While the holy Cetheus expounded the truth and defended himself with these statements, the aforementioned Umblo, not wishing to hear Cetheus any longer, ordered the previously mentioned Alahis to be brought in chains into the midst of the city and for his head to be cut off before the entire populace.[47]

10. When Alahis had been conducted to the place for his decapitation, the holy Cetheus then exclaimed, in a loud voice, "My heart and my flesh cry out for the living God," and likewise, "God have mercy upon me, have mercy upon me, for in you my soul takes refuge, and I shall take refuge in the shadow of your wings, until the disaster has passed." And again, "O God, whom I praise, do not remain silent, for wicked and deceitful men have opened their mouths against me."[48] When he reached the end of that psalm, the executioner [*speculator*] was completely terrified from fear. He cut off Alahis's head, but did not dare raise his hand against Cetheus. The most wicked Umblo was utterly furious when he heard this, and ordered Cetheus to be brought before him, and in the presence of the people gathered there he said to him, "O Bishop Cetheus, a little while ago you were a preacher, yet what has happened that you now appear before the people in chains?" The holy bishop responded, "I was never able to separate you, vilest of men, from the devil, because you dwell with him, and will do so eternally. And now I tell you with the word of Christ, that you will be a homeless exile on earth, just as Cain who killed his righteous brother, Abel, and so you will die, possessed by the devil. I, however, am the unworthy servant of the servants of God, and I shall save by the power of he whose voice raises the dead." Raising his eyes up to heaven he said, "God the creator of everything seen and unseen, who examines the kidneys and hearts of all men that you may know their faith and minds, examine and see the mind of your servant, if there is any truth in what they say against me, because deceitful men

47 Instead of "before the people," *Marc.* reads "at the eastern gate"; likewise, codex C, Papebroch, AA. SS. Iun. II, 692 e.

48 Ps. 83:3; 56:2; 108:2. The Marciana version contains a longer speech by Cetheus paraphrasing Ps.108:2–7; likewise codex C, though Papebroch did not provide the text: AA. SS. Iun. II, 692. Cf. Everett 2015a.

have surrounded me, and have had me bound and whipped without cause, and there is no one to help besides you God, whom I beg to judge my case."

11. And so he perspired in prayer and singing psalms while held fast in chains, never once afraid to speak to the most evil Umblo, or to his subordinates, because he was filled with the spirit of God.[49] Eventually a voice from heaven called out to him, saying,

> Bishop Cetheus, do not be afraid; behold you have the precious crown before the throne of your God. For the suffering you have endured, the holy archangels Michael, Gabriel, and Raphael will summon you. And because you have been an excellent preacher to the people, the Lord has heard your prayers, which you never ceased to pour out to him day and night.

After he heard this voice, the athlete of Christ received a boost of courage, and then spoke even more to the enemies, because of his destiny to be summoned to the kingdom of heaven, where he longed to be with an ineffable desire, every day hoping for the reward of martyrdom.

12. Therefore he said to the subordinates who kept him bound,

> Why, o sons of iniquity and ministers of hell, do you hold me in chains? Perhaps you do so because you know I am a servant of God? But in his name I would gladly suffer not only chains but death itself. You, however, Arian and faithless, will have your repose with Judas Iscariot, among inextinguishable fires. Your fate will be that of the lost and lonely, you will be accursed forever, because you often spurned my preaching and refused to hear the censure of truth. And as for you, Umblo, most abominable of them all, may there be no one to even offer you the kiss of peace. And may whoever blesses you be cursed, for he who cursed and expelled Satan from the community of the just will surely curse you.

13. Then Umblo was wild with fury and ordered him to be lead in chains to the river that is called the Pescara,[50] and there to be hurled off the bridge that is

49 *Marc.* adds "And so he argued while chained for a long while with the Arian and sacrilegious people" (*Itaque cum diu cum arriano atque sacrilego populo uinctus altercaretur*).

50 *Piscaria.*

called the Marble.[51] The blessed Cetheus, heading for death with joy, began to intonate psalms, saying, "Do not cast me from your presence, or take your holy spirit from me. Restore to me the joy of your salvation and grant me a willing spirit to sustain me."[52] He was then thrown into the river, but protected by God's help, he was swept onto the shore safe and sound. The people were furious, and at the order of the tyrant they seized him and hurled him into the river again and again, and like the first time, the holy bishop was protected by God's help and was swept onto dry ground. The most evil Umblo saw this and ordered him brought before his presence. When the man of God was brought forward, Umblo ordered his wicked followers to tie him to a miller's grindstone, which weighed almost five hundred pounds, so that he would sink to the bottom. But again Cetheus raised his eyes to heaven and began to intonate a psalm, saying, "O Lord God who saves me, day and night I cry out before you. May my prayer come before you, and save me from those going down into the pit."[53] When he had completed these prayers he was hurled into the river, and immediately rendered his spirit. But his holy body floated about on the water, the grindstone still attached to his neck.[54] At God's command and through the hands of his angels, the body of the blessed martyr was borne between the water's depths and the dry land until one night it was ejected near the city of Zadar.[55]

14. There was a fisherman in that place by the name of Valerianus who one night was wading through these same waters to repair his nets as he usually did,

51 *marmoreus*. *Marc.* reads "marmoriolus," probably reflecting its local name in spoken Latin. This Roman bridge, dating from the imperial period but refurbished in the fourth or fifth century, was still in use in the sixteenth century: see Staffa 1991, 2006a–b, and introduction above.

52 Ps. 50:13–14.

53 Ps. 87:2–3; 27:1

54 *Marc.* reads "And the most wicked Umblo went out of the city with the people and his ministers and waited (*aspitiebat*) for a long while until the blessed body was carried off into the distance." The word *aspitiebat* may be late Latin/early Romance? (cf. mod. Italian *aspetto*.)

55 Latin *Iadera*, Croatia, which became the capital of the Byzantine province of Dalmatia after the destruction of Salona (mod. Solin) in the 640s by Avar and Slav invasions. The diocese of Iadera/Zadar was founded in 381: a bishop of Zadar, Sabinianus, corresponded with Gregory the Great (*Reg.* VI.48; VII.17; VIII.11, 24; IX.179, 234). A late ninth-century church there dedicated to St Donatus reflects Carolingian influence in the area, although the Franks formally granted the city to the Byzantine empire in the treaty of Aachen in 812.

when suddenly a bright light beamed from the shore where the blessed body lay on the sand-dunes. Amazed, he quickly headed out in his boat to see who it might be. He carefully looked over the body, but did not recognize it, so hurried back and announced to the bishop and the consul of the city how he had seen a corpse with a stone tied to his neck lying on the dunes. When he heard this the bishop instantly gathered the clergy of the city together and hurried off with them to the shore, where they found the holy body lying on dunes, just as they were told, with a stone tied around his neck.[56] Noticing his angelic face, which had been suffocated in water for the name of our Lord Jesus Christ, they decided to pick him up with all due reverence and care and bury him with appropriate respect. But because his name was unknown, they called him *Peregrinus* [foreign, foreigner], since his body was found like some unknown foreigner.[57] They buried him amid sweet fragrance in a place near the shore where he was found by the sea.

15. Thereafter when fishermen sailed along the shoreline in their habitual way they frequently saw a lantern glowing where his head lay, which omnipotent God deigned to exhibit because of his servant's merits.[58] In these days a man in the city of Zadar who had been blind since birth said to some of the nobles of the city, "I am going to that corpse buried on the shore, and if God grants me my sight there, know for sure that it is holy." To this they responded, "Go, just as you say, and see if God deigns to show you the effects of his mercy." They took the hand of the blind man and led him to the tomb of the blessed martyr. Sinking to his knees he prayed in tears, saying, "God who made heaven, earth, and the sea, and all things in these, who rescued Adam from the fire after 5,552 years, who freed Jonah from the belly of the whale, who restored sight to the blind man at the pools of Siloam,[59] restore sight to me, a sinner, through the merits of the foreign fellow buried here, if there is any merit in you. Then

56 *Marc.* includes an episcopal speech: "The bishop of Zadar said to the leader (*consul*) and the people of the city, 'Listen to me, my sons. Have a boat brought to us and let us get to that body, before wild beasts and animals devour it. For that would be a great sin for us and for the city.' They responded to him, 'do as you wish father, we all will support you.'" Likewise, codex C: Papebroch, AA. SS. Iun. II, 693 c.

57 *Marc.* adds "All were weeping over him as they carried him in great lamentation and no damage to him was found." Likewise, codex C: Papebroch, AA. SS. Iun. II, 693 d.

58 *Marc.* adds, "The wise and fearful (*sapientes et timorati*) were saying that the Lord has deigned to show miracles through him [Cetheus's body]." Likewise, codex C: Papebroch, AA. SS. Iun. II, 693 e.

59 John 9:7–8.

all will know that his body is holy and should be venerated." As soon as he stopped speaking, he opened his eyes, and saw light. He got up and hurriedly ran back to the city shouting and saying, "I thank you, Lord Jesus Christ, King of kings and Lord of lords,[60] who have deigned to show unto me such a miracle, through the body of your most blessed servant Peregrinus!"

16. When they heard this all the inhabitants of the city went to the bishop and the consuls, and adopting their advice they all went together giving glory to God by singing psalms and carrying crosses to the place where they first consigned his consecrated body to the tomb.[61] They respectfully removed him from there and placed him in another place at the nine-mile mark from the city. As for the most evil Umblo, he was seized by a demon, and just as the blessed Bishop Cetheus predicted to him, he and all of his followers died, and all of his wealth came to nothing. *The blessed Bishop Cetheus suffered in the city of Aternum, and as we said above, and was then carried across the swirling waters to the city of Zadar, where he was called Peregrinus, with our Lord Jesus Christ reigning, to whom go glory and honour forever. Amen.

[Marciana codex reads, *"The blessed Bishop Cetheus suffered under the most wicked consul Umblo on the Ides (13th) of June and in the city of Zadar is called Peregrinus the martyr, with our Lord Jesus Christ reigning ..."]

60 Deut.10:17; 1Tim. 6:15–16; Apoc. 19:16.

61 The Marciana codex differs considerably here (continued from ch.15: italics at the end signal the return to ch.16 as found in AA. SS.): "And let everyone know that this body should be recognized and venerated"; [ch.16] "And rising up he quickly returned to the city of Zadar. And when the citizens saw that he had been healed and could see clearly, they were all amazed that such miraculous things can happen through the blessed martyr Peregrinus, so that a man blind from birth was lightened by his prayers. Then together they all hurried from the town to his tomb and prostrated themselves. They asked that they might be worthy to receive the blessed body into the city of Zadar to rest there in peace. Later on the bishop of the city came with its priests and consuls singing psalms and giving glory to God. They arrived with crosses at the holy body of Peregrinus, who had travelled [peregrinatus fuerat] through the sea with a stone tied to his neck, and they lifted him from that place. *They buried him* with aromatics *in another place at the nine mile mark from the city of Zadar.*"

26 JUNE

The Passion of Vigilius of Trent

The *Passion of Vigilius of Trent, Bishop and Martyr*[1] records how its hero, Vigilius, the third bishop of Trent (c.385–400/405), evangelized the town and surrounding region, including Verona and Brescia, and also deep in the countryside, where he was killed by pagans: when Vigilius smashed up their statue, they smashed in his head with rocks. Outside of the *Passion* we know little about Vigilius, a contemporary of Ambrose, who wrote to Vigilius upon his consecration with pastoral advice for ministry in a diocese infused with paganism.[2] Even more prescient is that Vigilius himself was a hagiographer who wrote about three martyrs he knew who also died at the hands of wild pagans in Anaunia (Val di Non, thirty-five kilometres north of Trent), as mentioned in this *Passion* (ch.5). Vigilius's account of the three martyrs served as source for another, later *Passion* concerning the three martyrs, and, spookily, as a source for the *Passion of Vigilius,* which has been dated variously from the sixth to the ninth century.[3] The chain of textual dependence in these three works provides us with a glimpse of hagiographic traditions at work, and how local legends of early Christians suffering were readapted and employed to reconstruct the region's past. The key to the text's date lay in its claims that the relics of the three martyrs were at Trent, that Vigilius founded over thirty churches in the territories of Verona and Brescia, and that Vigilius was consecrated by the "bishop of Aquileia" (ch.2), which suggest the *Passion* was written in the early eighth-century, when these four cities shared in an unprecedented geopolitical unity under Lombard rule, and "Old" Aquileia (Cormons/Cividale) held primacy over Trent.

1 BHL 7976; AA. SS. Iun. IV (Venice, 1774) 163–168; Cesarini-Sforza 1905.
2 Ambrose, *Ep.* 62, ed. Banterle 1988; PL 16: 1025. On the letter, see Martini 1997.
3 See Forlin Patrucco 1986 (late sixth or early seventh century); Costa 1975 (sixth century); Picard 1988, 667 (eighth or early ninth century).

City and Cult

Vigilius's status of patron saint of Trent has endured through the Middle Ages to the present day, and his relics rest in the cathedral of Trent, dedicated to Vigilius, along with those of the martyrs of the Val di Non,[4] which Vigilius originally interred at Trent also, according to the *Passion* (ch.6). Underneath the cathedral are the remains of a palaeo-Christian church, possibly that founded by Vigilius himself, and built "at the gate that leads to Verona," according to the *Passion* (ch.9). The structure under the cathedral appears to date from the sixth century and presents a basilica 50x14 metres, with a singular nave, and presumably a trussed roof. The pavement floor was completely occupied by graves, which preserved some 175 individuals, some in multiple burials, and some with slab epitaphs neatly arranged. The site has also preserved a late antique sarcophagus and fragments of inscriptions that date to the fifth century; hence, it would appear that Vigilius's original foundation was enlarged by his successors in the sixth century.[5] This may be a reason the *Passion* was written, to promote the new church and the antiquity of its patron. But competition may also have played a role: surprisingly, excavations (1974–1978, 2007–2009) under the church of Santa Maria Maggiore, just to the north of the cathedral, have uncovered yet another sixth-century church, with mosaics and *opus sectile* flooring in late antique style, that was in use until the ninth or tenth century.[6] Who built this church and its relation to the church under the cathedral is unclear, for the early ecclesiastical history of Trent is largely unknown, and our earliest surviving sources date from the turn of the millennium.[7] Our earliest episcopal list from Trent (c.1039) places Vigilius as the eighteenth bishop of Trent, which is clearly an error: the *Passion*'s claim that Vigilius was the third bishop is more

4 The key studies are Rogger 1966, and Quacquarelli and Rogger (eds) 1985. See also below.

5 The initial excavations in 1964–1977 were co-ordinated by I. Rogger (1974a, 1974b). See now Rogger and Cavada (eds) 2001, which contains individual studies of aspects of the church: inscriptions (D. Mazzoleni, 379–412), mosaic (S. Tavano, 413–436), sculpture (P. Porta, 413–544). For other early medieval archaeological sites in Trent, see Cavada 1993, 1998; on palaeo-Christian churches in the Veneto region, see Gonzato Debiasi 2000.

6 See Guaitoli and Lopreite 2013, which supersedes earlier studies. Picard 1988, 667, suggests this church was the cathedral church until the ninth century and is that referred to in the *Passion*. Cf. Rogger 1992.

7 Collected in Rogger and Dell'Oro (eds) 1983–1984, 1988.

likely.[8] That and information such as the location of the church demonstrate how precious the *Passion* is for this undocumented period and place in Italian history. Arguably, the *Passion* has played a large role in spreading the cult of Vigilius to other parts of Italy, especially Lombardy and the Tyrol, with a rich iconographic tradition, often including the motif of Vigilius holding one of his shoes (clogs), reflecting his paraphrase of Luke 1:79, "to go on naked foot to a naked people" in facing vicious unbelievers (ch.6).[9]

Vigilius, the Three martyrs of Anaunia (Val di Non), and Hagiographic Tradition

The two letters of Vigilius that survive, one addressed to Simplicianus of Milan (Ambrose's successor, 397–400/401), and another addressed to John Chrysostom (397–407), the latter of highly doubtful authenticity, both describe the recent martyrdom in Anaunia (c.397) of three missionaries from Cappadocia by the names of Sisinnius, Martyrius, and Alexander.[10] The letters were written in high-rhetorical, late antique style, full of abstract moralizing and metaphors of good and evil, and provide little historical detail: we glean from the letter to Simplicianus that Sisinnius was old, Martyrius ("with a name that is promise to commend him," writes Vigilius[11]) was once a soldier and now a *lector* with a beautiful voice, and his brother, Alexander, was a deacon. Vigilius claimed no responsibility for their presence in Anaunia – they were simply "clergy in churches that had recently been founded" (*ministri in ecclesiis quae nuper fun-*

8 Picard 1988, 295–296, 502–504, 533–534, 665–666.

9 Spinelli 1993; on iconography, see Primerano (ed) 2000.

10 On the letters, see BHL 7794–7795; text in PL 13: 543–558. Critical edition by Menestó 1985, 151–170. Their manuscript tradition is late: the earliest witness for the letter to Simplicianus is Verona, Biblioteca Capitolare XCV (90), dating from ninth century, where it immediately follows the *Passio Vigilii* (see below); manuscripts for the Chrysostom letter date from the fifteenth century. Note the Bollandists: "Vtrobique stylus inflatior & obscurior est" (AA. SS. Mai. VI, 38). Doubts have been raised and dismissed for both letters: see Dekkers 1997; Forlin Patrucco 1997; Grégoire 2000. In my opinion the Latinity of the letter to Chrysostom suggests a different author who elaborated on the letter to Simplicianus. Nonetheless, the *Passion of Vigilius* seems to have used both: Everett 2000, 82 n99. On their style and content, see Pizzolato 2000 (for classical references) and Raurell 2000 (exegesis). On the martyrs of Anaunia, see Rogger 1966; Quacquarelli and Rogger (eds) 1985; Grégoire (ed) 1997.

11 *iam nominis pignore commendante eum*, picked up by the *Passio Sisinni* et al. (see n.16 below), "qui nominis sui natalem meretis consummavit."

datae fuerant) – and says nothing about relics in the letter to Simplicianus, despite the common assertion that he sent the relics with the letter. The letter to Chrysostom, although probably inauthentic, was used by our hagiographer, and it implies that Vigilius sent relics to Constantinople. But this was not the only difficult claim our hagiographer needed to whitewash. Bishop Gaudentius of Brescia (387–410), who was also consecrated by Ambrose in 387, wrote a sermon called the *Council of Saints* (*Concilium Sanctorum*) for the dedication of his church in Brescia (c.401/407), in which he had proudly gathered together his collection of relics from his tours of Italy and the Middle East, and claimed that among these were

> the holy ashes of Sisinnius, Martyrius, and Alexander, who were recently killed by the sacrilegious people in Anaunia while they were diligently performing religious services, and were tied up and burned, so that they became a burnt sacrifice to God, who with a just rebuke prevented his Christians from becoming victims to demons.[12]

This claim may explain why the Brescians appear in the *Passion of Vigilius* (ch.8) as armed thugs who threatened to steal the body of Vigilius as his followers carried it back over the river Sarca, and had to be bought off with a silver vase. The legend of the martyrs quickly became a *cause célèbre* among major churchmen. In a letter (c.410) to his friend, the imperial commissioner Marcellinus, Augustine of Hippo mentions the martyrs when advising leniency against Donatists who had committed acts of violence and even murder: "... for I know that in the case of the clergy in the valley of Anaunia, who were slain by the pagans, and are now honoured as martyrs, the emperor granted readily a petition that the murderers, who had been discovered and imprisoned, might not be visited with a capital punishment."[13] The hagiographic tradition makes no mention of this imperial intervention. Bishop Maximus of Turin (d.c.420) wrote a sermon about the martyrs in celebration of their feast day in his church.[14] Within a decade of Augus-

12 Gaudentius, *Sermo* 17, ed. Glück 1936, 141–151, at 143; PL 20: 964. The martyrs joined high company in Brescia. Gaudentius also claimed to have relics of the apostles Andrew, Luke, Thomas, and John the Baptist. On Gaudentius and the Brescian church, see Picard 1988, 226–230, 273–275, 590–592.

13 *Ep.* 139 (158), ed. Mutzenbecher 1970. On Marcellinus, who later suffered capital punishment for conspiracy, see Brown 2009, 290–291, 332–338.

14 Maximus, *Sermo* 82, ed. Mutzenbecher 1962; PL 57: 695–698. Maximus preached it a "few days" after the feast day, but the textual tradition provides no day or year.

tine's letter, Paulinus, the notary and biographer of Ambrose, claimed in his *Life of Ambrose* (c.422) that the bodies of the martyrs were in Milan:

> Also at Milan we received with deepest devotion the remains of the martyrs, Sisinnius and Alexander, who in our time, that is, after the death of Ambrose, gained the crown of martyrdom in the pagan persecutions in the regions of Anauni. At this time, there came a certain blind man, who, by touching the coffin in which the remains of the saints were being carried, that same day received sight. From his report we learned that in a vision he had seen a ship approaching the shore, in which were a great number of men clothed in white. When, as they were disembarking, he asked one of the crowd to learn who the men were, he found that they were Ambrose and his companions. And upon hearing the name Ambrose, when he was praying that he might receive his sight, he heard from Ambrose, "Proceed to Milan and contact my brothers who are about to go there" (indicating the day) "and you will receive sight." The man was, as he himself said, from the Dalmatian coast. And he further declared that he had not come to the city before he met with the remains of the saints on the highway, at which time he still lacked sight, but upon touching the bier he began to see.[15]

The Dalmatian story here perhaps reflects the same legends behind the merchants of Salona who appear in the *Passion of Vigilius* (ch.9) and who mop up some blood of Vigilius to take back to Dalmatia. As with the "Zadar epilogue" in the *Passion of Cetheus*, the importance of Dalmatia to Italian ecclesiastical history is again evident.

Hence, within decades of Vigilius's death, two other north Italian cities had claimed the martyrs' relics as their own, and a letter spuriously attributed to Vigilius that claimed that he sent them to Constantinople may also have been circulating. This may explain why another martyr narrative, the *Passion of Sisinnius, Martyrius, and Alexander*,[16] of indeterminable date and which used Vigilius's letters, mentions nothing about the martyrs' relics. This *Passion of Sisinnius et al.* acknowledges that their martyrdom took place during Vigilius's

15 *Life of Ambrose*, ch.10. Martyrius has been dropped from the legend, probably because of confusion over his name.

16 BHL 7798; AA. SS. Mai. VII, 37–38, "ex aliis mss. codicibus," including Paris Bibliothèque nationale de France, lat. 5593, fol.r66–68r, used for their edition of the *Passio Vigilii* (see below).

bishopric, cursorily mentions Vigilius's own bloody martyrdom in the region, and that he "directed" (*direxit*) the three men to preach in Anaunia. It also mentions that Sisinnius, who was a deacon, built a church there at his own expense, in a place called "Metho."[17] After the martyrdom, "In that same place a church was constructed, so that the faithful might hasten to the doorway of these holy men, and whoever manages a capacity for the faith will find through the baptistery a medicine for many wounds." Relics play no part in this martyr text, and Vigilius's part is relegated to the shadows.

Our hagiographer therefore wrote to set the record straight: Vigilius received the three missionaries (after their stay in Milan), installed them as his clergy in Anaunia, was given a divine signal when they were martyred, and rushed to retrieve the burned remains, which he interred in his church at Trent.[18] The hagiographer claims he described their martyrdom "just as is recorded in their history," which may mean Vigilius's letters, or the *Passion of Sisinnis et al.*, since he appears to have used both. But he added the most important details that helped put Vigilius back into the centre of the popular story of martyrs, and their relics back in Trent, right next to those of Vigilius in his church.

Date of Composition

The *terminus ante quem* for the *Passion of Vigilius* is provided by a citation in Usuard's *Martyrology* (c.860) and earliest manuscripts from the late ninth or early tenth century, but there are solid grounds for dating the text much earlier. Just how early is difficult to determine: it may have been written in response to the early fifth-century claims for the relics in Brescia and Milan cited above. It may also have been written in conjunction with the construction of either (or both) of the sixth-century churches found under today's cathedral and under Santa Maria Maggiore. Another issue is dating the *Passion of Sisinnius et al.*, which the author seems to have used, but nothing in that text betrays a determinable date, and the *terminus ante quem* is the citation of it by Ado of Vienne (870s) and manuscripts of similar date.

17 We are told that Martyrius and Alexander were "at the grade" of *lector* and *hostiarius* respectively and that they had worshipped in the church there for some time.

18 The reliquary that housed the martyrs was opened and analysed in 1977: inside were bones, in various states of being burnt, of at least two adult males, another body of indeterminable sex, and possibly a fourth body that was female: see Corrain and Capitanio 1979.

Some details in the *Passion of Vigilius*, however, suggest an eighth-century date. The claim that the "bishop of the city of Aquileia consecrated Vigilius as bishop outside the walls of Trent" (ch.2) is difficult to square with the surviving letter of Ambrose congratulating Vigilius on his consecration, suggesting the bishop of Milan consecrated Vigilius, as chief metropolitan authority of northern Italy. Jurisdiction over Trent passed to Aquileia during the fall out from the Three Chapters schism, when the "new Aquileia" at Grado was created in response to "old" Aquileia's defiant stance against reconciliation with Rome and Ravenna. Trent, as with most other northern Italian bishoprics (near Cividale), sided with "old" Aquileia, located firmly in Lombard territory (transferred to Cormons by 607), as early as the synod of Marano (c.588–590), and remained loyal. Secundus of Trent, a monk and Three Chapters schismatic, was a close confidant of the King Agilulf and Queen Theudelinda, whose son he baptized.[19] Pope Gregory II recognized "old" Aquileia's status as a metropolitan in 723, though limited its jurisdiction to Lombard Veneto.[20] The *Passion*, therefore, seems to have been written sometime when Trent was subject to Aquileia, during the Lombard period, before or after Pope Gregory II's recognition of old Aquileia. The hagiographer's use of the word *episcopus* may be significant: the *Passion* promotes Vigilius's connections to Rome, even to the extent that some of his relics and a copy of his *History* were archived there by the pope (ch.2, 10–11). The choice of *episcopus* may be a diplomatic choice for a church either seeking or having recently gained reconciliation with the head of Christendom, for the papacy appears to have reserved the use of the term *patriarch* (of Aquileia) for the prelates of Grado.[21] Nonetheless, papal recognition in 723 of Aquileia's authority in the area, including over Trent, presents a suggestive period for the text's composition. The idea of a nameless pope advising a nameless emperor in Rome upsets modern historical sensibilities. But the advice, to place the *History* of Vigilius on the imperial standards battle, illustrates how hagiography delights in imagery of itself and its power to inspire.

The geographic focus of the *Passion* on Trent's relations with Brescia and Verona also suggest it dates from the Lombard kingdom. The duchy of Brescia, a heartland of Lombard aristocracy, according to Paul the Deacon, was united with Trent under the leadership of the usurper Alahis (688–689), who

19 Paul, *HL* IV.27. On Secundus, see Everett 2003a, 83–84; Gardiner 1983.

20 Everett 2000, 85–86.

21 Everett 2000, 85 n110.

was duke of both territories, a unique phenomenon in the history of the Lombard state, and all three cities were key military centres for guarding the Alps in this period.[22] We mentioned above the claims of Gaudentius of Brescia to possess the relics of the martyrs: the representation of Brescians as armed thugs intent on stealing the body of Vigilius (ch.9) may be a swipe at this legend. But there is also a clear claim to superiority in prestige and historical importance over both Brescia and Verona, whose bishops are portrayed as scared and inept, and who act as a foil to Vigilius's courageous actions. That Vigilius "founded more than thirty of God's churches" in their territories (ch.4) probably reflects claims over parochial churches on the borders of these neighbouring dioceses, of the type witnessed in the Siena–Arezzo dispute in this period.[23]

Text and Translation

The translation below is based on the critical edition of Cesarini-Sforza 1905, 5–29, who collated more than ten manuscripts, at least four of them dating from the ninth or tenth century. Cesarini-Sforza also collated readings from the previous editions of Resch (1755), Bonelli (1761), and Papebroch in AA. SS. Iun. IV, 163–168, all three of whom relied heavily on a twelfth-century manuscript ("Codex Maximi Trevirensis," now Paris, Bibliothèque national de France, lat. 9741), and were not aware of the earlier witnesses used by Cesarini-Sforza, among which he privileged St Gall, Stiftsbibliothek, 566, fols. 560–567 (which dates from the ninth century, and contains many grammatical and orthographical errors), and Verona, Biblioteca Capitolare, XCV (90), fols. 174–177 (ninth/early tenth century), in which Vigilius's letter to Simplicianus also appears. The irreconcilable imperial and papal dates and other aspects of the pope–emperor collaboration printed in earlier editions belong to later manuscript traditions: see notes to ch.10–12.

The hagiographer follows Vigilius's literary lead in his use of the imagery of fire (pagans) and water (Christian faith), military metaphors and similes, and some of the scriptural citations. Comparison with the letters of Vigilius and

22 Paul, *HL* V.36; Gasparri 1978, 47. On Brescia, Trent, and Verona as important military centres for guarding Alpine passes, see Cavada 2002; Christie 2006. The Val di Non served as a strategic location with a fortified *castrum* during the Frankish invasions of Italy in the 580s: *HL* III.9 (from Secundus of Trent?); Bassi 1998.

23 Everett 2003a, 150–153, 198–190.

the *Passion of Sisinnius et al.* reveals how the hagiographer of the *Passion of Vigilius* borrowed imagery and motifs but also simplified the language to create a short, racy narrative. Two examples of our hagiographer at work are pagans erupting in agitation and the martyrs representing the Trinity:

(a)

Passion of Vigilius: cumque se saepe tubarum vocibus excitassit truculenta gentilitas.

Passion of Sisinnius: "cumque sæpe tubarum clangoribus excitata fuisset truculenta gentilitas"

Ep. to Simplicianus: "Nam fumosa gentilitas contra vaporem fidei, zelo diaboli flamma furoris incaluit"

Ep. to Chrysostom: "tubis saepe excita truculenta gentilitas aemulo furore bellique clamoribus inflammatur"

(b)

Passion of Vigilius: "in tribus viris impletum est mysterium trinitatis"

Passion of Sisinnius: "ut in tribus viris Trinitatis perfecta gratia compleretur"

Ep. to Simplicianus: "[Alexander] tertius trinitatis hostias complens"

Ep. to Chrysostom: "Impletum est, fratres, in tribus ministris ... mysterium trinitatis"

The Passion of the Holy Vigilius, Bishop and Martyr

1. Most sacred praise of the martyrs should be brought forth in numerous proclamations,[24] so that by hearing their deeds the indolent might rouse their spirits to good, and so that priests be ever mindful that eager fighters poured out their blood for love of their Lord Jesus Christ. He willingly poured out his blood for them and for us all so that by his example the instructed of men also poured out their blood in seeking to give their souls to him, and so that we remember the examples of their strength.

2. At that time, Vigilius, a citizen of Trent and of Roman descent, although a man accomplished in Athenian liberal letters, his mind from infancy was dedicated to Christ, and he gave himself over to worship. Returning therefore from his studies in Rome and Athens, in the city of Trent he fulfilled the office of holy religion so that worthily he took up the third pontifical office in that same city and sat upon the episcopal throne in accordance with apostolic custom. At the age of about twenty both the love and choice of the people extolled him, for they learned of his many miraculous deeds. He, however, using the excuse of his youthful age, kept accusing himself of unworthiness. But the more he excelled his elders in works and sanctity, the more he was being praised as the more worthy by the shouts of the people. Compelled by such, the bishop of the city of Aquileia consecrated Vigilius as bishop outside the walls of Trent. When he re-entered the town, he began to preach the law of the Lord and to convert the people, so that daily the number of believers increased.[25] Once he had converted the whole city to the Catholic faith, he placed a church of the Lord inside the city, and there he founded a sanctuary of Christ, in which with his prayers he illuminated the blind, restored hearing to the deaf, and speech to the mute, and placing his hand upon those oppressed by demons, he relieved them with the standard of Christ.

3. His reputation for holiness began to flourish throughout the neighbouring cities. Up to this time the greater part of the population in the fields outside the city was constricted by the practice of diabolical traditions, worshipping and making sacrifices to mute idols and false statues of wood and stone. Vigilius,

24 *multifariis praeconniis.*
25 Cf. Acts 5:14.

however, filled with the holy spirit, softened the hard hearts of the gentiles with incessant, daily teaching until he brought the whole populace of his diocese to the church of Christ. [Even] his relatives and siblings devotedly served the Lord. One day, summoning his priests and deacons together he said to them, "Pious men, we must not hide away the talents given to us by the Lord like lazy servants placing one talent in their napkins, but instead should show the tenfold interest when our Lord comes, and as good servants increase the Lord's wealth and earn the right to enter into the joy of our God."[26] He then sent a legation to the bishops of Verona and Brescia to say on his behalf, "My Lords and most holy brothers, do not neglect the word of the God in whom Christ has ordained us to be heads of his church, but go out from your cities and preach the word of the Lord, so that no longer the devil, that old serpent, might bind the souls of men for whom our Lord Christ died and rose again."

4. To this they responded that they could not go. The blessed Vigilius, however, understanding their response, said, "I am prepared to die for him who chose to suffer the punishment of death for us. Nor will I suffer the crown prepared for me to be given away to others." Taken aback by his declaration, they responded, "Then you go, brother, into the territory of our cities to acquire souls for the Lord that are presently held captive, and demonstrate to those people the way of truth." Filled with confidence the blessed Vigilius went about their territories, to all parts of Verona and Brescia, preaching the word of the Lord, converting them to the faith of the Lord, and he founded more than thirty of God's churches.

5. When he went out into the territory of his city he took with him a certain Sisinnius, Martyrius, and Alexander, most Christian and devoted men who had come from across the seas. Cappadocian in origin, they had stayed for some time at Milan before our man of God established them as clergy of Anaunia,[27] leaving them there to preach, where they converted some of the populace and founded a church for the Lord. The Anaunians, however, seized the three men, afflicted them with diverse punishments, bound them in chains, and threw them half-dead into a fire. And there they were burned, their most holy bod-

26 Cf. Matt. 25:20; Luke 19:6, 19:20; Matt. 25:21, 23.

27 *cultores ordinavit Agagniae*. Anaunia (Val di Non) was a strategic military location with a fortified *castrum*: Paul, *HL* III.9; Bassi 1998.

ies weighed down, but they gave their spirit to God, just as is recorded in their history.[28]

6. While the blessed Vigilius was constructing a church of God, by gift of the holy spirit he saw their precious souls being carried to heaven by angels. Immediately, he himself began to burn with ardour for the glory of the martyrs so that he might have a share in their crown. He quickly took to the road, and together with his deacons set out for Anaunia. His own people tried to retain him, saying, "Where do you go, o pastor, while you abandon all of your sheep?" But he was now too deeply moved in spirit and stirred up inside.[29] When he came to a river, he said to his deacon, "Let's take off our shoes so that we may go with naked foot to a naked people, for their feet have not yet been set on the path of peace."[30] When they came to the place where the precious bodies of the martyrs had been burned, they gathered their ashes into clean linen shrouds[31] and took them back to Trent where they interred them with honour in the basilica of God that Vigilius himself had built.

7. Not long after this, when, as it has been told, Vigilius had gone out into the territories of Brescia and of course Trent, to find a number of pagans and turn them to God, there remained one place in which he had not been. A horrid place, positioned high up in the mountains, set amongst cliffs and cut off by a gully from which a river ran down, it had always been hostile to the Christian religion. The name of this valley was called Randena.[32] It was a slave estate of a certain rich man, upon which foolish and ignorant people worshipped as a god a statue of the devil, manufactured from a pitiful expense of bronze, evidently venerating this Saturn before them with fire ceremonies.[33] Upon learning this, the apostolic potentate said again with a sense of duty, "Why do we stand here idle, when we have now been called? Let us go to the joy of our Lord." And marking himself with the sign of the holy cross he set off and reached the gate of the city called Brescia, where he came to a bridge. The people and leaders of

28 *sicut gesta eorum continent*.

29 Cf. John 11:33, 38.

30 Cf. Luke 1:79.

31 *in sindones mundas*; cf. Matt. 27:59.

32 Val Rendena (German *Rhendenatal*), which follows the Sarca River in the Trentino, 30 km east of Trent.

33 *Saturnum in inferni iura proiectum venerantes*: *ius/iura* may also mean bowls/offerings [of fire].

the town escorted him a little, then, saying their goodbyes, they returned home. Vigilius, along with his brothers Claudian, Magorian, and Julian the priest, then came to the chosen place. All the Christians there who had been converted by his teachings came together to venerate and worship the Lord and asked if they could partake in a Eucharist of Christ's body consecrated by the holy hands of Vigilius. When he came to that place in which the idol stood, fired by faith he brought forth Christ's salutary host in the hope that he might enjoy the test of torment. Like a renowned soldier hurrying to the battle, the priest rushed to the conflict, about to accept the predetermined rewards of the Lord. Looking skywards he saw the glory of God and said, "Christ, I give you thanks, because it is by you I have desired to be found. And now I see with my eyes to the right of you what has been prepared for me."[34] All those standing about him heard him say all this in a clear voice, but they themselves saw nothing. Vigilius then struck down the idol in the name of our Lord Jesus Christ, smashed it into small pieces, and threw it in the river called Sarca. He then stood on top of the statue's stone base and began to preach the word of the Lord. As soon as they learned of this, a crowd of rustics came running wildly towards him with swords and rocks. The most blessed leader [*praesul*], armoured in the faith of Christ, merely looked down upon them as though they were no more than dirt. Their hearts now swollen by a diabolical inflammation, they smashed in his holy head with a massive shower of rocks. The most blessed martyr, looking again towards the heavens, his face covered in blood, gave thanks to the Lord and gave up his spirit. (Later in that place, above that very rock, Christians founded a church of the Lord.)

8. The priests and deacons who were with him also endured a great hailstorm of rocks, but not one of them suffered bruise or wound. Nevertheless, they earned the prize of being confessors. They gathered together his body and placed it on the horse that he himself rode and carried it back to the city. Everywhere they stopped along the way miraculous things occurred. When they came to the bridge over the river Sarca, they met a thick crowd of Brescians who were armed and ready to steal from them the body of the most holy martyr. The Tridentines, however, resisted them and bought them off with a silver vase, and quickly retook to the road with the holy body.

9. Before the news had even reached town, already demons had begun to confess through the mouths of those whom they had possessed, saying, "Behold

34 Cf. Acts. 7:55.

the holy martyr of Christ, Vigilius returns in triumph, and who expels us from our habitats." In the presence of everyone this was shouted by all of those who were liberated by the arrival of his sacred body. When it reached the town, the priests of all the neighbouring churches met together in great assembly and the Christian people rushed to attend the funeral rites. Raising his relics to be venerated, they interred them on the third day of his passion with great pride and aromas in the church that he had built earlier at the gate which leads to Verona.[35] There were some merchants from Salona who were trading in the city, one of whom collected his spilt blood on the road that is called "Vela" and placed it in a clean linen cloth, tidied it up, and took it with him to where many more miraculous things happen with Christ's assistance.

10. The *History*[36] of the most blessed martyr, as was customary, was transmitted to the archbishop of the city of Rome in order that it might be included amongst the holy records of the martyrs, which the Pope undertook with all veneration once he read through it.

11. At that time, Italy was being devastated by the tribe of the Alemans, against whom the emperor of the Romans sent an army. The Pope said to him, "Good emperor, take with you the recently received *History of the Holy Vigilius*, martyr of the city Trent, so that it might work its miracles."[37] With the greatest joy the august emperor accepted the *History* and handed the affair over to a soldier. Sowing the *History* and a few rags together, the soldier placed it roughly on top of his spear and carried it before him like a military standard. When they came close to the enemy, before the battle had even begun the strength of Christ was shown in this martyr, so that the adversaries turned in ignominious flight, abandoning all their booty so that they scarcely possessed any, as it was now in the hands of the Christians. With this, Caesar returned to the city of Rome in great triumph. Together with the pope they placed the

35 *porta veronensis*: clearly referring to the monumental entrance gate to the south, which was rediscovered in 1947. The limestone double-gate, flanked by diagonal brick towers, dates from the mid-first century AD and fell into misuse towards the end of the fourth century: Cavada 1993; Picard 1988, 666–667.

36 *gesta*: this may refer to the present text or another biography of Vigilius used by the author.

37 *ut manifestetur virtutes:* an example of the dual meaning of *virtus* as "strength/power" and "miracle." Cf. Matt. 11:21; 13:58, and Eugippius, *Vita Severini*, 18:17; 31:18.

history of the blessed martyr in the archives and at the same time interred some of his corporal relics.[38]

12. And thus suffered the most blessed Vigilius bishop and martyr on the sixth day of the Kalends of July, who conducted his episcopate in the town of Trent for twelve years, when Stilico held the consulship.[39] With our Lord Jesus Christ ruling for ever.

38 Cesarini-Sforza 1905, 27–28, notes that a number of later manuscripts add here "and from this it has been observed by other emperors that when they went out to fight against a pagan or barbarian people they carried the *History* of our blessed father Vigilius on their banners." Another manuscript used by Resch and Papebroch (Codex E, Treverensis) for their editions and dated to the twelfth century adds instead, "The *History* was then translated from Latin speech into Greek by the Roman pope, then [the emperor] took it back with him to Constantinople, along with some relics of the saint, having witnessed more of their miracles performed through the saint's kindness."

39 AD 400 or 405. The earlier manuscripts favoured by Cesarini-Sforza (1905, 27–28, A–D) only contain the consular dating, either of which is consistent with Vigilius's career (c.397–409). The earlier editions of Bonelli, Resch, and AA. SS. included the interpolations of later hands that inserted misdated chronological references here to "the time of Honorius and Arcadius the emperors" or to "Theodosius and Arcadius." Later codices also record Vigilius's episcopate for twenty years, which is rejected by Cesarini-Sforza 1905, 29–30, and Rogger 1992.

23 JULY

The Passion of Apollinaris of Ravenna

Located on the Adriatic, Ravenna's strategic importance brought it to prominence as the capital city of the Western Roman Empire in late antiquity. Despite scholarly attention lavished on Ravenna's monuments and mosaics from this period, the *Passion of Apollinaris of Ravenna* has received much less attention than it deserves from students of early medieval Italian history. There are two main reasons for this: first, the uncertainty of its date of composition, and second, the *Passion*'s obviously ahistorical claims, above all that Apollinaris was a disciple of Saint Peter in Rome and was sent to Ravenna in the time of the Emperor Nero – a claim that is difficult to reconcile with the history of Christianity in Italy. The *Passion* is therefore often dismissed as fanciful legend, and has been dated to different periods with different purposes – as anti-Arian propaganda among the Ostrogoths, as a literary complement to the construction of St Apollinare in Classe (530s), or as a statement of apostolicity to complement the church of Ravenna's grant of independence (autocephaly) from Rome by the Emperor Constans II in 666.[1] This last dating enjoys a consensus among most recent scholars, but it is challenged below as being inconsistent with the tenor of the *Passion,* which promotes a close relationship between Rome and Ravenna in the figure of Apollinaris. The *Passion* was certainly written before 725, when Bede cites it in his *Martyrology*. A review of the evidence for Apollinaris's cult discussed below suggests the most likely period for the composition of the *Passion* to be the mid-sixth century, and that the *Passion* was written both to represent the alliance of Rome and Ravenna in the Three

1 Zattoni 1904 was the first to date the text to the 660s; in tentative agreement, though not ruling out earlier origins, was Lanzoni 1927, 14–15, 18–19, 737–748; also Picard 1988, 116–123; Deliyannis (ed) 2006, 39–40; and Deliyannis 2010, 259–260. Lucchese 1969 argued for the 630s; Orioli 2001 dated the text to the 480s or 490s. Mazzotti 1952 was the first to argue that the *Passion* was written in conjunction with the church's construction at Classe, and therefore dated the text to the 530s. The arguments put forward below for Bishop Maximianus's involvement have not, to my knowledge, been seriously considered.

Chapters schism and to complement construction of Apollinaris's church in Classe: the mosaic there of Apollinaris (on the cover of this book) offers visual evidence. There are, however, also sound arguments for a later dating to the seventh century *before* and *after* the period of Ravenna's autocephaly (666–681), which will also be considered below, proceeding chronologically.

Unlike other hagiographic works in this book, the *Passion of Apollinaris* can be assessed against a range of surviving evidence – documentary, architectural, archaeological – due to Ravenna's capital status and patronage in late antiquity. A key piece of evidence is the *Book of Pontiffs of Ravenna* (*LPR*) by Agnellus of Ravenna (writing 830s–840s), who also summarized the *Passion* for his own biography of Apollinaris, even quoting the text in places, and whose account of Ravennate history is invaluable as much as it can be problematic.[2] Moreover, the *Passion of Apollinaris* is especially fortunate among our Italian texts in the survival of a particularly early manuscript, dating from the late seventh or early eighth century, which not only helps to establish the text of the *Passion*, but also relieves some scholarly concerns about using later manuscript traditions for other hagiographic texts, including those in this book.

City and Early Cult

Linked by a short canal to the Adriatic, Ravenna's strategic importance was recognized by Julius Caesar, who gathered his forces there before crossing the Rubicon, and subsequently by Augustus, who built the naval harbour in nearby Classe. The city was elevated to capital of Western Roman Empire when the Emperor Honorius moved the imperial court from Milan to Ravenna in 402. Ravenna remained the capital administrative city in Italy even during the barbarian governments of General Odoacar (476–493) and the Ostrogoths (493–550s). When it was recaptured by Roman (Byzantine) forces under Belisarius in 540, the Emperor Justinian (527–565) continued to use Ravenna as the administrative centre of Italy, but the civilian element was eclipsed, government was predominately in the hands of military personnel, and the Ravennate church became intrinsically linked with the city's administration and role as imperial headquarters in Italy – this close relationship between church and state is essential to consider in any assessment of the *Passion of Apollinaris*. After the Lombard

2 Agnellus, *LPR*, ch.1–2, also for Eleuchadius (ch.4) and Marcianus (ch.5). See Martínez Pizarro 1995, 44. On Agnellus as source, see Deliyannis (trans) 2004 and (ed) 2006.

invasions of northern and central Italy (568–590), Ravenna continued as the seat of the "exarch," or military governor, responsible for the Byzantine "duchies" still under Constantinople's protection, including that of Rome.[3]

Our first historical notice of Apollinaris's cult dates to this period from the archbishop of Ravenna, Peter Chrysologus (c.430–450), who gave a sermon on the occasion of Apollinaris's feast day. Ravenna was a minor bishopric until the imperial court was established there (402), when it subsequently become a metropolitan see and was granted jurisdiction over the churches of Emilia – a move opposed by the church of Milan. There was already a *basilica apostolorum* next to the town wall from as early as the fourth century.[4] Imperial presence in Ravenna also brought patronage of cults and construction, most notably by the princess Galla Placidia (392–450), who built three churches dedicated to the Holy Cross, St Zacharias, and St John the Evangelist, and probably also the mysterious and beautifully decorated mausoleum that bears her name, which served the cult of St Lawrence or St Vincent.[5] Chrysologus says nothing that would help date Apollinaris's life, but notes that Apollinaris was the city's first bishop, and a native of Ravenna. Significantly, Chrysologus makes no mention of St Peter or apostolic origins. Chrysologus also implies that Apollinaris's body is in Ravenna, not Classe, and that the saint is still "alive here, here as a good shepherd he is at his post in the midst of his flock," which suggests some sort of patron status for the town, though (as we shall see below) by the sixth century Ravenna had many well-established cults. Curiously, in his sermon Chrysologus seems defensive about Apollinaris's martyr status, explaining away Apollinaris's title of *confessor* and noting that "the enemy did not make him [Apollinaris] a martyr, since he did not inflict death, but he proved him to be a martyr, because he did not remove his faith."[6] Chrysologus emphasizes that Apollinaris's martyrdom was drawn out over repeated occasions on which he shed his blood. This suggests the *Passion* did not yet exist. On the other hand, Apollinaris in the *Passion* suffers many horrendous torments (beatings, hot coals, the rack, imprisonment, cruel restraints, starvation), is brought near to death several times, and seven days elapse between his last beating and death (ch.34–35). It is possible, therefore, that the *Passion* was composed in part because of the confusion over Apollinaris's martyr status, as voiced by Chrysologus in his sermon.

3 See Bovini 1970; Brown 1979, 1984; Deichmann 1969–1989; Deliyannis 2010.

4 Picard 1988, 154–160; Deichmann 1969–1989.

5 Mackie 1990; Deliyannis 2001.

6 Chrysologus, *Sermon* 128.1 (ed. Olivar 1975–1982).

Bishop Maximianus, Portraiture and Apostolicity

Our next attestation of the cult of Apollinaris is the construction in the mid-sixth century of the church dedicated to Apollinaris in Classe, and a number of factors strongly suggest that the *Passion of Apollinaris* was composed in this period, when the Ravennate church became a key agent of imperial authority in Italy after its recapture from the Ostrogoths in 540, and when Rome and Ravenna were in alliance doctrinally over the Three Chapters controversy. The church at Classe was built upon what was considered to be the original tomb of Apollinaris, and archaeology shows that the site was an ancient necropolis, with coins dating from the late second and early third century, which is consonant with other evidence for the possible dates of Apollinaris's career in historically verifiable terms, and inferences from Agnellus's chronology.[7]

Although the church at Classe was begun by Archbishop Ursicinus of Ravenna (533–536), there are strong grounds to attribute the *Passion* to the period, if not the intervention, of his successor, Archbishop Maximianus of Ravenna (546–556), for the mosaics inside the church at Classe, which were commissioned by Maximianus, and his other activities in promoting episcopal authority in Ravenna, match the tenor of the *Passion* and its promotion of Ravenna's close relationship with Rome.[8] However, Maximianus also promoted an astonishing number of other cults and their churches both in Classe and in the city itself, so that by no means did Apollinaris enjoy a privileged status as town patron during a boom period of church building for the period 540–600, when six major churches were constructed, along with several smaller buildings and numerous renovations of existing structures. Arguably Saint Vitalis, to whom Maximianus dedicated the extant church famous for its mosaics of Justinian and Theodora (and Maximianus himself), was Ravenna's "chief martyr"[9] in this

7 There is no evidence for a bishop in Ravenna before Severus (c.340s), the eleventh successor of Apollinaris, according to Agnellus of Ravenna. The average length of known episcopates at Ravenna has been calculated at 15.5 years, which would place Apollinaris in the later second or third century, which agrees with the archaeological data: Picard 1988, 116–123, 130–131. But the *Passion* seems to contain information that suggests earlier sources: see *Passion*, ch.14n, and ch.30n. The best discussion of the church at Classe and its decoration is Deliyannis 2010, 259–275.

8 The original study of buildings by Bovini 1970 has been updated by Johnson 1988, Moorhead 1992, 92–95, and Deliyannis 2010, 106–138.

9 Deliyannis 2010, 219–220ff., "chief martyr" established by construction of San Vitale, 223.

period. Maximianus himself was buried in the pre-existing church of St Andrew, whose beard he had obtained from Justinian, after asking for the body itself, according to Agnellus of Ravenna (writing c.830s), in a story rich with significance for the *Passion*: Justinian explained that since the body of St Peter "keeps Rome in first place, this one [Andrew] is to convey second place. The cities are both sisters, and the apostles are both brothers. I do not want to give him to you." Agnellus remarked that "if [Maximianus] had buried the body of blessed Andrew, brother of Peter the prince, here, the Roman popes would not have thus subjugated us."[10] While Agnellus's comment clearly looks forward to the autocephaly dispute, his story suggests interest in apostolic saints as patrons of capital cities in Maximianus's day, also reflected in the apostolic origins of Apollinaris in the *Passion*. On the other hand, it also might suggest that Apollinaris's apostolic origins were still not widely known (a cynic might say "not yet invented"), or they would have received more attention. In other words, the *Passion of Apollinaris* had not yet been written

Nonetheless, despite Maximinus's commemoration of other saints (and himself), some of his activities, the iconography of the figure of Apollinaris in the church at Classe, and aspects of text of the *Passion* itself suggest a very probable context for the composition of the *Passion of Apollinaris*. The startling image of "Apolenaris" (as he is entitled with an inscription) in the vault of the apse, underneath a curious representation of the Transfiguration and an enigmatic large cross, celebrates the martyr's role as bishop, for the saint stands with both arms raised in prayer, the pose adopted to begin the Eucharist ceremony, visually complementing the performance of the Eucharist on the altar underneath the image. Apollinaris wears a *pallium*, the symbol of his metropolitan authority. Maximianus also wears the *pallium* in the mosaic of him next to Justinian in San Vitale, which was made by the same artisans and was likewise commissioned by Maximianus. Agnellus informs us that among the relics of twenty different "apostles and martyrs" that Maximianus interred at his own church of St Stephen (now obliterated), which Maximianus built with his own money, were those of Apollinaris. Apparently Maximianus also decorated the apse of this church with a "multicoloured mosaic" of himself, "surrounded by wonderful glasswork": we can only wonder if this portrait of Maximianus matched in style the Apollinaris figure he commissioned in Classe, and that of Maximianus in San Vitale.[11] In any case, often overlooked by scholars is the careful

10 Agnellus, *LPR*, ch.76. On cult of Andrew, see Dvornik 1958.
11 Agnellus, *LPR* 72.

resemblance of the Apollinaris figure in Classe, with white tonsured hair and beard, to contemporary images of St Peter, thus associating the two apostles, as found in the *Passion*.[12] This same St Peter-like image of Apollinaris was used in the mosaics of the church of Saint Martin in Golden Heaven (today San Apollinare in Nuovo), commissioned by Maximianus's successor, Archbishop Agnellus (557–570), where Apollinaris appears as the seventeenth of twenty-six processing male saints on the south side of the nave, carrying a crown, identifying him as a martyr.[13] Curiously, there is no evidence of Apollinaris's martyr status in Classe, and an inscription placed on Apollinaris's tomb at the time of Maximianus records that the saint was *sacerdos et confessor*. An inscription placed by Maximianus in his own church of St Stephen declares that saint's privileged status as "the first who performed the act of martyrdom; the same palm is given to all for holy blood; however he benefits from it more who was earlier in time."[14]

Although hardly privileging the cult of Apollinaris, Maximianus's appreciation of a martyr's antiquity (Stephen, Vitalis) should be paired with his promotion of episcopal authority in other images and churches in Ravenna, and especially in Classe. Underneath the image of Apollinaris at Classe, in the jambs of the window arches, Maximianus also commissioned the images of four previous bishops of Ravenna, Severus (c.340s), Ecclesius (522–532), Ursus (c.450–478), and Ursicinus (533–536), all four holding books, evoking the four evangelists. Maximianus's selection of these four bishops seems curious: Ursicinus originally founded the church (532); Severus's growing cult was honoured with a church dedicated to him by the end of the century; Ursus founded the cathedral in Ravenna; and Ecclesius began the church of San Vitale with the mysterious Julianus the banker, who also sponsored the church in Classe – both churches were made from the same "Julian" bricks, as they are called by scholars. Ecclesius also invited the bishop of Rome to settle disputes between himself and his clergy concerning church property and doctrinal matters, as we learn from Agnellus.[15] Maximianus also refurbished an existing church in Classe

12 I owe this observation to Kristyna Zemanova, postgraduate (MA) in art history, University of Toronto.

13 On the complicated history of this church, originally built by King Theoderic, and dedicated to Apollinaris in the ninth century when his relics were transferred from Classe, see Urbano 2005 and Deliyannis 2010, 146–173.

14 Agnellus, *LPR* 72. Cf. inscription for the church of the "blessed martyr Vitalis," ibid., 77.

15 *LPR* 60. On the other bishops, see Deliyannis 2010, 257–274.

dedicated to Probus (either the seventh or fourteenth bishop of Ravenna, both called *Probus,* and probably dating from the third century or second half of the fourth century, respectively), including decorating its facade with mosaics of bishops Probus, Eleucadius, and Calocerus,[16] the last two of which appear in the *Passion* (ch.7, 13).

Maximianus's decoration programme to promote the authority of Ravenna's archbishops throughout the city, along with the mosaic of Apollinaris and the four bishops he commissioned at Classe, certainly suggests fertile ground for the *Passion*'s composition. Other aspects of Maximianus's episcopacy are suggestive: he wrote chronicles, and seems to have been the first to compose a history of the see of Ravenna, much as the *Liber Pontificalis* of Rome emerges from this period. This historical interest extended to fashioning an altar cloth with depictions "woven in gold" of his predecessors (much like the Velo di Classe for Verona's bishops: see *Zeno of Verona*). His literary interests included promotion of Jerome's Vulgate Bible (among the earliest indications of its use in Italy), the production of a missal "for the whole cycle of the year and for all the saints." Curiously, a text known as the *Discovery and the Passion of the Holy Martyrs Gervasius and Protasius* emerged from Ravenna in this period, which claims that the martyrs' father was a soldier called Vitalis, who was martyred in Ravenna: "even today" in Ravenna Vitalis responds to prayers and intercedes for believers. As Deliyannis has noted, "By making Vitalis the father of Gervasius and Protasius, the author demonstrates the superiority of Ravenna over Milan."[17] The *Passion of Apollinaris*, another hagiographic promotion of Ravenna's prestige, may have been another literary enterprise from this period.

16 *LPR*, ch.77; Picard 1988, 123–132, based on Agnellus [ibid., 130], cites Aderitus (first successor to Apollinaris), Calocerus (fourth), Datus (seventh), Liberius I (eighth), Agapitus (ninth), and Marcellinus (tenth). Towards the end of the century, Classe also was endowed with a church dedicated to Saint Severus (bishop c.342): Agnellus, *LPR* ch.93; Picard 1988, 132–143. There was also a church dedicated to Eleucadius, the second successor of Apollinaris (and mentioned in the *Passio*), of uncertain date, though certainly well established before King Aistulf raided it (c.750) for Eleucadius's body, which he brought back to Pavia, according to the *Vita Probi*, AA. SS. Nov. IV.481–482, of twelfth-century date. It was still there in Agnellus's time (*LPR*, ch.4); he does not comment on when the church was built, but it was located in Classe somewhere near St Apollinare and the *Basilica Probi*: see Picard 1988, 122–123. In the next half century, a church was built for the third bishop, Florentius.

17 BHL 3514; Ps. Ambrose, *Inventio et Passio SS. Gervasii et Protasi*. Text in PL 17: 744–746. See Picard 1988, 29–30, and Deliyannis 2010, 224.

Maximianus may have played some part in disseminating the Justinian Code in Italy,[18] but he certainly had to defend Justinian's religious policy in Italy, especially concerning the Three Chapters dispute, and this may have been another reason for the *Passion*'s composition. Justinian extended the jurisdiction of the Ravennate see to include Flaminia (probably *Forum Flamini*, today San Giovanni Profiamma), Forlimpopoli, Cesena, and Sarsina, and reconfirmed Maximinianus's title of *archepiscopus*. In 553 Justinian's Second Council of Constantinople condemned the work of three theologians in what is known as the Three Chapters schism, over which the metropolitan sees of Milan and Aquileia broke communion with Rome and Constantinople.[19] It is precisely from this period that we first hear the church of Ravenna being called "apostolic" because of its doctrinal unity with Rome and Constantinople. Pope Pelagius I (556–561) lamented the "lonely partnership" between himself and the archbishop of Ravenna as they tried to exert their doctrinal authority to establish unity in Italy. Admittedly Pelagius also refers to Milan and Aquileia as "apostolic" sees, even as he arranged for their bishops to be physically intimidated by Byzantine forces.[20] Nonetheless, the term "apostolic" was being used for sees with metropolitan authority, at a time when Ravenna became the most powerful (and theoretically the only legitimate) metropolitan church in Italy. The *Liber Pontificalis*, the surviving version of which was written about this time (540s), records that Pope Symmachus (498–514) endowed an "oratory of St Apollinaris" in the basilica of St Andrew he built at St Peter's in Rome with thirty-one pounds of silver for "the *confessio* with the arch."[21] The association of Apollinaris with Andrew in Rome, combined with Agnellus's story of Maximianus obtaining Andrew's beard from Justinian, suggests apostolic identity had become an important symbol of episcopal authority among chief administrative cities of the empire. Apollinaris's banishment and travels to Illyricum, Moesia, Thrace, and Dalmatia in the *Passion* seems to cover the area of Europe

18 Agnellus, *LPR* 78–81; Picard 1988, 489–490; Deliyannis 2010, 212–213.

19 Chazelle and Cubitt (eds) 2007; Everett 2003a, 80–84.

20 Pelagius, *Ep.* 50 (ed. Gassó and Batlle 1956; also PL 69: 395A): "Quisquis ergo ab apostolicis divisus est sedibus, in schismate eum esse non dubium est"; " et dimittitis eos in contemptum apostolicarum sedium de sua rusticitate gloriari"; "ab eisdem apostolicis sedibus [Milan and Aquileia]." See also *Ep.* 10, 19, 24, 35, 39, 52, 60. Pelagius cites Augustine's definition of "apostolic churches and those who received letters" as the highest authorities in the church: Markus 1997, 147; Markus 1981, 567–568.

21 *LP* 53.6.

under Byzantine control at the time of Justinian, but also an area thrown into great instability by Avar, Slav, and other barbarian invasions during Justianian's reign, and churches's reactions to the Three Chapters schism.[22]

There is also some support for a pro-Second Council of Constantinople stance in the text of the *Passion* itself: in his confession before Messalinus the *vicarius* (an office relevant to the period c.284–530),[23] Apollinaris explains Christ's nature as both God and man: "He was God while he remained in the flesh, and performed miracles that amazed the world, for which he was seized by the Jews and crucified, and suffered in the flesh, which was assumed from the Virgin. As God he remained unperturbed and immortal; on the third day he revived that flesh from the dead, and after appearing to many, he ascended to heaven, from where he descended as God" (ch.18). The expounded creed reads as a statement of neo-Chalcedonian orthodoxy on Christology – that Christ has two natures, divine and human, united in one hypostasis – the issue at the heart of the Three Chapters schism, and may well be an attempt to defend the Second Council's decisions on the matter and demonstrate its orthodoxy.[24]

A Late Sixth- or Seventh-Century Date

One strong argument against attributing the *Passion* to the time of Maximianus is that it was never cited before Bede. The poet Venantius Fortunatus (c.530–600), who was educated in Ravenna in the 550s, wrote poems celebrating the cults of saints Vitale and Martin there, but only mentions Apollinaris in passing in his metrical *Life of St Martin*: "Then seek the sweetly pleasing city of Ravenna, and visit the religious pulpits of the saints, worship at the tomb of the blessed exceptional martyr Vitale, and of mild Ursicinus, blessed with the fate of Paul; then turn back and humbling yourself on the ground kiss the threshold of precious Apollinaris, then hurry through the rest of the churches. And seek the little locale of Martin, who through his shrine gave me back my

22 Apollinaris's journey to Illyricum may reflect Justinian's foundation there of a new see, Prima Justiniana, which was granted the status of a papal vicariate, without defining its relationship to the old vicariate of Thessalonica: Procopius, *Buildings* 4.1.15–27.

23 Cantarelli 1964; Jones 1964. On Messalinus, see note below, *Passion* ch.16.

24 Cf. canons 2,3,5,6, 10, and 14 of the council of Constantinople, ed. and trans. Price 2009. My thanks to Ben Wheaton, PhD student at the University of Toronto, for this observation and discussion of the texts.

failing eyesight."[25] Pope Gregory I likewise never mentions the *Passion*, but notices of the cult of Apollinaris in his correspondence demonstrate that the saint's martyr status was well established in his day (590–604), and that the cult was directly associated with the archbishopric of Ravenna. In a letter (Oct. 594) to Archbishop John II (578–595), Gregory granted him the privilege of wearing the *pallium* (the woollen cloak that symbolizes the metropolitan authority to ordain bishops) "on the days of the nativity of Saint John the Baptist, of Saint Peter the Apostle, and of Saint Apollinaris the martyr, and on the day of the celebration of your consecration." But this was only a temporary grant until Gregory could find out what the customary practice was in Ravenna. To this end he sent to Ravenna his notary Castor with instructions to gather together the senior members of the church and have them "come before the body of Saint Apollinaris, and touching his sepulcher, swear as to what the custom was before the time of Bishop John." Gregory even provides the formula for the oath: "I swear by the Father, Son, and Holy Ghost, the indivisible Trinity of divine power, and by this body of Saint Apollinaris the martyr."[26] Gregory's use of Apollinaris's body as a touchstone for an issue that reflects Ravenna's rise in authority suggests some sort of official role for the cult, just as Gregory used oaths before the body of St Peter in Rome for declarations of orthodoxy by clerics suspected of Three Chapters sympathies.[27] As mentioned in relation to the *Life of Cetheus of Pescara*, Gregory intervened in a disputed election at the church of Salona, the metropolitan authority of Dalmatia, and again relied on the body of Apollinaris, by having the rebel Bishop Maximus swear on the apostles' relics before the archbishop of Ravenna, Marinianus (596–606).[28] The dispute demonstrates not only how Gregory pro-

25 *Vita Martini* 4.680–688, ed. Leo (MGH Auct. ant. 1881: 4.1) "Inde Ravennatum placitam pete dulcius urbem/ Pulpita sanctorum per religiosa recurrens/ Martyris egregii tumulum Vitalis adora / Mitis et Urcisini Pauli sub sorte beati / rursus Apollinaris pretiosi limina lambe/ fusus humi supplex, et templa per omnia curre / Et pete Martini loculum, quo jure sacelli/ Jam desperatum lumen mihi reddidit auctor / Munera qui tribuit." Fortunatus goes on to describe the church of Paul and John, in which this shrine to Martin was situated, in detail to finish his *Life*. On the church, see Deliyannis 2010, 256–257; on Fortunatus's poem, see Roberts 2001, 2009.

26 Gregory, *Reg*. V.11, 6.31. On the issue of the *pallium,* see Markus 1981; 1997, 143–162.

27 Gregory, *Reg*. XII.7, authentic according to Norberg 1937, 2: 28. Possibly intended for Firminius of Istria, *Reg*. XII.13, but cf. XII.6 (concerning Ravenna, and see next note). Gregory seems to request such a document if travelling to Rome is difficult: *Reg*. IX.150; cf. IV.2. On clerical oaths, see Everett 2011.

28 Gregory, *Reg*. IX.178, 179, but see also I.10, I.19, II.17–20, II.44, III.22, III.32, III.46, IV.16, etc.; the dispute is well summarized in Markus 1997, 157–159.

moted the cult of Apollinaris as a necessary extension of Rome's authority in Ravenna but also the connections between Dalmatia and Ravenna, which may explain Apollinaris's journey to Dalmatia in the *Passion* (ch.24–25).[29] Gregory even granted temporary jurisdiction over sees in the Pentapolis to Archbishop John II of Ravenna, who was a personal friend.[30] Moreover, in the *Passion* (ch.3), Apollinaris's invocation, "God, you who belong to no one place but are everywhere" (*non localiter sed ubique es*), may have been inspired by a line of Gregory in the *Moralia* (see note to text), suggesting it was written after Gregory's time.

Yet another possible context for the *Passion*'s composition is during the pontificate of Pope Honorius (625–638).[31] The *Liber Pontificalis* (of Rome) records that Honorius built a church dedicated to "St Apollinaris the martyr" in the portico of St Peter's, and ordered that every Saturday a litany with hymns and chants be performed in procession from St Apollinaris's to St Peter's, which the people should join in, and it seems that the feast day of Apollinaris began to appear in Roman lectionaries around this time.[32] Honorius's pontificate also witnessed a degree of papal activity at the international level not seen since Gregory. Honorius openly endorsed the Emperor Heraclius's expulsion of the Jews from Jerusalem in 629 (which might explain the anti-Semitic statements in the *Passion,* ch.1[33]) and in 633 supported the promulgation of the *Ecthesis,* the theological formula promoted by Constantinople for reuniting Catholics with the Monophysites of Egypt. As a result, Roman missionary activity among the Croats in Dalmatia gained imperial support,[34] and Honorius pursued a vigorous policy of supporting Ravenna and suffragan Istrian churches against the Three Chapters schismatics. To this end, Honorius appointed a Roman subdeacon as patriarch of Grado, the "new Aquileia," as opposed to the "old Aquileia" (now Cormons, near Cividale) in Lombard hands. The legend of

29 Everett 2015a, 2015b.

30 *Reg.* II.25, II.28. Markus 1997, 147–148.

31 Here I build on the arguments of Lucchese 1969 for a date to the 630s, and collate more evidence.

32 *LP* 72.3–4, trans. Davis 2000. On the lectionaries, see Orchard 1996.

33 For Orioli 2001, 78, the anti-Semitism is further proof of the *Passion*'s Ostrogothic date, reflecting the "pesantissima tensione antiebraica" of the second half of Theoderic's reign.

34 The source is the tenth-century *De administrando imperii* (ch.30–31), by Constantine VII Porphyrogenitus (ed. Moravcsik, trans. Jenkins 1967). Curiously, it also records that some Croats also occupied Illyricum and Pannonia as well, both of which Apollinaris visited according to Agnellus (*LPR*, ch.2), not mentioned by the *Passion*.

Aquileia's apostolic foundations by Mark the Evangelist emerged around this time, and Grado's own house *Chronicle* (composed in the eleventh century) implicates Honorius in fostering the see's foundation by Mark.[35] The increasing strength of the Lombard kingdom and the threat it posed to Rome and Ravenna in this period may also have prompted composition of the *Passion*: the reference to Apollinaris evangelizing Emilia (ch.13) may reflect an attempt to shore up religious and political allegiance to Ravenna in the area, since the Lombards conquered much of the province in the campaigns of King Rothari (636–652).

More recent scholars have dated the *Passion* to a period soon after this, when the alliance between Rome and Ravenna fell apart. Pope Martin I (649–653) condemned the Monothelete doctrine of the reigning emperor, Constans II (641–668), who then arrested the pope and banished him to the Crimea, where he died in 655. Rome and Ravenna now found themselves on opposite sides of a theological division, and Ravenna sought to capitalize on its loyalty to Constantinople. When Pope Vitalian (657–672) demanded the appearance of the archbishop of Ravenna, Maurus, in Rome, on the threat of anathema, Maurus simply refused, issued his own anathema against the pope, and travelled to Constantinople to secure in 666 the privilege of autocephaly, which granted future archbishops of Ravenna freedom from papal consecration, or any papal interference, in the nomination and consecration of bishops. As Maurus instructed his priests on his deathbed, "Do not place yourselves under the Roman yoke. Choose a pastor from yourselves, and let him be consecrated by his bishops. Seek the *pallium* from the emperor."[36]

The same period produced a false diploma of Valentinian (425–455), which granted Ravenna metropolitan status. Some scholars see both texts as part of a *dossier* compiled by Maurus to support Ravenna's cause, because the privilege of Constans II twice calls the Ravennate church a "holy and apostolic church." We have already seen that Pope Pelagius I began to call Ravenna "apostolic" at the outbreak of the Three Chapters controversy; it is also possible that the false

35 The *Chronicle of the Patriarchs of Grado,* ch.6–7 (MGH SS rer. Lang., 394–395). It was Honorius's appointee, Primogenius, who brought the body of Hermagora (Mark's successor) to Grado, and Primogenius who petitioned the Emperor Heraclius for help and received the chair of St Mark from Alexandria. On the legend of St Mark's foundation of Aquileia, see Picard 1988, 414–422, 579, 583–556; Tomea 1993, 11–12 n23, 333–334 n17, 371–372; Cuscito 1992; Everett 2003b. The *Life of Sirus* appears to be the first attestation of it (p. 215).

36 Agnellus, *LPR*, ch.113; Picard 1988, 116–123, and Deliyannis 2010, 259–260, both date the *Passion* to this period.

privilege was drawn up then.[37] But the very text of the *Passion* argues against dating it to the autocephaly dispute, for its opening clearly promotes Rome's supremacy over Ravenna in the relationship between Peter and Apollinaris, and Petrine authority is invoked several times in the text (ch.5, 15, 24), including immediately before Apollinaris's martyrdom, when the saint proclaims his mission from Saint Peter to save Ravenna (ch.32). This is hardly the cry for independence from papal authority that we find in the evidence surrounding the grant of autocephaly to Ravenna in 666. Moreover, Agnellus reports that Archbishop Maurus brought the body of Apollinaris from the narthex of the church to its centre, "and set in silver sheets the history of that martyr." Two such silver plates were discovered in 1173 when the body of Apollinaris was transferred yet again, containing a text entitled *On the Discovery of the Body of the Blessed Apollinaris the Martyr* (given in Appendix below), which is, in effect, a summary of the *Passion of Apollinaris*. If we accept that this text and that mentioned by Agnellus are one and the same (and it is not certain that they are), then the *Passion* must have existed before Maurus had its contents inscribed on the silver plates.[38]

Finally, an argument that has not been seriously considered is that the *Passion* was written *after* Ravenna's short-lived period of autocephaly. After the condemnation of monotheletism at the Sixth Ecumenical Council of 680–681, Archbishop Theodore of Ravenna (677–691) abandoned independence altogether and appeared in Rome, where an imperial mandate had been received ordering that Ravenna's bishops be restored to the control of the papacy, that the requiem for Maurus no longer be observed in Ravenna, and the privilege of autocephaly be surrendered "to the apostolic see" of Rome.[39] This is an equally plausible setting for the composition the *Passion*, but is perhaps a little too close to our cut-off date of c.720 provided by Bede's citation of the text, and the possibly even earlier date of the *Codex Petropolitanus*, to which we now turn.

37 For the privilege, see Marini (ed) 1805, 94, no.57; Orioli 2001 argues that it was drawn up in the Justinianic period.

38 The silver plates have been variously dated to the ninth century by Mazzotti 1952, and to the eleventh by Testi Rasponi 1926, whom I follow here. Mauskopf Deliyannis (trans) 2004, 40–41, suggests that the original plates of Maurus may have been pictures, and that the plates found in 1173 were made on a later, erroneous reading of Agnellus's text. But Agnellus described the text as a *historia*: "... et ipsius martiris historiam laminis argenteis infixit" (*LPR* ch.114).

39 Brown 1984; Picard 1998, 187–188.

Text and Translation

The *Passion of Apollinaris* must have been written before the *terminus ante quem* provided by the *Martyrology* of Bede (composed 725–731), whose notice of Apollinaris seems to derive from the text of the *Passion*, since it includes events found only in that text: Apollinaris's ordination by Peter and dispatch to Ravenna, his preaching tour in Emilia and exile in Illyricum, the dating to Vespasian's reign, and the mention of Demonsten. There are also unmistakable similarities of phraseology between the two texts.[40] Just how Bede, writing in remote Wearmouth-Jarrow, obtained a copy of the *Passion* cannot now be retraced, but it is possible that the *Passion*'s presence in England was owed to the many book-buying trips to Rome of the monastery's founder, Benedict Biscop (d.681, with six trips to Rome between 643 and 679).[41] In any case, even if one were to doubt Bede's access to the *Passion*, the existence of the *Codex Petropolitanus,* dating from the eighth century (see below), proves that the text was in circulation. Interestingly, Agnellus clearly knew a version similar to the text in the *Codex Petropolitanus*, for he also records Apollinaris's episcopate as twenty-nine years, one month, and four days, and not the variants of other traditions (see *Passion* ch.35 noo).

Unlike many hagiographic works from Italy in this period, including those selected for this book, the text of the *Passion of Apollinaris* has an extraordinarily early manuscript witness, possibly written not long after the composition of the text and probably written in the saint's home of Ravenna. A manuscript now preserved in St Petersburg (National Library of Russia, V.1.12, fols. 47v–62) known as the *Codex Petropolitanus* (hereafter cited as *CP*) contains a copy of the *Passio* written in late seventh-century or eighth-century uncial script (see Plate 2). Some scholars have even dated the "solemn uncial" to the pontificates of Maurus (642–671) or Reparatus (671–677), the period in which Ravenna

40 For example, compare Bede, *Martyrology* (ed. Quentin 1908), Iul.3: "... saxo os eius constusum est, et cum gravissimo ferri pondere inclusus in carcere horrifico atque in ligno extensus: ubi ab hominibus quidem neglectus, sed ab Angelo publice pastus est," and *Passio,* ch.21: "Tunc indignatus iudex iussit saxo os eius contundi ... Apollinarem autem beatissimum cum gravissimo pondere ferri iussit in carcerem horrificum retrudi, et in ligno pedes eius extendi, et nihil ei ministrare, ut sic deficeret. Angelus autem Domini nocte veniens ad eum, videntibus custodibus, pavit eum." Quentin provides a diplomatic edition of Bede's text; there is no critical edition of the *Martyrology*. See the comments of Lifshitz (trans) 2001, 174–175, prefacing her English translation (ibid., 169–198).

41 On Bede's library, see Lapidge 2006, 34–37.

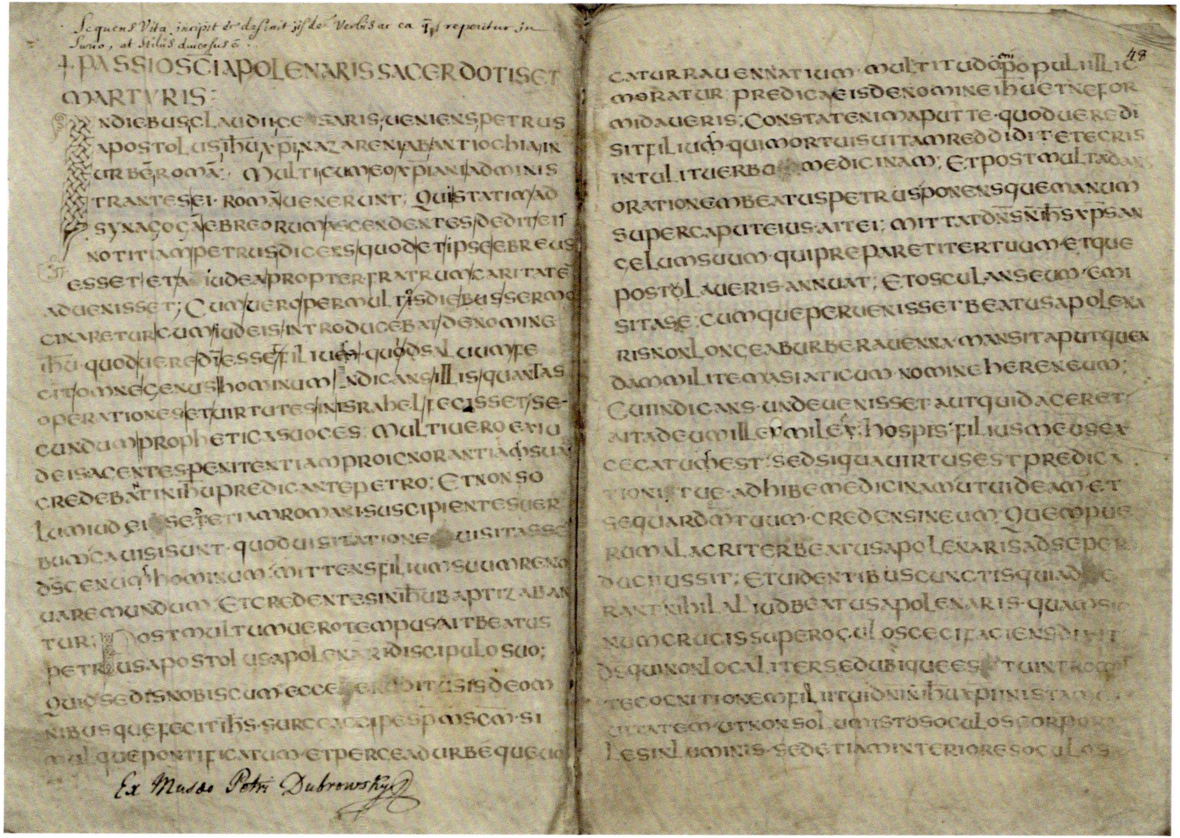

Plate 2: *Passio Apollinaris*. St Petersburg, National Library of Russia, MS Lat. F V.I.12, fols. 47v–48r.

claimed and was granted independence.[42] In the ninth or tenth century the text was bound with other hagiographical works in Corbie, though it is unclear how it arrived there.[43] The text of the *CP* differs from later manuscripts only slightly, mostly in the use of more humble epithets for Apollinaris such as "blessed" (*beatus*) often changed to the superlatives in the later versions ("most blessed" [*beatissimus*]), and in its use of vulgar orthography and grammar that predates the Carolingian reform of Latin – in the exchange of b/u (*liuera/libera, Iobis/Iovis, nouilium/nobilium,* etc.) and e/i (*hospis/hospes, sedis/sedes, advinit/advenit*); doubled or assibilated "t" (*cottidie, nunsiatum/nuntiatum, Vespatiano/Vespasiano*); the use of prepositions *ad* and *ab* for motion towards or away (*ad Emilia perexit, regressus est ab Emilia*); and some confusion between the accusative and ablative cases. For examples, see Orioli 2001, 32.

The text edited in AA. SS. Iul. V, 344–350, was based on a manuscript then preserved in Fulda, and this edition includes marginal notes recording variant readings from manuscripts originally preserved at the monastery of St Maximian in Trier (MSS Treverensis). Muratori used the "codice estense" for his version *RIS* I, 2 (Milan, 1725), col. 529–533, where it is entitled "Vita S. Apolenaris." In the translation below I have generally preferred the readings from *CP* (as given by Orioli 2001) and record in the notes only differences that alter the text or its meaning significantly.

42 CLA 11: 1608. Lowe compares its uncial to the liturgical fragment of Mombello (CLA 3: 371), also thought to be from Ravenna. Arguing for its early date is Cavallo 1992, 109–110.

43 The texts are (1) *Vita Fulgentii et Epistula Ferrandi*, fols. 1–38; (2) *Vita s. Marcellini,* fols. 39–46; (3) *Passio Apollinaris* fols. 47–62; (4) *Passio S. Dionysii, Rustici et Eleutheri*, fols. 63–68; (5) Venantius Fortunatus, *Vita S. Germani,* fols. 68–98 (cf. CLA 8: 1610); (6) *Vita S.Adomari*, fols. 99–106; and (7) *Dionysii Exigui Collectio Canonum, fols.* 106–147 (cf. CLA 8: 1061). The manuscript was in the library of Saint-Germain-des-Prés, Paris, by 1638. Prior to this it had been consulted by Lorenzo Surio for his edition in *De probatis sanctorum historiis* (Cologne, 1570–1575). See Orioli 2001, 55–57. The text may have been brought back from Ravenna among the books allegedly acquired by Charlemagne (Bischoff 1994, 131, 140–141; cf. Everett 2003a, 301) or by the Archbishop George (834–838), who took books and documents of the church with him to Francia: Agnellus, *LPR*, ch.173–174.

The Passion of Apollinaris of Ravenna

1. In the days of the Emperor Claudius, Peter the apostle of Jesus Christ of Nazareth came from Antioch to the city of Rome, bringing many Christians with him to administer the faith [and where he converted many to the Lord[44]]. Immediately they went down to the synagogue of the Hebrews, and Peter gave them notice saying that he himself was Hebrew, and that he had come from Judea because of concern for his brothers. For many days he preached to the Jews, introducing them to the name of Jesus, explaining how he is the Son of God, and how he has saved the entire human race. Peter pointed out to them the miracles and wonders that he worked in Israel, as told by the voices of the prophets. Many of the Jews were repentant about their ignorance and began to believe in the Christ because of Peter's preaching, and not only Jews but even Romans joyously received the word that by his embassy God visited the human race in sending his Son to renew the world. And so believing in Jesus they were baptized.

2. After quite some time the blessed Apostle Peter said to Apollinaris, his disciple, "Why do you sit here with us? Behold, you are well-learned about everything that Jesus did; get up and receive the holy spirit, and a bishopric along with it, and go to the town called Ravenna, where a great many people await, and preach to them about the name of Jesus. And do not be afraid, because he is with you, he who is truly the Son of God, he who has raised the dead, and he who brought the medicine of the word to the sick." The blessed Peter then prayed for Apollinaris for some time before blessing him and placing his hand upon his head, saying to him, "May our Lord Jesus Christ send his angel to prepare your journey, and may he grant you all that you request." He then kissed Apollinaris and sent him on his way.

3. When the blessed Apollinaris was close to the town of Ravenna, he stayed with an Asiatic soldier by the name of Hereneus, and told him all about how he had been sent and what he was about to do. His host the soldier said to him, "My son has gone blind. If there is power in what you preach, show us its medicine so that he may see again, and I will follow this God of yours and believe in him." Apollinaris ordered the boy to be brought to him immediately, and

44 Absent from the *Codex Petropolitanus* (*CP*).

before everyone who had gathered to watch, he did nothing more than make a sign of the cross over the eyes of the blind boy and say, "God, you who belong to no one place but are everywhere,[45] introduce this city to the knowledge of your Son our Lord Jesus Christ, so that you may illuminate not only this boy's corporal eyes, but also open the interior eyes of the heathen who live here, that they may swiftly know Jesus Christ the Son to be their Lord God, and that my preaching in this place may be truly effective." As soon as he finished this sermon the blind boy saw again and threw himself at the blessed Apollinaris's feet. Together with his parents they began to believe in Jesus Christ and were baptized in a river not far from the city of Ravenna.

4. A certain tribune's wife, who was called Thecla,[46] had suffered for many years from a terrible illness that no doctor could cure. One day the soldier, who was now Christian, was standing before the tribune when he heard him recount the story of his wife.[47] The soldier said to him, "I have staying with me right now a foreigner, of fairly advanced age, who cured my son's blindness without any medicine. If you grant him an interview, he will cure your wife." The tribune asked, "Where is this man from?" to which the soldier responded, "from the city of Rome." The tribune then asked, "so he is of Roman origin?" The soldier responded, "I don't know. He seemed more Greek to me." The tribune said to him, "Secretly bring this man to my house, so that I can determine whether what you have told me is the truth." As Apollinaris entered the city of Ravenna he crossed himself and said,

5. "God, you who have worked with my master Peter, now work with me, so I may make your name ring out, and your will be done." He entered the home of the tribune and was received with all due ceremony. The tribune said to him, "It's a good thing you have come, doctor, for nothing is sweeter than cold water to one who is parched."[48] The blessed Apollinaris replied, "May the peace

45 *non localiter, sed ubique es*: the passage seems to have been inspired by Pope Gregory, *Moralia,* 27.11 (PL 76: 409D): "Deus enim, qui persemetipsum non localiter ubique est, per praedicatores suos in mundi partes localiter ambulat." Cf. also Ps. Augustine, *Speculum* 27 (PL 40: 980).

46 Thecla (or "Tecla"), the subject of a second-century apocryphal text known as the *Acts of Ss. Paul and Thecla*, and whose cult was very popular among early Christians, is a common figure in many early hagiographical works: see Davis 2001.

47 Accepting the Bollandist reading of the "Trier" manuscript, *commemoravit de conjuge*: AA. SS., Iul. V, 344.

48 Cf. Matt.10:42; Prov. 25.1; Augustine, *Tract. in Ep. Ioh.*, 6:8 (PL 35: 2024).

of God and our Lord Jesus Christ rest within you." The tribune asked, "Who is this? Who are you talking about?" Apollinaris answered, "The Son of the living God, who renewed a world that was damned." The tribune then said, "I see you are a Galilean." The blessed Apollinaris responded, "yes." The tribune then said, "Are you aware of our cures for this?" Apollinaris responded, "There is nothing without the name of Christ." The tribune asked, "And what power is there in Jesus?" Apollinaris answered, "Summon your soldiers here, and before all of them watching you will come to know the power of my Lord Jesus Christ, and that he is the living God, for there is no other God except him." The tribune said, "Let the leading citizens be brought in, so that we all may know the power of Jesus." And when they were all standing before him the tribune said, "Look at my wife. She has been bedridden from illness many years now, and not one cure of the doctors has been able to help her. If there is any power in you, make it work!"

6. Apollinaris replied to him, "May God open the eyes of your heart so that you see his miracles and believe that Jesus is God." Then taking the hand of the women he said, "Rise, in the name of the Lord Jesus Christ, and believe in him, and say no more that there are others like him." Immediately the woman sat up and climbed out of her bed in full health, exclaiming, "There is no other God besides Jesus, just as Apollinaris preaches." Seeing all this the tribune and his soldiers were stupefied, and said, "This is truly God who could do such a thing. And since he is this powerful, worshiping him could really help us in battle." Subsequently, the tribune, his wife, his children, and the entire household believed in Jesus and were baptized, and likewise many other pagans who were present received the faith of Jesus Christ.

7. In the meantime the blessed Apollinaris took up residence at the home of the tribune in the city of Ravenna, and every day a great number of the people there came to him, and he instructed them in secret, saying, "Believe in Jesus, because he is the God of heaven and earth." Many believed and were baptized, and many nobles gave their sons to the blessed Apollinaris to be instructed by him in sacred letters. For those who believed in Christ, the blessed Apollinaris performed masses and baptisms with his disciples in the home of the tribune. Over the course of twelve years he ordained two priests, Aderitus and Calocerus. He made the noblest of men, Marcianus and the philosopher Eleu-

cadius, both deacons.[49] He established six clergy, with whom he sung psalms for the Lord day and night.

8. The reputation of Apollinaris for preaching Jesus Christ soon grew, and such great number of people believed in the faith of Christ that it could no longer be kept quiet, and so it was eventually mentioned to the commander,[50] Saturn, who had him brought before the pontiffs at the *capitolium*[51] of Ravenna. The commander interrogated him about what he wanted. Apollinaris replied in a clear voice,[52] "I am a Christian." The commander asked, "Who is Christ?" Apollinaris responded, "The Son of the living God, through whom live all creatures, in heaven, earth, and the sea." The duke said to him, "And did he himself send you to purge the temples of our gods? Do you not know of the sacred name of Jupiter? That he is mighty and inhabits the *capitolium* of this very city? You had better humble yourself before him." The holy[53] Apollinaris responded, "Who this inhabitant is, I do not know, nor do I know what temples he possesses."

9. The pontiffs then said, "Come and see the great temple marvellously decorated. You'll see there the statue of the invincible Jupiter." When he entered the *capitolium*, the blessed Apollinaris smiled and said to the pontiffs, "These fantastic ornaments of gold and silver would be better given to the poor than hung before the presence of demons." The pagan pontiffs and the people then

49 *CP* reads "He made the noblest of men, Marcianus, Leuchadius, and a philosopher, deacons." According to Agnellus, *LPR*, ch.3–4, Aderitus, Leuchadius, Marcianus, and Calocerus were the successors of Apollinaris (in that order) in the episcopacy, but he may have been influenced by the Roman *Liber Pontificalis* for the model of succession from St Peter: Deliyannis (trans) 2004, 21–29.

50 *dux*, as in some manuscripts, including *CP*; others read *iudex*, "judge."

51 It is unclear whether the *capitolium* was an area, a piazza, or, as suggested in the *Passion*, a residence for pagan priests dedicated to the worship of Jupiter. It appears to be in a different location from the temple of Apollo on the Porta Aurea and near the amphitheatre mentioned by Agnellus, *LPR*, ch.2. The *capitolium* has left no archaeological traces, though the term is mentioned in documents as late as the twelfth century. For its possible location, see Deichmann 1969–1989, 2: 27–28 (east of the Cardo and south of the Pons Augusti) and Orioli 2001, 19 n16 (area of the church of St Domenico today).

52 *CP*: "in an outspoken voice" (*libera voce*).

53 AA. SS.: "blessed" (*beatus*).

attacked him and beat him badly, and threw him out of the city and into the sea, leaving him half-alive. His disciples rescued him and hid him in the house of a widowed Christian woman while they attended to his wounds.

10. Six months later a very noble man by the name of Bonefacius, a citizen of Classe, suddenly went dumb. Many doctors were consulted, but they could do nothing for him. It was mentioned that the servant of God Apollinaris was still alive, and that he lived secretly with a widow. Bonefacius's wife immediately went to Apollinaris and pleaded with him to pay a visit to her husband. When he arrived at the house, he came across a girl of the household possessed by an evil spirit who shouted at him, "Get back, O servant of the living God! For I shall see to it that you are tied by the feet and dragged from this city." The holy Apollinaris said, "Shut up, devil, and leave this girl. You will no longer talk through men." The devil immediately departed from the girl. Then this most blessed man went up the stairs into the house of Bonefacius, saw him lying there unable to speak, and said,

11. "O Lord Jesus Christ, you who shut the mouth of this man that he may no longer invoke idols to come to his aid, open his mouth once again so that he make invoke your name, which is blessed, and let him believe that you are the living God until the end of time." Then all the Christians present said, "Amen," and immediately the man's tongue was freed, and he began to praise God, saying, "There is no other God except the one whom Apollinaris preaches." On that same day more than five hundred people began to believe in Jesus Christ, giving thanks to God and to his servant the blessed Apollinaris, through whom they were enlightened.

12. A few days later some of the pagans were ignited by an evil spirit, and according to its wishes they seized Apollinaris and beat him for a long time to stop him from ever mentioning the name of Christ again. He lay there on the ground shouting that surely he is truly God who by his own will wished to suffer in the flesh for the salvation of all. Unable to bear his testimony any longer, the pagans made the blessed Apollinaris stand barefoot on burning coals, but he simply shouted louder in praise of Christ. The wicked pagans then threw him out of the city of Classe, saying to him, "You may well have remedies, but do not enter our town, and you may live." And there the most blessed Apollinaris lay on the ground, outside city walls, and yet he continued preaching the name of Jesus Christ.

13. Many people, fearing God, came to him from the city and helped him recover, and not just the small number of Christian folk, but also a great number of the nobility. The Christians had a hut not far from the city walls, where the blessed Apollinaris baptized in the name of the Father, the Son, and the holy spirit. After many years there the most blessed Apollinaris set out for Emilia, where he taught in secret the people he caught with the word. In the meantime the priest Calocerus governed the church at Ravenna, and quietly performed many miracles in the name of Jesus Christ. Shortly after, the blessed Apollinaris returned from Emilia[54] to be received by the Christians with greatest joy.

14. At that time the consul and patrician Rufus[55] held the duchy of Ravenna,[56] and his only daughter was ill. He was told about this most blessed priest called Apollinaris, and immediately ordered for him to be summoned to his house and pay a visit to his daughter. But when Apollinaris entered the house with his clergy, [Rufus the patrician began shouting that[57]] the daughter immediately died. When he heard the lamentations, the holy Apollinaris immediately knew that she had passed away. Rufus the patrician came down the steps and in tears began to chastise him, saying, "I wish he had never entered my house! The gods have been greatly offended, and have refused to save my daughter. And now you, how could you cure her?" And everybody present was weeping along with Rufus. The most blessed Apollinaris said to him, "Patrician, faithfully entrust your oath on Caesar's health[58] unto me, and allow your daughter to follow her saviour, and then you will know the power of our Lord Jesus Christ." Rufus the patrician responded, "I know the girl is dead, and does not

54 AA. SS.: "from the town of Emilia." On the possible significance of Apollinaris's trip to Emilia, see introduction above.

55 *consul*: the Trier MSS read *proconsul*. *CP*, damaged here, seems to read *et consul* (Orioli 2001 reads *ex consul*) as do many later MSS. Orioli 2001, 30, notes that an L. Verginius Rufus was consul for AD 63, 69, and 97, C. Julius Rufus for 67, and Q. Petilius Cereale Cesius Rufus for 70, 74, and 83 – dates that do agree with the proposed chronology for Apollinaris in the *Passion*; hence, the author was possibly using local sources. In retelling this story, Agnellus, *LPR*, 1, mentions that the house of Rufus serves as the episcopal residence of Bologna in his day, and that Bishop Theodore of Bologna stole the stone sarcophagus in which Rufus and his daughter were buried to use for his own burial.

56 *ducatus Ravennae*. The term suggests a fifth-century date at least, *pace* Orioli 2001, 27.

57 Passage absent from *CP*.

58 On these oaths (also below, ch.18) and the problems they presented for Christians, see Beare 1978.

live, but if I should see her stand and speak, I will praise the power of your God, and will not stop her from following her saviour." [The entire crowd wept bitterly.[59]]

15. He who held faith in the Lord Christ went up and touched the girl, saying, "Lord Jesus Christ, my God, who gave to your apostle, Peter, my master, a place for promoting you as he requested, resuscitate this girl, because you are her creator, and there is no other God besides you." And looking over the girl he said to her, "Why do you lie there? Get up, and confess your saviour."[60] Immediately, she arose and began to speak with full voice, saying, "great is the God whom Apollinaris, his servant, preaches, and there is no other God besides him." At that moment there was great joy among all Christians, because the name of the Lord Jesus Christ had been magnified. The girl was baptized with her mother and their household of three hundred and twenty men and women. Even many of the pagans came to believe in Christ.

16. The patrician Rufus was fearful of Caesar, yet secretly loved the blessed Apollinaris and attended to his needs. His daughter was consecrated to Christ and remained a virgin. However, Caesar was eventually informed by pagans that a certain man coming from Antioch had introduced the name of Jesus Christ [the Jew[61]] to the town of Ravenna with magical incantations, and that a great number of people obeyed him, including the home of Rufus the patrician. Caesar decided to replace Rufus and wrote to the *vicarius*[62] by the name of Messalinus,[63] whom he then sent to Ravenna to determine whether an imposter of this sort should be made to bow to the gods or sent far into exile. The *vicarius* Messalinus summoned the blessed Apollinaris to his official

59 Absent from *CP*.

60 AA. SS.: "creator."

61 Absent from *CP*.

62 A *vicarius* was the head of a diocese, which may comprise several provinces: the term is relevant for the period c.284–530. See Cantarelli 1964 and Jones 1964.

63 Messal(l)inus was a noble Roman name shared by several important figures from the first century BC to the first century AD: Marcus Valerius Messalla Messallinus (36–21 BC) was commemorated in the poetry of Tibullus and Ovid as a priest of the Sibylline books and keen interpreter of Apollo (Cairns 1979, 74), which may have served as inspiration for our hagiographer. Appearances of the name in other hagiographic works (e.g., on Rufus of Capua, AA. SS. Aug. VI, 9–10; *Life of Placidus*, AA. SS. Oct. III, 70–120) seem dependent on the *Passion*.

residence[64] to be questioned, and said to him in the presence of the priests of the *capitolium*, "What is your name?" He responded, "I am called Apollinaris." The *vicarius* Messalinus said, "And from where have you come?" The most blessed Apollinaris responded, "from Antioch." The *vicarius* Messalinus said, "what art do you practice?" Apollinaris responded, "I am a Christian, and a disciple of the apostles of Christ."

17. The *vicarius* said, "And who is Christ?" Apollinaris responded, "The Son of the living God, who made heaven and earth, the sea, and every living soul."[65] The *vicarius* Messalinus said, "This Christ you speak of, is that the same who just a few years ago said he was the Son of God, and was killed by the Jews? Well, if he was God, he would not have been able to die, nor have suffered any injury. But instead he acted with arrogance, suffered injuries, and was put to death. With what reason you count him among the number of gods, we do not know." The holy Apollinaris responded, "The one about whom we speak, Jesus, was God, and he is eternity, but because he wanted to rescue the human race from slavery to demons, he emptied himself,[66] and was incarnated by the holy spirit. He was born from a virgin who had never known a man." The *vicarius* Messalinus said, "We have heard this before, but it is difficult to believe."

18. The holy Apollinaris responded, "Listen manfully,[67] judge, to what I say: he was God while he remained in the flesh, and performed miracles that amazed the world, for which he was seized by the Jews and crucified, and suffered in the flesh, which was assumed from the Virgin. As God, he remained unperturbed and immortal; on the third day he revived that flesh from the dead, and after appearing to many, he ascended to heaven, from where he descended as God.[68] He bestows so much power on those who believe in him that in his name demons are cast out, the sick are healed, the dead are revived." The *vicarius* Messalinus said, "You cannot persuade me to follow unknown gods that have not been approved by the senate. So now that these matters are out of the way, you are to approach the *capitolium* and with your own hands place incense

64 *praetorium*. Cassiodorus, *Var.* 11.8, refers to it a "building in which one judges."
65 AA. SS.: "... and everything which is in these."
66 Cf. Phil. 2:7, *semet ipsum exinanivit*.
67 *viriliter*.
68 This creed expounded by Apollinaris may be a statement of Christological orthodoxy reflecting Rome and Ravenna's alliance in the Three Chapters schism: see introduction above.

before the great god Jove the Thunderer, and then you shall live. Otherwise, by Caesar's health, I shall have you tortured by a range of torments and sent into exile."

19. The holy Apollinaris responded, "Fine, sentence me to be lead to the *capitolium*, but you can be sure that I won't be putting my hands on incense. I will, however, offer the incense of sweet praises to my Lord Jesus Christ." The pontiffs, however, began to shout, saying, "But judge, you don't know – this man has bestowed upon himself the title of pontiff, and under our title he seduces the crowd. You should examine him about his presumptions." The *vicarius* said to his secretaries, "Take him out, and say to him while you beat him, 'Come to your senses, and make an offering to the gods.'" Yet when they struck Apollinaris he exclaimed, "I am a Christian. Treat me as you see fit." While the servant of God was undergoing this, one of the demonic pontiffs said to the *vicarius*, "Stretch him on the horse-rack.[69] After a while in that agony he will honour the immortal gods." And while they tortured the most blessed Apollinaris for a long time, he repeatedly said, "I profess that the Lord Jesus Christ is the living God, and there is no other."

20. Then the *vicarius*[70] Messalinus said, "Tell me, pestiferous one, what reward do you get for suffering these torments?" The blessed Apollinaris responded, "It is written, that if any one perseveres until their death, they will be saved. For if they die in Christ, they live – this is the reward for Christians." Upon hearing this everyone who was present began to glorify God in heaven, because the blessed Apollinaris, even while being tormented, was stronger than those who administered the torture.[71] The judge said to the torturers, "While you give him another thrashing, pour boiling water into his wounds. Then with public announcement take him to a ship and chain him to a heavy weight of iron, and deport him to Illyricum in exile." One man who had been particularly cruel to the servant of God was suddenly seized by a demon and died instantly.

21. As he was being lifted from the ground the blessed Apollinaris said to the *vicarius*, "Most evil one, why don't you just believe in Jesus Christ the Son of

69 *eculeum (equuleum)*, a rack made of wood in the shape of a horse used for torture. Cf. Prudentius, *Steph.* 10, 109.

70 AA. SS: *comes*, "count."

71 AA. SS. records a vulgar use of the preposition *ab* (*fortior … ab his qui*), absent in *CP*.

God, then you can avoid eternal torment?" The judge was indignant, and ordered his mouth to be smashed in with rocks. The Christians were then so deeply disturbed at the sight of this ungodliness that they attacked the pagans. There was a great clash, yet quickly the Christians killed more than two hundred of the most wicked, and planned to kill the *vicarius* also. The judge was so disturbed, he hid and ordered that the most blessed Apollinaris be attached to the heaviest of weights and shut into a frightful prison with his feet stretched out on a board,[72] and that nothing be given to him, so he would just waste away. However, during the night an angel of the Lord came to him while the guards were watching and fed him, comforted him, and went away. On the fourth day the judge learned that Apollinaris was still alive, so had him chained and secretly placed on a ship and deported for exile. Three men of his clergy who had been attending to him followed.

22. In the meantime, the priests and deacons governed the church at Ravenna, and the number of Christians increased. While the ship sailed along the shores of the Gulf of Corinth, a storm suddenly welled up. The ship was thrown onto dry land and was smashed into pieces, and while the rest of the passengers perished at sea, the blessed Apollinaris, his clergy, and two soldiers were ejected onto the shore. The soldiers said to him,[73] "Lord father, where shall we go? What shall we do?" He answered them, "Be baptized in the name of Jesus Christ, and you will live." They immediately renounced their idols, and were baptized in the name of the Father, the Son, and the holy spirit.

23. They then began to go around from place to place, and reached Moesia,[74] where they preached the word, but no one received them. The brother of an important and wealthy man had contracted leprosy, and when the most blessed

72 *in ligno pedes eius extendi.*

73 AA. SS.: "... said to the most blessed Apollinaris ..."; "the most blessed Apollinaris answered."

74 The ancient Roman province of Moesia: its southern boundary was formed by the Balkan and Šar mountains, its northern by the Danube, and it extended east and west by the Euxine and Drina rivers respectively. There is no other testimony to Apollinaris's presence in this region. The ancient town of Apollonia Pontica (mod. Sozopol, Bulgaria) on the Thracian coast contained a giant statue of Apollo thirty cubits high, brought to Rome by Sulla's general Lucius Lucullus (c.86 BC), and this may have been a source of inspiration for our author. Agnellus, *LPR*, 2, seems to reverse the order of Apollinaris's journey (Ilyria to Salona, Panonnia, down Danube, into Thrace and Corinth on way back to Ravena).

Apollinaris had seen him, he said to him, "Do you want to be healthy?" He responded, "Yes, I do." The holy Apollinaris said, "Believe in the Lord Jesus Christ, and you will be healed." The fellow replied, "Whoever heals me shall be my god." So the [most] blessed Apollinaris called out the name of our Lord Jesus Christ and touched the leper, and immediately he was healthy again. The fellow renounced his statues, believed in the Lord Jesus Christ, and was baptized; he remained with Apollinaris for many days, and then journeyed to the banks of the Danube, and there introduced many people to the Lord.

24. When he[75] perceived that the pagans there wished to kill him, because he was the enemy of their idols, he fled to the area of Thrace, and remained there many days. A city there contained a temple of Serapis[76] which had refused to give any response to its followers throughout these days. They gave many offerings, until finally the demonic spirit spoke and said, "Don't you know that a disciple of Peter the apostle of Jesus Christ has come here from Rome, and has bound me by preaching about Jesus? We cannot give you a response unless that man is banished from this region." An investigation was begun, and the blessed Apollinaris was discovered. When they questioned him about what he was doing in this region, he said to them, "I am a Christian, and for the name of Christ I was exiled from the city of Ravenna."

25. They stripped his clothes off and beat him with clubs for a long time before leading him out to sea. They asked the rector of the province if they could place the blessed Apollinaris with all his followers on a ship already bound for Italy, saying, "It is better that he live there in the place from which he came and ruin those people, rather than empty the shrines of our gods here." And so after three years Apollinaris entered the city of Ravenna and was received there by the Christians who were overjoyed, and glorified God, who for them had

75 AA. SS.: "the most blessed Apollinaris."

76 The cult of Serapis was initially associated with Babylon and first reported in relation to Alexander the Great's death. Plutarch informs us that Ptolemy stole the statue from the town of Sinope (Sinop, Turkey) on the north shore of the Black Sea and brought it back to Alexandria, but modern Egyptologists have found evidence for the cult's local origins. Technically, Sinope was within the neighbouring province of Paphlagonia, close enough to be easily associated in legend with Thrace. Later Latin sources on the cult, however, seem unaware of the Sinopic origin, e.g., Firmicius Maternus, *De errore profanarum religionum* 14, or Augustine, *De civitate Dei* 18.5 (derived from Varro); Isidore, *Etym.* 8.11.85 (derived mostly from Augustine), offers the etymology of *serapis* from *Apis*, king of the Argives, which seems geographically apt.

recalled their father and teacher. And the Lord performed many miraculous deeds through him as he departed from the shores of Dalmatia.[77]

26. After a long time it happened that while he was conducting mass for the Christians on the suburban estate of the senator Pyreneus, a commotion was suddenly stirred up by the pagans about the celebrity of the blessed Apollinaris. The people rushed to attack him, bound him, and lead him to the forum, striking and wounding him along the way, so that when the pontiffs of the *capitolium* saw him they became indignant, saying, "He is not worthy to be presented to the great god Jupiter, since he frequently ridiculed him. Instead take him to the temple of Apollo,[78] and there he will learn of the power of the immortal gods." And when he was led there he was followed by a great number of nobles, as many pagan as Christian, together with the people. The pagans began to say, "Let's see if this man rejects us now." But when he arrived at the temple and saw the statue of Apollo, the holy Apollinaris said to those standing there, "Is this the god through whom you prophesy?" The pagans responded and said, "Yes, he's the first among the gods, and the very guardian of this city."

27. The holy Apollinaris responded, "Let nothing ever be well with this god. When he is destroyed, the Lord Jesus Christ, who is the true God, shall be the guardian of the Christians living in this place," and as he said a prayer over the statue it fell apart, and the temple of the devil was destroyed. Seeing what had happened the pagans began to exclaim, "The irreligious old man must be killed! Because of him everything has been violated." But the Christians simply gave thanks to God, saying, "Truly it is God who has performed these deeds through our Father." Some of the pagans were furious and handed Apollinaris over to a judge by the name of Taurus to have him killed. Taurus gathered the entire nobility of the city in his office along with Apollinaris and began to address him with these words: "We ask of you, that you deign to show us what powers you possess to do these things, where you have established a congregation, and what your symbol is. Also, why does such a huge crowd follow you?"

77 Agnellus, *LPR*, ch.2, specifies that Apollinaris went to Salona rather than Dalmatia in general. The appearance of Dalmatia in the *Passion* may reflect the ambience of its composition: see introduction above.

78 According to Agnellus, *LPR*, 2, this temple was "before the gate named Aurea, next to the amphitheater."

28. The holy Apollinaris responded, "The power is none other than that of the Lord Jesus Christ. We possess the house of the Lord in our hearts, but if it is a building you are after, there is one not far from the city where we Christians teach the divine word." The judge Taurus said, "Do you have any assistants?" The most blessed Apollinaris responded, "Yes, many." Judge Taurus said, "And where are they now?" The holy Apollinaris responded, "They are right here in this city of Ravenna." Judge Taurus said, "Is there any power of divinity within you yourself?" The most blessed Apollinaris responded, "I have already told you, the celestial power is that of our Lord Jesus Christ." Judge Taurus said, "You know, I have a son who was born blind. Invoke the name of this God, whom you allege was crucified by his own people, and open my son's eyes: we will then believe that this is really God. If otherwise, we shall consign you to be incinerated by fire for your crimes."

29. The holy Apollinaris then said, "Bring the blind one before us." When the boy arrived the [most] blessed Apollinaris said to him, "In the name of the Lord Jesus Christ, open your eyes and see." Immediately, he opened his eyes and received the light. Every aristocrat present began to say, "He is truly God, who does such things." Then many of them believed in the Lord Jesus Christ, so Judge[79] Taurus snatched Apollinaris away from the people and at night dispatched him to his private estate to keep him there under guard. And there he remained four years, just six miles from town. All the Christians came to visit him there and to be instructed by him, and whenever a sick person was taken there, no matter what infirmity they suffered, they returned in health.

30. During the reign of the Emperor Vespasian[80] a hateful report against the [most] blessed Apollinaris reached Rome from the pontiffs of the *capitolium* in Ravenna, where there were over three hundred altars. In the report the pontiffs stated, "If you do not kill this seducer Apollinaris, who preaches against your rule and against the well-being of the state, he will consign Roman ceremony to oblivion. For it is no small multitude whom he seduces every day into raging against the immortal gods by assaulting them. This man has destroyed temples with his magical tricks: it is necessary, therefore, to take only the life of this Apollinaris, already stooped from age, in order that the name of Rome

79 *praeses* (*CP*).
80 Vespasian (69–79). *CP* reads "Vespasian Caesar."

endures." The emperor[81] then sent out the following order: "Should anyone dare insult the gods even verbally, he must request pardon from the gods or be exiled from the town. For it is not right that we should vindicate our gods, when they can avenge themselves of their enemies if they are angered. Fair thee well."[82]

31. Soon after the order had been given it reached[83] Demonsten, a nobleman and a patrician, but completely and utterly pagan. In full compliance with the commands he ordered that the blessed Apollinaris be summoned before him. Although stooped from old age and the various tortures he had suffered, he stood before the judge as he had been ordered. The pagans shouted out, "Do not ask this man anything, for we all know that he is a Christian and a destroyer of temples; simply punish him, and send him far away from this city, lest we all perish."

32. The patrician Demonsten said, "Tell me, o ancient seducer, what is your religion?" Apollinaris said, "I do not deny your glory, but I speak the truth[84]; I am a Christian, taught by the blessed Apostle Peter, who himself sent me to this happiest of towns, so that its inhabitants might believe and deserve to be saved in the name of Jesus Christ." Demonsten the patrician said, "What more can be done? It is high time that you abandon your vanity and satisfy the gods." The blessed Apollinaris responded, "I offer myself as a sacrifice in order to save my children whom I have acquired for myself here."

33. "Anyone who does not abandon the worship of demons[85] to worship the God of heaven,[86] who rules in eternity together with the Lord Jesus Christ and the holy spirit, will be consumed in an eternal fire. But whosoever believes and is baptized will have eternal peace and everlasting wealth." Then the judge seethed with anger and handed him over to a certain centurion while he

81 "Caesar Vespasian" (AA. SS.).

82 The shift to direct speech and the apt wording of the decree (including the customary salutation *bene valete*) lends suspicion to an authentic document, even if used only as a model, behind this passage. See Zuccotti 2000, 46–47; and Wheeler 2016, 5–6, 10–11.

83 Reading *percurrit* (*CP*, MS *Estense*) instead of "*praecipet* ad Demonsten ..." (AA. SS.).

84 "I do not envy your eminence, and I shall speak the truth" (AA. SS.).

85 AA. SS.: "abandon the gods."

86 AA. SS.: "... of heaven, the earth and the sea ..."

thought about which tortures to inflict upon Apollinaris. But the centurion was secretly a Christian, and took him to his house in Classe, where after a few days he said to the blessed Apollinaris, "Lord Father, I do not want to hand you over to die so quickly, because your life is necessary for us. So leave at night and go into the district where the sick live, until the people's fury has abated." And silently, in the middle of the night, he untied him so that Apollinaris could escape.

34. When the pagans had learned of this, they set out after him, and captured him not far from the gates, where they repeatedly struck him until they thought he was well and truly dead, and so left him there. But before the break of day his disciples collected him and led him into the district where the lepers lived.[87] And there lying among the Christians he survived another seven days, admonishing the church never to forsake the faith of Christ, and proclaimed to them that the future held in store many more persecutions for the sake of Jesus Christ, and that after these many storms[88] the emperors themselves will turn to the faith of Christ, the power[89] of the demons will be emptied, and throughout the entire world Christians will be able to freely offer the host to the living God. Whosoever endures in the faith of Jesus Christ will fully live,[90] and who does not will die.

35. After he had said these things and much more, the most blessed martyr and bishop of Jesus Christ died, and was buried by his disciples outside the walls of Classe in a coffin made of stone, which they placed under the ground in fear of what the pagans might do. He had governed his church for twenty-nine years, one month, and four days.[91] The most blessed Apollinaris, priest of the Lord and martyr for Christ, was martyred in the city of Ravenna during the reign of the Emperor Vespasian, on the tenth day from the Kalends of

87 *vicus leprosorum*, also attested in the *Life* of Eletherius of Tournai (c.454–531), one of whose disciples died in Ravenna: "ibique sepultus est in vico qui vocabatur Vico Leprosorum" (AA. SS. Feb. III, 183). It is possibly the same "district where the sick live" (above, *Passion*, ch.33).

88 *tempestates* (*CP*, and MSS Estense and Vossius); AA. SS. amends to *tentationes*, "trials."

89 Reading *numina* (MS Maximini) instead of *nomina* (*CP*).

90 *vita vivet*, lit. "live with life."

91 Following *CP*, which agrees with Agnellus's account: *LPR*, ch.1. AA. SS. reads "twenty-eight years and four days."

August.[92] In the reign of Our Lord Jesus Christ, to whom be honour and glory, forever and ever. Amen.[93]

92 23 July.

93 Following *CP*, which then concludes with four phrases of "thanks be to God" arranged in the form of a cross. AA. SS. reads, "... under the rule of the Lord God and our Saviour Jesus Christ, who lives and rules as God together with the holy spirit for ever and ever. Amen."

Appendix

Text of the silver plates placed on Apollinaris's sarcophagus. Translated from the Latin text in Testi Rasponi 1926. The details given are taken from the *Passion*, following the order given below, cf. *Passion*, chapter 2 (sent); 3, 28–29 (blind); 4–6 (paralytics); 10–11 (mute); 10 (demons); 14–15 (raised dead); 23 (lepers); 26–27 (idols); 25 (clubs); 12 (coals); 19 (rack); 20 (boiling water); and 21 (iron and rock).

> Blessed Apollinaris born in Antioch, was sent to Ravenna by the highest prince of the apostles to preach the baptism of repentance for the remission of sinners. And there through him the Lord worked many miracles. For instance, he gave light to the blind, cured paralytics, made the mute speak, put demons to flight, raised the dead, cleansed lepers, and destroyed images and temples of idols. Here he was beaten with clubs. Still longer he stood barefoot over live coals. Hung from a rack he was beaten once more. He received boiling water over his wounds. He was banished into exile with a heavy weight of iron and his mouth smashed by a rock. He died under Vespasian Caesar, on the tenth day before the Kalends of August [21 July] in the reign of Our Lord Jesus Christ, with the Father and the holy ghost, forever and ever, Amen.

I AUGUST

The Passion and Life of Eusebius of Vercelli

The *Passion and Life of Eusebius of Vercelli* is the longest and arguably the most ambitious hagiographical work from early medieval Italy after Gregory I's *Dialogues*. Sometime between c.570 and c.890, an anonymous hagiographer of Vercelli assembled information on the first bishop of his city, Eusebius (episcopate c.345–371), in order to remind his congregation, and a wider audience, of the importance of their patron saint as one the great defenders of Nicene orthodoxy, and that thanks to Eusebius, their city church became the chief authority in western Christendom at the time. The hagiographer drew upon chronicles and histories that have come down to us, including Eusebius's own writings, but also upon local documents and other sources that have not survived, to highlight the saint's starring role on the historical stage: baptized by a pope, Eusebius defied an emperor, suffered imprisonment and exile in Palestine and Cappadocia, convened a council with Athanasius of Alexandria in that city, was granted oversight of the western church by another pope, and was violently martyred by Arians in revenge for his success against them. The *Life of Eusebius* allows us to witness a hagiographer at work in configuring his sources, filling in gaps, and even rearranging chronology to create a compelling portrait of a patron saint very much in the mould of Ambrose of Milan – and, what is more, a local patron saint who made Ambrose possible.

A Hero of Orthodoxy and His Cult

Eusebius of Vercelli (d.371) was undeniably an important historical figure in the fourth-century conflicts between state-sponsored Arianism and those who claimed to defend orthodox Christianity based on the Nicene Creed. Eusebius convened councils with Athanasius of Alexandria and Hilary of Poitiers, and along with them suffered exile for his defiance of the Emperor Constantius. Jerome, writing c.392, granted Eusebius a place in his *On Illustrious Men* of the church, and Ambrose hailed Eusebius as the first bishop to hold "clerical office while living under monastic rule."[1] As is duly noted in the *Passion and Life of Eusebius of Vercelli*, presented here, Eusebius held primacy over all churches in the West by papal authority, and is reputed to have written in his own hand the earliest known complete text of the Gospels in Latin (*Codex Vercellensis*: see *Life of Eusebius*, ch.17). Pieces of his correspondence with the Emperor Constantius, Pope Liberius, and his own suffragan clergy survive, and he is perhaps the author of a treatise on the Trinity.[2] Eusebius seems to have been the first bishop to have been buried in a church.[3]

But Eusebius's reputation, both as martyr and as staunch defender of orthodoxy, has enjoyed a mixed fortune. His cult was established quickly: within decades of his death, sermons (wrongly attributed to Bishop Maximus of Turin [d.465] but in all likelihood dating c.380–400) circulated commemorating his "martyrdom" at the hands of violent Arians. As we shall see below, Gregory of Tours (writing in the 590s) attests to the fame of Eusebius's cult and the saint's posthumous healing powers on his feast day. Gregory even claims that his mother had relics of Eusebius (which once prevented her house burning down), a claim at odds with the *Life of Eusebius*, which records Eusebius's express commands to his clergy not to distribute relics of his body or clothing (ch.42, below). But Gregory classified and described Eusebius not as a martyr but as a "confessor," and none of the historians and writers of the late fourth and early fifth century mention Eusebius's martyrdom. Instead, Rufinus of Aquileia, Sulpicius Severus, and the Greek historians whose works were collected and translated into Latin in the *Historia Tripartita* (Socrates, Sozomen, and Theodoret) all made brief mentions of aspects of Eusebius's career: his involvement at the Council of Milan in 355, his subsequent exile to Palestine, Cappadocia, and Egypt, and his involvement in the Council of Alexandria of 362. Their attention focused more on Eusebius's contemporaries, such as Hilary and Athanasius, as the holy heroes of orthodoxy in the mid-fourth century.

1 Jerome, *De viris illustribus* 96 (PL 23: 697B); Ambrose, *Ep.* 13 *extra coll.*, ed. Banterle 1988, 263–321.

2 The same *De Trinitate* has also been attributed to Athanasius, Vigilius of Thapsus, or Ambrosiaster. Bulhart's edition, 1957 (CCL 9), 3–99, revived the theory of Eusebian authorship but has not universally been accepted, for good reasons: see Simonetti 1963 and Dattrino 1976. A restatement of Eusebius's authorship is Williams 1995, 239–242.

3 Picard 1988, 271, 290–292. On the form and archaeological remains of the church, totally rebuilt first in the sixteenth and again in the eighteenth century, see Cantino Wataghin 1997, 28–34.

The career of Ambrose (bishop 374–397), and the subsequent elevation of Milan as the indisputable metropolitan authority of northern Italian churches, also contributed to the eclipse of Eusebius's historical importance. It was only towards the late nineteenth century that historians rediscovered his role, and that "Eusebius must have been a more important personage than we are accustomed to think."[4] In the twentieth century Pope John XXIII (1958–1963) recognized this by declaring Eusebius the patron saint of Piedmont. A similar sense of rediscovery, and the need to set the record straight, permeates the early medieval *Life of Eusebius* translated here.

There may be two other reasons why Eusebius was relatively neglected by contemporary and slightly later authors. The first is that, shockingly, Eusebius may not have been the strict advocate and enforcer of orthodoxy that his later reputation, and the *Life of Eusebius*, tried to project. Three separate testimonies from the period question his judgement on theological matters: Jerome noted that Eusebius translated into Latin a commentary on the Psalms by Eusebius of Caesarea, whom Jerome considered a heretic[5]; a contemporary writer known as "Ambrosiaster" recalled that a book by Eusebius claimed that "the holy spirit did not know the mystery of the birth of Jesus Christ, and I am amazed that a man of such learning should have cast this stain upon the holy spirit"[6]; and, finally, in a record of a debate (AD c.366) between the Arian bishop of Sirmium and an orthodox layman, the bishop defensively claims, "I expounded and revealed my creed to Eusebius, and it was pleasing to him."[7] It seems that Eusebius (of the historical record) was capable of finding room for theological compromise among the hair-splitting definitions of fourth-century theology.

The second reason for the neglect of Eusebius in favour of his contemporaries is his less impressive literary output. The *Historia Tripartita,* which the hagiographer clearly used for the *Life of Eusebius*, drew less-than-flattering comparisons between Eusebius and Hilary of Poitiers, as did Rufinus of Aquileia:

4 Turner 1899, 126. The same spirit animates Ferrari 1996.

5 Jerome, *De viris illustribus*, c. 96 (PL 23: 697B), named the work which Eusebius translated as that of Eusebius of Caesarea but voices the criticism in a letter defending his own translation of Origen: *Ep.* 61, ed. Labourt 1953, 3: 111 (PL 22: 603).

6 Ambrosiaster, *Quaest.*, ed. Souter 1905, 384–385. Schepens 1950 identifies the text in question as the *De Trinitate* mentioned above.

7 *Altercatio Heracliani laici cum Germinio episcopo Sirmiensi*, in Patrologiae cursus completus: *Supplementum*, ed. A.-G. Hamman, 5 vols. (Paris, 1958–1974), 1: 345–350, at 346. On this text, see Simonetti 1975.

> ... like two great lights of the world, [Eusebius and Hilary] lit up Illyricum, Italy, and Gaul with their brightness. The only difference was that Hilary, a man naturally gentle and peaceful and at the same time learned and most adept at persuasion, was achieving this purpose more skilfully. For Hilary also published some excellent books in which he so carefully expounded both the cunning of the heretics and the way in which our people had been deceived and their unfortunate gullibility that with this faultless teaching he corrected both those with him and those far away whom he could not address in person.[8]

Another key source used by the hagiographer, as mentioned above, was the Ps. Maximus of Turin sermon (written AD 380–400), which conceded that Eusebius was less artful with the written word, and should be venerated for translating doctrine into pastoral care:

> And now we wish to add something in praise of the holy martyr Eusebius. For he lived as a master of ineffable teachings, so that his merits are known more easily from his good works than from his sermons. For he retained such an amount of knowledge that it was beyond the power of speech to phrase it. Therefore the deeds of this man should not be embellished with words, but instead revealed for their meaning, especially since we know we should not adorn a thing in speech which we see already adorned by virtue, just as the apostle of the Lord says, "the kingdom of God lies not in speech but in virtues."[9]

Despite the sermon's moving description of Eusebius's harsh imprisonment, torture, and martyrdom, descriptions borrowed and elaborated upon by the author of the *Life of Eusebius* (ch.24–26, 29), this was not how Eusebius was remembered outside Italy. Our only other early medieval notice of Eusebius's cult is a curious chapter in one of Gregory of Tours's hagiographic works – not his *Glory of the Martyrs*, as one might expect, but instead *Glory of the Confessors*:

8 Rufinus, *Historia Ecclesiastica* 1.31 (PL 21: 501B). Likewise, Cassiodorus *HT*, 6.24 (Socrates 3.8) (PL 69: 1046A–B): "Both these men worked hard for the faith. But Hilary was so learned in his books that his writing completely settled the matter of the consubstantiality of the Trinity. He set this out so well that he utterly destroyed the beliefs of the Arians."

9 (Ps.) Maximus of Turin, *Serm.* 7, ed. Mutzenbecher (CCL 23 1962: 24) (trans. mine). On the origin and date of this sermon, see Everett 2006, 141 n25.

> Bishop Eusebius of Vercelli was a great supporter of Hilary against heresies. He shows that he is still alive after burial by his current miracles. For on his feast day many of the sick are cured, and the demonically possessed dance around the entire church in violent spins, plainly confessing that they are suffering from torments. They leap in the air and with their hands strike and smash the lamps which are lit to provide light. Once they are soaked in the oil that leaks out of the lamp, the demon immediately departs and they are cleansed. The people then know how many of the ill have been cured by the number of lamps they see broken. Moreover, everything that belongs to his church is considered to be guarded by his devout protection, so that no one steals anything from it. You might see that even among unjust enemies no one touches the herds of cattle, horses, or sheep, for as soon as someone touches anything, his voice calls out, "These things belong to the confessor Eusebius." My mother placed the relics of this saint in the oratory of her own house.[10]

Gregory goes on to describe how these relics of Eusebius saved his mother's house, and the whole town, from burning down after late night carousing by an unattended fire. Yet in Gregory's story Eusebius describes himself as a "confessor," and again he plays second fiddle to Hilary. As we shall see below, the *Life* can only be loosely dated 570–830 (and possibly pre-725). Perhaps this sort of appropriation of Eusebius's cult elsewhere, certainly earlier than the 590s when Gregory wrote, prompted the composition of the *Life* to reclaim Eusebius for Vercelli, and explains the hagiographer's comments on the lack of relics (*Life of Eusebius*, ch.42). We may well be looking at a late sixth- or early seventh-century context for the composition of the *Life*, when its heavy emphasis on combating Arianism would have found a ready audience among clerics concerned about the establishment of Lombard rule in northern Italy.

The almost hysterical portrayal of Arians as one-sided villains in the *Life of Eusebius* is common to anti-Arian diatribes from the fourth and fifth centuries, and here the *Life* reflects the language of its sources, particularly the letters of Eusebius, Hilary, and Pope Liberius, who often described themselves as "martyrs" ("of the true faith") for suffering exile. Most fourth-century emperors, including Constantine, were sympathetic to deviations from the Nicene for-

10 *Glor. Conf.* 3, ed. Arndt and Krusch (MGH SS rer. Merov. 1885: 3:750). The location of Gregory's mother's house is uncertain: most likely Chalon-sur-Saône. See Van Dam (ed and trans) 1988a, 20 n7, whose translation of Gregory's chapter differs slightly.

mula, and there were many views and factions.[11] Late fourth-century and fifth-century authors paint over these conflicts with a simple dichotomy between Niceans and Arians, and our hagiographer uses the same narrative framework. Anti-Arian polemic fades from the historical record after the conversion of the Visigothic monarchy to Catholicism in 589, and after some Lombard kings finished flirting with Arianism in the mid-seventh century – another context that suggests a sixth or seventh century date for the *Life of Eusebius*. It is difficult for the modern mind to understand why such fine theological distinctions caused such bitter hatred among churchmen. One prime reason was a perceived need for absolute unity of doctrinal belief throughout the empire, mentioned by the hagiographer with a scriptural allusion: "Every kingdom or house divided against itself cannot by any means stand" (*Life of Eusebius,* ch.26. Cf. Matt. 12:25).

The Council of Milan (355) and Lost Documents

The central event in the *Passion and Life of Eusebius*, around which much of the narrative is structured, is the Council of Milan in 355, when Eusebius was condemned to exile because of his opposition to Emperor Constantius II's attempts to enforce acceptance of the creed promulgated at the Council of Sirmium (351), and because of Eusebius's refusal to agree to the condemnation of Athanasius of Alexandria, the fiery prelate who had already been exiled by this emperor once before (330–346), and by his father, Constantine I, before him (335–337), for his staunch opposition to Arian clergy and ability to stir up trouble (he was later condemned by two more emperors).[12] Interestingly, we have two other accounts of events at the council that differ from the portrait offered in the *Life of Eusebius*. Sulpicius Severus records in his *Chronicle* (written c.400) that Dionysius of Milan agreed to condemn Athanasius so long as the assembly discussed matters of doctrine; instead, the assembly retired to the imperial palace and issued a synodal letter in the emperor's name, which Dionysius refused to accept, and he was thrown out of the city. Our other description is from Eusebius's colleague, Hilary of Poitiers, who was not at the council, but

11 Trusty guides to the events and theological debates of the fourth century, including the episodes referred to in the *Life*, are Hanson 1988; Brennecke 1988; Barnes 1993; Williams (trans) 1987; McLynn 1994; and Williams 1995. On the fifth-century rewriting of this period, see Ferguson 2005.

12 Barnes 1993.

gave Eusebius the starring role: Hilary claims that Eusebius tried to trick the council by saying that he would agree to the condemnation of Athanasius if everyone present signed a copy of the Nicene Creed, which Eusebius suddenly produced and placed before them. Dionysius was the first to pick it up and began to sign when the Arians "snatched the quill and parchment from his hands," and effectively shut down the council, retired to the palace, and issued the decree of exile.[13]

The account given by the hagiographer is similar, but was clearly based on other sources, some of which survive, but others have been lost. One recognizable source was the Ps. Maximus sermon on Eusebius's martyrdom: although it does not mention the council, it explains that Eusebius suffered exile because of a ruse he devised to rescue Dionysius of Milan, who had been tricked into signing some sort of chirograph – a story that matches that of Sulpicius Severus (above), who implied that Dionyisus was somehow tricked (or tricked himself) into signing the condemnation of Athanasius. The Ps. Maximus sermon then gives an account of Eusebius's behaviour from which the hagiographer borrowed to describe the council:

> Just as the apostle says, "To the Jews I am a Jew, so that I might win Jews" (1 Cor. 9:20), likewise the holy Eusebius lied and made himself a heretic for the heretics, in order to liberate his son [Dionysius] from heresy. For he said he would consent to their treachery, if this would make them happy, but the fact that they had placed his son Dionysius before him to subscribe [the document] gravely upset him. "For you," he said, "you say the Son of God cannot be equal to God, so why do you place my son before me?" This argument immediately disturbed them, and they deleted the autograph of Dionysius and asked Eusebius to sign in his place. But he then just mocked them and, laughing, said, "I will not pollute myself with your evil, nor do I permit my son to associate with you in any way."[14]

The hagiographer also used this sermon for his account of Eusebius's torment on the stairs of the palace (where the martyrdom took place, according to the sermon), along with the glib analogy to Jacob's ladder, and a mountain-top dream presaging Eusebius's martyrdom (*Life of Eusebius*, ch.25).

13 Sulpicius Severus, *Chronicon* 2.39 (PL 20: 150A–151B); Hilary, *Liber I ad Constantium*, 2.3, ed. Feder 1916, 186–187.

14 Ps. Maximus, *Sermo*, ed. Mutzenbacher, 1962, 25. Cf. *Life of Eusebius* ch.22.

But the hagiographer also had access to other sources on the council presumably preserved at Vercelli. The claim that Dionysius and "another twenty-nine bishops" signed the condemnation of Athanasius seems to refer to the same now-lost document seen by the sixteenth-century scholar Cesare Baronio.[15] Other claims, such as the forty-eight signatures on a creed (*Life of Eusebius* ch.21), may reflect more archival sources, but in this case the events seem quite muddled: Dionysius was supposedly ordained by Eusebius as a replacement for Auxentius, who was supposedly condemned earlier at the Council of Rimini (*Life of Eusebius*, ch.18), and Pope Liberius supposedly attended, along with 318 bishops, the legendary number of attendees at the Council of Nicaea. All of this is ahistorical nonsense – Rimini actually took place in 359, and Auxentius replaced Dionysius in 355 – but suits the hagiographer's purpose to create an idealized version of the council whereby Milan and Rome are united in Eusebius's suffering for the defence of the faith. The same artistry can be seen in the use of Eusebius's letters (ch.19 to Constantius, ch.28 to Patrophilus), which raise interesting questions about their disputed chronology and later transmission, and also Eusebius's subscription from the Council of Alexandria in 362, inserted into the proceedings of Milan (ch.21). Interestingly, our hagiographer also seems to have had a copy of the *Epistula Catholica,* the synodal decree issued from Alexandria but which survives only in fragmentary form. The *Life* claims that this decree gave Eusebius metropolitan authority over all of Europe, and that Eusebius deposited a copy in the papal archives (ch.34–35, and references cited); although these claims are not supported elsewhere, there seems little reason to doubt them.

The author of the *Life of Eusebius* therefore had access to documents and materials dating from Eusebius's career that have now been lost to us. Confirmation of this is Eusebius's letter to Patrophilus, which only survives because of its inclusion in the *Life of Eusebius* (see ch.28). It is also clear that he consulted the letters to Eusebius from Pope Liberius, Emperor Constantius, the papal legate at the Council of Milan, and the council itself.[16] The language and imagery from these letters infuse the *Life of Eusebius*, most notably in the repeated references to legitimate absenteeism (e.g., ch.11, 18, 20, from the exchange between Eusebius and Constantius) and the rhetoric of "martyrdom"

15 On the lost documents mentioned here, see Everett 2006, 157–163.

16 The letters are collected in Bulhart (ed) 1957 (CCL 9: 102–135). On their use in the *Life*, see Everett 2006, 148–150. The chronology and order of the letters is unclear: the revisionist views of Williams 1995, 53–58, are contentious; they are vehemently opposed by Simonetti 1997, 170–172.

for defending orthodoxy (*passim*, from Pope Liberius to Eusebius, and Eusebius to his clergy). Our ability to consult these and other surviving sources used by the hagiographer (the Ps. Maximus sermons, the *Historia Tripartita*, Jerome's *De viris illustribus*, etc.), offer us the rare chance to watch an early medieval hagiographer at work. Just when he worked is another question.

Date of Composition

Earlier historians such as Fedele Savio and Francesco Lanzoni dismissed the *Life of Eusebius* as a work of little or no historical value.[17] Part of the problem was the text's anonymous authorship and uncertain date of composition. The *termini* (*ante* and *post*) are provided by the *Life*'s use of Cassiodorus's *Historia Tripartita* (written 570s), and the earliest manuscripts dating from the late ninth or early tenth century (some are listed below). However, the evidence of martyrologies suggests a slightly earlier date: Bede's martyrology (written c.720s) merely notes that Eusebius was a martyr, but the notices in the Carolingian martyrologies of Florus of Lyon (c.830s), Hrabanus Maurus (c.845–855), Ado of Vienne (c.870–875), and Usuard (c.870–875) all seem to depend on the *Life* and its contents.

This closes the gap a little (570–830s), but evidence presented elsewhere in this book may close it more. As I argue above (pp. 20–22), the *Life of Gaudentius of Novara* can be dated to the period 685–725, despite the tendency of historians to date it later because of its rhetorical style of Latin, a high style also evident in the *Life of Eusebius*. But it is also possible that the author of the *Life of Gaudentius* knew the *Life of Eusebius*, from which he gained his information about Eusebius's exile. If the hagiographer behind the *Life of Gaudentius* did use the *Life of Eusebius*, then the *Life of Eusebius* must have been written between the 570s (the use of Cassiodorus's *Historia Tripartita*) and c.725 (the latest date for the *Life of Gaudentius*).

Unfortunately there are no further clues or hints in the text to any contemporary purpose, issue, philological or topographical reference that might help us to secure that date or any other, as has been possible with other hagiographical texts (e.g., *Sirus* and Pavia's disputes with Milan and Aquileia; *Michael*

17 Savio 1899–1932, 412–420, 514–552; Lanzoni 1927, 1038. Expressing cautious optimism about the text was Crovella 1961. More recent considerations of the text are Ferrari 1996, Saxer 1997, and Grégoire 1999.

and the dispute between Siponto and Benevento). Nevertheless, in the interest of future research that might help pinpoint the date, I would highlight two aspects of the text that also have historical significance. Firstly, the *Life* (ch.17) contains the earliest reference to the site of Crea (today Sacro Monte di Crea, in Serralunga di Crea, Piedmont), where Eusebius founded an oratory dedicated to the Virgin Mary – later medieval legends add that he installed a statue of the Madonna there also (which may be an elaboration from the *Life*). There is no reason to doubt that Eusebius founded the site – he had, after all, been thrown out of Vercelli and needed a safe haven from angry Arians. But further information on the site of Crea – the date when first occupied and clear evidence for a religious cult there – may well throw further light on the composition of the text. Secondly, the *Life* (ch.40) contains the earliest reference to a "martyr Theognistus," for whose relics Eusebius built a church dedicated to the saint, the same church in which they interred Eusebius's remains. We have almost no information on this martyr besides the *Life* (see below, n.72), but future discoveries may shed more light on the history of this cult, and subsequently on the *Life of Eusebius*.

Text and Translation

The following translation relies on the edition of Ferdinando Ughelli, printed in his monumental *Italia sacra; sive de episcopis Italiae et insularum adjacentium*, 2nd ed., 10 vols. (Venice 1717–1722), 4 [1719]: 749–761 (1st ed. = 1030–1040). The text is known as the *Vita antica* (BHL 2748) to distinguish it from later epitomes, particularly that used by Jacob de Voragine in the *Legenda Aurea*, ch.108 (103) and published in Mombritius 1910, 1: 460–461 (also BHL 2751; see also *Life*, ch.28 n63). A full list of editions and partial editions of epitomes is given by Maritano 1997, 426–427. The *Vita antica* has been translated into Italian by Capellino 1986, 28–52, and Bosco 1995, 234–252, both of which render the text in more simple language than the ambitious Latin really allows.

Ughelli's text remains the only serviceable edition of the *Vita*. He edited it "from a very old manuscript of saints lives from the monastery of Nonantola, which appears to have been written before the year 1000" (ibid., 4: 749C). The manuscript remains unidentified, but the most likely candidate is Turin, Biblioteca Nazionale e Universitaria, F.III.16, written in Emilia, possibly Nonantola. However, Saxer 1997, 145–146, notes that this manuscript contains different readings, suggesting either that Ughelli consulted another manuscript or that he "corrected" the text considerably. A new edition is needed, preferably based on the five manuscripts that are pre-1000 (as above, Turin, Biblioteca Nazionale e Universitaria, F.III.16, fols. 60–72, saec. X, plus, Ghent, Universiteitsbibliotheek, 244, fols.46v–55, saec. IX; Paris, Bibliothèque nationale de France, lat. 5321, fols.126v–133v, saec. X; Rouen, Bibliothèque municipale, 36, fols.41v–49v, saec Xex; Rouen, Bibliothèque municipale, 42, fols. 90–99v, saec. Xex). The Bollandist website lists thirty-seven manuscripts, most dating to the twelfth and thirteenth centuries.

The relatively lengthy *Life of Eusebius* shows signs of loose composition, with repetitions (e.g., the etymology of Eusebius's name, ch.3, 12) and jumbled themes (angelic assistance and chastity, ch.12), or at least adaptability for extemporal modification on the occasion (e.g., whether long or short sermon), particularly the block of obligatory miracles (ch.12–16), which read like later additions, more concerned to paint Eusebius in the traditional light of a martyr.

The Latin is rhetorically ambitious (e.g., *typicalis operatio* and "Passover" in ch.3, *transitus mutatio* in ch.38) and shows a preference for para-liturgical use of abstract nouns as agents ("God's grace provided Y," "Eusebius's sanctity caused X," "the madness of the Arians oppressed Liguria," etc.). For this reason it is often less successful in conveying a clear meaning for the purpose of narrative, and there are places where the text or tradition seems corrupted (e.g., Sardinia, ch.3 and Auxentius, ch.18). Of particular literary interest is the use of a *laus civitatis* passage coupled with claims to primacy (ch.9), which matches the civic pride expressed in other hagiographic works from this period (e.g., *Sirus*, *Zeno*, *Gaudentius*), and in praise poems such as the *Laudes Mediolanensis civitatis* and *Versus de Verona*.

The Passion and Life of Eusebius of Vercelli

1. Everything which, on the Lord's authority, has been written down in this, my first work, concerning the most blessed Eusebius, bishop and martyr of Vercelli, I have learned from the histories and chronicles of distinguished men, and also from the short works of the same most holy man that were sent to different places to inform the holy fathers. And in this work, dearest brothers, I shall try my hardest to tell his story from the very beginnings of his childhood. It is true that no mortal can describe the glory of the deserved praise of the saints. Nevertheless, to the extent that my powers are sufficient, my corporal tongue cannot remain silent, for long as the soul swells with love to sing praises of the saints for their interventions, even if they are not worthily performed, the reward will be denied to no one.

2. First we must describe the noblest birth of his innate character and how the pure innocence in that holy time, of the most blessed Eusebius, bishop of Vercelli, was rewarded for his service. It was the time when Diocletian and Maximian, emperors of Romans and persecutors of Christians, were celebrating triumphs with excessive pomp in Rome, while the blessed Eusebius was holding the papacy.[18] While those emperors were running riot throughout the entire world in their cruelty and savagery, Eusebius was worthily glorified by God with the summit of the priesthood. Now, in the midst of that storm, when the persecution by those emperors gripped the entire world, the father of this most blessed man, who is the subject of his work, was brought in chains from Africa to Rome. First separated from his family, he died en route, leaving behind a distinguished wife by the name of Restituta, and his most holy daughter, steadfast in virginity, but also a single surviving son. Now, although his distinguished parents, both father and mother, were steadfast in their Christianity, their children had not yet been reborn in the font of Christianity because of the pressure of the persecutions. Despite this, they secretly served the Lord, believing in their hearts, and as parents imitated those of Moses, the most holy prophet and leader of God, who was hidden for three months lest the Pharaoh

18 *apostolicatus*. Although not registered in the *Thesaurus Linguae Latinae*, Du Cange, *Glossarium* 1: 325, cites the *Vita Eusebii* as the first instance of this word to mean the papacy; his other reference is to the twelfth-century author Otto Morena. Pope Eusebius (18 April–17 August 309/310) was banished from Rome by the Emperor Maxentius and died in exile in Sicily.

murder him, and who afterwards was lifted up from the water and made the destroyer of Egypt and liberator of the most holy people.[19]

3. After the death of his most blessed father, this most blessed man, together with his distinguished mother, completed the journey they had begun in the company of God. Born of a noble family of Sardinians,[20] he headed for Rome, and was there made more noble by a second regeneration of faith thanks to Pope Eusebius, who shared the same name, which means "most pious man." This most holy pope remained strong in his faith throughout various persecutions, like a rose among thorns, living righteously among the threats of the persecutors, and forbidding the ordination of any of his ministry. Then, when holy Easter was being celebrated in the month of March, and the aforesaid pope was conducting the appropriate holy vigils and honouring the most sacred baptistery, the boy whom we mentioned, with his mother and sole sister, asked the holy pontiff if they might deserve to be washed in sacred baptism and anointed with holy chrism by the most blessed pope himself. As I have already said, the boy Eusebius was named after this pope, and not without reason. For this essential religious ceremony is not performed on the servants of God without purpose[21]: he made Eusebius his son in baptism, his kindred in name, and his companion in sanctity. But as the writings of the chronicles relate, so infinite was the brutality of the treacherous emperors Diocletian and Maximian at that time that, on that same holy day of Easter, just after he baptized the blessed Eusebius, Pope Eusebius was killed, and the churches of the Christians were collapsed upon Christians within by the same emperors. On that very day, the Christians celebrated the glorious transit and gained eternal rest, and soon thereafter those persecutors very swiftly learned of their eternal punishment. And so it came to pass. Indeed, the blessed Pope Eusebius, since he was completing the sacred ceremonies of the mass with Christians on the very day of Easter, "passed over," having accepted the body of Christ, and passed from death unto life: therefore "Passover" (*Pascha*) is interpreted as a "passing over." But then, the persecutors, after a short time conceded to them, also "passed over," but through temporal to eternal death, without chance of pardon. With the pass-

19 Cf. Heb. 11:23–29.

20 The information is from Jerome (*De uir. illust.* c. 96), and difficult to square with the claim that Eusebius's father was brought to Rome from Africa during the persecutions: see Grégoire 1999.

21 *nequaquam enim frusta agitur erga Dei servos typicalis operatio*. The phrase and meaning is obscure.

ing of Pope Eusebius, Melchiades was ordained pontiff of Rome, the same year in which Emperor Constantine began to rule.[22]

4. Now while the blessed man Eusebius was flourishing in the faith and work of Christ, he was also instructed in knowledge of the liberal arts, and perceptively taught about holy scripture, for he was as much as three or four times greater than his age in wisdom. He stayed by the side of the blessed Pope Melchiades day and night for three years, serving God without complaint. After the death of that most holy father, the holy Sylvester[23] succeeded to his throne, a man of the greatest sanctity, as writings inform us and as nearly everyone knows.

5. During this time, the blessed Eusebius was consecrated *lector* of the Roman church, ascending through the ranks one at a time, so that he deserved to go from strength to strength to see the Lord of gods in Zion.[24] For what he believed in his heart, he taught in words, and perfected in his works. And so living for a considerable time in the city of Rome, he was a faithful steward of his ministry, and astutely served the Lord. Everyone judged this most blessed man Eusebius to be most worthy of the Lord in his talents and words, and all gladly listened to his advice, all honoured him. For this servant of Christ taught the people just as the Gospel says about Jesus Christ, not like the scribes and Pharisees, but instead using his teaching as the source of authority.[25] For he who fulfils in deeds that which he says in words has the power to teach.

6. But as history relates, the Emperor Constantine, ruling by the will of God, was led from faithlessness to the faith of Christ, and through him almighty God worked many good deeds for the holy church, granting it peace and increasing the faith everywhere. At that time was born Jerome,[26] the interpreter of divine law, who from the very cradle was destined to benefit the church and became a doctor of the faith. But just as, thanks to the goodness of God, Jerome

22 The chronology is mistaken: Melchiades (Miltiades) was pope 311–314, Constantine 306–337 was sole ruler from 324.

23 Pope Sylvester (314–335).

24 Ps. 84:8.

25 The slightly obscure phrasing (*sed in potestate habens doctrinam suam*) is made clearer by the scriptural reference (Matt. 7:29, "Jesus taught as one who had authority, and not as their teachers of law").

26 Jerome (c.347–420).

became known everywhere to an increasing number of Christ's servants, so also the treachery of the devil polluted his own servants, if indeed it is right to call them servants at all. For at the same time as that emperor there arose Arius,[27] a priest of Alexandria, who dared to babble against the unity of God's divinity, saying that the Son was less than the Father, and that the holy spirit was less than the Father and the Son. He spoke as much perversity as he was perverse, claiming that human nature is not divine: this is the law of the flesh, that the begotten may not be equal to the begetter. But our faith believes that there was no time in the generation of God. For we believe and confess that the Father and the Son and holy spirit are one and the same nature or substance. We confess three persons, but believe in the single nature of the deity. In order to suppress his perfidy, a synod was convened of three hundred and eighteen fathers in the city of Nicaea,[28] where *homoousion*[29] was declared, just as the scriptures say, and there Arius himself, the heretic and Antichrist, was destroyed.

7. After the deaths of the Emperor Constantine and the most blessed Pope Sylvester, Constantius,[30] the son of the Emperor Constantine, began to rule jointly with his brothers. But by falling into the same heresy, Constantius not only destroyed himself with the same impiety, but also condemned to death or exile many of the holy who refused to believe. While Sylvester governed the Roman church for twenty-two years, the holy men of God enjoyed peace everywhere: some at the time may have been in trouble, but none were endangered. But upon his death the grieving Romans elected the blessed Mark as pontiff, who governed the church for eight months.[31] During that time Mark ordained the blessed Eusebius as priest, seeing Eusebius's steady persistence, sanctity, and his sound and most faithful doctrine, and believing him to be already mastering the mystery of the body and blood of Christ. Indeed, Eusebius's age demanded this of him now, for he was in his fiftieth year, the age when priests are ordered by the Lord, through Moses, to be the guardians of the vessels.[32] After the death

27 Arius (c.256–336).

28 AD 325, the first ecumenical council. On the legendary number of bishops (oddly repeated below for Milan, ch.21), see Chadwick 1966.

29 The term (used again ch.21) is not scriptural; on its use and history, see Stead 1994.

30 Constantius II (337–361).

31 Pope Mark (18 January 336–7 October 336).

32 The reference appears to be to Num. 8:23–26, "The Lord said to Moses, 'This applied to the Levites ... at the age of fifty, they must retire from their regular service and work no longer.'"

of the blessed Pope Mark, Pope Julius presided for sixteen years and four months.[33]

8. And so from the time of the Emperor Constantius the perfidy of the Arians, bolstered with his support, persecuted all the bishops not on their side, with exile, as I have said, as well as with imprisonment and different kinds of torment. The highest apostolic, Julius, perceiving that the emperor and the entire world was corrupted by Arian perfidy, summoned our man Eusebius to him, expounded everything to him in order, and asked him whether he had been clothed in an ankle-length tunic[34] like the blessed Joseph – that is, whether he had resolved to maintain the right faith even unto death. In response the holy Eusebius, strong in faith, merely smiled, and calmly replied that he would rather suffer death of the body than deviate from the right faith. Then with the prayers of the people, blessed Eusebius was consecrated bishop by Julius, the supreme bishop. Just like a strong athlete seeking the victory prize of divine reward, he began to wage war against the mendacious Arians, protected not by any body-shield or helmet, but by the right faith and works. He pierced through the enemies of Christ with the holy lance of the word.

9. The perfidy of the Arian sect, which arose in the time of the Emperor Constantine, nearly corrupted the entire world. For Constantius had been enticed by the madness of Arius himself, and gravely assaulted the canonical faith and afflicted the preservers of it in all sorts of ways, as I have already said. But the very depravity of the Arians oppressed Liguria in particular. At that time, the city of Vercelli still held the primacy among the other cities of Liguria: since then, Milan has obtained the primacy.[35] Consecrated with the pontifical stole by Julius, the supreme pontiff, Eusebius was sent to destroy the aforementioned heresy in Vercelli. From this pestilence he liberated not only the city but the entire world. Now, the noblest city of Vercelli was rich in wealth, well-wooded with trees and vineyards, abundant in pastures, and irrigated by clean rivers. But it was also contaminated with the Arian pestilence. In this city, holy Euse-

33 Pope Julius (337–352).

34 *talarica*. Cf. Gen. 37:3.

35 This exaggerated claim rests on Eusebius's later authority to oversee the restitution of orthodoxy in the western churches (see below, ch.34), the precise nature of which is unclear (see Milano 1987 and Ferrari 1996). Nevertheless, the claim reflects some truth, since Milan was controlled by the Arian (or *homoian*) faction. On the relation between the two cities, see Cracco Ruggini 1997.

bius occupied the pontifical chair, and governed the same Catholic faith wisely. He not only cared for the welfare of his city by preaching the right faith to it, but also bestowed faith on all cities by sensibly performing proper ordinations for the bishops of neighbouring towns. For at that time, under so great a pastor, his city canonically held the primacy, and it nourished itself and the other neighbouring cities in the region with the unity of true salvation and faith. For just as from exaltation of the holy there arises the vengeance of the evil, so by the envy of the devil the heart of the Emperor Constantius was inflamed against the most holy man Eusebius, and also against Athanasius, the bishop of Alexandria,[36] both of whom were persevering in the defence of the Catholic faith day and night, one governing the realms of the East, the other those of the West. The emperor wanted to expel them from the church, but could only do this secretly and deviously for he feared being denounced by the people. Nevertheless, he tried every way he could imagine to expel them.

10. For father Eusebius, truly caring for the welfare of his children, situated in the sheepfold of Christ, amidst the sheep, obeyed the apostolic precept: "correct, rebuke, and encourage,"[37] and likewise, concerning the heretics, after their first and second censure: do not eat with such men.[38] For he prohibited the Arians from the church and from the company of Christians, repelling them not only from heavenly feasts but also from worldly gatherings. He soothed the Catholics, while he rebuked and corrected the profane and the schismatic, knowing that their conversation was useful for nothing except the ruination of those who listened. Furthermore, he eliminated the Arians from the churches of the faithful. And in order to anathematize them, he barricaded the doors, so that none of them could enter into the church. Not only did they flee from his glance, they hardly dared to stand their ground when he became aware of their presence and approached them. And so it happened that the holy Eusebius ordained a most holy man, whom he himself had trained, by the name of Dionysius, in the place of the damned Ariomaniac Bishop Auxentius,[39] who had been prattling madness in Arian Milan. Justly, then, was Auxentius, who

36 Athanasius of Alexandria (c.328–373).

37 2 Tim. 4:2.

38 Cf. 1 Cor. 5:11.

39 Auxentius (355–374) was the Arian bishop who replaced Dionysius and who preceded Ambrose: the chronology and events given in ch.18 and elsewhere in the *Life* are confused. Auxentius enjoyed considerable popularity and support: see McLynn 1994, 22–31.

refused to believe in the unity of the Holy Trinity, condemned and cut off from the unity of the church.

11. Meanwhile the Emperor Constantius, already entangled in the chains of the Arians, learned that a man of such talent and authority was freely doing all these things, and he began to seethe with rage, and asked around inquiringly how he might destroy him. The emperor gave notice that divergent councils were to be celebrated in different places. But because there is no counsel against the Lord, the same holy man, content with God, fled the fellowship of the evil ones resentful of the Catholic faith. However, letters were sent out, both by the synods and also by the emperor himself, inviting this most holy prelate to come if at all possible to condemn *in absentia* by his own authority Athanasius, who was already condemned by the Ariomaniacs. But he excused himself from joining their company, offering the excuse of age and implying bodily infirmity, for he knew that he would not be allowed to complete anything to the church's advantage. But he also considered that no one can be condemned *in absentia.* He repeatedly made these acquittals or excuses for himself and for the most blessed Athanasius, mindful that it is written, "Leave room for God's wrath."[40] But the ancient enemy, whose hot breath makes coals burn, and whose sneezing is like an unquenchable fire,[41] inflamed the heart of the Emperor Constantius with the desire to destroy these men, and he began to inquire how he might erase their memory from the face of the earth. And so it was decreed and frivolously arranged that, because of the inconvenience to such an old man – hence using the excuse given by the most holy father himself – a council would be celebrated in Milan, in the same manner as the Council of Rimini. No one without unavoidable cause[42] was excused from attendance, and the emperor announced that even he would take part in their council, and so he did.

12. Although I have sought to abridge wherever possible the narrative of this most holy father's history, I have not forgotten about his miracles, which must be described, if not each one individually, then at least as many as I can, with the help of the Lord. For instance, among other miracles of his youth, which he performed because of his innate goodness, this miracle was especially

40 Rom. 12:19.

41 Cf. Job 41:18–21.

42 *nullus excusatur nisi inevitabili causa.* The language reflects that of Constantius's summons recorded in a letter of Pope Julius (PL 130: 265B, *absque inevitabili causa*). On the hagiographer and his sources for the council, see introduction above and Everett 2006.

famous. Now, the blessed Roman Pope Eusebius was informed by an angel before he baptized this Eusebius about who and how holy this man would become, and by what name he should call him. And so it happened that this same boy possessed the most sacred authority of the blessed John the Baptist, since his sanctity was predicted not by the name of his parents, but rather granted by divine will in the Greek name of Eusebius, which is properly translated in Latin as "the most pious one."[43] It was reported that at his sacred baptism angelic visions were seen. Alongside the apostolic hands that lifted him up from the font, other hands were seen. No doubt these hands were angelic, and it was their support that sustained him through every adversity with divine help. After his own baptism, he sparkled with such excellence that he lived the life of an angel placed on earth among men. Although he gave nourishment to his body sparingly, he did so not for the beauty of his body, but merely so that he did not lose his inner life. He was a virgin from birth not only in the mind but also in the body. For after his baptism he neither touched nor kissed the flesh of any woman, not even his holy mother or sister, not in rejection of nature but in flight from sin. And so it happened that, kept safe by divine judgement, he never donned the noose of sin in the company of women, maintaining in himself the divine testimony "just as a lily among thorns, so is my love among maidens."[44]

13. Now it is said that a certain noble wife, admiring his youthful beauty, planned to enter his bedroom secretly. All night she searched everywhere, wandering the streets of the city, trying to get access to his bedroom. On the following day, prostrating herself at his feet, she confessed before everyone. Now, it is clear here that the protection of the angels was with him incessantly.

14. However, he himself was no less than evidence of a third miracle. For he pursued the apostolic life without regard for any distinction between the sexes. Restoring all things to common ownership and regarding nothing as his own, he gave his people everything that they needed. He maintained this apostolic life constantly even while living together with men and women, and was never accused of any sin whatsoever. It is said that many came to him falsely, posing as imitators of his life, giving away their property. But he recognized them

43 *piissimus* Cf. Luke 1:56–57. Curiously, a similar phrase (*Eusebius namque Attice, Romane dicitur pius*) appears in the (anonymous) *Life of Jerome* (BHL 3870; PL 22: 201).

44 Song of Sol. 2:2.

from a mile off, and publicly revealed to everyone their falsity. He preached to them about the death of the soul, just as Peter preached to Ananias and Saphira.[45] Now, a certain pseudo-anchorite promised to be his disciple, but also tried to keep a sum of gold and silver for himself to enjoy. But he was caught out in his falsehood by the most blessed man, who sharply chastised him for it. He was suddenly seized by the spirit of mendacity and shook violently before everyone, so that he nearly exhaled the breath of life. But he was cleansed by the holy man, and chastised never to act so falsely again.

15. But I have heard of a fourth famous miracle. After he was ordained priest, with the assistance of God, he reached such a level of sanctity that he frequently performed the solemnities of the mass with angelic singing as accompaniment, and visions of holy angels were seen around him. For when he broke the body of Christ, often the hands of angels were seen joined with his, and likewise in the distribution of the body and blood of Christ. Many people had their vision restored by applying to their eyes the water he used to wash his hands after he had completed the sacred mysteries. Many wounded and lepers were also cleansed, and in the process became his disciples without him knowing it. He saw nothing advantageous to himself in this, but rather was made to be all things to all men,[46] that he might win over everyone. He never desired control over anyone, but only sought be useful to everyone. He who held conversation with Christ in heaven upheld the life of an angel on earth.

16. And I know of a fifth miracle: when he arrived in Vercelli at the beginning of his consecration, Auxentius was then the presiding bishop of Milan. Other Arians who remained in this city of Vercelli were partisans of this Auxentius, and they barricaded with bars all the doors of the church, preventing entrance to anyone. When blessed Eusebius learned of such great malevolence and sacrilegious temerity, he prayed to the Lord on bended knees for the deliverance of the people before the doors of the great church, which was built in honour of the blessed Virgin Mary, the mother of God. Next he entered the oratory and offered a sacrifice to the Lord for the rescue of the people. By labouring like this every day, he led that city to the true and Catholic faith.

17. However, he was fighting against the most savage of the Ariomaniac beasts, and they expelled him from the city by stirring up the people to persecute him.

45 Cf. Acts 5:1–11.
46 1 Cor. 9:19–23.

But to avoid letting the people, whom afterwards he delighted to have as his sons, sin against him, and knowing that it is written, "If you are persecuted in one city, flee to another,"[47] he crossed to the other side of the river Po. Arriving at the fortress which is called Credonium,[48] and staying there for three months, he built an oratory in honour of the blessed mother of God. Remaining still longer, he wrote out the Gospel of Christ in his own hand.[49] And there is a miracle of his in that codex of four Gospels: not simply the words of Christ but also the miraculous power of this father sparkles from it, so that if anyone seduced by the devil swears a false oath over it, very quickly his body is covered in wounds, and he is further punished with death, or loses his eyes and therefore corporeal light along with spiritual light, or is made crippled or lame by the withering of his limbs, or is rent to pieces by an attack of demons until near death.

18. At the same time when the blessed Eusebius was staying in that fortress together with his disciples, he[50] was condemned together with his followers by the council held in Rimini. Letters from the aforesaid blessed father Eusebius and the most holy Athanasius intervened, on the authority of which the most holy fathers who had convened at Rimini both condemned that man [Auxentius] and threw him out of the city of Milan. Now, the blessed Eusebius, as soon as he learned this, returned to his own city, for he had not gone outside his diocese, but he had travelled twelve miles to the aforesaid fortress. Now, his most holy disciples shone like the brightest stars in heaven, among whom Dionysius was exceptional in his sanctity. Shining like the sun, he illuminated everyone with the rays of his miracles and words. Therefore the blessed Eusebius proceeded to Milan and ordained Dionysius as bishop, in place of

47 Matt. 10:23

48 This is the earliest mention of the sanctuary at Crea, north of Monferrato (35 km NW of Vercelli), the foundation date of which is unknown, otherwise the reference might help to date the *Life* more accurately. Later legends attribute the statue of Mary there to Eusebius bringing it back from exile, a legend also applied to the Marian sanctuary on nearby Mount Oropa: see Maccono 1951, 5–18. The word *Credonium* may derive from Celtic *dunum* ("temple") and *Creo* (a local deity).

49 Undoubtedly referring to the *Codex Vercellensis* preserved at the city's Biblioteca capitolare, N.S. (CLA 4.467). The text itself has been published several times: a good edition is Gasquet 1914. See Vian 1997.

50 The text here seems corrupt or simply confused: grammar dictates that the subject ("he") is Eusebius, but the sense seems to refer to Auxentius of Milan (355–374), given what is said below. But it was Auxentius who replaced Dionysius as bishop of Milan in 355, and the synod of Rimini took place in 359.

Auxentius. The blessed Dionysius, famous for his miracles, unhesitatingly preached the Catholic faith, which he had learned from his teacher, and vigorously eliminated the Arians from that city. But the ancient enemy, seeing the two candelabra shining before the Lord, grieved over the advancement of the Catholic people, so increasing the merit of these fathers. For the time had now come that, in return for their service in battle, they should both receive their palm of victory, and be enriched with the crown of eternal blessedness, just as the outcome of this affair proved afterwards.

19. So Emperor Constantius hurried to arrive in Milan, where he had already called a council of ten bishops. There he learned about the blessed Eusebius, bishop of Vercelli. He began to inquire on what pretext this pontiff was being detained, since he had not come to the synod with the others. The emperor was informed that it was either on account of arthritis or from some other bodily infirmity. However, the same emperor had arranged that Pope Liberius in Rome, the successor of Julius, should attend this council, and also Hilary, bishop of Poitiers; Paulinus, archbishop of Trier; and Lucifer, bishop of Cagliari. The blessed Eusebius, receiving letters from the emperor, or from the synod itself, and reading them through, wrote the following letter to the emperor:

> I, most merciful emperor, received your letter with great joy, and see that your heart is devoted to God, and that you desire a lasting ecclesiastical peace that will endure throughout the world. I also received letters from my brothers and fellow bishops, in which they deigned to suggest that those whom they sent should give me a full account, and that I should do what they want. But because a full account could not be given to me, and because I ought to be obedient to your clemency, I consider it necessary to come immediately to Milan. But I promise, Lord Emperor, that when I have come into your presence, I shall do whatever seems just and pleasing to God.
>
> May God protect you, most glorious Emperor.

20. Meanwhile, the envoys of the Romans, the priest Pancratius, and the deacon Hilary were being detained in custody until Pope Liberius arrived. While Emperor Constantius held them back, awaiting the arrival of Pope Liberius and the other bishops who were also yet to arrive, he took action together with the Arian bishops, to the effect that they subscribed to a statement of their faith,

and Athanasius was condemned. In fact Dionysius, the bishop of Milan itself, and after him another twenty-nine bishops, also subscribed to this, for the Catholic bishops had not yet arrived. So it happened that both Pope Liberius and the other Catholic bishops exchanged letters and chose a day to gather together unanimously in Milan. It was still another seven days after Eusebius had sent his letter to the emperor and synod before he left Vercelli to go to the synod. With prophetic spirit he predicted everything that was supposed to happen to him at that synod. He said that he will be far away from them, will go into exile, and will afterwards return to his city. Once he confirmed his church was in order and blessed the people, he bade farewell to all the priests and deacons, and began the journey to Milan on foot. While he was heading to Milan to destroy the church of the Arians with the help of his colleagues, he came to a river named Civida, but there was no bridge with which he might quickly reach the opposite bank. The insensible river obeyed him whom sensible men refused to obey. There is as much sorrow in this as there is wonder. Behold, while his band of disciples marvelled at how they crossed directly over that river without oarsmen or helmsmen, Catholic men arrived from the city of Milan announcing that hurrying out to meet him was Dionysius the pontiff, whose lapse had deeply wounded the most blessed Eusebius and his followers and caused them to weep. Having crossed the river, Dionysius came out to meet him, holding in his hands the Gospel of Christ and the cross of the Lord. Throwing himself on the ground before him, Dionysius said, "Father, I have sinned. Absolve me if you can."[51] Once he had made the confession and received guidance, they walked on together.

21 So they came to Milan. They settled into their lodgings and began to discuss the rescue of the same Bishop Dionysius. On the following day, all the bishops arrived in the church of Milan.[52] Pope Liberius and the other Catholic bishops took their seats, three hundred and eighteen Catholics in number. In a public statement they proclaimed the true, apostolic, and Catholic faith, in support of which they all subscribed, endorsing that our Lord Jesus Christ was the

51 This passage subsequently appeared in liturgical texts from Vercelli into the modern period, e.g., *Corpus antiphonalium officii*, ed. Hesbert 1963–1979, no. 5171: "Transacto uero flumine, obuiauit eum Dionysius episcopus dicens: Pater, peccavi; libera me si vales."

52 It is unclear whether the large, imperially sponsored *Basilica Nova* (80x45 m) had been constructed by 355: see Krautheimer 1983, 74–77. In any case, Auxentius was the first to enjoy it: McLynn 1994, 24. On the number 318, see above, *Life*, ch.6 n28.

true Lord, and of one substance with the Father, which in Greek is called *homoousion*. Eusebius was the first to subscribe to that creed, stating,

> I, Eusebius, bishop of the city of Vercelli, confirm and hold this creed, expounded to us by the Father, and anyone who does not consent to this creed I judge and pronounce to be estranged from the Catholic church.[53]

Similarly after him came Dionysius, his son in baptism and bishop of Milan, and the envoys of the Romans, the priest Pancratius, and the deacon Hilary. The other holy fathers also subscribed, forty-eight in number, for Eusebius had already petitioned the emperor to secure the release of Bishop Lucifer and the legates of the Romans from custody and have them returned to Eusebius.

22. The blessed Eusebius was then summoned by the Emperor Constantius, who received him with honour, since he wished to sway him from the true faith with threats, or flattery, or gifts. But the holy father, standing firm despite now being very old, considered his threats and flattery as worthless, nothing more than excrement, and refused to consent to him. Instead he said before all, "Since you say that the Son of God cannot be equal to God the Father, why do you pretend to me to be my son and disciple? For no disciple is above his teacher, nor any son above his father." Disturbed by his line of reasoning, they brought out the handwritten document that Dionysius had subscribed. But he said, "I shall not sign after the son whom I precede in name. Burn it, and write up a new one if you want me to sign it." And so it happened by divine will that the document which Dionysius and the other twenty-eight bishops signed was burned. Once the first document was burned, another was drawn up straightaway which Eusebius and the other bishops were meant to sign. As soon as it was brought before them, the blessed Eusebius saw that no one else had subscribed it, and said that this exposed the stupidity of those who ordered him to sign it or commanded him to support it.

53 This subscription seems to be inspired by parts of the *De Trinitate* attributed to Eusebius and modelled on Eusebius's subscription to the decree from the council of Alexandria in 362, partly preserved for us in the document known as the *Tomus ad Antiochenos*: see Everett 2006, 159–160. On the *Tomus*, see Armstrong 1921 and Barnes 1993, 156–158.

23. The Emperor Constantius said to Eusebius, "It is right that you sign first of all, after which the others may honour your paternity by following." But the blessed Eusebius said in reply, "You slither like a snake, O emperor, who tickles with his tongue but strikes with his tail. For this is how the ancient enemy deceived our first ancestors with flattery, then dragged them to the edge of the abyss. But I will not filthy myself with your crimes, nor do I permit my son Dionysius or any of my other colleagues to participate in this insanity with you!"

Now the confessors of Christ who had previously signed the offending document – or, if you will, those who did not render thanks to God their Creator – exulted in the holy man, for Father Eusebius had damned the divisions between the Father and Son dictated by the Arians, and had caused them and their sayings to burn with fire, and the unity of the Catholic faith, of those who believe in the Father and the Son, endured unconquered. While they praised the Lord, they also all promised to remain Catholics in unity. Then full of rage, the Emperor Constantius said to Eusebius, "You old dog! I had judged you to be a man of sanctity, but now I realise you are a sacrilegious magician and a poisonous wizard! Indeed, you have deceived everyone more with one speech than our entire conference had made progress with them over the course of ten days."

In response to the emperor, the blessed Eusebius said,

> My Lord Jesus Christ, one with God the Father, and the equal Son, responded with one speech to your father, the devil, when he promised to give him many things – all the kingdoms of the world, all their honour and glory. But he confounded him, saying, "Stand back, Satan. You will worship our Lord God, and serve him alone."[54] Therefore, if God is one and only, why have you dared to yap like a little dog that there are three Gods? You wish to destroy the flock of God that Christ redeemed with his own blood. For if you believe this when you depart from this world, you will never achieve eternal life. You do not believe in his words, so how do you expect to share in Christ? You speak falsely that you are a Christian, for you do not believe in Christ. And when you oppose his words, you are the Antichrist. What the blessed John the Evangelist says in his epistle is therefore about you and your followers: "Even now many Antichrists

54 Cf. Matt. 4:8–11.

have come: repent, and do not wish them to destroy those for whom Christ has died."[55]

24. Hearing this, the emperor rose from his throne and summoned the Arians together. He ordered them to take Eusebius into their custody and force him to consent and subscribe. He grieved for that decree which he himself and the other bishops had signed with their own hands, and which Eusebius so frivolously and so cleverly had burned. Hurrying over to Eusebius, the Arians dragged him off, snatching the blessed man from the company of bishops, and forcefully thrashed him with whips, leaving him half-alive. There were huge staircases in that building, and the blessed Eusebius was dragged up and down the stairs on his back by the Arians. With the blunt stone injuring his face and head, he shed his blood for Christ, yet bravely proclaimed the unity of the Holy Trinity. They kept dragging him from the top all the way to the bottom, and then from the bottom to the top again, saying to him, "Now join with us, and consent to our decrees." But he gracefully rejoiced that he deserved to endure some abuse for the truth that is God. So then the Arians, after such acts of humiliation, after cracking his skull, after shedding his blood, dragged along the pontiff and martyr of God by a leather strap bound around his throat, with his hands bound behind his back. Again beating him with blows they interrogated him, asking whether he would now consentingly confess. But he wisely responded that he would remain in his confession and happily die for it. When they reported his completely unyielding resolve to the Emperor Constantius, it was decreed that he be deported into exile, not only Eusebius himself but also those who, because of his virtues, had become confessors of Christ with him, that is, Liberius the pope of Rome, Hilary of Poitiers, Paulinus of Trier, Lucifer of Cagliari, Dionysius of Milan, and the other pontiffs of Christ who had gathered at this synod and who, because they were witnesses of Christ with him, merited to suffer martyrdom with him. Tied up with leather straps in the council itself, the holy pontiffs and martyrs of God were deported into exile together with Dionysius and Pope Liberius, for the sake of the unity of the faith.[56]

55 Cf. 1 John 2:18–27.

56 Neither Pope Liberius nor Paulinus of Trier attended the Council of Milan. Paulinus was exiled at the previous council of Arles in 353: Hilary was actually exiled at the council of Béziers in 356, but here the hagiographer was following his source, the *Historia Tripartita*.

25. Now because of his grave old age, Eusebius was confined to a cage, as if he were a devastator of the vine of Christ and of the peace of the whole empire. He was then taken to Scythopolis and was handed over to the Arians to do as they wished with him. He was rightly confined to a cage, which he took on for the glory of the heavenly kingdom, because the holy men of God happily endure small spaces for Christ, so they earn the right to receive eternal rewards, as the Apostle Paul said, "The sufferings of this time are not worth comparing to the future glory of eternal life."[57] Also, his being dragged up and down the length of the staircase, from bottom to top and back down again, was prefigured in another way, for the holy Jacob saw a staircase set up, the top of which reached the heavens, and angels were ascending and descending on it.[58]

26. Indeed the blessed Eusebius was like an angel, ascending and descending on that staircase, but he ascended because he truthfully professed the Son of God to be God and man joined together in one person, and born equal to God the Father, before the creation of the world.[59] He descended again because he affirmed that the same invisible Son of God took on our visible and mortal flesh, so the same Son of God was in and of two natures, as I have said. He also believed and confessed that one God was with the Father and the holy spirit. Therefore, he rightly ascends to him whom he worships and loves as God. The Arians rightly fall, plummeting into hell, for they neither worshipped God with love nor believed at all in the unity of his nature. The stupidest of all people did not believe in the truth that says what we have seen with our very eyes. Every kingdom or house divided against itself cannot by any means stand.[60] Those who preach division are divided from God, and are closely related to him who desires division and schism, who is, without doubt, the devil himself.

27. Now Scythopolis is a well-known city in Palestine, situated in the territory of the tribe of the Manasseh; it is also known by another name, Beth Shan, and holy scripture gives it the epithet "the house of Nyssa." In our tongue, Beth

57 Rom. 8:18.

58 Cf. Gen. 28:12. The motif and imagery here was adapted from the Ps. Maximus's sermon (7) on Eusebius: see introduction above.

59 *ante saeculum genitum*. The sentiment is that of the Nicene Creed (*ex Patre natum ante omnia saeculum*) but also resembles the creed of the Fourth Council of Toledo (633) (*ex substantia Partris ante saecula genitum*).

60 Cf. Matt. 12:25.

Shan means "the house of enemies," because the Manasseh, who were a people of Israel, could not inherit it, just as is said in the Book of Judges. It is also a Scythian city, for the Scythians founded this city after they left the kingdom of the Egyptians and relentlessly waged war in every direction far and wide, coming to hold nearly all of Asia.[61] It is indeed a metropolis, as can be read in the same book.

28. And so, as I have said, the blessed Eusebius was brought to this city in exile and confined in a cage. Although he could not move himself about with any comfort, nevertheless he could turn himself about and look around. But the Arians noticed this and dragged him away from there and shut him up in a narrow chamber where they kept him confined and withheld his rations of food and drink, so that he endured starvation for many days, and was nearly undone by hunger. Then he wrote a note [*librum*] to Patrophilus, the guard[62]:

> From Eusebius, the servant of God, together with his co-servants, to Patrophilus, their guard.
>
> The Ariomaniacs have taken me captive and with the strength of many in complete fury have stripped my body and dragged me on my back along the ground to my holding cage, and are now holding me prisoner in other quarters. Since they will offer me neither bread to eat nor water to drink until I give in to them, it seems right for me to depart this body before consenting to such things. Know that you have acted contrary to divine and public law, for it has already been seven days, and unless you correct this, you will be murderers, without a doubt.[63]

61 The information here is taken from Judg. 1:27 and the comments on such by Jerome, *De situ et nominibus locorum Hebraicorum* (PL 23: 883A), and Augustine, *Quaestiones in Heptateuchum* 7.8 (PL 34: 796).

62 Patrophilus was the (Arian) bishop at Scythopolis. Epiphanius of Salamis (d. 403) records that he met Eusebius in Scythopolis staying at the estate of Josephus, a Jew who had converted to Christianity and was granted the rank of count by Constantine, and who was the only other orthodox Christian in the city: Epiphanius, *Panarion*, 1..5.1, trans. Williams 1987, 1: 23.

63 This is a truncated version of the "letter to Patrophilus," which Eusebius himself included in a long letter to the churches of northern Italy while in Italy (*Ep.* 2, ed. Bulhart et al. 1957, 104–106) and is probably that referred to below (ch.30) as "most treasured." The longer version appears in the later medieval epitome of the *Vita Eusebii* (BHL 2751) edited by Mombritius (AD c.1480, rev. ed. 1910), 1.462. It is unclear whether the antiquarian copies made of the letter by Baronius and Gallandi relied on

29. On the fourteenth day Patrophilus intervened, having been softened by this short note [*libellum*]. He consulted with his subordinates over what action to take, and they decided to take Eusebius to another lodging, allowing those who had come for the sake of a visit to speak with him. But not long after, on the twenty-fifth day, they rushed out again armed with clubs and came and seized him from his quarters and transferred him to an even smaller cell. They shut him back up in a prison cell that was shorter and narrower than him in length and width, so he could not even look at his feet by straightening out his bended knees. His head was so pressed down by the prison ceiling that it was impossible for him to look up at the heavens. Nor could he move his shoulders or elbows at all, and remained immobile in these conditions. If not maintained by a visitation of angels, there is no way that the human body could bear this punishment for so many days. But almighty God, who preserved the prophet Jonah in the belly of a whale,[64] guarded this his most holy athlete no less in his many sufferings. And he endured his situation there in that cruellest of prisons right up until the death of the Emperor Constantius.

30. Those who were with him report that he was so spirited, nourished by divine food, that he did not feel the punishment of that prison at all, nor starvation, and he constantly advised his followers to return quickly to their own homes. Instead he managed to call on Catholic churches everywhere by sending them letters: he even sent to the city of Vercelli a most treasured letter, reminding all its citizens to be on their guard, to act cautiously, and not to believe in anything other than what he had taught them. Similarly he sent a letter to the church of Milan with his own endorsements that they should not believe in anything other than what they have heard from him or from their Bishop Dionysius.

31. After the death of Emperor Constantius, his successor, Emperor Julian, went to Constantinople and began to think about how he might capture the affections of the people and acquire their favour. And he did this skilfully, for he understood that Constantius was hated by all people who embraced the name of the consubstantiality of God, for the sake of which Catholic bishops had been expelled from the church and their ecclesiastical properties confis-

this later version of the *Vita Eusebii* or upon its survival in some other format, such as a dossier, now lost: the letter survives only via hagiography. Eusebius's reference to law, here concerning homicide and in the longer letter concerning also prison conditions, has resonance with surviving late Roman legislation: see Everett 2006, 161–163.

64 Cf. Jon. 1:17–2:10.

cated. Since the holy fathers were unjustly suffering exile, the children of their churches were quite depressed. Julian knew that the Jews and pagans were upset about the prohibition of their sacrifices – that is to say, of the former's laws and the latter's idols – and that they longed for a time when their temples might be thrown open and they would have ample offering of sacrifices. And so, observing that both these peoples were wounded with sorrows, he seemed to come to their rescue like a conscientious physician to the injured. But as a false physician, he wounded them more gravely with poisonous puss. For he empathized with the people who had been oppressed by the violence of the soldiery, commended himself to them under false pretence, and rejected and censured the harsh cruelty of Constantius to his victims, rejecting it as inimical to peace. He decreed that the bishops in exile be recalled and returned to the locations of their churches, that they have full enjoyment of peace under whichever law each chose, and that their confiscated property be returned to them. He further commanded that the temples of the pagans and Jews be opened up immediately, instructing the people that they should injure no Christian, Jew, or pagan, and neither compel an unwilling man to sacrifice nor prevent a willing man from sacrificing, for only this would secure peace. Meanwhile, it so happened that he himself was wholly converted to paganism. At the same time, the holy prelates in exile returned to their homes.

32. And so it came to pass that blessed Eusebius, whom I have been commemorating up to now, left the city of Scythopolis for Alexandria. There he found Athanasius unharmed, and told him all about the different kinds of punishment he had suffered in exile. Now once they had assembled a council in the city of Alexandria, the blessed prelates Athanasius and Eusebius considered how they should repair the corrupt rule of the church. But blessed Lucifer, bishop of Cagliari, bade goodbye to Athanasius and Eusebius, for he was sent by them to Antioch to confirm the churches there in the consubstantiality of the divinity, leaving his deacon with them in Alexandria to take his place in the council, and through whom Lucifer declared that he would consider valid whatever was established by the order of the council. But Bishop Lucifer also healed the divisions of the church in Antioch, ordained Paulinus as bishop there, then departed to return to his home.[65]

65 The *Historia Tripartita* along with Rufinus and Sulpicius all record that Lucifer and Eusebius quarrelled over the ordination of Paulinus by Lucifer, who never attended the Alexandrian council, and the two men refused communion with each other: see Everett 2006, 154–156.

33. As I was saying, Eusebius and Athanasius wanted to convene a council in Alexandria, and bishops from different regions assembled to debate highly important and necessary matters. They did not introduce a new religion into the church, but rather just affirmed what ecclesiastical tradition has taught Christians from the beginning. For they confirmed the faith of the Council of Nicaea, so that it might be preserved sacrosanct, and acknowledged the consubstantiality of the Father and the Son and the holy spirit, and so defined the Trinity.

34. Immediately afterwards the blessed Eusebius, bishop of Vercelli, left Alexandria for Antioch, and journeyed throughout the East like the best of physicians: everywhere he healed those who were infirm in faith, resuscitated those who were dead in faithlessness, and cured those who had been infected with the poison of the Arians, instructing and educating everyone in the proclamations of the church. Departing from there, he went to Illyricum, where he asserted the Nicene doctrine everywhere. From there, he travelled by sea to Italy and preached the same things there. For it had been arranged in the council of the Alexandrians that Athanasius would provide for the regions of the easterners under his care, and by the same decision, Eusebius, the bishop of Vercelli, was to take care of the lands of Europe, in regular consultation with the pope in Rome. And so it was done. Heading to Rome, Eusebius visited Pope Liberius, who received him with the greatest joy, and congratulated him on becoming his future colleague. The blessed Eusebius showed him the statement of faith which he himself and the distinguished man Athanasius had drawn up together with the other eastern bishops. The pope himself, along with his clergy and all of the people subject to him, responded that they too would stand by this statement forever. He confirmed with solemn guarantee everything regarding Eusebius's sole responsibility for the lands within the borders of Europe,[66] just as had been arranged in Alexandria.

35. Once the holy Eusebius, athlete of Christ, had delivered the creed of his faith and deposited it in the holy archive of Rome, he bade farewell to Pope

66 *De monarchia autem providentiae illius in Europae finibus terrarum omnia sub stipulatione subnixa firmavit.* No other source attests to this authority, but it is not unlikely that Eusebius was granted some form of papal authority for overseeing the restoration of orthodoxy in the West: see above ch.9 n35; Everett 2006, 157–158; Ferrari 1996; and Milano 1987.

Liberius together with the other brothers and went to leave when Pope Liberius said to him,

> I know you are a truthful priest, and I believe you are a good soldier, so toil like one, because before long you will gain the reward of eternal life. I pray to God that you may return to your home safe and happy, and I entrust to you the sheep of Christ, for whom Christ died in courageous suffering, rose again, and resides in heavenly glory together with the Father. For I know that the spirit of God is with you to secure his church, which you have snatched from the jaws of the devil by your deeds and words, and which will rejoice and exult in the strengthened unity of belief in the divinity. May Christ the Lord preserve you here in eternity, distinguished brother.

Saying these things, he then kissed him, and allowed him to leave.

36. Now, at the same time, the Arian madness was lying low, as though dormant: it had been suppressed by the Emperor Jovian, for by then the Emperor Julian had incurred divine retribution. The blessed Eusebius entered Vercelli, and the people were consumed with such great happiness that they even wept for joy. They hurried out to meet him with hymns of praise, saying, "Blessed be the Lord our God, who had restored you to our church and taken pity upon us. He has restored you to us, our liberator and saviour, lest we be destroyed by the poison of the devil. For we declare that, just as you taught us by word of mouth, and confirmed in the words of your letters from exile, so is our faith in God our Creator safe, and may your rewards from us also be safe." So chanting a melodious litany, they led him to his chair.

37. When the Milanese clergy, people, and *vicarius* Serneus heard that blessed Eusebius of Vercelli had returned, they sent an embassy to him, saying, "We have just heard that your sanctity has arrived, and we resolutely pray that you consent to visit us, most blessed Lord Father, because Auxentius, the supporter of the Arians and the bishop of Milan, has been ejected from the city by Catholic men, and was killed in some sort of riot." So blessed Eusebius went to Milan, and was received with honour by the *vicarius*, clergy, and people. He taught and fortified them, then proceeded on to other places, travelling around and diligently investigating whether they persevered in the right faith in all matters, just as he had once taught them.

38. Meanwhile the perfidy of the Arians began to rise up and rage, with Valens[67] as their exuberant patron. Now while the blessed Eusebius was travelling around various parishes, the recovering Arians, on the authority of Valens, prepared a rebellion against him. But since the time had come when the actions of both would be rewarded, it came to pass at the instigation of God that both the merit of the holy father Eusebius multiplied in reward, and the faithlessness of those Arians, by increasing, plunged them into the depths of hell. For it happened that, one particular night, while Eusebius was travelling, he saw himself in a dream sitting on top of a mountain, and he flew with wings from that mountain to an even higher one, and then entered a type of palace, brighter than the sun, which had been constructed with indescribable skill. On awakening, the holy man of God at once understood the vision, and recognized without a doubt that he would cross over from his lofty lifestyle to the loftier glory of eternal blessedness. He accepted this as due reward of faith, just as the prophet once desired, saying, "Make my end known to me, Lord, and the measure of my days."[68] Such a blessed martyr received that which the prophet once deserved, and still more, for he both realized the day and recognized without doubt the glory that he would assume after the end. And let it not be suggested that this vision is contrary to the words of the Lord, "It is not for you to know the times or the seasons, which the Father has set by his own power,"[69] and indeed, "no one knows about that day, neither the angels of heaven nor the Son,"[70] since all these things were said about the last judgement, not about the passing of each holy man. This passing is really a transformation, for this holy man was rightly both transferred and transformed,[71] that is, from suffering to rest, from the pain of death to eternal repose.

39. Therefore the blessed Eusebius called a meeting of the clergy who were staying with him, and predicted to them everything that was coming in the next few days. Once he had interpreted his dream, he began to comfort them with his cheerful expression, since after the example of the Saviour he was

67 Emperor Valens, 364–378, who ruled the eastern half of the empire and perished in the battle of Adrianople against the Goths, supported Arian clergy. His brother Valentinian I, who ruled the western empire 364–375, supported the Nicene faction.

68 Ps. 39:4.

69 Acts 1:7.

70 Cf. Matt. 24:36, Mark 13:32.

71 Difficult passage: *Nam hic transitus mutatio est: hic autem sanctus merito translatus est atque mutatus.*

going to die and pray for them. They should not be so afraid, but should follow his example, for they would remain alive and unharmed: he alone would meet death.

40. After a few days had passed, he returned again to Vercelli. A violent and frenzied gang of Arians surrounded the house of holy Eusebius himself, where they knew he was resting. Seizing him, they dragged him outside of the house on his back. As they pummelled him with stones and pelted him from overhead with rocks, the holy head of that martyr was smashed, along with the rest of his body, and as his sacred blood gushed out of his skull, his holy soul was set free of his flesh and immediately soared upward towards the glory that he himself had foreseen only a short while before. His disciples collected his sacred body, and interred it in the basilica that the holy man himself had previously built in honour of the holy Theognistus the martyr, where the body of holy Theognistus himself rests.[72]

41. Ever since then, divine miracles have occurred at the tomb of holy Eusebius. For example, on the day when he was killed, there was such bright lightning and such heavy storm-clouds that hardly any Arians were believed to have escaped. And so it was granted by divine grace that no Arian could live in that city ever after, nor enter its church. Furthermore, as a gift from the Lord, different ailments are cured at his tomb. The blind are given light, demons are cast out from within, the sick are healed, the lame and the paralytic are restored, the deaf truly recover their hearing and the mute their speech, and the servants of God day and night sing psalms of divine eloquence in that church in different melodies. Visions of angels are often seen there, and the glorious martyr himself frequently seems to appear to the attendants of his church in their sleep, and instruct them about many matters. On the day of his burial, such a strong and sweet fragrance billowed out over everyone that it was as if a rivulet of balsam was coursing into that church. For it was his blood that was poured out and

72 The *Life of Eusebius* is the only source to mention this saint and cult before the discovery in 1581, when the church mentioned here was demolished, of a tombstone with the inscription "S. MARTIR THEONESTUS," along with another tombstone inscribed with Eusebius's name; both went missing in the early seventeenth century: Picard 1988, 291–293. Theognistus may have been martyred in the Diocletian persecutions; Eusebius may have learned of his cult during his period in exile: see E. Crovella, "Teonesto," *Bib. Sanct.* 12: 358–359. On the remains of the church, the form of which resembles the Constantinian basilica of St Peter's in Rome, see Cantino Wataghin 1997.

his skull that was so redolent, as though every kind of balsam and incense mixed together. Since then, whenever something happens there involving his blood or skull, those who frequently come to stand by his tomb can recognize it immediately by the same fragrance.

42. However, when he was still alive in the flesh, he made his disciples swear that all the vestments which he used, or aprons or stoles, or whatever came off or concerned his body, would all be placed in his tomb, and that they would permit no clippings or offerings of his hair or beard to be made. It is because of this that relics of him are seldom encountered. His feast day is celebrated on the Kalends of August, in the reign of our Lord Jesus Christ, who together with the Father and the holy spirit, lives and reigns, one God, forever and ever, Amen.

The most blessed Eusebius ordered that this sentence be written as his final words[73]:

> I, Eusebius the bishop, implore you who have read these words, by the Father and the Son and the holy spirit, not to suppress what has been written here, but to pass it on to others to read.

Through his prayers and merits, may the Lord almighty have mercy upon me, the author of this history [*gesta*].

73 The quotation is a modified version of the end of Eusebius's letter (*libellus*) to Patrophilus (above, ch.28), as contained within the letter of Eusebius to his suffragans that was preserved by Hilary of Poitiers: see Everett 2006.

12 SEPTEMBER

The Life of Sirus of Pavia

The anonymously written *Life of Sirus of Pavia* claims that Sirus was a contemporary of St Peter, Mark the Evangelist, and the Emperor Nero, established his episcopate at Pavia in the apostolic era, propagated the Christian faith in the cities of Verona, Lodi, and Brescia, and arranged for the burials of the saints Nazarius, Celsus, Protasius, and Gervasius, all of whom were martyred during Sirus's bishopric of fifty-six years. These claims are difficult to reconcile with what we know of early ecclesiastical history in Italy and the diocese of Pavia. There is no evidence for the existence of an episcopate in Pavia prior to the late fourth century and no mention of Sirus in written sources until the first quarter of the ninth century, and only well into the tenth century do we find evidence of Sirus's status as the patron saint of the town: the text has been dismissed as myth, a falsification of history.[1] A date for the text's composition is difficult to determine and has ranged from the early seventh to the early ninth century[2]: a *terminus ante quem* of c.830 is secured by Florus of Lyon's use of the *Life* in his martyrology, and its use in a later *Translation* text (*Translatio Siri*), which celebrates the relocation of Sirus's relics to the cathedral sometime after 832. However, the text can be dated to the early eighth century, for it reflects the conflict between the churches of Pavia and Milan, its metropolitan author-

1 BHL 7976. See Billanovich 1986, 1993, who locates the historical Sirus in the late fourth century. On earlier antiquarian attempts to legitimate the text's claims, see Everett 2002a, 857–860.

2 The debates and earlier literature are fully reviewed in Everett 2000, 2002a; Prelini 1880 (seventh century); Savio 1932, 321–326 (first half of ninth century); Lanzoni, 1927, 985, and Bognetti 1966–1970, 1: 143–217, 4: 301–338 (eighth century); Orselli 1978; Picard 1988, 601–603, 645–647; and Tomea 1993, 547–549. Most recently, Vocino 2014 (and 2010) repeats the arguments of Orselli and others for a ninth-century date, which are based on two main justifications: (a) the Carolingian period produced more documents than the Lombard, and (b) apostolic legends in hagiography only surface in the Carolingian period. These arguments are refuted in Everett 2002a, 858–876; cf. *Passion of Apollinaris*. On apostolic origins in southern Italian hagiography, see Granier 2012b.

ity, as Pavia grew in prestige as the Lombard capital and its bishop claimed a direct jurisdictional relationship with Rome in 711.

City and Cult

Although there is no evidence (besides the *Life*) for the cult of Sirus at Pavia before the tenth century, his status as town patron never wavered in the Middle Ages and has persisted until today.[3] Such success was partly owing to our hagiographer's efforts in the *Life of Sirus*, and underlines the earlier failure of Ennodius of Pavia to achieve town patron status for his hero, Epiphanius of Pavia (466–496), about whom Ennodius wrote a hagiographic work that should have made Epiphanius "the natural candidate" to be patron saint of Pavia.[4] Why Sirus should have succeeded where Epiphanius failed is a difficult question: the late antique vocabulary of Ennodius's *Life of Epiphanius* cannot have helped its somewhat limited reception in the centuries to come.[5] But perhaps more importantly, Ennodius's text was not a conventional hagiographic work, in that it was more a political biography, with hardly any element of divine majesty or miracles changing the course of events. Paul the Deacon was aware of both Ennodius and Epiphanius, and appears to have used the *Life of Epiphanius* as a source for his *Historia Romana*, but he made no mention of Sirus anywhere in his corpus, though he was partial to extolling the virtues of Italy's holy heroes, particularly those associated somehow with Pavia.[6] This eighth-century silence on Sirus is the main reason his *Life* is commonly misdated to the ninth century, but its historical context places it squarely in early eighth-century ecclesiastical politics.

3 On the cult, see Picard 1988, 199–202, 264–265, 645–648, 697–698, and Billanovich 1993.

4 *Vita Epifanii*, ed. Vogel (MGH Auct. ant. 1885: 7, 84–109); another edition with Italian trans. is Cesa (ed) 1988. English trans. in Cook 1942. "candidato naturale," Orselli 1978, 33. On Ennodius, see Kennell 2000.

5 Edited by Vogel (MGH Auct. ant. 1885: xxvi–xxvii); Cesa (ed) 1988, 32–36. Otto I's theft of the saint's cadaver demonstrates some popularity: see Dupré Theseider 1964.

6 Paul, *Historia Romana*, 16.3.5 (Ennodius), 15.17 (Epifanius). For Paul's use of the *Vita Epiphanii*, see Vogel (ed) (MGH Auct. ant. 1885: xxvii), though some citations are strained. On saints and Italians mentioned and praised by Paul, cf. *HL* I.25 (Cassiodorus), 26–27 (Benedict), II.13 (Venantius Fortunatus), and for Pavia in particular, V.38, VI.4 (Damian), V.38 (Thomas), VI.58 (Peter), IV.16 and VI.58 (Sabinus), and VI.48 (Liutprand and Saint Augustine's relics).

Date and Purpose

The keys to establishing the date and provenance of the text lie in this implicit assault on Milan's religious history, the sense of civic pride in Pavia's position among neighbouring cities, and the explicit criticism of Aquileia, forcefully expressed by means of Sirus's prophecy when he first enters the city that was to become his diocese (ch.2). Why Aquileia should "never be rebuilt to rise again" remains unexplained: the text never mentions the city again. The anti-Milanese tone of the text and the outright condemnation of Aquileia are not unrelated, and it is this connection that allows the redaction of the text to be placed within a particular historical milieu. Sometime around 712, Archbishop Benedict of Milan presented himself in Rome before Pope Constantine (708–715) to complain that the bishop of Pavia refused to be consecrated by him. The pope responded that indeed the bishop of Pavia was in his rights, for his consecration was dependent upon the apostolic see of Rome and Rome only, as it had been "from ancient times" (*a priscis temporibus*).[7] Yet there is secure evidence that the diocese of Pavia was always subject to Milan, and was still so as late as 680 – independent status could hardly have been "ancient."

Complicated theories have been put forward to explain these developments: Bognetti saw Pavese independence from Milan as arising from papal missionary activity against Arians in north Italy and the adherents of the Three Chapters schism; Duchesne suggested Pavia was granted the privilege of direct communication as a reward for the restoration to the papacy of the patrimony of the Cottian Alps by King Aripert II during the pontificate of John VII (705–707).[8] But the most compelling reason is the capital status of Pavia itself, for under the Lombards Pavia had become one of the most important cities of Europe, where kings and queens patronized artists, grammarians, and masons to celebrate the rule of the most powerful military force in Italy.[9] The *Life of Sirus* can be seen in the context of other expressions of civic pride in the sources of this period. In 698 the Lombard King Cunincpert presided over the Synod of Pavia, which put an end to the Three Chapters dispute, a source of division in Italian churches since the dispute first erupted in the mid-sixth century. The contemporary *Carmen de synodo Ticinensi*, which celebrates the conclusion of the synod, records that

7 *LP* 90.9. Also recorded by Paul, *HL* VI.29, using the *LP* as his source. On the events, see Bertolini1970, 396ff.

8 Bognetti 1966–1970, 4: 245–291; Bertolini 1960; *LP*, 385 n8, 395 n27; Hauptfeld 1983.

9 Majocchi 2008, 17–67; Everett 2003a, 64–65, 283–285.

> A schism long ago arose in the north, as the prophet Isaiah once warned (Jeremiah 4:6), which spread utter evil across the earth and caused the proud to fall from the throne. Although at the baptismal font they too accepted to believe in the Trinity in the same manner as us, the Aquileiese dissenters refused to believe in the fifth synod, which is in complete agreement with the fourth synod, and so have scorned everything altogether. [King Cunincpert] decreed that the faith should be united in all of Hesperia, and so summoned the Aquileiesi to the city where he resides, which is called Ticinum because of the river that flows through it, but which is commonly known as Pavia.[10]

Aside from sharing a common theological position against Aquileia, the *Carmen*'s reference to the nomenclature of *Ticinum/Pavia* (*Papia*) is similar to that which we find in the *Life of Sirus* (ch.1), as well as in a few other texts that date from the mid-seventh century, thus providing some further clues to dating the text.[11] Sirus's pro-Pavese and anti-Aquileiese prophecy, which itself went on to enjoy a considerable degree of popularity as a topos amongst later Pavese ecclesiastics, appears to place the composition of the text of the *Vita* at the earliest after the conclusion of the Synod of Pavia. Some Christological references in the text, and more importantly, in the words of Sirus himself in the long doxology (ch.11), further suggest an ecclesiastical ambience infused with controversy over Christ's nature.[12]

The *Life of Sirus*'s overt concern with Aquileia forms something of a diversionary subplot that distracts the reader's or listener's attention away from the covert anti-Milanese claims of the text: it dates the martyrdoms of Nazarius, Celsus, Protasius, and Gervasius to the same time as Sirus (Nero's reign), has Sirus arrange for the burial of the martyrs through his subordinate and even

10 *Carmen* ed. Waitz (MGH SS rer. Lang. 1878: 190). On its transmission, see Everett 2002a 86 n76.

11 The earliest references are Fredegar, 4:71 and the Ravennate Cosmographer 4.30. Cf. Paul, *HL* II.15; for references and discussion, see Everett 2002a, 863–865. Further confirmation of the Pavese church's concern in this period to subdue schismatic Aquileia is found in the epitaph of the Pavese deacon Thomas, mentioned in the *Carmen de synodo* as one of the key players in settling the dispute. Composed probably sometime in the early eighth century, the epitaph refers to Aquileia as "long blinded by error" and extols Thomas's achievement in subduing the schismatics: Everett 2001; cf. Paul, *HL* V.38.

12 Orselli 1978, 35–36, 59–67 (Excursus A) draws attention to interesting similarities with Pope Leo's *Tomus*.

tual successor Iuventius, who secured some of the blood of Nazarius for Pavia, and claims that some of the relics of Protasius and Gervasius were brought to Pavia, where Sirus performed miracles with them and built a cruciform church to house them outside the walls of the city, the "first banner of the heavenly king to be erected in this town" (ch.7, 5, 6). The hagiographer was clearly aware of previous hagiographic literature, including by Ambrose himself, which celebrated the martyrs' relics at Milan and their miraculous powers.[13] From these works our author developed the leitmotif of *litterae supultae*, inscriptions and books in graves, as a means of associating Sirus and Pavia with the famous Milanese martyrs. The claims for Sirus's early evangelization of northern Italy, his involvement with the martyrs, and his procurement of their relics for Pavia effectively rewrite history to subvert the authority of the Milanese see to the pre-eminence of Pavia, a church of apostolic stature, and in no need of Milan's metropolitan authority.

The anti-Milanese orientation of the text suggests a date of sometime around 711, when the Pavese bishop went to Rome to be consecrated. We cannot be more precise than that[14], but, curiously, a civic praise poem about Milan (entitled *Laudes Mediolanensis civitatis)* written around 739 appears to have been answering the proud exaltations of the Pavese *Carmen* in some instances. The first stanza emphasizes Milan's "*antiquitus*," then proceeds to describe the city's walls, turrets, ramps, buildings, and aqueduct, before breaking into unrestrained boasts:

13 Ambrose's letter on the discovery of the martyrs: *Ep.* 77. ed. Banterle and Zelzer 1988; Ps. Ambrose, *Passio Gervasii et Protasii* (BHL 3515–3519; text in PL 17: 820–825); *Passio Nazarii et Celsi* (BHL 6039–6042), text in Mombritius 1910, 2: 326–334. Another text that seems to have been consulted is the *Passio Narboris et Felicis* (BHL 6029), ibid., 2: 289–290. The various recensions are discussed by Zanetti 1979 and Zangara 1981. Another source was Paulinus, *Life of Ambrose*, ed. Pellegrino 1961 (also PL 14: 29–50). SeeTomea 1998. On the use of these sources in the *Life of Sirus*, see Everett 2002a, 877–883. Vocino 2014 attributes the anti-Milanese sentiment of the *Vita Siri* to the later ninth century, because Milan was favoured by Frankish rule. She does not engage with any of the arguments concerning the events of 712, Aquileia and the Synod of Pavia, Papia/Ticinum, or the codicological evidence in Everett 2002a, despite using that edition of the text.

14 It is worth noting that the opening quote from James 1:17 in the *Life* (below, ch.1) was also used by King Liutprand in 713 in the prologue to his first batch of legislation, likewise paired with a quotation from Proverbs. Liutprand was a patron of Bobbio (Everett 2003a, 250–253; 2001), where Vatican City, Biblioteca Apostolica Vaticana, Vat. lat. 5771 was written: see Everett 2002a and below.

> She is the queen of towns, mother of the realm, whom all nations of this world now praise together, and who bears the eminent title of metropolis. The immense dignity of her power endures, so that all the bishops [*presules*] of ancient Italy come to her to be instructed according to the dictates of canon law.[15]

Reference in the poem to the saints mentioned in the *Life of Sirus* (Nazarius, Celsus, Protasius, and Gervasius), along with another ten saints, and the proud claim that "no other town in this province" has as many holy corpses guarding it as Milan, all seem to indicate that the poem was directed against Pavia: *Ticinum* was, after all, as the poem tells us, the Lombard's second choice chronologically for the capital of the kingdom (it was actually third). These literary expressions of intercity rivalry betray a fierce civic pride so well known to later Italian history, but obscured in this period by the lack of sources. The *Life of Sirus* is another example of how hagiography was harnessed to express civic pride by associating the town's identity and history with its bishop and his authority.

The Life of Iuventius and Translation of Sirus

The *Life of Sirus* was followed by two other texts of interest. The *Life of Iuventius,* which appears alongside the *Life of Sirus* in our earliest manuscript (Vatican City, Biblioteca Apostolica Vaticana,Vat. lat. 5771), seems to have been written not long after the Sirus biography, for it continues its themes. Iuventius (feast date 8 February) established the clergy at Milan, which "remained under his jurisdiction," and built a church dedicated to Nazarius in Pavia (in which he was buried), and Sirus appears alongside the four Milanese martyrs in prophesying Iuventius's death.[16] There are differences in language and style, however, to suggest it was composed by a different author working in the same milieu. Another text, the *Translation of Sirus* (*Translatio Siri*) records the relocation of Sirus's relics to the cathedral sometime after 826, although the text may

15 MGH Poetae 2, 24–26. On the poem and its genre, see Hyde 1993, 1–32. On rivalry between Milan and Pavia, see Majocchi 2008.

16 BHL 4619. Text (ed and trans) in Everett 2002a, 937–942, 954–957; analysis at 872–877. Although also appearing in Vatican City, Biblioteca Apostolica Vaticana, Vat. lat. 5771, *Vita Iuventii* was less popular, appearing in sixteen manuscripts (compared to thirty-nine for *Vita Siri*).

have been written sometime in the second half of the ninth century.[17] The *Translation* is a clumsy, derivative text that borrows heavily from the *Life of Sirus*, though omits Iuventius and makes no mention of Milan, and other aspects of the text suggest a completely different ambience of composition from that of the lives of *Sirus* and *Iuventius*.

Text and Translation

The text translated below is that established by Everett 2002a, 921–936, a diplomatic edition of the text (and the *Life of Iuventius*) based upon its earliest surviving witness, Vatican City, Biblioteca Apostolica Vaticana, Vat. lat. 5771, a ninth-century manuscript from the monastery of Bobbio which had been overlooked in the earlier editions of Prelini 1880, Surius (1581), and Mombritius (1480). Everett 2002a also consulted and collated ten other manuscripts preserved in Rome, and collated the readings of the ten manuscripts used by Prelini 1880, which were mostly northern Italian, dating from the eleventh century onwards.[18]

The manuscript Vat. lat. 5771 is something of a landmark in the history of hagiographic production and preservation: it contains the earliest recensions of nearly half of the one hundred or so hagiographic works it preserves, including martyr narratives and the lives of Egyptian and Syrian saints, and it is one of the earliest examples of a passionary set out *per curriculum anni*, that is, containing texts arranged according to the feast days throughout the year, which became standard from the tenth century onward[19] (and is used in this book).

17 BHL 7978. The text is edited in Prelini 1880, 234–269. On the date, see Picard 1988, 646–647; analysis in Everett 2002a, 872–876. Orselli 1978 envisioned the composition of the *Translatio* and the *Vitae* of Sirus and Iuventius as simultaneous in the ninth century.

18 Everett 2002a, 914–920. MSS of Rome consulted include Vatican City, Biblioteca Apostolica Vaticana, Barb. lat. 586, s.XI–XII; Vat. lat. 1190, s.XII; Vat. lat. 1194, s.XII; Vat. lat. 6933, s.XII; Rome, Biblioteca nazionale centrale Vittorio Emanuele II, Sessoriana 5, s.XI; Sessoriana 48, s.XII; Rome, S. Giovanni in Laterano Archivio del Vicariato, 81, s.XI; Rome, Biblioteca Vallicellana, T. III, s.XII/XII; Rome, Biblioteca Casanatensis, 718, s.XI/XII; and Rome, Biblioteca Angelica, 1269, s. XV. Prelini's edition privileged the recension of the *Life* in Turin, Biblioteca Nazionale e Universitaria, F.II.10, an eleventh-century passionary.

19 The hagiographic contents of Vatican City, Biblioteca Apostolica Vaticana, Vat. lat. 5771 are analyzed in Everett 2002a, 904–913; on the development of passionaries and legendaries, see Philippart 1977 (on *per curriculum anni*, 68–72), 1994; Degl'Innocenti 1999, 2012; and Dolbeau 2008.

Moreover, Vat. lat. 5771 was written at Bobbio, which was founded by the Lombard monarchy, had strong links with the Lombard court, and owned a considerable amount of property in Pavia by the ninth century.[20] It is therefore likely that the *Life of Sirus* in Vat. lat. 5771 was copied from an earlier exemplar at Bobbio written closer to the events of 712, and that the monks of Bobbio were among the earliest readers and recipients of the text (see notes 14 and 22).

20 Documented in Everett 2002a, 884–887; Polonio 1962; and Bullough 1966.

The Life of Sirus of Pavia

1. Divine fortune arisen from on high, recounted with sweet eloquence, rings clear in the ears of the faithful everywhere. For the weakness of human declaration is unable to recount the sacred mysteries unless instructed by authority, as the wisest Solomon says, "The Lord gives wisdom, and from his very mouth comes knowledge and prudence."[21] This is further affirmed by the blessed Apostle James when he says "Every good endowment, and every perfect gift is from above, coming down from the Father of light."[22] With these declarations of truth in mind, let it now be recounted how the city of Ticinum, which usually is called Pavia, was once illuminated by divine compassion and by the visitation of heavenly grace, in which times past and by which preachers. For the written acts of the most blessed Sirus and Iuventius, the first preachers and bishops of this town, inform us how from the very beginnings of the nascent church in apostolic times the people of the city of Ticinum were converted to the faith of the Lord. For our Redeemer, as part of the mysteries for which he came to us in the flesh, suffered, and returned to the heavens, recruited disciples, twelve in number. Ennobled by the advent of the holy spirit, these then divided the world among themselves by lots, and whoever was chosen undertook to go to their province of origin. With the disciples preaching the incarnation of the Lord, so the number of the faithful grew, and in abandoning their error of faithlessness, they joined the disciples in teaching. And so it came about that there were helpers and successors to the apostles, through whom the church of Christ was instructed in the true religion and proceeded to the faith of Christ and the cult of heaven. It was at this time that the most blessed apostle of Christ, Peter, having founded the church of Antioch, in which the name of Christians was first used to describe a new people, sought to found the Roman church, and made his way to the city of Rome. There he preached of Christ crucified, and he performed all sorts of wonders and miracles before all of the Jews, so that many were converted to believe in his precepts. In these days Mark the Evangelist was his pupil and acted as his interpreter, and everything that he learned from the mouth of Peter concerning the marvels of our saviour Jesus Christ, Mark recorded in his Gospel. Many believe the Gospel to be the work of the blessed

21 Prov. 2:6 (*luminum*).

22 James 1:17. The same passage was quoted by King Liutprand in the prologue to his first legislative acts in 713. See introduction above, n14.

Peter, because although Mark the Evangelist wrote the Gospel, he did so steeped in Peter's teaching, and Peter's authority was then given for it to be handed over and read in the church. But after this Mark the Evangelist left Rome and set out for Egypt where he toiled to spread the truth from the teachings of the Master and founded the church of Alexandria in wondrous unity and most holy fellowship. Taking with him the Gospel which he had completed at the request of his brothers in Rome, he established in his place in Italy[23] the blessed Hermagora, a man whom Mark himself had trained and taught and who was renowned for his sagacity and holiness. Hermagora's students and ministers were the venerable men Sirus and Iuventius. And lo, inestimable lucidity poured from the very font of light was drawn into the blessed hearts of these two men and set alight the spirits of the people of Ticinum, so that it flowed from Christ to Peter, from Peter to Mark, from Mark to Hermagora, and from Hermagora to the most blessed men Sirus and Iuventius, thus fulfilling the cry of the psalmist: "Whoever sends his word to earth, swiftly his message runs."[24]

2. Having related these things according to the tradition of divine scripture, we shall now follow the course that we have learned from the narration of their lives by others.[25] While the blessed Hermagora was in Aquileia introducing the Lord Christ to a people who knew nothing about him, a mass of people, of infinite number, began to flock together from various directions to learn of his creed. With the swift word of divine inspirations, the church of Christ began to grow, as their minds, receiving the erudition of his word, were easily swayed to believe in that which he preached. Summoning his disciple Sirus, he bestowed upon him the title of bishop, and entrusting to his care the blessed Iuventius to evangelize the name of our Lord Jesus Christ, he directed Sirus to the town of Pavia, in order that he might perform his ministry there, demonstrate the faith to those living there, and unite the souls of pagans with the grace of Christ. Thus charged by the father and strengthened by his blessings, they took to the road for their holy mission. In the course of their travels, they entered the town of Verona, a town in which things cannot be hidden, for it is a city that, as the Gospel has it, "sits on top of a hill."[26] For a most noble

23 *ordine uicis suae Italiae*: *suae* ("his") may agree with *vicis* or *Italiae*.

24 Ps. 167:4. On the Hermagora and Marcian legends, see Everett 2002a, 865–867; Everett 2003b; Tomea 1993, 548; Vocino 2014.

25 *ex sermonis vitae eorum narratione didicimus*. The author could be suggesting that he obtained his information from recitations of written works concerning the two men.

26 Matt. 5:14.

woman, informed, I believe, by divine notice, and learning of their arrival, rushed towards them with great haste and, weeping bitterly, declared that she had lost her one and only son. She threw herself at the feet of the most holy Sirus, and promised him that she and all her family would join the Christian religion, if she saw her dead son restored to her by his prayers. To her request the man of God promptly responded, "If you believe with your whole heart, all things are possible." She promised to keep her word, and straightaway the man of God went to her house, where he began to pour out prayers to the Lord over the lying corpse, and restored the dead boy to life and pristine health. The lad began to glorify the Lord, for by the prayer of his servant he had been snatched from the prison of darkness. Many people came together on account of the miracle and said, "True is the God of the Christians, of whom his servant preaches here. It is he whom we should worship." And the noble widow, seeing her son restored to her, fulfilled her promises as she had made them. Immediately she was baptized along with her son, and both the men and women in her family abandoned the sacrilege of idolatry, and joined the fellowship of Christ. At the sight of this miracle an immense number of pagans was baptized, trusting in Christ the Lord.

3. When the man of the Lord Sirus then left that town and headed for Pavia, his fame preceded him and announced his coming. For before his arrival a huge crowd of townspeople had gathered in eager expectation of the arrival of so great a father and preacher of their salvation. When he came they threw themselves at his feet and cried, "Come, come desirable father, reclaim those who err, raise up the fallen, teach the ignorant, free those held captive by the cruellest of enemies. Rescue us and instruct us in the ways to salvation, and bring us into the presence of the true God so that we might know whom we should worship." At that very moment, by the power of God's clemency, the sick there who touched him were instantly restored to their full health. Sirus then entered the town and announcing its future prosperity he delivered a prophecy: "Rejoice, city of Pavia, because rejoicing will come to you from the eternal mountains, and no longer will you be called smallest, but rather the richest among neighbouring cities. But woe unto you, Aquileia, for you will fall into the hands of the wicked and be destroyed. You shall never be rebuilt to rise again."[27] The crowd of people were shouting, "The true and only God is the one whom this most blessed father preaches. Those who worship idols are full

27 Cf. Mic. 5:2; Matt. 2:6.

of vain stupidity." Turning to all those gathered together, the man of God said, "Be firm, my dear children, and be sure to fulfil the duty that you have professed in speech. Believe that Christ is the Son of God, eternally existent with the Father, God from God, invisible from the invisible, all powerful from the all-powerful. Who for our redemption was incarnate of the Virgin, and who grew through time and with age as a real man, nevertheless remaining the true God in his divinity. He suffered death, was resurrected, and ascended into heaven." Soon enough he revealed to all those who listened the mystery of the passion and resurrection of the Lord, informing them of the day of judgement and the eternal glory for believers and the saints, saying, "If you believe in these things, God shall always be with you as with us, and whatever you seek in his name with faith will be granted to you."[28] With these and many other holy exhortations the people were converted to the faith of Christ. All who followed on from this with the grace of baptism then venerated this father, the herald of their salvation, with tremendous affection.

4. At that time, a thoroughly pagan count called Anolinus had stirred up the persecution of Christians in the city of Milan. While many Christians were punished for their love of Christ, this cruellest of rulers arranged for the blessed Protasius and Gervasius, men outstanding in their Christian devotion, to be shut away in a dark prison, but many of Christ's faithful kept them hidden. The most blessed Nazarius, of illustrious birth, went about throughout this storm constantly preaching the name of Christ and illuminated many souls, caring nothing for the affairs of this wretched life. Seized by the hands of the wicked, he was thrown into the waves of the sea. Freed by divine intervention, this true athlete of Christ was soon saved from the shipwreck of grave danger. After this divinely inspired miracle, he immediately began to preach that the Lord Jesus Christ was the Son of God and headed back to Milan. There, by the order of the most contemptible Nero and that same count, he was sentenced to death. Fearing repercussions because of Nazarius's high birth and noble lineage, the most savage persecutor, one stormy night, ordered his head to be cut off, along with that of one of his followers, a boy called Celsus.

5. When the most blessed Sirus learned of these things from the reports of many people, he turned to the venerable Iuventius and said, "Go with all speed and haste to Milan, diligently seek out the Christians there and address them in

28 Cf. John 16:24; Matt. 21:22.

the following manner: 'May the ardour of divine charity compel you and bind you to revere the martyrs of Christ. Let the dear bodies of our brothers Nazarius and Celsus, whose blood has been spilt in the name of Christ, receive the burial they deserve, one of the highest honour, and be sure to place in their tomb an epitaph upon which their struggle is written in sacred letters. As for those most worthy confessors, Protasius and Gervasius, who are currently being held in prison by that pestiferous ruler, when they too shall have been crowned with martyrdom for their Christian faith, bury them with due and deserved honour, and compose for them a little book recording their passion and place it next to their heads for the future praise of our Lord Jesus Christ and for their glory. For it has been predestined by God that the bodies of these saints will be revealed to men of faith at a time when their faith needs to be confirmed. For their corpses will be resplendent in repute and miracles and restore health and strength to many of the infirm.'"

6. Accepting all of the advice of the father with a cheerful heart, Iuventius with joy and all readiness took to the road to fulfil his special mission and arrived at Milan when it was already night, despite his hurrying. When Iuventius found those faithful of whom the holy father spoke, he informed them of all he had been commissioned to do. But they responded that they had already buried the bodies of the martyrs Nazarius and Celsus. To which the blessed Iuventius replied, "I beseech you, then, so that when the most blessed Protasius and Gervasius, who are still alive at present, should come to the end of their struggle, retain for us some relic of their clothing or bodies and offer it to us out of the sweetness of love and reverence for them." Upon hearing this, those that were present replied that they had seen a woman, a servant of God, who had managed to gather up some blood of the holy Nazarius into a linen cloth when his head was cut off by that iniquitous butcher, and then ran away. At this news the man of God Iuventius was greatly impressed and anxious to find this servant of Christ, and he immediately set upon her trail until he found her. Inspired by divine admonition, she happily gave to Iuventius the blood of the martyr that she was carrying. Iuventius received the great gift for which he had searched as though treasure,[29] and joyfully returned to the walls of Ticinum. When the bearer of so great a gift entered the gates, a boy was suddenly possessed by the

29 Cf. *Vita Ambrosii*, c. 33; on the hagiographer's manipulation of earlier Milanese hagiographic literature in these chapters, see Everett 2002a, 877–883. On the Milanese literature, see Tomea 1998.

devil and ran about in the street groaning and wailing. In a mourningful voice he shouted, "Woe unto me, for I am tortured at the entrance of the blood of the martyr!" When the soldier of Christ Iuventius heard this, he placed the blood of the holy martyr Nazarius over the vexed boy, and immediately expelled from the boy the demon who had spoken. With Christ's guidance and for the confirmation of the Catholic faith of many, the most wise Iuventius made the blood of the holy martyr Nazarius famous through the performance of many miracles. For when he placed it over the eyes of the blind, he restored their sight, and frequently cured the different illnesses that were brought before him. From this time on, through the powerful protection and intercession of the blessed Nazarius, the people of this city of Ticinum were fully confirmed in their belief.

7. Not long afterwards, when the trials of the holy martyrs Protasius and Gervasius at Milan were over, their precious bodies were buried by the Christians in secret so that dead they might not suffer atrocities of the wicked as they had when alive. Then a certain man named Liberius, a faithful Christian who out of love and reverence for the martyrs had taken what little he could of their relics in an act of rash piety, gave them happily to the most blessed Sirus, father of the city of Ticinum and wise teacher, when Sirus asked him. The venerable man took possession of the relics of the blessed and used them to perform miracles. As the fame of their healing powers spread far and wide, crowds of sick rushed to him in full throng even from unexpected places. While the distinguished priest of God was rejoicing in the miracles which Christ the Lord was busily performing through the merits of his martyrs, he began to conceive the idea of building a temple of the Lord dedicated to their memory not far outside the walls of this city, which he set out to build in the form of a cross.[30] Completed, it was the first banner of the heavenly king to be erected in this town. And the Lord's flock, whom the most faithful pastor ruled under his sheep folds as lambs of the Lord, with careful watch snatched them from the jaws of the evil serpent. As had been told of the most powerful David, when he broke the arms of bears and ground down the necks of lions, keeping the hostage flock from their bloody fangs.[31]

30 On this church, thought to date from the sixth century, see Bullough 1966, 118–119, and Majocchi 2008.

31 Cf. 1 Sam. 17.

8. Once the ceremonies concerning the dedication of the church and altar were completed, Sirus began to perform the daily offerings of the host and praise of God. One day, when the excellent pontiff was celebrating the mass before a large gathering of his children whom, as the apostle of God says, he had cultivated from the seed of the word[32] and who were now devoted to the holy mysteries, a Jew, inspired by a malign spirit, boldly entered the church and attempted to receive the Lord's Body so that he might throw it in the dung heap. Moving through the crowds of the faithful he came before the man of God and with wicked effrontery received the holy host in his filthy mouth. As he opened his mouth to spit out the host, he was suddenly struck down by righteous revenge. He tried to call out to all those who were present, but he could not form any words. He tried to close his mouth but could not. He attempted to express words, but his rigid tongue would not lend itself to the power of speech. It was as though a fiery javelin had speared his mouth and now tortured him with immense pain. The whole church echoed with the shouts of his deranged voice, and the gathering of Christ's faithful were overjoyed to witness such a miraculous wonder, so fulfilling what is written: "he himself scorns those who scorn him,"[33] and as the apostle writes to the Galatians, "Do not be deceived. God is not mocked. For man shall reap what he has sown."[34] The unbelieving Jew, who had neither heard nor read these precepts of the Scriptures, therefore tried to play tricks with the holy spirit. The man of God ordered that the Jew be brought before him and said, "Is your mind so full of disbelief and wickedness from having listened to the counsel of the evil enemy that you thought the body of Christ to be completely worthless? Behold how the secret solicitor has deceived wretched you to act so and how divine virtue then revealed all to his faithful." But the Jew continued to gargle noises in excessive pain without mouthing a proper word, the agony of his evil now stuck in his throat. As the prophecy of the most holy Simeon reminds us, just as the word of God is wreck and ruin for the unbelievers, so it is life and joy to his faithful.[35] For as those who were watching attentively saw, the Lord's Host appeared to be miraculously freed by being suspended in the Jew's mouth so that it hovered above the tongue without touching his palate. On account of his misery the faithful asked the man of God to intervene. Sirus took the mystery of the holy Eucharist from his sacrilegious mouth, saying, "Behold now you are free. Be careful not to do anything simi-

32 1 Cor. 4:15.

33 Cf. Prov. 3:34: *inlusores ipse deludet*.

34 Cf. Gal. 6:7–8.

35 Luke 2:34.

lar or presume to try this again." The Jew then threw himself at Sirus's feet and swore that he was ready to believe in Christ the Lord if Sirus would wash him in the water of sacred baptism and join him with the community of the faith. "I give thanks," said Sirus, "to you, God, Almighty Father, you who do not disdain to correct the Jewish treachery but instead with great compassion turn it towards belief in your only Son." After his baptism, many other Jews who thought likewise were reborn by holy baptism and were united in the spiritual brotherhood of Christ's faithful.

9. While God was showing many praiseworthy acts through this Father of ours who was distinguished for being enlightened with the spirit of prophecy, an arrogant man came to him under the pretence of piety. Sirus considered the man before him and said, "It would be better for you to remain silent rather than speak, because that which you think is revealed." The man was dumbstruck. Not being able to utter a word, he fell at the feet of the holy man and with tears and groans confessed all the secrets of his evil mind. The man of the Lord, moved by the fellow's tears and groans, soon restored his ability to speak and made him a minister in divine service. The grace of God then spread throughout the Pavese town,[36] and along with it the fame of this holy man, so that from everywhere crowds of many peoples came to him. In this happiest of towns he then established ecclesiastical orders, and made his disciples the gentlest Iuventius and Pompeius deacons. He also ordained as priests the illustrious man Crisantius and the eminent Fortunatus. Sirus himself held the bishop's see for the course of fifty-six years, during which he gained many souls lost to the most pagan cults of idols and brought them to the faith and service of God.

10. One day when he headed out from the abovementioned city and was going around the neighbouring villages and estates imbuing the hearts of the ignorant with the words of his holy preaching, a certain man threw himself at Sirus's feet and cried out that he had a son who was deaf and dumb. He begged Sirus to grace the boy with his holy presence, so that gift of speech and hearing might be granted. With Sirus's agreement the boy was brought to him, and he began to pour out his prayer to the Lord aloud, saying, "Lord Jesus Christ, you who deigned, along with the Father and the holy spirit, to fashion the human form without blemish in your own likeness,[37] and who gave to him the gift of free

36 *civitate papiana*.
37 Cf. Gen. 1:25.

will, who restored speech to the dumb, sight to the blind, hearing to the deaf, and life to the dead, watch over this boy and open his mouth and blocked-up ears, because this restitution can only come from you, the Creator, by whose finger[38] all parts of the human being are put together so as to be congruent. At the end of his prayer he made a sign of the cross with his fingers over the boy's ears and mouth. Suddenly the boy's ears were opened and his tongue was loosened so that in a loud voice he began to confess and bless the Lord. All the unbelievers who witnessed the miracle believed in the Lord Jesus Christ and his creed and were baptized in the faith.

11. Later on a horrid persecution of Christians was underway, and much blood was spilt throughout a number of different places. The purveyors of this wickedness eagerly hastened to the town in which the man of God was performing such miracles. But knowing that nearly all of the citizenry was already Christian, they did not dare attack the town nor lay their iniquitous hands upon the citizens. Instead they hurried to find the man of God and in a threatening manner said, "Who gave you the power to coerce by oppression both nobles and commoners into the Christian sect, and to frighten the unwilling with your magic tricks, so that they worship Christ whom the Jews crucified as though the Son of God? A god whom they have not seen nor shall see, so that they then despise the true gods that Roman religion professes? If we told this to the almighty emperor, he would at once decree a punishment of many tortures for you and all those who listened to your message and believe in your teachings. Take our advice: cease this stupidity and stop subverting souls who live quite peacefully serving their gods." To this speech the most blessed Sirus responded with the most charming courtesy:

> Do not deceive yourselves, my beloved children, nor let that ancient error which blinded the hearts of your ancestors remain in your mind any longer. Do not worship mute, deaf, and completely vacuous idols, made by human effort, at the devil's suggestion, and without sense or soul, for these cannot provide you with the remedy of salvation. Instead, believe in God, creator of heaven and earth, and of all creatures, he who made the world from nothing, who established the earth upon the waters, and lined the seas with beaches, and made all things above in heaven, and all things below on earth and in water; who compacted land over the abyss and made the waters run from the cliffs and mountains; who produced rivers from secret [caverns]

38 Cf. Luke 11:20.

and mixed their currents with the waves of the sea. Believe in this Christ, the Son of God, who for our salvation deigned to assume the form of a slave, and whom the undefiled Virgin Mary conceived at the annunciation of the Archangel Gabriel, who grew in the womb of the Virgin Mary for the full nine months – his birth was known to the wise men through the appearance of a new star that guided them to come in adoration to Bethlehem in Judea, where they brought him gifts as King of kings – for whom Herod searched to find and kill, and who was persecuted among the holy innocents. He shone with miracles, raised the dead, cleansed lepers, and restored sight to the blind, hearing to the deaf, mobility to the lame, and speech to the mute, and by whose command and will all ailments were healed. He slept like an ordinary man, yet commanded the gusts of the wind like the true God. As an ordinary man he felt hunger, yet as true God satisfied five thousand people with fives loaves of bread and two fish. As a real man he thirsted, yet as true God he has given an inexhaustible fountain to those who believe in him. Because of jealousy the leaders of the Jews had him flogged and crucified under Pontius Pilate. At his crucifixion a darkness was drawn over the whole world from the sixth hour of day until the ninth. What more? He died and was buried, but rose again on the third day, and spoke with his disciples for forty days, who then witnessed in wonder his ascent into heaven. He promised his disciples that, in believing in him, they too would follow him in his glory; those who did not believe, however, were destined to face the punishments of the eternal flame that had been prepared for them and for their father the devil. For whoever does the devil's deeds is his child. But I promise to you in the Lord that if you believe in the Son of God Jesus Christ, and you renounce evil deeds and the vacuous idols, then you will possess eternal life with the holy angels, the life in which light is never lacking and darkness had no place, the life in which there is no hunger or lack of clothing but in which Christ himself is true respite for his faithful, who gives to those who believe in him the whitest of robes and the eternal glory of everyday happiness.[39]

12. When the man of the Lord had spoken these words, the minds of all were converted by the aspect of his divine tranquillity so that they all said with one

39 For the above scriptural references, cf. Luke 1:26; Matt. 2:1–18; John 2:11; Luke 17:12–19; Matt. 8; John 6:1–14, 6–15; Matt. 27; Acts 2:11; Matt. 18:20; John 8:37–40; Apoc. 7:14–17.

accord, "It's better for us to believe in the sort of God who lives in heaven, not in rocks." Then they all fell at the feet of the holy man and asked to obtain the grace of baptism. The man of the Lord, revealing the mysteries of the Catholic faith and endowing all with the gift of holy baptism, united them with the body of the Catholic church. One day, when he had left the city of Ticinum for the sake of holy preaching, and was among the people of the city of Brescia, a little boy called Eustasius, who was possessed by a demon, shouted, "Who is this who enters this city, and of what race is he who subdues my brothers and fellow citizens to his rule?" Running up to Sirus, he said, "It's enough for you, Sirus, to have persecuted me throughout so many places. At least grant me permission to live here. Who sent you to evict me from my homes? You have come from far away, and you have no relatives here, our possession is your inheritance." The man of the Lord simply laughed in his face and said, "What wretch gave you any right of possession here? Eternal fire is your possession!" The demon responded, "Don't think that this fire is my possession only, because many people of this town, who obey my commands in all things, will enter it with me. Only you fight against me and bother much with my destruction." Immediately the man of God raised his eyes to the heavens in prayer and commanded the demon, saying, "Vile spirit and deceiver of souls, leave him, and do not dare to return to him again, but go to the eternal tortures that await you." As soon as he uttered the command the demon, groaning and weeping, knocked the boy down and left him, not daring to return. Then many of those who saw these miraculous events believed in Jesus Christ. The boy and his entire family, and a great crowd of people, now believers, were baptized. The holiest of fathers remained a few more days in this town among the faithful Christians and added more spiritual children to the holy church.

13. Leaving the city of Brescia, he then entered the town of Lodi, when a man, blind from birth, rushed up before Sirus and begged him with prayers for help. The man of God said to him, "Do you believe in the Lord Jesus Christ, Son of God?" The blind man responded, "I believe, so long as my eyes will be illuminated." The most blessed Sirus said, "If you believe with your whole heart, he in whom you believe will open your eyes." Immediately his eyes perceived the light, and the blind man began to praise the Lord Jesus Christ as the one and true Son of God. Baptized with his entire family along with a great number of witnesses, he remained strong in the faith of Christ. On the following day when he returned to Pavia many people who had followed him for the love of his holy words and who had stayed many days with him began to understand the

foundation of true faith. The citizens, who knew of the holy man's return and of the miracles he had performed in the aforesaid towns, came out to greet him, men and women, praising and glorifying the Lord who had deigned to give them so great and such a father as this. He then returned to the seat of his ministry and called before him the wisest of men Iuventius and said, "Let it be no secret to you, my dearest son, that you will be the third to obtain the honour of this ministry after me. Strengthen your resolve, and do not let the frenzy of the confused frighten you."[40] Instructing him in all ecclesiastical duties, he passed over to the Lord, having lived 112 years in all. An assembly of the faithful, whom the venerable father had acquired for the Lord with his preaching, accompanied by priests and a multitude of clerics, buried the remains of his holy body with due honour and the utmost attentiveness in the church of the holy martyrs Gervasius and Protasius, which Sirus himself had constructed.

14. After his death, Pompeius, outstanding in his simplicity and humility, and whom Sirus himself had raised to the level of deacon, obtained the honour of that see. Living only a few but peaceful years, he passed over to the Lord.

40 Iuventius's career, which included establishing clergy at Milan and founding a church dedicated to Nazarius in Pavia, is recorded in the *Life of Iuventius*, ed. and trans. Everett 2002a.

Bibliography

Manuscripts

Gaudentius
Intra, Archivio capitolare, 12 (10).
Milan, Biblioteca Ambrosiana, S 55 Sup.
Naples, Biblioteca nazionale, XV AA 12.
Barbatus
Naples, Biblioteca nazionale VIII B 6.
Vatican City, Biblioteca Apostolica Vaticana, Vat. lat. 7810.
Zeno
Paris, Bibliothèque nationale de France, lat. 5593.
Vatican City, Biblioteca Apostolica Vaticana, Barb. lat. 586.
Michael
Paris, Bibliothèque nationale de France, lat. 2873A.
Senzius
Lucca, Biblioteca Capitolare, C, 174v–176v.
Rome, Archivio del Capitolo di S. Giovanni in Laterano, 79.
Cetheus
Venice, Biblioteca Nazionale Marciana, lat. Z 356.
Vigilius
Paris, Bibliothèque nationale de France, lat. 9741.
St Gall, Stiftsbibliothek, 566.
Verona, Biblioteca Capitolare, XCV (90).
Apollinaris
St Petersburg, National Library of Russia, V.1.12.
Eusebius
Ghent, Universiteitsbibliotheek, 244.
Paris, Bibliothèque nationale de France, lat. 5321.
Rouen, Bibliothèque municipale, 36.
Rouen, Bibliothèque municipale, 42.
Turin, Biblioteca Nazionale e Universitaria, F.III.16.

Sirus

Vatican City, Biblioteca Apostolica Vaticana, Vat. lat. 5771.
Vatican City, Biblioteca Apostolica Vaticana,Vat. lat. 1190.
Vatican City, Biblioteca Apostolica Vaticana,Vat. lat. 1194.
Vatican City, Biblioteca Apostolica Vaticana, Vat. lat. 6933.
Vatican City, Biblioteca Apostolica Vaticana, Barb. lat. 586.
Rome, Biblioteca nazionale centrale Vittorio Emanuele II, Sessoriana 5.
Rome, Biblioteca nazionale centrale Vittorio Emanuele II, Sessoriana 48.
Rome, S. Giovanni in Laterano, Archivio del vicariato, 81.
Rome, Biblioteca Vallicellana, T. III.
Rome, Biblioteca Casanatensis, 718.
Rome, Biblioteca Angelica, 1269.
Turin, Biblioteca Nazionale e Universitaria, F.II.10.

Printed Sources

Ancient and medieval sources are listed by name for authored texts with reference to modern editions, where the full citations will appear under the editors' names: e.g., Paul the Deacon. *Historia Langobardorum*. *See* Waitz and Bethmann (eds) 1878. Anonymous texts and/or texts with titles that vary among manuscripts (as often in hagiography) are also listed under the name of their modern editors as cited.

Agnellus of Ravenna. *Liber pontificalis ecclesiae Ravennatis*. *See* Holder-Egger (ed) 1878; Deliyannis (ed) 2006; Deliyannis (trans) 2004.

Ambrose, (Saint) of Milan. *See* Banterle (ed) 1988.

Amore A. 1968. "Senzio" (voce) *Bib. Sanct.* 9: 496–498.

Andenna, G. and G. Picasso (eds) 1996. *Longobardia e longobardi nell'Italia meridionale: Le istituzioni ecclesiastiche*. Milan: Vita e Pensiero.

Anti, E. 1996. "Zeno di Verona e Geminiano di Modena: Due Vitae a confronto." *Annuario storico zenoniano* 13: 27–52.

—. 1998. *Santi e animali nell'Italia padana (Secoli IV–XII)*. Bologna: CLUEB.

—. 2000. "Mondo contadino e vite dei santi: Alcuni esempi delle fonti agiografiche dell'Italia padana altomedievale." In Golinelli (ed) 2000: 65–78.

Antonopoulos, P. 2010. *The Reign of Cunincpert: Saga, Reality, Stability and Progress in Lombard Italy at the End of the Seventh Century*. Camberley, UK: Porphyrogenitus.

Arecchi, A. 2006. *I mausolei dei re Longobardi a Pavia*. Milan: Mimesis Liutprand.

Armstrong, C.B. 1921. "The Synod of Alexandria and the Schism at Antioch in A.D. 362." *Journal of Theological Studies* 22.2: 206–221; 22.4: 347–355.

Arndt, W.F. and F. Wilbur Gingrich 1979. *A Greek-English Lexicon of the New Testament and Other Early Christian Literature*. 2nd ed. Chicago: University of Chicago Press.

Arnold, J.C. 2000. "Arcadia Becomes Jerusalem: Angelic Caverns and Shrine Conversion at Monte Gargano." *Speculum* 75: 567–588.

—. 2013. *The Footprints of Michael the Archangel: The Formation and Diffusion of a Saintly Cult, c. 300–c. 800*. New York: Palgrave Macmillan.

Ashbrook Harvey, S. 2004. "Women and Words: Texts by and about Women." In *The Cambridge History of Early Christian Literature*, ed. F. Young, L. Ayres, and A. Louth, 382–390. Cambridge: Cambridge University Press.

Aulisa, I. 1994. "Le fonti e la datazione della *Revelatio seu apparitio S. Michaelis Archangeli in monte Tancia*." *Vetera Christianorum* 31: 315–331.

Aureli, P., M.A., De Lucia Brolli, and S. Del Lungo (eds) 2006. *Orte (Viterbo) e il suo territorio: Scavi e ricerche in Etruria meridionale fra antichità e Medioevo*. Oxford: John and Erica Hedges.

Avesani, R. 2004. "Il re Pipino, il vescovo Annone e il *Versus de Verona*." In P. Golinelli and C.G. Brenzoni (eds) 2004: 57–65.

Balzaretti, R. 2013. 1996. "Cities, Emporia and Monasteries: Local Economies in the Po Valley 700–875." In *Towns in Transition: Urban Evolution in Late Antiquity and the Early Middle Ages*, ed. N. Christie and S.T. Loseby, 213–234. Aldershot, Hants: Scolar Press.

—. *Dark Age Liguria: Regional Identity and Local Power, c. 400–1020*. London: Bloomsbury Academic.

Banterle, G. (ed) 1988. *Opera Omnia di Sant'Ambrogio*. Milan; Rome: Città Nuova.

Banterle, G. and M. Zelzer (eds) 1988. *Sancti Ambrosii episcopi mediolanensis opera*. Volume 21: *Epistulae* 3. Milan: Biblioteca Ambrosiana.

Barbiera, I. 2005. *Changing Lands in Changing Memories: Migration and Identity during the Lombard Invasions*. Florence: Edizioni All'Insegna del Giglio.

Barnay, S. 1992. *Les apparitions de la Vierge*. Paris: Cerf.

Barnes, T.D. 1993. *Athanasius and Constantius: Theology and Politics in the Constantinian Empire*. Cambridge, MA: Harvard University Press.

Bartholdy Glenthøj, J. 1997. *Cain and Abel in Syriac and Greek Writers (4th–6th Centuries)*. Corpus Scriptorum Christianorum Orientalium 567. Subsida Tomus 95. Louvain: Peeters.

Bassi, C. 1998. "Il problema della continuità dell'insediamento umano tra età tardoantica ed altomedievale in Val di Non (Trentino)." In *Dalla tarda latinità agli albori dell'Umanesimo: Alla radice della storia europea*, ed. P. Gatti and L. de Finis, 307–344. Trent: Dipartimento di Scienze Filologiche e Storiche.

Baynes, N.H. 1949. "The Supernatural Defenders of Constantinople." *Analecta Bollandiana* 67: 165–177.

Beare, R. 1978. "The Meaning of the Oath by the Safety of the Roman Emperor." *American Journal of Philology* 99: 106–110.

Beccaria, B. 2011. "La 'questione di san Gaudenzio' nell'ultimo mezzo secolo: I problemi intorno alla figura del primovescovo e la loro soluzione." *Novarien* 40: 9–26.

Bede, *Martyrology. See* Quentin (ed) 1908; Lifshitz (ed) 2001.

Belting, H. 1962. "Studien zum beneventanischen Hof im 8. Jahrhundert." *Dumbarton Oaks Papers* 16: 141–193.

Berschin, W. 1986. *Biographie und Epochenstil im lateinischen Mittelalter.* Volume 2: *Merowingische Biographie Italien, Spanien und die Inseln im frühen Mittelalter.* Quellen und Untersuchungen zur lateinischen Philologie des Mittelalters 9. Stuttgart: A. Hiersemann.

Bertolini, O. 1960. "Le chiese longobarde dopo la conversione al cattolicesimo ed i loro rapporti con il papato." In *Le chiese nei regni dell'Europa occidentale*, 455–492. Centro italiano di studi sull'alto Medioevo: Settimane di studio 7. Spoleto: Presso la sede del Centro.

—. 1970. "Il 'Liber pontificalis.'" In *La storiografia altomedievale*, 387–455. Centro italiano di studi sull'alto Medioevo: Settimane di studio 17. Spoleto: Presso la sede del Centro.

Bettocchi, S. 1994. "Note su due tradizioni micaeliche altomedievali: Il Gargano e Mont Saint-Michel." *Vetera Christianorum* 31: 333–355.

Bianchetti, C. 1997. *Pescara.* Rome: Laterza.

Billanovich, M.P. 1986. "San Siro: Falsificazioni, mito, storia." *Italia medioevale e umanistica* 29: 1–54.

—. 1993. "Le tradizioni sull'apostolicità di San Siro." *Rendiconti del Istituto Lombardo, Accademia di scienze e lettere* 127: 139–159.

Bischoff, B. 1994. *Manuscripts and Libraries in the Age of Charlemagne.* Trans. and ed. M.M. Gorman. Cambridge: Cambridge University Press.

Bluhme. F. (ed) 1868. *Leges Langobardorum.* MGH Leges (in Folio) 4. Hannover: Hahn.

Boesch Gajano, S. 2000. "L'identità storica di Vigilio e il suo destino storiografico." In Codroico and Gobbi (eds) 2000: 19–30.

Boesch Gajano, S. and M.R. Berardi (eds) 1990–1992. *Civiltà medioevale negli Abruzzi.* Volume 1: *Storiografia e storia*; 2: *Testimonianze.* L'Aquila: Colacchi.

Bognetti, G.P. 1966–1970. *L'età longobarda.* 4 vols. Milan: Giuffre.

Bonnet, M. 1889. "Narratio de miraculo a Michaele Archangele Chonis patrato." *Analecta Bollandiana* 8: 289–307.

Bosco, M.L. et al. (eds) 1988. *Le pergamene degli archivi di Bergamo a. 740–1000.* Bergamo: Edizioni Bolis.

Bosco, T. 1995. *Eusebio di Vercelli nel suo tempo pagano e cristiano.* Turin: Editrice Elle Di Ci.

Bosworth, A.K. 2010. "'Learning from the Saints: Ninth-Century Hagiography and the Carolingian Renaissance."' *History Compass* 8.9: 1055–1066.

Bouet, P., G. Otranto, and A. Vauchez (eds) 2003. *Culte et pèlerinages à Saint Michel en Occident: Les trois monts dédiés à l'Archange.* Rome: École française de Rome.

Bove, F. 2000. "L'architecture de la cathédrale de Bénevént." In *La cathédrale de Bénevént*, ed. T.F. Kelly. Ghent: Ludion.

Bovini, G. 1970. *Edifici di culto d'età teodoriciana e giustinianea a Ravenna*. Bologna: R. Pàtron.

Brand, B. 2008. "John Hothby and the Cult of St Regulus at Lucca." *Early Music History, Studies in Medieval and Early Modern Music* 27: 1–46.

—. 2014. *Holy Treasure and Sacred Song: Relic Cults and Their Liturgies in Medieval Tuscany*. Oxford: Oxford University Press.

Brennecke, H.C. 1988. *Studien zur Geschichte der Homöer: Der Osten bis zum Ende der homöischen Reichskirche*. Tübingen: J.C.B Mohr.

Brigaglia, M. and S. Tola (eds) 2006. *Dizionario storico-geografico dei Comuni della Sardegna*: 1 (A–D). Sassari: Carlo Delfino.

Brogiolo, G.P. and S. Gelichi 1998. *La città nell'alto medioevo Italiano: Archeologia e storia*. Rome; Bari: Laterza.

Brown, P. 1981. *The Cult of the Saints: Its Rise and Function in Latin Christianity*. Chicago: Chicago University Press.

Brown, T.S. 1979. "The Church of Ravenna and the Imperial Administration in the Seventh Century." *English Historical Review* 94: 1–28.

—. 1984. *Gentlemen and Officers: Imperial Administration and Aristocratic Power in Byzantine Italy, A.D. 554–800*. Rome: British School at Rome.

—. 2009. "Lombard Religious Policy in the Late Sixth and Seventh Centuries: The Roman Dimension." In *The Langobards before the Frankish Conquest*, ed. G. Ausenda, P. Delogu, and C. Wickham, 289–308. Woodbridge: Boydell Press.

Brown, W. et al. (eds) 2013. *Documentary Culture and the Laity in the Early Middle Ages*. Cambridge: Cambridge University Press.

Brown Tkacz, C. 2002. "A Possible Source for the Casket's Program of Types: The Libera Petitions of the *Commendatio animae*." In *The Key to the Brescia Casket: Typology and the Early Christian Imagination*, ed. Brown Tkacz, 109–137. Notre Dame, IN: University of Notre Dame Press.

Brugnoli, P. (ed) 1986. *L'abazia e il chiostro di S. Zeno Maggiore in Verona: Un recente intervento di restauro*. Verona: Banca popolare.

—. (ed) 1987. *La Cattedrale di Verona nelle sue vicende edilizie dal secolo IV al secolo XVI*. Venice: Arsenale Editrice.

Brugnoli, P. and G. Maroso 1986. "L'abazia di San Zeno e il suo chiostro monumentale." In P. Brugnoli (ed) 1986: 11–81.

Brunelli, V. 1913. *Storia della città di Zara*. Vol. 1. Venice: Istituto Veneto di Arti Grafiche.

Brunori, E. 1993. "Sant'Agostino alla Fontenella." *Bollettino della Società Tarquiniese di Arte e Storia* 22: 211–237.

Bulhart, V. et al. (eds) 1957. *Eusebius Vercellensis, Filastrius Brixiensis, Hegemonius (Ps.), Isaac Iudaeus, Archidiaconus Romanus, Fortunatianus Aquileiensis, Chromatius Aquileiensis: Opera quae supersunt*. CCSL 9. Turnhout: Brepols.

Bullough, D.A. 1966. "Urban Change in Early Medieval Italy: The Example of Pavia." *Papers of the British School at Rome* 34: 82–130.

Burattini, V. 1990. *San Senzia di Blera: Studio critico.* Viterbo: Agnesotti.

Burchi, P. 1965. "Gaudenzio." *Bibliotheca Sanctorum* 6: 61–63.

Burleigh, J.H.S. (trans) 1953. *Augustine: Earlier Writings.* Library of Christian Classics. Vol. 6. Philadelphia: The Westminster Press.

Cagiano de Azevedo, M. 1979. "Le due 'Vite' del vescovo Lorenzo e il mosaico della città a Siponto." *Puglia paleocristiana* 3: 47–57.

Cairns, F. 1979. *Tibullus: A Hellenistic Poet at Rome.* Cambridge: Cambridge University Press.

Camici, M. 2010. *Monastero ed abbazia di San Mamiliano nell'isola di Montecristo.* Turin: Seneca Edizioni.

Campione, A. 1992. "Storia e santità nelle due *Vitae* di Lorenzo vescovo di Siponto." *Vetera Christianorum* 29: 169–213.

Cantarelli, L. 1964. *La diocesi italiciana da Diocleziano alla fine dell'Impero occidentale.* Studia Historica 8. Rome: Bretschneider

Cantino Wataghin, G. 1997. "Fonti archeologiche per la storia della chiesa vercellese." In Dal Covolo et al. (eds) 1997: 23–61.

Capellino, M. 1986. *Le suore eusebiane: La vita antica.* Vercelli: [publisher not identified].

Capra, R. 2010. "Le origini cristiane e la *basilica Apostolorum.*" In Capra (ed) 2010, 21–32.

— (ed) 2010. *La basilica di San Gaudenzio a Novara.* Novara: Interlinea.

Carletti, C. 1980. "Iscrizioni murali." In C. Carletti and G. Otranto (eds) 1980: 7–180.

Carletti, C. and G. Otranto (eds) 1980. *Il Santuario di S. Michele sul Gargano dal VI al IX secolo: Contributo alla storia della Langobardia meridionale.* Vetera Christianorum Scavi e Ricerche 2. Atti del convengo tenuto a Monte Sant'Angelo il 9–10 dicembre 1978. Bari: Edipuglia.

— (eds) 1994. *Culto e insediamenti micaelici nell'Italia meridionale fra tarda antichità e medioevo.* Scavi e Ricerche 7. Atti del convegno internazionale Monte Sant'Angelo 18–21 Nov. 1992. Bari: Edipuglia.

Casini, P. 2013. *Devozione popolare nell'Arcipelago Toscano nelle immagini dei tabernacoli e delle chiese.* Florence: LoGisma.

Cassani, L. 1954. "Dov'era la basilica-sepolcro di San Gaudenzio." *Bollettino Storico per la provincia di Novara* 45: 1–4.

Catallo, T. 1991. "Sulla datazione delle *Vitae* di Lorenzo vescovo di Siponto." *Studi Medievali* 32.1: 129–157.

Cattin, G. 1990–1992. *Musica e liturgia a San Marco.* 4 vols. Venice: Fondazione Levi.

Cavada, E. 1993. "La città di Trento tra l'età romana e il medioevo: Campione stratigrafico nell'area di Piazza Duomo." *Archeologia delle Alpi* 1: 75–110.

—. 1994. "Trento in età gota." In *I Goti*, ed. V. Bierbrauer et al., 224–231. Milan: Electa.

—. 1998. "Cimiteri e sepolture isolate nella città' di Trento (secoli V–VIII)." In *Sepol-*

ture tra IV e VIII secolo, ed. G.P. Brogiolo and G. Cantino Wataghin, 123–141. Documenti di archeologia 13. Mantua: Società Archeologica Padana.

—. 2002. "*Militaria tardoantichi* (fine IV–V secolo) dalla valle dell'Adige e dalle aree limitrofe: L'informazione archeologica." In *Miles Romanus dal Po al Danubio nel tardoantico*, ed. M. Buora, 139–162. Atti del convegno Internazionale. Pordenone-Concordia Saggitaria 17–19 Marzo 2000. Pordenone: Lucaprint.

Cavada, E. and I. Rogger (eds) 2001. *See under* Rogger.

Cavallo, G. 1992. "La cultura scritta a Ravenna tra antichità tarda ed alto Medioevo." In *Storia di Ravenna*. Volume 2.2: *Dall'età bizantina all'età ottoniana: Ecclesiologia, cultura et arte*, ed. A. Carile et al., 109–110. Venice: Marsilio.

Cervato, D. 2004. "La chiesa di Verona dalle origini al Mille." In P. Golinelli and C.G. Brenzoni (eds) 2004: 69–81.

Cesa, M. (ed) 1988. *Ennodio: Vita del beatissimo Epifanio vescovo della chiesa pavese*. Biblioteca di Athenaeum 6. Como: Edizioni New Press.

Cesarini-Sforza, L. 1905. "Gli atti di San Vigilio." In *Scritti di storia e d'arte: Per il XV centenario della morte di S. Vigilio vescovo e martire*, 5–29. Trent: Comitato diocesano.

Chadwick, H. 1966. "Les 318 pères de Nicée." *Revue d'Histoire Ecclésiastique* 61: 808–811.

Chazelle, C. and C. Cubitt (eds) 2007. *The Crisis of the Oikoumene: The Three Chapters and the Failed Quest for Unity in the Sixth-Century Mediterranean*. Turnhout: Brepols.

Christie, N. 1991. "Invasion or Invitation? The Longobard Occupation of Northern Italy, A.D. 568–569." *Romanobarbarica* 11: 79–108.

—. 2006. *From Constantine to Charlemagne: An Archaeology of Italy, AD 300–800*. Aldershot, Hants: Ashgate.

Ciaralli, A., V. De Donato, and V. Matera (eds) 2002. *Le più antiche carte del capitolo della cattedrale di Benevento: 668–1200*. Fonti per la storia dell'Italia medievale. Regesta chartarum 52. Rome: Istituto storico italiano per il Medio Evo.

Cicco, G.G. 2006. "La scuola cattedrale di Benevento e il vescovo Urso (secolo IX)." *Rivista di storia della Chiesa in Italia* 60: 341–373.

Clementi, A. 2003. *Amniternum dopo la distruzione*. L'Aquila: Libreria Colacchi.

Codroico, R. and D. Gobbi (eds) 2000. *Vigilio vescovo di Trento: Tra storia romana e tradizione europea*. Atti del convegno, Trento 12–13 ottobre 2000. Trent: Civis.

Collavini, S.M. 2007. "Da società rurale periferica a parte dello spazio politico lucchese: S. Regolo in Gualdo tra VIII e IX secolo." In *Un filo rosso: Studi antichi e nuove ricerche sulle orme di Gabriella Rossetti in occasione dei suoi settanta anni*, ed. G. Garzella and E. Salvatori, 231–247. Pisa: GISEM Edizioni ETS.

Colombo, G. 1974. "Le date e le denominazioni delle feste di San Gaudenzio." *Novarien* 6: 3–52.

Colombo, G., T. Temporelli, and M. Perotti (eds) 1983. *San Gaudenzio*. Novara: Tip. San Gaudenzio.

Conte, P. 1978. "Osservazioni sulla leggenda di san Cerbonio vescovo di Populonia." *Aevum* 52: 235–260.

Conti, P.M. 1982. *Il ducato di Spoleto e la storia istituzionale dei Longobardi*. Spoleto: Edizioni dell'Accademia spoletina.

Cook, G.M. (trans) 1942. *The Life of Saint Epiphanius by Ennodius: A Translation with an Introduction and Commentary*. Washington, DC: Catholic University of America.

Coon, L. 1997. *Sacred Fictions: Holy Women and Hagiography in Late Antiquity*. Philadelphia: University of Pennsylvania Press.

Corrain, C. and M. Capitanio 1979. "Resti scheletrici Paleocristiani e medievali nell' antica basilica di S.Vigilio in Trento." *Studi Trentini di Scienze Storiche* 58: 97–154.

Corsi, P. 1975. "La spedizione in Italia di Costante II: Fonti e problem." *Nicolaus: Rivista di teologia ecumenico-patristica* 3.2: 343–392.

Costa, A. 1975. *San Vigilio, vescovo e patrono di Trento*. Trent: Edizioni Diocesane.

Courcelle, P. 1973. *Recherches sur Saint Ambroise: "vies" anciennes, culture, iconographie*. Paris: Études Augustiniennes.

Cracco Ruggini, L. 1997. "Vercelli e Milano: Nessi politici e rapporti ecclesiali nel IV–V secolo." In Dal Covolo et al. (eds) 1997: 91–120.

Crook, J. 2002. "The Enshrinement of Local Saints in Merovingian and Carolingian Francia." In Thacker and Sharpe (eds) 2002: 45–62.

Crovella, E. 1961. *S. Eusebio di Vercelli: Saggio di biografia critica*. Vercelli: Soc. Ed. Tip. Eusebiana.

Curta, F. 2001. *The Making of the Slavs: History and Archaeology of the Lower Danube Region, ca. 500–700*. Cambridge: Cambridge University Press.

Curti, C. 1981. "La vita di San Senzio di Blera." *Atti del Convegno Il Paleocristiano nella Tuscia: Viterbo, Palazzo dei Papi, 16–17 Giugno 1979*, 23–42. Biblioteca di studi viterbesi 5. Viterbo: Consorzio per la gestione delle biblioteche.

Cusack, C.M. 2011. *The Sacred Tree: Ancient and Medieval Manifestations*. Newcastle upon Tyne: Cambridge Scholars Publishing.

Cuscito, G. 1992. "La tradizione marciana aquileiese come problema storiografico." In *Martiri cristiani ad Aquileia e in Istria*, ed. G. Cuscito, 17–49. Udine: Del Bianco.

Dal Covolo, E., R. Uglione and G. Vian (eds) 1997. *Eusebio di Vercelli e il suo tempo*. Biblioteca di Scienze Religiose 133. Rome: LAS.

D'Angelo, E. 2006. "Agiografia latina del Mezzogiorno continentale d'Italia (750–1000)." *Hagiographies* 4: 41–134.

Dattrino, L. 1976. *Il 'De Trinitate' pseudoatanasiano*. Studia ephemeridis "Augustinianum" 12. Rome: Institutum patristicum Augustinianum.

Davis (trans) 1992. *The Lives of the Eighth-Century Popes (Liber Pontificalis)*. Liverpool: Liverpool University Press.

— (trans) 1995. *The Lives of the Ninth-Centiry Popes (Liber Pontificalis)*. Liverpool: Liverpool University Press.

— (trans) 2000. *The Book of Pontiffs (Liber pontificalis): The Ancient Biographies of the First Ninety Roman Bishops to AD715*. 2nd ed. Liverpool: Liverpool University Press.

Davis, S.J. 2001. *The Cult of Saint Thecla: A Tradition of Women's Piety in Late Antiquity*. Oxford: Oxford University Press.

De Blois, L. 1976. *The Policy of the Emperor Gallienus*. Leiden: Brill.

Degl'Innocenti, A. 1999. "I leggendari agiografici latini." In *I santi patroni: Modelli di santità, culti e patronati in Occidente*, ed. C. Leonardi and A. Degl'Innocenti, 73–80. Rome: Ministero per i beni e le attività culturali.

—. 2012. "I leggendari agiografici latini." In *Forme e modelli della santità in Occidente dal tardo antico al Medioevo*, ed. M. Bassetti, A. Degl'Innocenti, and E. Menestò, 137–158. Spoleto: Fondazione Centro italiano di studi sull'alto Medioevo.

Deichmann, F.W. 1969–1989. *Ravenna: Hauptstadt des spätantiken Abendlandes*. 3 vols. Wiesbaden: F. Steiner.

Dekkers, E. 1997. "De la disparition des lettres épiscopales de l'Eglise ancienne." In Grégoire (ed) 1997: 83–90.

Deliyannis, D.M. 2001. "Bury Me in Ravenna? Appropriating Galla Placidia's Body in the Middle Ages." *Studi Medievali* 42: 289–299.

— (trans) 2004. *Agnellus of Ravenna: The Book of Pontiffs and the Church of Ravenna*. Washington, DC: Catholic University of America Press.

— (ed) 2006. *Liber pontificalis ecclesiae Ravennatis*. Corpus Christianorum, Continuatio Mediaevalis 199. Turnhout: Brepols.

—. 2010. *Ravenna in Late Antiquity*. Cambridge: Cambridge University Press.

Del Lungo, S. 1994. "Santa Maria del Mignone." *Archivio della Società romana di storia patria* 117: 5–95.

Delooz, P. 1969. *Sociologie et canonisations*. Liège: Faculté de Droit de l'Université de Liège.

Dennis, G.T. (trans) 2001. *Maurice's Strategikon: Handbook of Byzantine Military Strategy*. Philadelphia, PA: University of Pennsylvania Press.

De Prisco, A. 2000. "Il pubblico dei santi nei "Miraculorum libri octo" di Gregorio di Tours." In Golinelli (ed) 2000: 23–51.

De Rossi, G. 1887. "Memorie e monumenti antichi cristiani di Bieda nella Tuscia." *Bullettino di archeologia cristiana* 4: 90–103.

De Vogüé, A. (ed) 1978. *Dialogues Grégoire le Grand: Texte critique et notes par Adalbert de Vogüé; traduction par Paul Antin*. Sources chrétiennes 251, 260, 265. Paris: Éditions du Cerf.

Diehl, C. 1888. *Études sur l'administration byzantine dans l'exarchat de Ravenne (568–751)*. Paris: Ernest Thorin.

Di Muro, A. 2009. *Economia e mercato nel Mezzogiorno longobardo (secc. VIII–IX)*. Società salernitana di storia patria, Nuovi quaderni salernitani 1. Salerno: Laveglia & Carlone.

Dolbeau, F. 2008. "'Naissance des homéliaires et des passionnaires: Une tentative d'étude comparative." In *L'antiquité tardive dans les collections médiévales: Textes et représentations, VIe–XIVe siècle*, ed. S. Gioanni and B. Grévin, 13–35. Collection de l'École française de Rome 405. Rome: École française de Rome.

Draghi, A. 1998. "Gli affreschi della ex Chiesa di San Nicola." *La Torretta* 5: 58–60.

Dronke, P. 1984. *Women Writers of the Middle Ages: A Critical Study of Texts from Perpetua to Marguerite Porete*. Cambridge: Cambridge University Press.

Dubois, J. (ed) 1965. *Le Martyrologe d'Usuard*. Subsidia Hagiographica 40. Brussels: Société des Bollandistes.

Duchesne, L. (ed) 1981. *Le "Liber Pontificalis."* 3 vols. Paris: E. de Boccard.

Dunbabin, K.M.D. 1990. "*Ipsa deae vestigia*... Footprints Divine and Human on Graeco-Roman Monuments." *Journal of Roman Arachaeology* 3: 85–109.

Dupré Theseider, E. 1964. "La 'grande rapina dei corpi santi' dall'Italia al tempo di Ottone I." In *Festschrift Percy Ernst Schramm*, ed. P. Classen et al., 1: 420–432. Weisbaden: F. Steiner.

Duval, N. 1999. "Le culte des martyrs de Salone à la lumiere des recherches récentes à Manastirine." *Comptes rendus de l'Academie des Inscriptions et Belles-Lettres* 134: 432–453.

Dvornik, F. 1958. *The Idea of Apostolicity in Byzantium and the Legend of the Apostle Andrew*. Cambridge, MA: Harvard University Press.

Dzino, D. 2010. *Becoming Slav, Becoming Croat: Identity Transformations in Post-Roman and Early Medieval Dalmatia*. Leiden: Brill.

Elm, E. 2003. *Die Macht der Weisheit: Das Bild des Bischofs in der Vita Augustini des Possidius und anderen spätantiken und frühmittelalterlichen Bischofsviten*. Leiden: Brill.

Ennodius of Pavia. *Life of Saint Epiphanius*. *See* Cesa (ed) 1988; Cook (trans) 1942.

Eusebius of Vercelli. *See* Bulhart (ed) 1957.

Everett, N. 2000. "The *Hagiography* of Lombard Italy." *Hagiographica* 7: 49–126.

—. 2001. "Liutprandic Letters amongst the Lombards." In *Roman, Runes and Ogham: Medieval Inscriptions in the Insular World and on the Continent*, ed. K. Forsyth, J. Higgitt, and D.N. Parsons, 175–189. Donington, Linc: Shaun Tyas.

—. 2002a. "The Earliest Recension of the Life of S. Sirus of Pavia (Vat. lat. 5771)." *Studi Medievali* 43: 857–957.

—. 2002b. "The *Liber de Apparitione S. Michaelis in Monte Gargano* and the Hagiography of Dispossession." *Analecta Bollandiana* 120: 364–391.

—. 2003a. *Literacy in Lombard Italy, c. 568–774*. Cambridge: Cambridge University Press.

—. 2003b. "Paulinus, the Carolingians and *famosissima* Aquileia." In *Paulino d'Aquileia e il contributo italiano all'Europa carolingia*, ed. P. Chiesa, 115–154. Udine: Forum.

—. 2006. "Narrating the *Life* of Eusebius of Vercelli." In *Narrative and History in the Early Medieval West*, ed. R. Balzaretti and E.M. Tyler, 133–165. Turnhout: Brepols.

—. 2009. "Literacy from Late Antiquity to the Early Middle Ages, c. 300–800 AD." In *The Cambridge Handbook of Literacy*, ed. D.R. Olson and N. Torrance, 362–385. Cambridge: Cambridge University Press.

—. 2011. "Paulinus of Aquileia's Sponsio episcoporum, Written Oaths and Ecclesiastical Discipline in Carolingian Italy." In *Textual Cultures of Medieval Italy*, ed. W. Robbins, 167–216. Toronto: University of Toronto Press.

—. 2015a. "The Passion of Cetheus of Pescara and the Lombard Invasions of Italy: With a Diplomatic Edition of the Passio Cethei based on Venice, Biblioteca Marciana, lat. Z 356." *Hagiographica* 22: 79–132.

—. 2015b. "The Cult of Saint Peregrinus in Early Medieval Zadar/Kult svetog Peregrina u ranosrednjovjekovnom Zadru." *Journal of Dalmation Archaeology and History* 108: 1–22.

—. 2015c. "The Life of Senzius of Blera and Episcopal Appropriation in Early Medieval Tuscany." *Rivista di Storia della Chiesa in Italia* n.2: 315–334.

Fabbri, M. 1999. "La basilica paleocristiana." In Mazzei (ed) 1999: 179–187.

Fainelli, V. 1958. "L'abbazia di San Zeno nell'alto medioevo." In *Miscellanea in onore di Roberto Cessi*. Rome: Edizioni de Storia e letteratura 1: 51–62.

Fanning, S.C. 1981. "Lombard Arianism Reconsidered." *Speculum* 56.2: 241–258.

Feder, A. (ed) 1916. Hilarius Pictaviensis, Tractatus mysteriorum, Fragmenta, Ad Constantium Imperatorem, Hymni; Pseudo-Hilarius, Epistula ad Abram filiam, Hymni. CSEL 65. Vienna: Akademische Verlagsgesellschaft.

Federici, V. (ed). 1925. *Chronicon Vulturnense*. Rome: Tip. del Senato.

Ferguson, T.C. 2005. *The Past is Prologue: The Revolution of Nicene Historiography*. Leiden: Brill.

Ferracci, E. 2001a. "Seconda e terza campagna di scavo a Petrolone." *La Torretta* 16.1.

—. 2001b. "Blera, prime indagini sull'abitato altomedievale." In *Dalla Tuscia romana al territorio valvense: Problemi di topografia medievale alla luce delle recenti ricerche archeologiche*, ed. L.P. Ermini, 29–56. Miscellanea della Società Romana di Storia Patria 43. Rome: Società Romana de Storia Patria.

Ferracci, E. and M.L. Agneni 1998. "Blera (VT) – loc. Petrolone: I campagna di scavo." *Archeologia Medievale* 25: 157.

—. 2000. "Blera (VT) – loc. Petrolone: II e III campagna di scavo." *Archeologia Medievale* 27: 268–269.

Ferrari, M.C. 1996. "Eusebio di Vercelli e il suo tempo." *Bollettino storico Vercellese* 46: 113–125.

Fine, J.V.A. 1991. *The Early Medieval Balkans: A Critical Survey from the Sixth to the Late Twelfth Century*. Ann Arbor: University of Michigan Press.

—. 2000. "Croats and Slavs: Theories about the Historical Circumstances of the Croats' Appearance in the Balkans." *Byzantinische Forschungen* 26: 205–218.

Fiocchi Nicolai, V. 1988. *I cimiteri paleocristiani del Lazio*. Volume 1: *Etruria meridionale*. Vatican City: Pontificio Istituto di Archeologia Cristiana.

Fioretti, P. 2010. "L'eredità di un maestro: Genesi ed edizione della grammatica di Orso beneventano." In *Libri de scuola e pratiche didattiche: Dall'antichità al Rinascimento*, ed. L. Del Corso and O. Pecere, 285–319. Cassino: Ed. Università di Cassino.

Fiorio Tedone, C. 1987. "La basilica di S. Zeno." In Brugnoli (ed) 1987: 82–123.

Fischetti, F.P. 1973. *Mercurio, Mithra, Michael: Magia, mito e misteri nella Grotta dell'Arcangelo*. Prima pubblicazione di iscrizioni e affreschi paleocristiani e longobardi. Monte Sant'Angelo: Tip. La garganica.

Foerster, H.P. (ed). 1958. *Liber diurnus Romanorum pontificum*. Bern: Francke Verlag.

Fontaine, J. (ed) 1967–1969. *Sulpice Sévère, Vie de Saint Martin*. 3 vols. Sources chrétiennes 133–135. Paris: Éditions du Cerf.

Forlin Patrucco, M. 1986. "Agiografia nel Trentino altomedievale: La *Passio sancti Vigilii episcopi et martyris*." In *Congresso La regione Trentino-Alto Adige nel Medio Evo* 1: 155–165. Atti del Accademia Roveretana degli Agiati, ser. 6.25. Rovereto: Accademia Roveretana degli Agiati.

—. 1997. "Echi di un antico dibattito: Le lettere di Vigilio e il problema del martirio 'recente." In Grégoire (ed) 1997: 91–102.

Fouracre, P. 1990. "Merovingian History and Merovingian Hagiography." *Past and Present* 127: 3–38.

—. 1999. "The Origins of the Carolingian Attempt to Regulate the Cult of Saints." In *The Cult of Saints in Late Antiquity and the Middle Ages: Essays on the Contribution of Peter Brown*, ed. P.A. Hayward and J. Howard-Johnston, 143–165. Oxford: Oxford University Press.

Fouracre, P. and R.A. Gerberding 1996. *Late Merovingian France: History and Hagiography, 640–720*. Manchester: Manchester University Press.

Frattaroli, P. 2004. "Il velo di Classe." In P. Golinelli and C.G. Brenzoni (eds) 2004: 45–55.

Freeman, C. 2011. *Holy Bones, Holy Dust: How Relics Shaped the History of Medieval Europe*. New Haven: Yale University Press.

Gardiner, K. 1983. "Paul the Deacon and Secundus of Trent." In *History and Historians in Late Antiquity*, ed. B. Croke and A.M. Emmett, 147–154. Sydney; Oxford: Pergamon Press.

Garrison, E.B. 1953–1962. *Studies in the History of Medieval Italian Painting*. 4 vols. Florence: L'Impronta.

Gasparri, S. 1978. *I duchi longobardi*. Studi Storici dell'Istituto storico italiano per il Medio Evo 109. Rome: Istituto storico italiano per il Medio Evo.

—. 1983. *La cultura tradizionale dei longobardi: Struttura tribale e resistenze pagane*. Spoleto: Centro italiano di studi sull'alto Medioevo.

Gasquet, F.A. 1914. *Codex Vercellensis*. Collectanea Biblica Latina 3. Rome; Ratisbon; New York: F. Pustet.

Gassó P.M. and C.M. Batlle (eds) 1956. *Pelagii I Epistulae quae supersunt*. Scripta et documenta 8. Montserrat: Abbatia Montisserrati.

Gavinelli, S. 2001. "Per una edizione della *Vita Sancti Gaudentii*: I codici carolingi." *Hagiographica* 8: 35–86.

—. 2007. "Testi agiografici e collezioni canoniche in età carolingia attraverso codici dell'Ambrosiana." In *Nuove ricerche su codici in scrittura latina dell'Ambrosiana*, ed. M. Ferrari and M. Navoni, 53–78. Atti del convegno, Milano, 6–7 ottobre 2005. Milan: Vita e Pensiero.

—. 2010. "La vita di san Gaudenzio nella più antica trasmissione carolingia." In Capra (ed) 2010: 41–45.

—. (ed) 2013. *La Vita sancti Gaudentii nella più antica trasmissione manoscritta del secolo IX*. Italian trans. G. Benedetto. Analecta Gaudentiana 1. Milan: Fabbrica Lapidea della Basilica di San Gaudenzio.

Geary, P.J. 1979. "The Ninth-Century Relic Trade: A Response to Popular Piety?" In *Religion and the People, 800–1700*, ed. J. Obelkevich, 8–19. Chapel Hill, NC: University of North Carolina Press.

—. 1994. *Phantoms of Remembrance: Memory and Oblivion at the End of the First Millenium*. Princeton: Princeton University Press.

Gianni, A. (ed) 2000. *Santità ed eremitismo nella Toscana medievale*. Atti delle giornate di studio, 11–12 giugno 1999. Siena: Cantagalli.

Gioanni, S. 2010. "Hagiographie d'Italie (300–550): 2: Les Vies de saints latines composées en Italie de la Paix constantinienne au milieu du Vie siècle." *Hagiographies* 5: 371–445.

Giuliani, R. 1999. "I mosaici del complesso archeologico di Santa Maria di Siponto." In Mazzei (ed) 1999: 197–223.

Glück, A. (ed). 1936. *Gaudentii episcope Brixiensis tractatus*. Corpus Scriptorum Ecclesiasticorum Latinorum 68. Vienna: Akademische Verlagsgesellschaft.

Godding, R. 1994. "Italia hagiographica: (I) Chronique d'hagiographie italienne." *Analecta Bollandiana* 112: 401–422.

—. 1996. "Italia hagiographica (II) Chronique d'hagiographie italienne." *Analecta Bollandiana* 114: 411–430.

—. 1998. "Italia hagiographica (III) Chronique d'hagiographie italienne." *Analecta Bollandiana* 116: 404–429.

Goffart, W.A. 1980. *Barbarians and Romans, A. D. 418–584: The Techniques of Accommodation*. Princeton: Princeton University Press.

—. 1988. *The Narrators of Barbarian History (A.D. 550–800): Jordanes, Gregory of Tours, Bede, and Paul the Deacon*. Princeton: Princeton University Press.

Golinelli, P. 1989. "Il Cristianesimo nella 'Venetia' altomedievale: Diffusione, instituzionalizzazione e forme di religiosità dalle origini al sec. X." In *Il Veneto nel medioevo: dalla "Venetia" alla Marca Veronese*, ed. A. Castagnetti, and G.M. Varanini, 1: 237–331. Verona: Banca popolare de Verona.

—. 1996. *Città e culto dei santi nel medioevo italiano*. 2nd rev. ed. Bologna: CLUEB.

—. 2000a. "I santi vescovi tra tardo antico e alto medioevo nell'Italia Annonaria." In Codroico and Gobbi (eds) 2000: 195–208.

—. 2000b. "Il pubblico di santi: Uno sconosciuto inconoscibile? Discorso di apertura." In Golinelli (ed) 2000: 7–22.

— (ed) 2000. *Il pubblico dei santi: Forme e livelli di ricezione dei messaggi agiografici*. Rome: Viella.

—. 2004. "Passione e Traslazione dei santi Fermo e Rustico." In P. Golinelli and C.G. Brenzoni (eds) 2004: 13–23.

Golinelli, P. and C.G. Brenzoni (eds) 2004. *I santi Fermo e Rustico: Un culto e una chiesa in Verona; per il XVII centenario del loro martirio (304–2004)*. Verona: Parrochia di San Fermo Maggiore.

Gonzato Debiasi, A. 2000. "Strutture ecclesiali nella X *regio* del secolo IV." In Codroico and Gobbi (eds) 2000: 183–194.

Granier, T. 1996 "Napolitains et Lombards aux VIIIe–XIe siècles: De la guerre des peuples à la 'guerre des saints' en Italie du Sud." *Mélanges de l'École française de Rome. Moyen Âge* 108.2: 403–450.

—. 2001. "L'hagiographie napolitaine du haut Moyen Âge: Contexte, corpus et enjeux." *Bulletin du CRISIMA* 2: 13–40.

—. 2006. "Conflitti, compromessi e trasferimenti di reliquie nel mezzogiorno latino del secolo IX." *Hagiographica* 13: 33–71.

—. 2007a. "San Gennaro e compagni nelle fonti dei secoli X–XII." In *San Gennaro nel XVII centenario del martirio (305–2005)*, ed. G. Luongo, 1: 251–274. Atti del Convegno internazionale (Napoli, 21–23 settembre 2005). Campania Sacra 37. Naples: Editoriale Comunicazioni Sociali.

—. 2007b. "La captivité de l'empereur Louis II à Bénévent (13 août–17 septembre 871) dans les sources des IXe–Xe siècle: L'écriture de l'histoire, de la fausse nouvelle au récit exemplaire." In *Faire l'événement au Moyen Âge*, ed. C. Carozzi and H. Taviani-Carozzi, 13–39. Aix-en-Provence: Publications de l'Université de Provence.

—. 2009. "La *renovatio* du modèle rhétorique antique dans les éloges urbains de l'Italie du haut Moyen Âge." In *Au Moyen Âge: entre tradition antique et innovation*, ed. M. Balard and M. Sot, 35–56. Actes du 131e Congrès national des Sociétés historiques et scientifiques, Grenoble, 2006. Paris: Éditions du CTHS.

—. 2012a. "*Si quilibet lector idoneus affuisset, incunctanter ad rei veritatem pertigissemus*: Identifier et authentifier les reliques (IXe–XIIe siècle)." In *Experts et expertise au Moyen Âge: Consilium quaeritur a perito*, 47–58. Paris: Publications de la Sorbonne.

—. 2012b. "Saints fondateurs, récits d'origine et légendes apostoliques dans l'Italie méridionale des VIIIe–XIIe siècles." In *Hagiographie, idéologie et politique au Moyen Âge en Occident*, ed. E. Bozóky, 165–183. Turnhout: Brepols.

Grégoire, R. 1983. "L'agiografia spoletina antica: Tra storia e tipologia." In *Il ducato di Spoleto* 1: 335–365. Atti del IX Congresso Internazionale di studi sull'alto medioevo (Spoleto, 27 settembre–2 ottobre 1982). Spoleto: Centro italiano di studi sull'alto medioevo.

—. 1987. *Manuale de agiologia: introduzione alla letteratura agiografica*. Fabriano: Monastero San Silvestro Abate.

— (ed) 1997. *L'Anaunia e i suoi martiri: XVI centenario dei martiri d'Anaunia 397–1997*. Bibliotheca Civis 10. Trent: Civis.

—. 1999. "Agiografia e storiografia nella *Vita antiqua* di Eusebio di Vercelli." In *La Sardegna paleocristiana tra Eusebio e Gregorio Magno*, ed. A. Mastino, G. Sotgiu, and N. Spaccapelo, 187–200. Atti del convegno nazionale di studi, Cagliari 10–12 Ott. 1996. Cagliari: Pontificia Facoltà teologica della Sardegna.

—. 2000. "Vigilio di Trento, agiografo dei martiri d'Anaunia." In Codroico and Gobbi (eds) 2000: 155–182.

Gregory I, Pope. *Dialogues*. *See* De Vogüé (ed) 1978.

—. *Letters/Registrum*. *See* Norberg (ed) 1937; Martyn (trans) 2004.

Grierson, P. and Blackburn, M.A.S. 1986. *Medieval European Coinage*. Volume 1: *The Early Middle Ages (5th–10th centuries)*. Cambridge: Cambridge University Press.

Gryson, R. 1982. *Le recueil arien de Vérone: Ms. LI de la Bibliothèque Capitulaire et feuillets inédits de la collection Giustiniani Recanati, Étude codicologique et paléographique*. Hague: Nijhoff.

Guaitoli, M.T. and Lopreite E. 2013. *La città e l'archeologia del sacro: Il recupero dell'area di Santa Maria Maggiore*. Trent: TEMI; Museo diocesano tridentino.

Hadrian I, Pope. *See* Hampe (ed) 1899.

Haldon, J.F. 1999. *Warfare, State, and Society in the Byzantine World, 565–1204*. London: UCL Press.

Halkin, F. (ed) 1957. *Bibliotheca Hagiographica Graeca*. 3rd ed. Brussels: Société des Bollandistes.

Hampe, K. (ed) 1899. "Epistolae selectae pontificum Romanorum Carolo Magno et Ludowico Pio regnantibus scriptae." MGH Epistolae Karolini Aevi 3: 1–84. Berlin: Weidmann.

Hanson, R.P.C. 1988. *The Search for the Christian Doctrine of God: The Arian Controversy 318–381*. Edinbugh: T&T Clark.

Hauptfeld, G. 1983. "Zur langobardischen Eroberung Italiens: Das Heer und die Bischöfe." *Mitteilungen des Instituts für Österreichische Geschichtsforschung* 91: 37–94.

Head, T. 1999. "Discontinuity and Discovery in the Cult of Saints: Apulia from Late Antiquity to the High Middle Ages." *Hagiographica* 6: 171–211.

— (ed) 2001. *Medieval Hagiography: An Anthology*. London: Routledge.

Head, T. and T.F.X. Noble (eds) 1994. *Soldiers of Christ: Saints' Lives from Late Antiquity and the Early Middle Ages*. University Park, PA: Pennsylvania State University Press.

Heene, K. 1989. "Merovingian and Carolingian Hagiography: Continuity or Change in Public and Aims?" *Analecta Bollandiana* 107: 415–428.

Herman, J. 1988. "La situation linguistique en Italie au VIe siècle." *Revue de linguistique romane* 52: 55–67.

Hesbert, R.-J. (ed) 1963–1979. *Corpus antiphonalium officii*. 6 vols. Rome: Herder.

Hilary of Poitiers. *See* Feder (ed) 1916.

Hlawitschka, E. 1972. "Die Diptychen von Novara und die Chronologie des Bischöfe dieser Stadt vom 9.–11. Jahrhundert." *Quellen und Forschungen aus Italienischen Archiven und Bibliotheken* 52: 767–780.

Hodgkin, T. 1892–1896. *Italy and Her Invaders.* 2nd ed. 8 vols. Oxford: Clarendon Press.

Holder-Egger, O. (ed) 1878. "Agnelli qui et Andreas *Liber pontificalis ecclesiae ravennatis.*" MGH Scriptores Rerum Langobardicarum, 265–391. Hannover: Hahn.

Hummer, H. 2013. "The Production and Preservation of Documents in Francia: The Evidence of Cartularies." In Brown et al. (eds) 2013: 189–230.

Hyde, J.K. 1993. "Medieval Descriptions of Cities." In *Literacy and Its Uses: Studies on Late Medieval Italy*, ed. J.K. Hyde and D.P. Waley, 1–32. Manchester: Manchester University Press.

Innes, M. 2013. "Archives, Documents and Landowners in Carolingian Francia." In Brown et al. (eds) 2013: 152–188.

Isidore of Seville, *Etymologiae. See* Lindsay (ed) 1911.

Jenal, G. 1995. *Italia ascetica atque monastica: Das Asketen- und Mönchtum in Italien von den Anfängen bis zur Zeit der Langobarden (ca. 150/250–604).* 2 vols. Monographien zur Geschichte des Mittelalters 39. Stuttgart: Hiersemann.

Johnson, M. 1988. "Towards a History of Theodoric's Building Program." *Dumbarton Oaks Papers* 42: 73–96.

Johnson, R.F. 2005. *Saint Michael the Archangel in Medieval English Legend.* Woodbridge, UK; Rochester, NY: Boydell and Brewer.

Jones, A.H.M. 1964. *The Later Roman Empire 284–602: A Social, Economic, and Administrative Survey.* 2 vols. Oxford: Basil Blackwell.

Kaegi, W.E. 2003. *Heraclius: Emperor of Byzantium.* Cambridge: Cambridge University Press.

Kelly, T.F. 1989. *The Benevantan Chant.* Cambridge: Cambridge University Press.

Kennell, S.A.H. 2000. *Magnus Felix Ennodius: A Gentleman of the Church.* Ann Arbor: University of Michigan Press.

Keresztes, P. 1975. "The Peace of Gallienus: 260–303 A.D." *Wiener Studien* 9: 174–185.

Klaić, N. and I. Petricioli 1976. *Zadar u srednjem vijeku do 1409.* Zadar: Sveučilište u Splitu, Filozofski fakultet.

Krautheimer, R. 1983. *Three Christian Capitals: Topography and Politics.* Berkeley: University of California Press.

Kreutz, B.M. 1996. *Before the Normans: Southern Italy in the Ninth and Tenth Centuries.* Philadelphia: University of Pennsylvania Press.

Kurelac, M. 1999. "Narrative sources [of early medieval Croatia]." In Supičić (ed) 1999: 117–146.

Labourt, J. (ed) 1949–1963. *Lettres: Saint Jérôme.* 8 vols. Paris: Les Belles Lettres.

Lampe, G.W.H. (ed) 1976. *A Patristic Greek Lexicon.* Oxford: Oxford University Press.

Lanéry, C. 2010. "Hagiographie d'Italie (300–550). Volume 1: Les Passions latines composées en Italie." In *Hagiographies*, ed. G. Philippart, 5: 15–369. Turnhout: Brepols.

Lanzoni, F. 1915. "Le fonti della leggenda di Sant'Apollinare di Ravenna." *Atti e memorie della deputazione di storia patria per le provincie di Romagna*, ser. 4, 5: 111–176.

—. 1927. *Le diocesi d'Italia dalle origini al principio del secolo VII (an. 604) studio critico*. 2 vols. 2nd ed. Studi e testi 35. Faenza: F. Lega.

Lapidge, M. 2006. *The Anglo-Saxon Library*. Oxford: Oxford University Press.

La Rocca, C. 1995. *Pacifico di Verona: Il passato carolingio nella costruzione della memoria urbana*. Rome: Istituto storico italiano per il Medio Evo.

—. 2009. "I silenzi dell'agiografia: La mancanza di sante in età longobarda." In *Giustina e le altre: Sante e culti femminili in Italia settentrionale dalla prima età cristiana al secolo XII*, ed. A. Tilatti and F.G.B. Trolese, 163–174. Rome: Viella.

La Rocca Hudson, C. 1986. "'Dark Ages' a Verona: Edilizia privata, aree aperte e strutture pubbliche in una città dell'Italia settentrionale." *Archeologia Medievale* 13: 31–78.

Lazzarini, V. 1904. *Scuola calligrafica veronese del secolo IX*. Venice: Reale Istituto veneto di scienze, lettere ed arti.

Leanza, A. 1985. "Una versione greca inedita *dell'Apparitio S. Michaelis in monte Gargano*." *Vetera Christianorum* 22: 291–316.

—. 1994. "Altre due versioni greche inedite." In Carletti and Otranto (eds) 1994, 85–93.

Leonardi, C., A. Degl'Innocenti, and F. Santi (eds) 2011. *Agiografie medievali*. Florence: SISMEL Edizioni del Galluzo.

Lifshitz, F. (trans) 2001. "Bede, *Martyrology*." In Head (ed) 2001: 169–198.

—. 2006. *The Name of the Saint: The Martyrology of Jerome and Access to the Sacred in Francia, 627–827*. Notre Dame: University of Notre Dame Press.

Lindsay, W.M. (ed) 1911. *Isidori Hispalensis episcopi Etymologiarvm sive Originvm libri XX*. Oxford: Oxford University Press.

Lizier, A. 1910. "Episcopato e comitato in Novara nell'alto medioevo." *Bollettino Storico per la Provinica di Novara* 4: 211–255.

Lizzi, R. 1990. "Ambrose's Contemporaries and the Christianization of Northern Italy." *Journal of Roman Studies* 80: 156–173.

Llewellyn, P.A.B. 1974. "The Roman Church in the Seventh Century: The Legacy of Gregory I." *Journal of Ecclesiastical History* 25: 363–380.

Lodi, E. 1967. "Le due omelie di San Petronio vescovo di Bologna." In *Miscellanea liturgica in onore di sua eminenza il Cardinale Giacomo Lercaro* 2: 263–301. Rome: Desclée.

Löfstedt, B. (ed) 1971. *Zenonis Veronensis tractatus*. CCSL 22. Turnhout: Brepols. Reprinted 2008 with updates and Italian translation by G. Banterle, G. Fedalto, and R. Ravazzolo (eds) Corpus scriptorum Ecclesiae Aquileiensis/Scrittori della chiesa di Aquileia 3. Rome: Città nuova; Gorizia: Società per la conservazione della Basilica di Aquileia.

Lo Iacono, S. 1995. *Bominaco: Spiritualità, cultura, fierezza di un'abbazia benedettina*. Bominaco: S. Lo Iacono.

Lombardi, E. 1953. *S. Cerbone nella leggenda, nel culto e nell'arte.* Parma: Edizioni "La Torre Massetana."

Lončar, M. 1999. "On the Description of the Churches of St. Anastasia and St. Donat in Zadar in *De Administrando Imperio* by Constantine Porphyrogenitus." *Hortus Artium Medievalium* 5: 235–243.

Lucchesi, G. 1962. "Apollinare di Ravenna." *Bibliotheca Sanctorum* 2: 239–246. Rome: Città Nuova.

—. 1969. "La missione petrina di S. Apollinare ovvero il conflitto delle metropoli." In *Atti dei Convegni di Cesena e Ravenna* 1: 371–389. Cesena: Centro Studi e Ricerche sulla antica provincia ecclesiastica Ravennate.

Lusuardi Siena, S. 1987. "Il primo impianto di culto (Chiesa A)." In Brugnoli (ed) 1987: 26–36.

Maccono, F. 1951. *Il Santuario di N. S. di Crea nel Monferrato.* 3rd ed. Casale Monferrato: Fratelli Tarditi.

Mackie, G. 1990. "New Light on the So-Called Saint Lawrence Panel at the Mausoleum of Galla Placidia, Ravenna." *Gesta* 29: 54–60.

Maggi, S. 1995. "Il Foro di Novara." In Mirabella Roberti (ed) 1995: 395–409.

Majocchi, P. 2008. *Pavia città regia: Storia e memoria di una capitale altomedievale.* Rome: Viella.

Manselli, R. 1972. "Gregorio Magno e due riti pagani dei Longobardi." In *Studi storici in onore di Ottorino Bertolini*, ed. O. Banti et al., 1: 435–440. Pisa: Pacini.

Marazzi, F. 1998. "The Destinies of the Late Antique Italies: Politico-economic Developments of the Sixth Century." In *The Sixth Century: Production, Distribution, and Demand*, ed. R. Hodges and W. Bowden, 119–159. Leiden: Brill.

Marcelli, M.T and F. Santoni 1996. "Case medievali di Blera: L'esempio di Via Roma." In *Case e torri medievali*, ed. E. De Minicis and F. Guidoni, 2: 143–151. Atti del III convegno di studi "La città' e le case: Tessuti urbani, domus e case-torri nell'Italia comunale (secc. XI–XV)," Città' della Pieve, 8–9 novembre 1996. Rome: Kappa.

Marchi, G.P. 1972. "Le antiche storie di San Zeno." In *Il culto di San Zeno nel Veronese*, ed. G.P. Marchi, A. Orlando, and R. Brenzoni, 11–61. Verona: Banca mutua popolare di Verona 1972.

Marin, E. 1989. "La topographie chrétienne de Salone: Les centres urbains de la pastorale." In *Actes du XIe congrès international d'archéologie chrétienne*, ed. E. Duval, 2: 1117–1131. Rome: Pontifico Istituto di archeologia cristiana.

Marini, G. (ed) 1805. *I Papiri Diplomatici.* Rome: Stamperia della sacra congregatione de propaganda fide.

Maritano, M. "Bibliografia eusebiana." In Dal Covolo et al. (eds) 1997: 415–471.

Markus, R.A. 1979. "Carthage – Prima Justiniana – Ravenna: An Aspect of Justinian's *Kirchenpolitik.*" *Byzantion* 49: 277–302.

—. 1981. "Ravenna and Rome, 554–604." *Byzantion* 51: 566–578.

—. 1997. *Gregory the Great and His World.* Cambridge: Cambridge University Press.

Marović, I. 1984. "Reflexions about the Year of the Destruction of Salona." *Vjesnik za Arheologiju i Historiju Dalmatinsku* 77: 293–314.

Martin, J.-M. 1974. "À propos de la *Vita de Barbatus*, Évêque de Bénévent." *Mélanges de l'École française de Rome: Moyen Âge – Temps Modernes* 86: 137–164.

—. 1993. *La Pouille du VIe au XIIe siécle*. Collection de l'École française de Rome 179. Rome: L'École française de Rome.

Martindale, J.R. 1992. *The Prosopography of the Later Roman Empire*. Volume 3: *A.D. 527–641*. Cambridge: Cambridge University Press.

Martínez Pizarro, J. 1995. *Writing Ravenna: The Liber Pontificalis of Andreas Agnellus*. Ann Arbor : University of Michigan Press.

Martini, C.M. 1997. "La lettera di Ambrogio a Vigilio: Un esempio di 'genus epistolare." In Grégoire (ed) 1997: 43–49.

Martyn, J.R.C. (trans) 2004. *The Letters of Gregory the Great: Translated with Introduction and Notes*. 3 vols. Toronto: Pontifical Institute of Mediaeval Studies.

Mastrangelo, M. 2010. *The Roman Self in Late Antiquity: Prudentius and the Poetics of the Soul*. Baltimore: John Hopkins University Press.

Matijević-Sokol, M. 1999. "Latin Inscriptions [of Early Medieval Croatia]." In Supičić (ed) 1999: 239–256.

Maximus of Turin. Sermons. *See* Mutzenbecher (ed) 1962.

Mazzei, M. (ed) 1999. *Siponto antica*. Foggia: C. Grenzi, 1999.

Mazzotti, M. 1952. "Per una nuova datazione della 'Passio S. Apollinaris." *Studi romagnoli* 3: 123–130.

—. 1986. "S. Apollinare in Classe: Indagini e studi degli ultimi trent'anni." *Rivista di Archeologia Cristiana* 62: 199–219.

McCulloh, J. (ed) 1979. *Martyrologium Rabani Mauri*. Corpus Christianorum, Continuatio Mediaevalis 44. Turnhout: Brepols.

McLynn, N.B. 1994. *Ambrose of Milan: Church and Court in a Christian Capital*. Berkeley: University of California Press.

McNamara, J.A., J.E. Halborg, and E. Gordon Whatley 1992. *Sainted Women of the Dark Ages*. Durham: Duke University Press.

Meaolo, G. 1996. *I Vescovi di Chieti e i loro tempi*. Vasto: Editrice il Nuovo Vasto.

Mellini, G.L. 1992. *I Maestri dei Bronzi di San Zeno*. Verona: Banca popolare di Verona.

Menestó, E. 1985. "Le lettere di S. Vigilio." In Quacquarelli and Rogger (eds) 1985, 151–170.

Milano, E. 1987. "Eusebio di Vercelli, vescovo metropolita: Leggenda o realtà' storica?" *Italia medioevale e umanistica* 30: 313–322.

Miller, M.C. 1993. *The Formation of a Medieval Church: Ecclesiastical Change in Verona, 950–1150*. Ithaca: Cornell University Press.

—. 2000. *The Bishop's Palace: Architecture and Authority in Medieval Italy*. Ithaca: Cornell University Press.

Mincione, G. 1967. "*Tractatus de Passione Domini facta in Civitate Aternensi* di Attone Vescovo di Chieti." *Abruzzo* 5: 99–122.

Mirabella Roberti, M. (ed) 1995. *Forum et basilica in Aquileia e nella Cisalpina Romana.* Antichità altoadriatiche 42. Udine: Arti Grafiche Friulane.

Mombritius, B. 1910. *Sanctuarium seu Vitae Sanctorum.* Rev. ed. Monachi Solesmenses. Paris: Fontemoing.

Mommsen, T., et al. (ed) 1853– . *Corpus Inscriptionum Latinarum.* Berlin: De Gruyter.

Montesano, M. 1991. "La 'Vita Barbati': Culti longobardi e magia a Benevento." *Studi Beneventani* 4–5: 39–56.

— (ed and trans) 1994. *Vita di Barbato.* Parma: Pratiche Editrice.

Monticolo, G. 1892. "L'inventio e la translatio dei SS. Ermagora e Fortunato." *Nuovo Archivio Veneto* 3: 117–156.

Moorhead, J. 1985. "*Papa* as 'Bishop of Rome." *Journal of Ecclesiastical History* 36: 337–350.

—. 1992. *Theoderic in Italy.* Oxford: Oxford University Press.

Mor, C.G. 1967. "Osservazioni sulla più antica lista episcopale di Novara (Dittico di San Gaudenzio)." Studia Gratiana 14. In *Collectanea Stephan Kuttner*, ed. G. Forchielli, 4: 1–12. Studia Gratiana 14. Bologna: Institutum Gratianum.

Moravcsik, G. (ed) and R.J.H. Jenkins (trans). 1967. *Constantine Porphyrogenitus: De Administrando Imperio.* Washington, DC: Dumbarton Oaks Center for Byzantine Studies.

Mores, F. 2011. *Invasioni d'Italia: La prima età longobarda nella storia e nella storiografia.* Pisa: Edizioni della Normale.

Moro, P. 2004. *I Longobardi e la guerra: Da Alboino alla battaglia sulla Livenza, secc. VI–VIII.* Roma: Viella.

Muehlberger, E. 2013. *Angels in Late Ancient Christianity.* Oxford: Oxford University Press.

Musurillo, H. 1972. *The Acts of the Christian Martyrs.* Oxford: Oxford University Press.

Mutzenbecher, A. (ed) 1962. *Maximi Episcopi Taurinensis: Collectionem sermonum antiquam nonnullis sermonibus extravagantibus adiectis.* CCSL 23. Turnhout: Brepols.

— (ed) 1970. *Sancti Avrelii Avgvstini de diversis quaestionibus ad Simplicianum.* CCSL 44. Turnhout: Brepols.

Nef, A. and V. Prigent 2006. "Per una nuova storia dell'altomedioevo siciliano." *Storica* 35–36: 9–63.

Neff (ed) 1908. *Die Gedichte des Paulus Diaconus: Kritische und erklärende Ausgabe.* Munich: C.H. Beck.

Nikolič, Z. 2003. *Rodaci i bližnji: Dalmatinsko gradsko plemstvo u ranom srednjem vijeku* (Relatives and Neighbours: Dalmatian Town Nobility in the Early Middle Ages). Zagreb: Matica hrvatska.

—. 2004. "The Formation of Dalmatian Urban Nobility: Examples of Split, Trogir, and Zadar." PhD Thesis: Central European University.

Noble, T.F.X. 1984. *The Republic of St. Peter: The Birth of the Papal State, 680–825*. Philadelphia: University of Pennsylvania Press.

Norberg, D. 1937. *In Registrum Gregorii Magni Studia critica*. Uppsala: Almqvist & Wiksell.

Obelić, B. and A. Sliepčević 2000. "Correction of Radiocarbon Age of Wooden Beams from St. Donat's Church in Zadar by Dendrochronological Method." *Vjesnik Arheološkog muzeja u Zagrebu*, 3rd ser., 32–33: 197–206.

Ó Cróinín, D. 1995. *Early Medieval Ireland, 400–1200*. London: Longman.

Oldfield, P. 2014. *Sanctity and Pilgrimage in Medieval Southern Italy, 1000–1200*. Cambridge: Cambridge University Press.

Oldoni, M. 1972. *Anonimo Salernitano del X secolo*. Naples: Guida.

Olivar, A. (ed) 1975–1982. *Sancti Petri Chrysologi Collectio sermonum a Felice episcopo parata sermonibus extravagantibus adjectis*. 3 vols. CCSL 24, 24A, 24B. Turnhout: Brepols.

Orchard, N. 1996. "The Medieval Masses in Honour of St Apollinaris of Ravenna." *Revue Bénédictine* 106: 172–184.

Orioli, G. 1986. "La Vita sancti Apolenaris di Ravenna e gli antecedenti storici dell'organizzazione ecclesiastica ravennate." *Apollinaris* 59: 251–267.

—. 2001. "La Passio Sancti Apolinaris secondo Il codice Petropolitano." *Ravenna: Studi e Ricerche* 8: 13–62.

Orlandi, A. 1990. "Altri edifici sacri intitolati a S. Zeno in Italia." *Annuario storico zenoniano* 7: 37–44.

—. 1991. "Il culto di S. Zeno fuori d'Italia e le chiese a lui intitolate." *Annuario storico zenoniano* 8: 33–40.

—. 2003. "Un rapido sguardo alle vicende dei testi liturgici per le celebrazioni di San Zeno." *Annuario storico zenoniano* 20: 21–26.

Orselli, A.M. 1976. "Il santo patrono cittadino: genesi e sviluppo del patrocinio del vescovo nei secoli VI e VII." In *Agiografia altomedioevale*, ed. S. Boesch Gajano, 85–104. Bologna: Il Mulino.

—. 1978. "La città altomedievale e il suo santo patrono: (ancora una volta) il 'campione' pavese." *Rivista di storia della chiesa in Italia* 32.1: 1–69.

—. 1989. "Santi e città: Santi e demoni urbani tra tardoantico e alto medioevo." In *Santi e demoni nell'alto Medioevo occidentale (secoli V–XI)*, 725–768. Settimane di studio del Centro italiano di studi sull'alto Medioevo 36. Spoleto: Centro italiano di studi sull'alto Medioevo.

Otranto, G. 1981. "Il *Liber de apparitione* e il culto di S. Michele sul Gargano nella documentazione liturgica altomedievale." *Vetera Christianorum* 18: 423–442.

—. 1983. "Il *Liber de apparitione*, il santuario di San Michele sul Gargano e i Longobardi del Ducato di Benevento." In *Santuari e politica nel mondo antico*, ed. M. Sordi, 210–245. Milan: Vita e Pensiero.

—. 1988. "Per una metodologia della ricerca storico-agiografica: Il santuario micaelico del Gargano tra Bizantini e Longobardi." *Vetera Christianorum* 25: 381–405.

Palmieri, S. 1996. "Duchi, principi e vescovi nella Longobardia meridionale." In Andenna and Picasso (eds) 1996: 43–100.

Paoli, E. 1997. *Agiografia e strategie politico-religiose: Alcuni esempi da Gregorio Magno al Concilio di Trento*. Spoleto: Centro italiano di studi sull'alto Medioevo.

—. 2002. "Tradizioni agiografiche dei Ducati di Spoleto e Benevento." In *I Longobardi dei ducati di Spoleto e Benevento* 1: 289–315. Atti del XVI Congresso internazionale di Studi sull'alto Medioevo: Spoleto, 20–23 ottobre 2002, Benevento 24–27 ottobre 2002. 2 vols. Spoleto: Centro italiano di studi sull'alto Medioevo.

Paredi, A. (ed) 1964. *Vita e meriti di S. Ambrogio: Testo inedito del secolo nono illustrato con le miniature del Salterio di Arnolfo*. Fontes Ambrosiani 37. Milan: Editrice Ceschina.

Patzold, S. 2008. *Episcopus: Wissen über Bischöfe im Frankreich des späten 8. bis frühen 10. Jahrhunderts*. Mittelalter-Forschungen 25. Ostfildern: Thorbecke.

Paul the Deacon. *History of the Lombards*. *See* Waitz and Bethmann (eds) 1878.

Paulinus of Milan. *Life of St. Ambrose*. *See* Pellegrino (ed) 1961.

Peers, G. 1996. "Apprehending the Archangel Michael: Hagiographic Methods." *Byzantine and Modern Greek Studies* 20: 100–121.

Pellegrini, M. 2009. *Vescovo e città: Una relazione nel Medioevo italiano (secoli II–XIV)*. Milan: B. Mondadori.

Pellegrino, M. (ed) 1961. *Paulinus Mediolanensis: Vita di Sant'Ambrogio*. Rome: Editrice Studium.

Peria, G. and S. Ferruzzi 2010. *L'isola d'Elba e il culto di San Mamiliano: Le chiese di Capoliveri e Campo*. Portoferraio: Centro grafico elbano.

Petricioli, I. 1995. "Sculpture in Zadar between the Late Roman and Pre-Romanesque Periods." *Hortus Artium Medievalium* 1: 74–83.

Petrucci, A. 1963. "Aspetti del culto e del pellegrinaggio di San Michele sul Monte Gargano." In *Pellegrinaggi e culto dei Santi in Europa fino alla prima crociata*, 166–180. Convegni del Centro di Studi sulla Spiritualità Medievale 4. Todi: Accademia tudertina.

Petrucci, E. 1984. "Pievi e parrocchie del Lazio nel basso Medioevo: Note e osservazioni." In *Pievi e parrocchie in Italia nel basso Medioevo (sec. XIII–XIV)* 2: 893–1017. Italia sacra: Studi e documenti di storia ecclesiastica 35–36. Rome: Herder.

Philippart, G. 1977. *Les Légendiers latins et autres manuscrits hagiographiques*. 2 vols. Typologie des sources du Moyen Âge 24–25. Turnhout: Brepols.

—. 1994. "Martirologi e leggendari." In *Lo spazio letterario del medioevo: 1 Il medioevo Latino*. Volume 2: *La circolazione del testo*, ed. G. Cavallo, C. Leonardi, and E. Menestò, 605–648. Rome: Salerno.

Picard, J.Ch. 1988. *Le souvenir des évêques: Sépultures, listes épiscopales et culte des évêques en Italie du Nord des origines au Xe siècle*. Bibliothèque des Écoles françaises d'Athènes et de Rome, fasc. 268. Rome: École française de Rome.

Picard, J.-M. 1982. "The Purpose of Adomnán's *Vita Columbae*." *Peritia* 1: 160–177.

Piemontese, G. 2000. *I Longobardi: Arte e religiosità lungo le vie del pellegrinaggio micaelico*. Foggia: Bastogi.

Pighi, G.B. 1960. "La vita ritmica di san Zeno." *Memorie dell'Accademia di Bologna,* 5th ser. 8: 25–53.

—. 1974. "La letteratura zenoniana dell'VIII e del IX secolo." In *Studi zenoniani in occasione del XVI centenario della morte di S. Zeno,* 13–32. Verona: [publisher not identified].

Pilsworth, C. 2000. "Sanctity, Crime and Punishment in the 'Vita Walfredi.'" *Hagiographica* 7: 181–199.

Pizzolato, L.F. 2000. "Vigilio di Trento e l'elaborazione delle fonti." In Codroico and Gobbi (eds) 2000: 49–76.

Pohl, W. 1997. "The Empire and the Lombards: Treaties and Negotiations in the Sixth Century." In *Kingdoms of the Empire: the Integration of Barbarians in Late Antiquity*, ed. W. Pohl, 75–133. Brill: Leiden and Cologne.

Polonio, V. 1962. *Il monastero di san Colombano di Bobbio dalla fondazione all'epoca carolingia.* Genova: [publisher not identified].

Pomaro, G. 2015. *I manoscritti medievali della Biblioteca capitolare feliniana di Lucca.* Florence: SISMEL, Edizioni del Galluzzo.

Poncelet, A. 1886–1889. *Catalogus codicum hagiographicorum bibliothecae regiae bruxellensis: Pars I Codices latini membranei.* Subsidia Hagiographica 1. Brussels: Societé des Bollandistes.

—. 1889–1893. *Catalogus codicum hagiographicorum latinorum antiquiorum … in Bibliotheca nationali parisiensi.* 4 vols. Subsidia Hagiographica 2. Brussels: Societé des Bollandistes.

—. 1906. "San Michele al monte Tancia." *Archivio della R. Società romana di storia patria* 29: 541–548.

—. 1909. *Catalogus codicum hagiographicorum latinorum bibliothecarum Romanorum praeter quam Vaticanae.* Subsidia Hagiographica 9 (Reprinted 1979). Brussels: Societé des Bollandistes.

—. 1910. *Catalogus codicum hagiographicorum latinorum bibliothecae Vaticanae.* Subsidia Hagiographica 11. (Reprinted 1961). Brussels: Societé des Bollandistes.

Possenti, E. 2002. "La tipologia delle sepolture tardoantiche-altomedievali; I corredi delle sepolture tardoantiche-altomedievali." In *Testimonianze archeologiche a S. Stefano di Garlate*, ed. G.P. Brogiolo, G. Bellosi, and L. Vigo Doratiotto, 195–213. Garlate: Parrocchia di S. Stefano.

Pratesi, A. 1964. "Barbato, santo." In *Dizionario biografico degli italiani*, 6: 128–130. Rome: Istituto dell'Enciclopedia Italiana.

Prelini, C. 1880. *San Siro, primo vescovo e patrono della città e diocesi di Pavia: Studio storico-critico.* Pavia: Fusi.

Price, R. (ed and trans) 2009. *The Acts of the Council of Constantinople of 553, with Related Texts on the Three Chapters Controversy.* Liverpool: Liverpool University Press.

Primerano, D. (ed) 2000. *L'immagine di San Vigilio, tra storia e leggenda.* Trent: Edizioni Museo Diocesano Tridentino.

Quacquarelli, A. 1975. *Il leone e il drago nella simbolica dell'età patristica*. Quaderni di Vetera Christianorum 11. Bari: Istituto di letteratura cristiana antica, Università di Bari.

—. 1980. "Gli apocrifi nei riflessi di un graffito del Calvario e il *Liber de apparitione*." In Carletti and Otranto (eds) 1980: 207–254.

Quacquarelli, A. and I. Rogger (eds) 1985. *I Martiri della Val di Non e la reazione pagana all fine del IV secolo*. Bologna: Istituto di Scienze Religiose in Trento.

Quentin, H. (ed) 1908. *Les Martyrologes historiques de Moyen Age: Étude sur la formation du Martyrologe Romain*. Paris: J. Gabalda.

Quieti, G. 2010. *Pescara antica città*. Bari: Carsa.

Quilici Gigli, S. 1976. *Blera: Topografia antica della città e del territorio*. Mainz am Rheim: Von Zabern.

Rački, F. 1877. *Documenta historiae Chroaticae periodum antiquam illustrantia*. Monumenta Spectantia Historiam Sclavorum Meridionalium 7. Zagreb: Academia Scientiarum et Artium.

Rapp, C. 2005. *Holy Bishops in Late Antiquity: The Nature of Christian Leadership in an Age of Transition*. Berkeley: University of California Press.

Raspi Serra, J. 1987. *Economia e territorio: Il patrimonium Beati Petri nella Tuscia*. Naples: Nella sede dell'Istituto.

Raurell, F. 2000. "Metodo esegetico-ermeneutico di Vigilio nella lettera a Simpliciano." In Codroico and Gobbi (eds) 2000: 125–154.

Reynolds, R.E. 1995. "The Organisation, Law and Liturgy of the Western Church, 700–900." In *The New Cambridge Medieval History*, ed. R. McKitterick, 2: 587–621. Cambridge: Cambridge University Press.

Riché, P. 1976. *Education and Culture in the Barbarian West: Sixth through Eighth Centuries*. Trans. J. Contreni. Columbia: University of South Carolina Press.

—. 1979. *Écoles et enseignement dans le haut Moyen Âge: Fin du Ve siècle – milieu du XIe siècle*. Paris: Aubier Montaigne.

Roberts, M.J. 2001. "The Last Epic of Antiquity: Generic Continuity and Innovation in the Vita Sancti Martini of Venantius Fortunatus." *Transactions of the American Philological Association* 131: 257–285.

—. 2009. *The Humblest Sparrow: The Poetry of Venantius Fortunatus*. Ann Arbor: University of Michigan.

Rogger, I. 1966. *I Martiri Anauniesi nella cattedrale di Trento*. Trent: Museo diocesano tridentino.

—. 1974a. "Un sarcofago longobardo nel sottosuolo del Duomo di Trento." *Studi Trentini di Scienze Storiche* 53.1: 102–107.

—. 1974b. "Scavi e ricerche sotto la cattedrale di Trento." *Studi Trentini di Scienze Storiche*, 53.4: 387–409.

—. 1992. "Il Vescovo di Trento e la sua Chiesa." In *Il Duomo di Trento*, ed. E. Castelnuovo and A. Peroni, 21–33. Trent: Terni.

Rogger, I. and E. Cavada (eds) 2001. *L'antica Basilica di San Vigilio in Trento.* 2 vols. Trent: Museo diocesano tridentino.

Rogger, I. and F. Dell'Oro (eds) 1983–1988. *Monumenta liturgica Ecclesiae Tridentinae saeculo XIII antiquiora.* Vols. I–IIA, IIB, III. Trent: Società di studi Trentini di scienze storiche.

Roma, G. (ed) 2010. *I Longobardi del Sud.* Rome: Giorgio Bretschneider.

Rossetti, G. 1973. "Società e istituzioni nei secoli IX e X: Pisa, Volterra, Populonia." In *Lucca e la Tuscia nell'alto medioevo*, 209–338. Atti del V Congresso internazionale di studi sull'alto medioevo. Spoleto: Centro italiano di studi sull'alto medioevo.

Sala, G. 1989. "Il culto di S. Zeno fino al secolo VIII." *Annuario storico zenoniano* 6: 19–26.

—. 1990. "Il culto di S. Zeno nei secoli 8 e 9." *Annuario storico zenoniano* 7: 19–36.

—. 1991. "Il culto di S. Zeno dal 10. al 12. secoli." *Annuario storico zenoniano* 8: 15–32.

Salisbury, J.E. 1997. *Perpetua's Passion: The Death and Memory of a Young Roman Woman.* New York: Routledge.

Salsotto, C. 1937. *Le più' antiche carte dell'Archivio di S. Gaudenzio di Novara (sec. IX–XI).* Turin: Tip. de E. Cattaneo.

Santella, L. 1981. *Blera e il suo territorio.* Blera: Associazione Pro-Loco Blera.

Sardella, T. and G. Zito (eds) 2006. *Euplo e Lucia 304–2004: Agiografia e tradizioni culturali in Sicilia.* Catania: Studio Teologico S. Paolo.

Savio, F. 1899–1932. *Gli antichi vescovi d'Italia dalle origini al' 1300 descritti per regioni.* Vols. 1–2. Biblioteca istorica della antica e nuova Italia 111, 139. Bologna: Formi.

Saxer, V. 1984. "La Tuscia nel Martirologio Geronimiano: osservazioni sulla storia del martirologio e su quella della Tuscia." In *Il paleocristiano nella Tuscia*, 19–45. Atti del II Convegno Il Paleocristiano nell Tuscia, Viterbo. 7–8 maggio 1983. Rome: Herder.

—. 1997. "Fonti storiche per la biografia di Eusebio." In Dal Covolo et al. (eds) 1997: 121–152.

Schepens, P. 1950. "L'Ambrosiastre et saint Eusèbe de Verceil." *Recherches de Science Religieuse* 37: 295–299.

Schmidt, K. (ed) 1991. *Vita Walfredi und Kloster Monteverdi: Toskanisches Mönchtum zwischen langobardischer und fränkischer Herrschaft.* Tübingen: Niemeyer.

Segala, F. 1982. *Il culto di San Zeno nella liturgia medioevale fino al secolo XII.* Verona: Archivio storico Curia vescovile.

—. 2004. "Documenti liturgici veronesi del culto dei santi Fermo e Rustico (secoli VIII–XIII)." In P. Golinelli and C.G. Brenzoni (eds) 2004: 25–38.

Sennis, A. 2013. "Documentary Practices, Archives and Laypeople in Central Italy, Mid Ninth to Eleventh Centuries." In Brown et al. (eds) 2013: 321–335.

Sensi, M. 2014. *Santuari e pellegrini lungo le "vie dell'Angelo": Storie sommerse del culto micaelico.* 3 vols. Nuovi studi storici 94. Rome: Istituto storico italiano per il Medio Evo.

Sicard, D. 1978. *La liturgie de la mort dans l'église latine des origines à la réforme carolingienne.*

Liturgiewissenschaftliche Quellen und Forschungen 63. Münster Westfalen: Aschendorff.

Simonetti, M. 1963. "Qualche osservazione sul *De trinitate* attribuito a Eusebio di Vercelli." *Rivista di cultura classica e medievale* 5: 386–393.

—. 1975. *La crisi ariana nel IV secolo*. Studia Ephemeridis Augustinianum 11. Rome: Institutum patristicum Augustinianum.

—. 1981. "Note sulla tradizione agiografica di S. Regolo di Populonia." In *Il paleocristiano nella Tuscia*, 107–130. Viterbo, Palazzo dei papi, 16–17 giugno 1979. Biblioteca di studi viterbesi 5. Viterbo: Consorzio per la gestione delle biblioteche comunale degli Ardenti e provinicale "Anselmo Anselmi."

—. 1997. "Eusebio nella controversia ariana." In Dal Covolo et al. (eds) 1997: 155–180.

Sivo, V. 1994. "Ricerche sulla tradizione manoscritta e sul testo dell'*Apparitio* latina." In Carletti and Otranto (eds) 1994: 95–106.

—. 1995. "Un nuovo testo sul culto di San Michele (cod. Parisinus B.N. lat 2873A)." *Vetera Christianorum* 32: 395–400.

Skinner, P. 2001. *Women in Medieval Italian Society 500–1200*. London: Longman.

Smith, J.M.H. 1992. "Early Medieval Hagiography in the Late Twentieth Century." *Early Medieval Europe* 1.1: 69–76.

—. 1995. "The Problem of Female Sanctity in Carolingian Europe c. 780–920." *Past & Present* 146: 3–37.

—. 2000. "Old Saints, New Cults: Roman Relics in Carolingian Francia." In *Early Medieval Rome and the Christian West*, ed. J.M.H. Smith, 317–340. Leiden: Brill.

Soprintendenza archeologica dell'Abruzzo (eds) 1993. *Pescara antica: Il recupero di S. Gerusalemme*. Pescara: Carsa.

Sot, M. 1978. "Historiographie épiscopale et modèle familial en Occident au IXe siècle." *Annales: Économies, Sociétés, Civilisations* 33.3: 433–449.

—. 1981. *Gesta episcoporum, Gesta abbatum*. Typologies des sources du Moyen Âge Occidental 37. Turnhout: Brepols.

Souter, A. 1905. *A Study of Ambrosiaster.* Cambridge: Cambridge University Press.

Speller, L.A. 1985. "A Note on Eusebius of Vercelli and the Council of Milan." *Journal of Theological Studies* 36: 157–165.

Spinelli, G. 1993. "Annotazioni sul culto di San Vigilio di Trento in Lombardia." *Civis* 17: 79–98.

Staffa, A.R. 1991. "Scavi nel centro storico di Pescara: 1 Primi elementi per una ricostruzione dell'assetto antico ed altomedievale dell'abitato di 'Ostia Aterni-Aternum.'" *Archeologia Medievale* 18: 201–367.

—. 1993. "Le origini antiche di Pescara: L'abitato di Ostia Aterni-Aternum." In Soprintendenza archeologica dell'Abruzzo (eds) 1993: 8–29.

—. 2000. "Alcune considerazioni sulla presenza Longobarda nell'Italia centrale Adriatica (secc. VI–VII)." In *Il Congresso Nazionale di Archeologia Medievale: Musei civici,*

Chiesa di Santa Giulia, Brescia, 28 settembre–1 otobre 2000, ed. G.P. Brogiolo, 117–126. Florence: All'insegna del giglio.

—. 2004. "Ortona fra tarda antichità ed alto medioevo: Un contributo alla ricostruzione della frontiera bizantina in Abruzzo." *Archeologia Medievale* 31: 365–404.

—. 2006a. "Il porto romano ed altomedievale di Pescara." *Journal of Ancient Topography/Rivista di Topografia Antica* 16: 7–58.

—. 2006b. "Quindici anni di ricerche archeologiche a Pescara (1990–2005): Un bilancio." *Congresso Nazionale di Archeologia Medievale* 4: 157–167.

—. 2010. "I Longobardi nell'Abruzzo adriatico fra VI e VIII secolo." In Roma (ed) 2010: 175–240.

Staffa, A.R. and W. Pellegrini 1993. *Dall'Egitto copto all'Abruzzo bizantino: I Bizantini in Abruzzo (secc. VI–VII)*. Crecchio: Castello Ducale.

Stancliffe, C. 1983. *St Martin and His Hagiographer: History and Miracle in Sulpicius Severus*. Oxford: Oxford Clarendon Press.

Stead, G.C. 1994. "Homoousios." In *Reallexikon für Antike und Christentum*, ed. F.-J. Dölger, E. Gassmann, and T. Klauser, 16: 364–443. Stuttgart: A. Hiersemann.

Sterk, A. 2004. *Renouncing the World Yet Leading the Church: The Monk-Bishop in Late Antiquity*. Cambridge, MA: Harvard Unversity Press.

Stouck, M.-A. (ed) 1999. *Medieval Saints: A Reader*. Peterborough, ON: Broadview Press.

Sulpicius Severus. *Life of Martin*. *See* Fontaine (ed) 1967–1969.

Supičić, I. (ed) 1999. *Croatia in the Early Middle Ages: A Cultural Survey*. London: Philip Wilson.

Supino Martini, P. 1987. *Roma e l'area grafica romanesca (secoli 10.–12)*. Alessandria: Edizioni dell'Orso.

Susi, E. 1995. "La 'Vita beati Mauri Syri abbatis et Felicis eius filii apud Vallem Narci prope Naris ripam' del Codice Alessandrino 89." *Hagiographica* 2: 92–136.

—. 1997. "Strategie agiografiche altomedievali in un leggendario di Farfa." *Cristianesimo nella Storia* 18: 277–302.

—. 2000. "San Mamiliano eremita nelle fonti agiografiche dell'Alto Medioevo." In Gianni (ed) 2000: 11–28.

—. 2004. "Osservazioni preliminari sul dossier agiografico dei santi Senzias e Mamiliano." *Sanctorum* 1: 79–87.

—. 2005. "Africani, cefalofori e 'saraceni': I cicli agiografici populoniesi dall'alto Medioevo al XII secolo." In *Da Populonia a Massa Marittima: I 1500 anni di una diocesi*, ed. A. Benvenuti, 23–66. Florence: Mandrogora.

—. 2006. "Memorie agiografiche e cultuali africane nella Tuscia dell'Alto Medioevo." In *Per una storia di Orte e del suo territorio*, ed. A. Zuppante, 145–166. Orte: Ente Ottava Medievale Orte.

—. 2007. "Storia religiosa, dinamiche cultuali e questioni agiografiche di Vulci nell'Alto Medioevo." In *Montalto di Castro: Storia di un territorio*. Volume 1: *Dalle origini al Medioevo*, ed. C.A. Falzetti and D. Mattei, 183–215. Tarquinia: Zetacidue.

—. 2010. "'Fare dicte reliquie nectare et pulire': La dispersione delle spoglie di san Mamiliano e santa Ninfa tra Porto e Pisa." *Archivio della Società romana di storia patria* 133: 53–159.

Susi, E. and A. Galdi 2008. "Santi, navi e Saraceni: Immagini e pratiche del mare tra agiografia e storia dalle coste campane a quelle dell'Alto Tirreno (secoli VI–XI)." In *Dio, il mare e gli uomini*, ed. L. Fanin, 53–101. Quaderni di storia religiosa 15. Verona: Cierre.

Testi Rasponi, A. 1926. "I documenti 'De inventione corporis beatissimi Apolenaris.'" *Felix Ravenna* 31: 1–11.

Thacker, A. 2002a. "Loca Sanctorum: The Significance of Place in the Study of the Saints." In Thacker and Sharpe (eds) 2002: 1–43.

—. 2002b. "The Making of a Local Saint." In Thacker and Sharpe (eds) 2002: 45–73.

Thacker, A. and R. Sharpe (eds) 2002. *Local Saints and Local Churches in the Early Medieval West*. Oxford: Oxford University Press.

Thesaurus Linguae Latinae. Leipzig; Munich; Berlin: 1900– .

Tjäder, J.O. 1955–1982. *Die Nichtliterarischen lateinischen Papyri italiens aus der Zeit 445–700*. 3 vols. Stockholm: P. Åstrom.

Tomea, P. 1993. *Tradizione apostolica e coscienza cittadina a Milano nel Medioevo: La leggenda di San Barnaba*. Biblioteca erudita 2. Milan: Vita e Pensiero.

—. 1998. "Ambrogio e i suoi fratelli: Note di agiografia milanese altomedievale." *Filologia Mediolatina* 5: 149–232.

Tosi, G. 1995. "Gli edifici per spettacolo di Verona." In Mirabella Roberti (ed) 1995: 467–491.

Toubert, P. 1973. *Les structures du Latium médiéval: Le Latium méridional et la Sabine du IX. siècle à la fin du XII. siècle*. Rome: École française de Rome.

Troiano A. 1989. *L'arcangelo guerriero: S. Michele e il culto speciale del papa e della Chiesa*. Foggia: Michael.

Tron, F. 1982. *I monti della Tolfa nel Medioevo: Preliminari di ricerca storico-topografica*. Rome: Gruppo archeologico romano.

Trotta, M. and Renzulli, A. 1998. "I luoghi dei Liber de apparitione di S. Michele al Gargano: L'ecclesia beati Petri." *Vetera Christianorum* 35: 335–359.

Turner, C.H. 1899. "On Eusebius of Vercelli." *Journal of Theological Studies*, o.s., 1: 126–128.

Ughelli, F. 1643–1662. *Italia sacra; sive de episcopis Italiae et insularum adjacentium, rebusque abiis praeclare gestis* ... 9 vols. Rev. ed. N. Coleti. 1717–1722. Venice: Apud Sebastianum Coleti.

Uglietti, M.C. 2010. "La Novara romana." In Capra (ed) 2010: 17–20.

Urbano, A. 2005. "Donation, Dedication, and *Damnatio Memoriae*: The Catholic Reconciliation of Ravenna and the Church of Sant'Apollinare Nuovo." *Journal of Early Christian Studies* 13.1: 71–110.

Usuard. *Martyrology*. *See* Dubois (ed) 1965.

Van Dam, R. (ed and trans) 1988a. *Gregory of Tours: Glory of the Confessors*. Liverpool: Liverpool University Press.

— (ed and trans) 1988b. *Gregory of Tours: Glory of the Martyrs*. Liverpool: Liverpool University Press.

Van Uytfanghe, M. 1987. *Stylisation biblique et condition humaine dans l'hagiographie mérovingienne (600–750)*. Brussels: Paleis der Academiën.

Varrasso, A.A. 2012. "La Storia di San Cetteo." *Notizie d'Abruzzo* (8 October 2012). http://archivio.notiziedabruzzo.it/itinerari-abruzzo/la-storia-di-san-cetteo.html#.VvKQHUs2bwI (accessed 22 March 2016).

Vedriš, T. 2005. "Communities in Conflict: The Rivalry between the Cults of Sts. Anastasia and Chrysogonus in Medieval Zadar." *Annual of Medieval Studies at CEU* 11: 29–48.

Vežić, P. 1995. "The Early-Medieval Phase of the Episcopal Complex in Zadar." *Hortus Artium Medievalium* 1: 150–161.

Vian, G.M. 1997. "L'evangelario eusebiano." In Dal Covolo et al. (eds) 1997: 347–364.

Viscardi, A. 1939. *Le origini*. Storia letteraria d'Italia. 3rd ed. Milan: Francesco Vallardi.

Visonà, G. 1999. "San Gaudenzio e le origini della chiesa di Novara." In *Il cristianesimo a Novara e sul territorio: Le origini*, ed. R. Corti and G. Wataghin Cantino, 137–159. Atti del convegno, Novara 10 Ottobre. Novara: Interlinea Edizioni.

Vocino, G. 2010. "Santi e luoghi santi al servizio della politica carolingia (774–877): Vitae e Passiones del regno italico nel contesto europeo." PhD thesis: Università Ca' Foscari Venezia.

—. 2014. "Under the Aegis of the Saints: Hagiography and Power in Early Carolingian Northern Italy." *Early Medieval Europe* 22.1: 26–52.

Vuolo, A. 1996. "Agiografia beneventana." In Andenna and Picasso (eds) 1996: 199–237.

Waitz, G. and L. Bethmann (eds) 1878. *Pauli Diaconi Historia Langobardorum*. MGH Scriptores Rerum Langobardicarum, 12–187. Hannover: Hahn.

Weigel, R. 1990. "Gallienus' 'Animal Series' Coins and Roman Religion." *The Numismatic Chronicle* 150: 135–143.

Westerbergh, U. (ed) 1956. *Chronicon Salernitanum. A Critical Edition with Studies on Literary and Historical Sources and on Language*. Stockholm: Almqvist & Wiksell.

Wheeler, N. 2016. "Perjury and False Witness from Late Antiquity to the Early Middle Ages." PhD thesis: University of Toronto.

Wickham, C. 1981. *Early Medieval Italy: Central Power and Local Society, 400–1000*. London: Macmillan.

—. 2005. *Framing the Early Middle Ages: Europe and the Mediterranean, 400–800*. Oxford: Oxford University Press.

Williams, D.H. 1995. *Ambrose of Milan and the End of the Nicene-Arian Conflicts*. Oxford: Oxford University Press.

Williams, R (trans) 1987. *The Panarion of Epiphanius of Salamis, Book I (Sects 1–46)*. Leiden: Brill.

Williams, R. 2001. *Arius: Heresy and Tradition*. Rev. ed. Grand Rapids, MI: Eerdmans.

Wilson, S. 1983. *Saints and Their Cults: Studies in Religious Sociology, Folklore and History*. Cambridge: Cambridge University Press.

Woods, J.C. 1997. "Six New Sermons by Hrabanus Maurus on the Virtues and Vices." *Revue Bénédictine* 107: 280–306.

Wright, R. 1982. *Late Latin and Early Romance in Spain and Carolingian France*. ARCA 8. Liverpool: Francis Cairns.

— (ed) 1991. *Latin and the Romance Languages in the Early Middle Ages*. London: Routledge; University Park, PA: Penn State Press.

Zamboni, A. 2000. *Alle origini dell'italiano: Dinamiche e tipologie della transizione dal latino*. Rome: Carocci.

Zanetti, U. 1979. "Les passions des Ss. Nazaire, Gervais, Protais et Celse." *Analecta Bollandiana* 97: 69–88.

Zangara, V. 1981. "L'*inventio* dei corpi dei martiri Gervasio e Protasio: Testimonianze di Agostino su un fenomeno di religiosità popolare." *Augustinianum* 21: 119–133.

Zanini, E. 1998. *Le Italie Bizantine: Territorio, insediamenti ed economia nella provincia bizantina d'Italia (VI–VIII secolo)*. Bari: Edipuglia.

Zattoni, G. 1904. "La data della 'Passio S. Apollinaris' di Ravenna." *Atti della R. Accademia delle scienze di Torino* 32: 364–378.

—. 1905–1906. "Il valore storico della Passio di S. Apollinare e la fondazione dell'episcopato a Ravenna e in Romagna." *Rivista storico-critica delle scienze teologiche* 1 (1905): 661–777; 2 (1906): 179–200; 3 (1906): 677–691.

Zeno of Verona. *Sermons; Tractatus*. *See* Löfstedt (ed) 1971.

Zielinski, H. (ed). 1986. *Codice diplomatico longobardo*. Volume 5: *Le chartae dei Ducati di Spoleto e di Benevento*. Fonti per la storia d'Italia 66. Rome: Tipografia del Senato.

— 1996a. "Auszeichnungsschriften, graphische Zeichen und Symbole in den Urkunden der langobardischen Fürsten von Benevent, Salerno und Capua (774–1077)." In *Graphische Symbole in mittelalterlichen Urkunden*, ed. P. Rück, 385–398. Sigmaringen: Thorbecke.

—. 1996b. "Fra 'charta' e documento pubblico : gli atti dei vescovi della Longobardia meridionale," in Andenna and Picasso (eds) 1996, 149–170.

Zuccotti, F. 2000. *Il giuramento nel mondo giuridico e religioso antico*. Milan: Giuffrè.

Index